The Story of Thornby

HOW ORDINARY PEOPLE TOOK ON GOVERNMENT

THE GRASSROOTS SAGA OF A COMMUNITY'S GRIT,
GUTS AND DETERMINATION TO PRESERVE ITS HISTORY

BY **SANDRA WALTERS**

A BLACKWYRM BOOK
LOUISVILLE, KENTUCKY

THE STORY OF THORNBY

Copyright ©2011 by Sandra Walters

All rights reserved, including the right to reproduce this book, or portion thereof, in any form. Written permission must be secured from the publisher to use or reproduce any part of this book, except for brief quotations in critical reviews or articles.

A BlackWyrm Book
BlackWyrm Publishing
10307 Chimney Ridge Court
Louisville, KY 40299

Printed in the United States of America.

ISBN: 978-1-61318-120-1
LCCN: 2011944764

From Front Cover:
Left to right: Carolyn Watson; Ernie Watson (in background); unknown; Annette Watson; Wesley (last name unknown); Dwayne Watson (standing)

Dedication

With love and endless gratitude, this book is dedicated to my husband, Dr. Roy A. Walters, my partner in life, in adventures, and in the all-consuming process that became "The Story of Thornby." You gave me patience when I lost mine, encouragement when things got tough, help when I floundered, and a push when I needed it. Graphics editor, researcher, business manager, mentor, teacher, best friend: without you, this book simply would not exist.

Foreward

The voice kept creeping into my head. Waking in the middle of the night, I heard it. Sitting through yet another public hearing, it found me. On a business trip to South Korea with my husband, it climbed hundreds of steps to a mountaintop Buddhist monastery with me. Praying for Thornby in a Gothic cathedral in the center of Zurich, I was at its mercy. "There's a book here," it clamored and it wouldn't shut up. "No matter how the story ends, it deserves to be told," insisted the voice. Finally, when all the prayers and traveling and hearings were over, I couldn't ignore it any longer.

I did not want to write the book myself. I tried to find someone else to do it, but eventually I came to realize that my husband was right. You lived it in a way no one else did, he said. It's your story to tell.

And so, in a process almost as complicated and agonizing, although not nearly as lengthy, as the Thornby saga, the story of Thornby became this book. My hopes for this book are several:

First, that Friends of Thornby's massive efforts and years of immense labor will be recognized and remembered. Second, that people in Volusia County who are familiar with the story gain an understanding of what it took to do what we did. Third, to encourage and assist people in Florida and elsewhere to stand up and fight for their own communities — whatever the odds against you, and no matter the outcome.

Contents

PART ONE: GATHERING MEMORIES
Prologue 7
Chapter 1. A Happy Little Lakeside Town. 11
Chapter 2. Famous for Children and Chickens 31
Chapter 3. To Live in Hearts We Leave Behind is Not to Die 49
Chapter 4. How Thornby Came to Be 59
Chapter 5. Train up a Child in the Way He Should Go 69

PART TWO: WITH RIGHTS COME RESPONSIBILITIES
Chapter 6. You Will Find That the Truth is Often Unpopular 91
Chapter 7. Enterprise Needs a Voice 113
Chapter 8. Around the Kitchen Table: The Friends of Thornby . . . 129
Chapter 9. Behind the Woodshed 155
Chapter 10. Once It's Gone, It's Gone 173
Chapter 11. This is No Time to Make New Enemies 187
Chapter 12. The Credit Belongs to Those in the Arena 211
Chapter 13. To Everything There is a Season . . . and then Another . . 227
Chapter 14. Politics as Unusual 237
Chapter 15. Why Can't We Just Say We Aren't Accepting It? 247

PART THREE: ENTERPRISE RETURNS WHAT IT RECEIVED
Chapter 16. Out of the Frying Pan and Into the Mire 273
Chapter 17. Indecision: The Thief of Opportunity 291
Chapter 18. Politics: The Art of the Possible 305
Chapter 19. Someday I'll Meet You Down at Thornby Park 321

Epilogue 339
Selected Pages from the Thornby Guest Book 340
List of Sources 344
Acknowledgments. 347
Photo Credits 349
Walters' Top 11 List 350
The ABC's of Land Use Activism 351
About the Author 360

Thornby

> *Orlando was the biggest,*
> *Sanford was the busiest,*
> *Deland was the liveliest, but*
> *Enterprise was the most beautiful.*
>
> **Unknown Author**

Prologue

I. Volusia Growth Management Commission: November 2, 2005

My dead grandmother's rosary beads hung around my neck. I looked at the floor because I couldn't look at their faces. Matter-of-factly, our attorney, Scott Selis, leaned over and whispered, "Save your speech, we've got them," but I couldn't absorb his words. My heart and stomach were trading places.

Five incredible years of meetings, phone calls, emails, speeches, travel, bills, experts, bureaucrats, politicians, letters, lies, arm twisting, civic campaigns, tears, elation, and disappointment, all came down to this moment — my final words, an anxious "Hail Mary" on Nana's rosary, a lawyer's last entreaty to the Volusia Growth Management Commission, and its simple response — "yes" or "no" — and the fight to preserve the 40-acre historic Thornby property would be won or lost.

As I sat there, I thought back to when it all began... that is, when I thought, *at the time,* that it all began...

II. How I Got Involved

A long time ago, I used to be normal. By "normal," I mean I didn't sit at the computer well into the night, crafting letters to newspaper editors about the latest land planning disaster; I didn't organize my social life around public meetings, and I most definitely never talked politics with friends, wondering who would run for office, and what to say to boards, commissions, and other officials (usually trying to kill or delay the latest chapter of Florida's shameful overdevelopment story).

All that pretty much changed one gorgeous Sunday afternoon about 10 years ago. My husband, Roy, and I were building a house on Stone Island in Enterprise and driving between there and Orlando frequently. Since we used Lakeshore Drive along Lake Monroe to get to I-4, I traveled past a mysterious bit of Old Florida often. I didn't know then that it had a name, an enticing past and a potentially murderous future. I just knew it was an old, vacant, two-story white house mostly shrouded from skinny, tree-lined Lakeshore Drive and wrapped in who-knew-how-many-acres of virtual Florida jungle.

Empty houses have always beckoned me, and this one was no exception. Once or twice, I stopped the car, ambled along the beat-up front walk, and poked around inside. It was a casual house, not elegant or pretentious, with old fireplaces, nice heart-of-pine floors and a beat-up kitchen that screamed "half-hearted cheap remodeling job." It was dirty, deserted and surprisingly intact, and its story fascinated me. Who built this place, who owned it, who left it behind? and why?

So, as Roy and I passed the vacant house on that fateful Sunday, we noticed a bright orange sign out front and couldn't resist stopping to read the "Notice of Public Hearing" that gave the date and time. It's the kind of sign that's all too familiar to me now, but back then I had little idea what it represented. Or of the "long and winding road" (thanks, Paul McCartney) that lay before me.

Roy was R&D Director of an instrument company he'd help start, and I'd been a paralegal for more than 30 years, when we came to Stone Island. We were just getting settled in our new house and getting to know our neighbors. One of the first people we met was Carol Aymar, a director of the Enterprise Preservation Society. Even before moving to the Island, we'd attended the first Old Enterprise Festival. There was never a doubt that we'd get involved with EPS: along with Lake Monroe, wild turkeys, and community get-togethers, the allure of historic Enterprise had brought us to Stone Island, with the promise of a lifestyle very different from the one we'd left behind in an Orlando suburb.

"Oh yea," said Carol with a sigh, when I asked about the orange sign. "That's the Thornby property, and we've been expecting this."

PART ONE

Gathering Memories

On the northern shore of beautiful Lake Monroe the quiet little village of Enterprise is situated among flourishing orange groves and her people, happy and contented, are prosperous.

The Florida Times Union
September 9, 1891

CHAPTER ONE

A Happy Little Lakeside Town

Dear Reader: This is a history book recounting events in Central Florida specific to the north shore of Lake Monroe. If you're anticipating a narrative about the Indian Wars, or steamboats, or how once-incorporated Enterprise lost its county seat-hood to DeLand in the 1890s, I respectfully refer you to the Enterprise Preservation Society's website or to Volusia County's Enterprise website (see List of Sources at the end of this book). In addition, any area museum, or any of the fine writings penned by local historians over the years will also satisfy your curiosity. This isn't that kind of history book, after all, except that it tells the story of how determined people changed the course of what happened to a pristine, historic and long-coveted 40-acre parcel of land in Enterprise called "Thornby."

B.P. (Before Present) History

In our story, the first people who called Thornby — or Enterprise — home were Native Americans living on Lake Monroe. Let's stop right here and say "thanks." Why? Because those folks created the Thornby Midden, and even a garbage dump, if it's old enough, is something to be thankful for. For all of Florida's modern history, remains of ancient shell middens have been shoveled up and carted off for septic fields, soil amendments and roadbeds. The Thornby Midden, or what's left of it, is important enough to be registered in the Florida Master Site File, the database of the state's archeological and cultural resources. It was likely part of a better-known site on Lake Monroe's north shore: the Enterprise Midden, which was the size of a football field and 20 feet tall. When Jeffries Wyman, curator of Harvard's Peabody Museum of Archeology and Ethnology, excavated the Enterprise Midden in 1860, he found pottery, shells and bones. Wyman was distinguished for being the first scientist to understand that the shell mounds were human made, and not the result of natural events. Pottery shards (fragments) that he dug out of the Enterprise Midden were shipped to the Peabody Museum, and are now included in its permanent collection. They can be viewed online. Nearly the entire midden has disappeared, used up by locals long ago for fertilizing orange groves and making shell walks.

Enterprise Indian midden,
sketch by Count Louis Francois de Poutales, 1848

Fort Kingsbury

Most of the Second Seminole War (1835-42) was fought in Central Florida. U.S. Army forts were established from New Smyrna to Tampa, intended to push the Seminole Indians southward. One was Fort Kingsbury, believed to have been on the north shore of Lake Monroe, although its precise location has never been ascertained. Named for 2nd Lt. Charles E. Kingsbury, who died of fever at Fort Mellon (now Sanford) in 1837, the log stockade fort was built around 1838. It is generally thought to have been a temporary camp or an outpost of Fort Mellon. One source says it was a recreation area for Fort Mellon's soldiers. Square nails and glass fragments dating to the 19th century, found in 2009 during archeological testing on Thornby could be associated with Fort Kingsbury.

"There is a possibility (based on historic description) that the remains of Fort Kingsbury are within the confines of this parcel (Thornby)," wrote University of Central Florida archaeologist David Butler in a Feb. 16, 2004 letter written for the Friends of Thornby, the grassroots group of Enterprise and Deltona residents who, 160 years later, were fighting their own war on the site. "If so," he continues, ". . . the fort site associated with this conflict (is an) irreplaceable component of our shared history."

Possible site of Fort (Camp) Kingsbury

He put the enterprise in Enterprise

The Florida Armed Occupation Act of 1842 conveyed the U.S. Government's pledge that "any man willing to bear arms for their country" would become owner of 160 acres of land south of Palatka by "squatting" there, clearing and cultivating the land for five years, and building a house in the first year. The land had to be more than two miles from a fort. It was an early economic recovery program, designed to boost Florida's population and chances for statehood, while at the same time getting rid of those pesky Indians once and for all.

Back Then They Gave the Land Away for Free/
Just Run Off any Seminole You See[1]

One settler who took advantage of the Act was entrepreneur/opportunist Major Cornelius Taylor of Jacksonville. Born about 1785 in what became West Virginia, he was a successful government timber agent, postal route operator and Indian fighter. He secured a land grant of 160 acres and brought his wife and three children, about 20 other families, and their slaves, livestock and personal belongings up the St. Johns River to Lake Monroe (once known as Lake Valdez). There, he founded the town of Enterprize (original spelling) on Christmas Eve 1841, four years before Florida became a state. Its location on the St. Johns River on "one of the finest bluffs in the state" attracted

Cornelius Taylor

---

1 Lyrics in this and subsequent chapters from "St. Johns Lullaby," copyright 2007 by Rog Lee.

them to the spot. As Enterprise resident Chris Elmer explains, Taylor had a U.S. Navy contract to supply wood for shipbuilding. In those days, the strong, curved limbs of ancient live oak trees were prized for use as "ribs" on ships, and "Taylor and his crew would roam through" the area, says Elmer, picking out pieces with the right specifications and cutting them from the trees. This was the "Enterprize" that named "Enterprize, Florida."

Despite Indian threats, Taylor and his band built the town on top of the old, 20-foot high Indian mound and began farming the fertile soil. Shortly after settlement, however, the government reneged on its promise to provide the colonists with rations and troops from Fort Mellon for protection from Indians. At that point, many returned to their homes, but Taylor and a few other hardy souls stayed and prospered in what is now referred to as "Old Enterprise." They were 80 miles from the nearest white settlement in St. Augustine.

How much did Old Enterprise resemble the present-day Thornby property? A March 28, 1843 letter in the *Florida Journal* stated that Lake Monroe was "skirted on every side by extensive bodies of fertile land," which was "covered with cabbage palmetto, live oak, hickory, yam, etc., together with shrubbery, a variety of plants and vines." That's a lot like the native vegetation on Thornby today.

Cornelius Taylor, elected a state legislator in 1843, managed to get Enterprise chosen as the seat of what was then known as Mosquito County. In a few years, Enterprise had the necessities of pioneer life: a sawmill to cut timber, a gristmill to grind grain into flour, a blacksmith shop, a store and a wharf for ferry service to Fort Mellon. Taylor's own plantation featured several springs, a sugar boiler, and orange groves. His cotton, sugar cane, and live oak harvest prospered. Stores and public buildings appeared, as well as Taylor's own two-story "pleasant and commodious inn" for steamboat clientele — one of Florida's earliest health spas, built to attract tourists who were beginning to come by steamboat in search of good times and good health. A visiting lawyer, Whitfield Brooks of South Carolina, called Taylor's settlement at Enterprise "one of the most picturesque and romantic spots that I have ever seen." At least one writer attributed the early name "Fountain City" to Enterprise because of its numerous natural springs.

Another early visitor to Enterprise (1843) wrote these words:

> At this place the lake is four miles wide, skirted on every side by extensive bodies of very fertile land, extending back for a mile or more, is covered with cabbage palmetto, live oak, hickory, yam... a variety of plants and vines...is the prospect for the new town of Enterprise...in a high state of cultivation. Corn, cotton, sugar, and most of the tropical fruits...

Even though Cornelius Taylor's town was peaceful, the man himself was not. Known as "The Thunder of Enterprise," he stood tall and broad, an immense man with red hair and a quick temper. Although he founded Enterprise, he didn't stick around long. His political dabbling led to feuds and a deadly fight with a Mellonville (Sanford) man. Taylor was charged with murder and then acquitted on grounds of self-defense. After that, he took his family and left Enterprise for south Texas, leaving behind the grave of daughter Polly. Her weathered tombstone still stands on property near Thornby, inscribed: "Sacred to the memory of our beloved Polly, daughter of C. & C. Taylor, who departed this life of typhus fever September 21, 1842, age 13 years and 13 days." It's the oldest recorded burial of a white person south of St. Augustine. A few years after leaving Florida, Taylor himself was reportedly lost at sea while sailing toward dreams of a new fortune from the California Gold Rush.

One member of Taylor's original group, William Fail, settled in 1843 on what is now Stone Island, originally called "Fail's Island" and eventually became a county judge.

After Cornelius Taylor's death, his widow, Catherine, came back to Enterprise, where her married daughter, Mary Virginia Houston, was living. The original Taylor home had been destroyed by fire. Catherine ran a boarding house for a while (possibly the original inn on the Indian mound) but eventually moved to Jacksonville with her widowed daughter, Elizabeth Carroll, to run the Taylor Hotel.

Mrs. Taylor sold her Enterprise land to Dr. James D. Starke, a Confederate Civil War veteran who founded the Orange County town of Ocoee in the mid-1850s. After the war, he moved to Enterprise and built an impressive home on high ground next to a bountiful spring. He named his 10-room, two-story pine home "Bueno Retiro" (Good Rest). The house, with eight fireplaces, was touted as "the most magnificent residence at the time in Volusia County."

The property was surrounded by extensive citrus groves, in the days when fruit was packed into barrels and hauled over sandy roads by oxcart or wagon to waiting ships. Starke's groves originated the "Enterprise Seedless Orange," a medium-sized, early-season variety still cultivated today.

As Central Florida counties were organized and reorganized, Enterprise was, at various times, the county seat of three different counties: Mosquito (1843-5), Orange (1845-54), and finally, it became Volusia County's first seat in 1854. In 1877, 25 citizens voted to incorporate Enterprise as a city. The town seal shows what might be the old shell mound. The ax to the left of the tree may be a reference to Taylor's occupation as timber agent.

Enterprise seal

In the 19th century, doctors in northern states commonly prescribed a change of climate for patients with tuberculosis and other lung diseases. If they could afford it, those people often went to Florida for the winter, hoping to regain their health from the warmer weather and beneficial mineral springs. Dr. Starke took advantage of the natural sulphur spring on his land and built a sanitarium for those seeking a cure for rheumatism or lumbago in the spring's healing waters. That spring is now just a muddy depression, with conflicting explanations for what happened to it. Enterprise old-timers often said the spring dried up after a horse and carriage fell in, blocking its source and diverting the stream. Local historian Bill Dreggors says the effects of an 1887 South Carolina earthquake caused the spring to move. Either way, the spring re-surfaced nearer to Lake Monroe, and its mysterious, green-tinged beauty attracted swimmers by the dozens in the 1930s and 40s, who for 10 cents got use of the bathhouse, too. Just as lovely today as it was then, Green Spring is now a Volusia County Park, but swimming is off-limits.

Green Spring, Enterprise

The once-gracious Starke home was converted to a boarding house for railroad travelers in the late 1800s; it later became the site of Walter Trapp's dairy farm. The former spring deteriorated into a dumping ground for unwanted items like old car parts. The Cobb family bought the house and property in the 1960s. Over the years, they extensively remodeled the 80-year-old "Bueno Retiro." "It's not a beautiful place," said Harold Cobb, "but it's full of history." He uncovered old kitchen utensils that may have belonged to the Taylors. In 1980, the Cobbs invited members of the Volusia County Anthropological Society to conduct archeological digs on the land. In a way, it was a modern-day midden, except the artifacts were pushed down instead of piled up. The team was thrilled to unearth parts of a brick foundation near a spring, probably part of Dr. Starke's health spa for invalids. Wine and ginger beer bottles, a china plate dated 1850 were among the items found, as were old nails and cast iron. The most intriguing find took them by surprise: buried under five feet of dirt was a 360 ft. long log flume made from cypress and wrought iron nails, maybe once part of Taylor's Enterprise grist mill.

The Monte Carlo of the South

Enterprise was settled because of its location on the St. Johns River. Sometimes called "The Nile of America" because it flows northward, the St. Johns River was, and is, a major transportation artery. Around 1852, a new era began for Florida and Enterprise when Captain Jacob Brock of New England, the "father of steamboat traffic on the St. Johns River," came to town. He bought 140 acres on Lake Monroe west of Old Enterprise and Thornby, where he built what eventually became a 150-room hotel. Described as "small, alert and heavily bearded," Jacob Brock at first had the Midas touch when it came to making money. His hotel, called the Brock House, was praised as a "genuine northern-looking hotel."

The Brock House Hotel, Enterprise, circa 1876

The Brock House served guests who traveled there on Jacob Brock's own sleek steamboats — the first regular line of steamboats from Jacksonville to Lake Monroe began service in 1859. In the summer, three or four boats arrived daily on the 206-mile, overnight trip from Jacksonville; in the winter, there were as many as five or six. The round-trip fare in 1869 was $9. Enterprise was also the landing spot for folks heading to New Smyrna, Mosquito Inlet, and Indian River. Like Walt Disney 100 years later, Brock pretty much had the tourist market captured, and he made the most of it.

The Brock House, and the dwellings and businesses built around it, then became known as "Enterprise," as opposed to Taylor's original settlement called "Old Enterprise." In effect, says local historian Bill Dreggors, the townspeople moved their town one mile westward because the Brock House had earned its place as Enterprise's commercial core.

Unlike the Seminole Indian Wars, the Civil War did not have a significant effect on Enterprise. One intriguing account relates an 1864 skirmish when the side-wheeler *Hattie Brock*, loaded with 1,500 head of cattle and hundreds of cotton bales, was captured in Lake Monroe by Union gunboats as she headed for Rebel forces and towed back to Enterprise. From her perch on her father's hotel veranda, Hattie Brock watched the ship being unloaded by Yankee marines and gave them a rigorous tongue-lashing. By coincidence, her name was strikingly similar to that of a woman who 40 years later would become a permanent part of Enterprise history.

Jacob Brock, a Southern sympathizer, was taken prisoner by Union forces and held for most of the Civil War. After the war, he managed to buy back his confiscated steamboats, and then it was business as usual.

Brock's hotel became one of the most famous hotels in Florida, if not the whole country, catering to "sportsmen, pleasure seekers and invalids" and advertised in the distinguished *Harpers Weekly* and other magazines. One early visitor to Enterprise was Albert Edward, Prince of Wales, the first member of the British royal family to visit North America. The Brock House's guest log is on display at the DeLand House Museum.

One guest extolled:

> It stands broadside to the lake, 110 feet long and two stories and a half in height, with a veranda its entire front, broad and airy.

While the rooms — for common folk anyway — were said to be plain (at $4 per night, according to an 1875 Florida guidebook), the hotel featured a bowling alley. At night, the dining room became a ballroom with an orchestra for dancing. Croquet on the lawn was hugely popular with hotel guests. Besides that, guests got free oranges (presumably picked from the hotel's grove.) The amenities, however, did not include bathrooms. Those were out back — one for men and one for ladies.

Brock House Hotel advertisement, Florida State Gazetteer (sic), 1883

BROCK HOUSE,

ENTERPRISE, FLORIDA,

Situated on the Right side of Lake Monroe. Excellent Fishing and Hunting. Good Livery and Boats.

WARM, SULPHUR, IRON AND SALT SPRINGS.

Hotel Enlarged. Many Guests at the Hotel every Winter from five to thirty years,

OLDEST AND FINEST GROVES IN THE STATE AT ENTERPRISE. LARGE AND WONDERFUL MINERAL SPRINGS, SHELL MOUNDS, Etc.

Oranges, Strawberries, Vegetables and Milk from the Hotel Farm. Hotel stands in an Orange Grove, fruit free to its guests.

Ladies' bathroom at the Brock House

Brock House lunch box

Outside, a long, wide pier with a warehouse at the end reached from the hotel out into Lake Monroe. In addition to loading and unloading boat passengers and cargo, the pier was a place for social get-togethers and church services. Even now, during the dry season when lake levels dip, the ragged ends of wooden dock pilings pop up from the water, giving those of us who missed it, a tantalizing glimpse into Enterprise's glamorous and colorful past.

Tourists gambled at the Brock House or in town, and raced horses on Main Street. (Perhaps they were persuaded that, "What happens in Enterprise stays in Enterprise.")

For guests on a day-long excursion, the hotel supplied a box lunch — literally. Brown cardboard, sandwich-sized lunchboxes bearing the Brock House logo were manufactured by the inventor of the folding carton, Robert Gair of Brooklyn, New York.

Whether it was the free fruit or the lavish entertainment, the Brock House was filled to capacity during the November-April season. In this sportsman's paradise, one could hunt deer, snipe, quail (it's reported that one hunter bagged 65 quail in a day) and turkey in the woods, shoot alligators, or while away the day fishing for black bass. Female guests might enjoy picnicking, boating on the river, or swimming in the cool, relaxing natural springs under massive, moss-draped live oaks.

Satisfied tourists sent letters to the folks back home, describing the delights of Enterprise:

> ...The most delightful sail from Palatka to this place up the St. Johns. It was a scene of enchantment. . . the grand old oaks draped in its (sic) long graceful gray moss... the bright sunlight, the singing birds & the rippled river. The [Brock] house is on a lovely lake, an orange grove one side... the house is quite primitive, no carpets, curtains nor luxuries, but when outdoors is so charming you can wink at the discomforts inside. (Mary Birchard, 1867)

The side-wheeler Fannie Dugan and two other steamships, circa 1882

In 1876, Jacob Brock, in financial trouble due to heavy competition for river travel, sold his hotel to Luther Caldwell, who expanded the building in order to attract more tourists traveling by rail.

"It is well known that Enterprise is one of the prettiest places in South Florida," said the *Enterprise Herald* on October 6, 1887, a statement as true as it was self-promoting. The Brock House reached the peak of its popularity from 1895 through 1905, but the rich and famous signed its guest register for many years. Among the notables were General Ulysses S. Grant, a honeymooning President Grover Cleveland, the Vanderbilt Family, writer Harriett Beecher Stowe, and artist Winslow Homer.

Still, the Brock House wasn't the town's only fine building during Enterprise's days as the queen of Volusia cities. A 1989 historical property survey of the area concluded that, ". . . several significant hotels and residential buildings were constructed in the 1850s and late 1860s in Enterprise." Unfortunately, no trace of those structures exists today.

Enterprise and the Brock House have been immortalized in art and literature. New York-based landscape artist Alexander H. Wyant (1836-1892), a member of the Hudson River School, painted "Enterprise at Lake Monroe" while staying at the Brock House in 1871. This oil painting is one of only two known "Florida" works by the artist. His work is on exhibit in museums across the country, including the National Gallery of Art in Washington, D.C. The original of "Enterprise at Lake Monroe" is in a private collection in Jacksonville.

Alexander H. Wyant, Enterprise at Lake Monroe, oil on canvas, 1871

Mary Jane Holmes (1825-1907) was one of the 19th century's most popular writers of "women's" novels. Her 1899 book, *The Cromptons*, is a genteel potboiler set in Enterprise. The first chapter, "The Stranger at the Brock House," sets the tone for a tale of romance, the Steamship "Hatty," long-lost heirs, and a happy ending. In another coincidence, one of its characters is "Miss Dory," a name almost identical to that of the woman who 60 years later would become an irreplaceable part of Enterprise and Thornby. (*The Cromptons* is free online, courtesy of Google Books.)

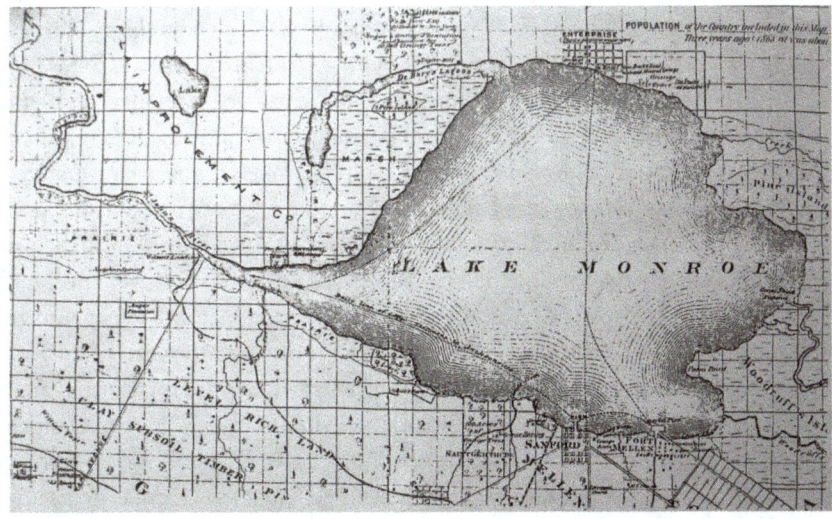

Steamship routes, 1871

Downtown Enterprise from the Brock House Hotel, 1880

Enterprise wasn't just another pretty face. Those seeking rejuvenation, or a cure for what ailed them, showed up in droves to soak in, or drink from, the healing waters of natural springs bubbling from the ground all around Enterprise. One tourist marveled over Basin Springs — 80 feet around, very deep, and perfectly transparent. Deservedly or not, the Benson Salt Springs (on the Turner Power Plant grounds) had a reputation for curing rheumatism; thousands of gallons a day flowed from it. The bathhouse at the Brock House was spring-fed. Although no one ever totaled all the springs in Enterprise and environs, an early writer counted 20 first-magnitude springs (64.6 million gallons a day or more). One of Florida's few green sulphur springs (now Green Spring Park) was on "Count" Frederic DeBary's land. Another, on the Parker property, discharged five million gallons a day. In 1931, two bubbling springs on the property supplied the Florida Methodist Orphanage with all the water it needed. That's how it was, before Florida's craze for over-development weakened the discharge of virtually every strong-flowing spring to a trickle.

The Brock House's eventual downward spiral parallels that of many historic Florida buildings. As the years passed, the hotel suffered fire damage, became a treatment center for invalids called the Benson Springs Inn, and then a Christian retreat center called the Epworth Inn. In 1935, owners Mr. and Mrs. Ellis Phillips of New York City donated it to the Florida Methodist Orphanage for expansion of its facilities. The Orphans Friend newsletter cheered: "This is a realizing of the dream that the Board of Trustees has had for many years." When the old Brock House hotel was demolished in 1937, the orphanage's good fortune was Enterprise's bad luck, although probably nobody saw it that way at the time. To Depression-era residents, it meant good riddance to a run-down eyesore. To us today, it means goodbye to the Brock House, a priceless icon of Enterprise, Florida and American history.

A few remnants of the Brock House survive. Its main staircase was saved and incorporated into the Barnett Methodist Church; salvaged wood from the hotel was used to build the church's communion table. Hotel contents were scattered, either sold or given to locals. For instance, Catherine Bruce of Enterprise has proudly inherited two quilts from the Brock House.

This lavish bed, displayed at the Florida Methodist Children's Home, came from the Brock House's "Presidential Suite," where presidents and other notables slept. The hotel's guest register, as well as its hunting log, are in the collection of the Henry A. DeLand House Museum in DeLand, Florida.

Bed from Brock House Hotel Presidential Suite

A number of Jacob Brock's descendants now live in the Jacksonville area. Well acquainted with the significant role their river-running ancestor played in local history, several have visited Enterprise, sharing Brock family stories and photos with members of the Enterprise Preservation Society. Several also attended the 2009 dedication ceremony for the newly named "Jacob Brock Avenue," including the smiling little boy named for the famous river man, his great-great-great-great grandfather, Captain Jacob Brock.

Jacob Brock, age 9, 2009

Rich in History and Community

From Cornelius Taylor's tiny settlement on top of an Indian midden, through the Brock House's status as a "celebrity hotel" and its heyday as a steamboat and tourist mecca, Enterprise was arguably the most significant city in Volusia County. In 1882, Enterprise boasted the Volusia County Courthouse, a drug store, three dry goods stores, a post office, real estate firms, a jewelry store, a blacksmith, livery stable, three hotels, several boarding houses, and two churches. There was even a local newspaper, the *Enterprise Herald*, until "the publisher's head swelled and he moved to Sanford," (as reported in the *Florida Times-Union*).

Enterprise Herald, November 10, 1883

Enterprise railroad station, circa 1890

In addition to citrus, farmers made comfortable livings growing celery, lettuce, strawberries, watermelon, persimmon, arrowroot, peas, corn, potatoes and tobacco. Thayer & Sauls was a something-for-everyone place — the 19th-Century version of a big box store. Elijah Watson operated a steam-powered sawmill from the 1860s to the 1880s. Just like today, however, happy little towns can have big-city problems. The town's postmaster was killed in 1886, and a jailbreak captured headlines in 1887. Most of the news was more cheerful, though. Residents socialized at the hotel, attended church and enjoyed picnics, hayrides and boat trips. They joined worthy groups like the Ladies Improvement Society and the Village Improvement Association. In the 1890s, Enterprise residents contributed to refurbishing the old courthouse as a normal (teacher training) school. The town's population was then at its peak — close to 1,000 people.

However, there were setbacks. The first to go were the steamboats — the railroads served Enterprise beginning in the 1880s, gradually replacing riverboats as the preferred means of travel.

Northerners began investing in land farther south, and when tourists flocked to the new luxury hotels surfacing along Florida's east coast, the town's main source of income — steamboat tourists — sailed away. Enterprise was apparently spared the disastrous effects of the yellow fever epidemic that swept Florida (causing almost half of Jacksonville's population to flee the city in panic), although a local paper reported quarantines and disrupted river traffic in 1887. Next were the freezes. Oranges were a profitable commercial crop in Enterprise, second only to tourism. Rare freezes in 1894 and 1895 killed many trees, forcing growers to give up or move further south. But the strongest blow came when two DeLand attorneys began circulating petitions to have the county seat moved from Enterprise "over violent protests from

Enterprise merchants," according to a 1957 newspaper article. In the ensuing 10-way vote, the winner was DeLand with 1,003 votes. Enterprise, site of the county seat for 34 years, placed second. (Tied for last place were Ormond and New Smyrna, with one vote apiece.) Understandably, it was a very big deal. When results were tallied, the good citizens of DeLand partied so hard that a local lawyer was severely burned by gunpowder exploding in the street.

The population loss and economic decline that resulted from losing the county seat caused Enterprise to de-incorporate as a city in 1895. Soon, people were calling it "the ex-queen of Volusia County." The town's 1900 population of 284 had dwindled to 188 by 1910. Although it would never return to its former glory, neither did it become a ghost town.

In 1908, when Enterprise's future seemed inescapably bleak, the Florida Methodist Orphanage opened. Father James Fisher, writing in the *Volusian* in 1996, opined that at the turn of the century, Enterprise probably would have been too small even to have a public school, had it not contained the orphanage. He believed that the orphanage rescued the near-failing town of Enterprise as surely as it rescued helpless children.

As later chapters will reveal, in 1908, "Mother" Hattie Brooks settled in Enterprise. Two years later, a little girl named Doris Faber arrived; in 1917, Dr. and Mrs. James Glass from Utica, New York bought the property that would become Thornby. Their separate and combined impacts, good works and enduring legacies were profound and far-reaching. Was it extraordinary good fortune, or a heavenly blessing, or a little of both, that brought them to the "happy little lakeside town" just when things were darkest? They solidified the community and held it together into the new century and beyond.

It wasn't that many years later when the survival of Enterprise as a community was again in danger. This time, though, its enemies were not freezes, railroads or epidemics. This time, it was official rules and policies and people who discourage — even penalize — those who find themselves on the "wrong" side of Florida's pro-development land use system.

> *As the March wind softly moved the white curtain to and fro, I caught a glimpse of my mother's white face, with closed eyes, and her lovely dark hair about her face. As I stood there looking in at her, all at once I knew what death meant.*
>
> **Doris Faber, "The Doris Story,"**
> unpublished manuscript, undated

CHAPTER TWO

Famous for Children and Chickens

In the early 1900s, Florida's Methodist Conference decided to establish a home for orphaned children from all over the state, an idea that had been in the works since 1896. "No one knows exactly why they chose Enterprise," said a 1992 newspaper article, but in fact, there were plenty of reasons to do so. For one thing, Enterprise was easy to reach by boat or railroad. The "medicinal" waters of Benson Springs (at the former Turner Power Plant site) were considered an asset, as was a proposed nearby religious training center. In addition, the land was a bargain. Enterprise resident Emma Tucker, a patron of children's causes, sold the Methodists a big, old hotel building, eight town lots, and 40 acres of "fine rich land," all for just $1,250. (about $30,000 today).

While the official reasons for siting the orphanage in Enterprise weren't recorded, the human reasons seem apparent. Claribel Cason, daughter of an early orphanage superintendent, recalled that the orphanage grounds were a "wonderful looking setting for children." The trustees picked "one of the most beautiful garden spots of Florida," it was said. Opened in 1908, The Florida Methodist Orphanage soon became an integral part of the Enterprise community. Its sturdy buildings snuggled along Lake Monroe under thick, protective trees provide an aura of peace and safety to those who need it the most: generations of rootless children who have found shelter there. Obviously, the trustees made a wise choice in choosing Enterprise, because the Home has stood in the same location for more than 100 years.

Hattie Greene Brooks, affectionately called "Mother" Brooks, was born in Missouri around 1863 and married Dr. Francis L. Brooks in 1885. Documented records indicate that Dr. Brooks was the first postmaster of Lakeland, Florida, practiced as a physician and druggist, and owned a furniture store. Mrs. Brooks was a founding member of the Lakeland First Methodist Church.

After Dr. Brooks died sometime after 1900, his widow moved to Tampa. There, she worked with the Wolff Settlement, a Methodist organization that operated day care, kindergarten, and after-school programs for children whose parents worked in the cigar factories of Ybor City. Thus, she began a life of inspired dedication to children in need. Why, then, did she leave Tampa and come to Enterprise? Most likely, the Rev. Dr. John Cason was the connection. Dr. Cason was a member of the Methodist committee charged with organizing the new orphanage. He was also pastor at the Lakeland church that Hattie Brooks helped start. He would have known of her devotion to the church and her leadership qualities, and enlisted her help in getting the orphanage project in Enterprise off the ground.

The original Methodist Orphanage (later picture)

Hattie Brooks with some of her orphans

When she arrived in Enterprise, Mrs. Brooks began caring for 12 orphans on Emma Tucker's property. When the property was sold to the Methodist Church, Hattie Brooks, age 47, simply stayed on and started receiving children from the Methodist churches in Florida. Once she was settled, it seems Mrs. Brooks intended to live permanently in Enterprise. With no Methodist church in town, she did what she'd done in Lakeland: helped to organize one. Although it would be years before that church, called Barnett Methodist, would have its own building, services were regularly held at the orphanage, or sometimes at the Brock House Hotel.

As superintendent of the new orphanage, Hattie Brooks was paid $10 per month per child. The first children brought to her by the Methodists were two sisters from Lakeland, orphaned children of recent Danish immigrants. Dr. Cason took them by train to Sanford, then ferried them across Lake Monroe to the orphanage by rowboat. One of those children, Benia Clemons, grew up to become a matron at the orphanage; every year, one of her descendants has attended the annual Children's Home reunions.

After a year in charge of the fledgling orphanage, though, Mrs. Brooks wasn't entirely happy. Perhaps she missed making her own decisions about what was best for the children she was raising. It's certain she was less than happy with the children's living arrangements. Mrs. Brooks desired to live in her own home where she cared for her rapidly growing family of orphans. With Louise Gramling replacing her as "matron in charge," she left the orphanage in 1909 and bought a house on Main Street from Mr. Voss to serve as her private home for homeless children. "The Old Yellow Hotel," as the building was known, was a boarding house in the Red Light district of Enterprise and rooms were rented by day or longer. Records indicate the orphans may have lived upstairs and two saloons were downstairs. Thought to have been built around 1870, the building ended up as an apartment complex and was demolished in 1987. It was to this home that Doris Faber and her sisters came in 1910.

The Doris Story

Over the years, newspapers have published articles and interviews about the life of Doris Faber, a remarkable woman whose personality and character are woven into the very fabric of Enterprise and Thornby. At the turn of the century, Charles Faber and his wife, Alice, lived in West Palm Beach with their young daughters, Doris, Euretta, Zona and Alma. Charles helped run Faber Brothers Grocery & Butchers. In addition to caring for four children, Alice used a wood stove to bake bread, cakes and pies that were sold at the store. As the oldest, Doris was already adept at helping her mother with baby care and chores — despite being so small that she washed dishes while standing on a chair. Doris' earliest memories included Sunday school, a Fourth of July watermelon big enough for four kids to sit on, and visits from her German grandfather, a retired farmer who could peel an orange despite having just one thumb. She remembered watching the solar eclipse in June 1908 through pieces of glass her mother smoked in the fire for eye safety.

Shortly thereafter, a tragedy all-too-common in those days overtook their lives. Alice Faber, 31 years old, had complications from the birth of a fifth daughter. Alice must have known she would not survive. One morning, she asked little Doris to take care of her youngest sister, and that night she died. Days later, once 6-year-old Doris understood that her mother was gone forever, she bravely took on responsibilities far beyond her years, including caring for year-old Alma. Relatives tried to decide which child would live with which aunt or grandparent, but their father wanted to keep his family together. Amid the household and family chaos, (one of his brothers and a sister-in-law died the same year Charles' wife died), Charles Faber tried to keep the children and the store in good working order. Hiring a housekeeper seemed the best solution but, as Doris lamented, "these came and went. Four little girls under six years old were too much for the average woman to handle." Later, she recalled when one of a series of housekeepers took the girls to a revival meeting. The woman marched Doris and her sisters dressed in their second-hand clothes, to the front of the tent, and addressed the preacher for all to hear: "These are four motherless girls I am caring for." The preacher's response: "Do a good job and the Lord will reward you." When Doris wrote about the incident some 40 years later, the housekeeper's name was long forgotten. She didn't say if she'd felt embarrassed at the time; she mostly kept her emotions private. However, what she did say goes a long way toward explaining who she was and why she chose the life she did. At that moment, as young as she was, she resolved that "nothing would be motherless if I could help it."

Sad and grieving for their mother, Doris' sisters had difficulties, frequently "acting out" as she described later. One sister professed to have a toothache every week at Sunday school. Another sister refused to eat dinner unless she had dessert first. Charles Faber was losing his struggle to hold the family together when a family friend told him about a woman in Enterprise who took children in need and gave them a "happy normal life." A letter was sent to Mrs. Hattie Brooks with a photograph of 2-year-old Alma. The girl's "big brown eyes" and "shoes two sizes too big" persuaded Mrs. Brooks to add four more youngsters to her brood. For his daughters' upkeep, Mr. Faber agreed to pay $2 plus an order of groceries from the Faber Brothers grocery store every week.

Four little girls, wearing their Sunday best, were put on a train. Though they did not know it then, they were leaving home and family behind forever.

Since first hearing her father's plan, Doris' mind was filled with confusion about what would happen and where they would go. She was a scared 8-year-old. Although she'd been raised Episcopalian, for some reason her mind filled with bewildering images of convents and Catholic nuns, enveloped in black from head to toe. But then,

> When the train stopped and we got ready to get off, there was Miss (sic) Brooks. She was all dressed in white with a big, broad-brimmed white hat and she reached up and took my baby sister down from my arms. She looked like an angel.

On the day their new life began, Doris, Euretta, Zona and Alma joined about 15 other children under Mrs. Brooks' care. Doris' first sight was of boys and girls of all ages coming out into the bright sun to welcome the new arrivals, from "the biggest white house I had ever seen." The house was located in Enterprise, on the west side of Main Street, close to Lake Monroe. Pigs and cows roamed freely on Main Street, Doris said. Many years later, she described the place as a former "house of ill repute" and wrote:

> At the time I came, Mrs. Brooks was still cleaning up the rooms and papering the walls. The walls were written all over with unseen remarks. That early age we were all learning to read and enjoyed finding them. Mother Brooks tried to wash the walls before we children got to them but we would outrun her.

"Mrs. Hattie Brooks will make many improvements to her training school by building new verandas and painting her house," announced the *Enterprise Herald* in August 1910.

One of Doris' biggest adjustments was sleeping in a bed by herself. She said that at age 7, "I'd slept most of my life with a baby by my side." As she promised her dying mother, she'd taken on duties far beyond her years, so much so that Mrs. Brooks called her "little mother," even though she was only five years older than the baby sister she cared for! Clearly, a life full of nurturing, and guiding children had its beginnings very early for Doris.

The Faber sisters at least had each other, and they had Hattie Brooks. "After many nights of crying ourselves to sleep," Doris said, "four little girls became content." She learned to sleep in a bed without a baby, and Zona learned to eat dinner before dessert. They had to adapt to life without mother, father, grandparents, home and friends, and so they did. One of Doris' saddest moments came when the baby clothes her mother had made, had to be put away because they were outgrown or worn out. She kept them as mementoes all her life, along with locks of hair, her father's childhood toys, and other "things too numerous to mention." One wonders what became of that priceless treasure trunk.

While no child in normal circumstances wants to live apart from their parents, sometimes tragedy, poverty and other sad happenings make it so. Today's vision of a 1900's "orphanage" might invoke a dark, dismal place, full of sadness or even cruelty. Without modern child-protection laws, we can picture a Charles Dickens, chore-filled life of meager meals in sterile surroundings. In her later years, Doris reminisced about those years spent with Mrs. Brooks in at least two newspaper interviews, and in her own typed 12-page manuscript, "The Doris Story." Life as she described it didn't resemble a gloomy Victorian-era orphanage. Instead, she described a "happy lakeside town," with group dances, boat trips and tree-fresh oranges. Mrs. Brooks showered the children with love and affection and the townspeople opened their hearts and homes, too. Locals provided food for the annual school picnic for Mrs. Brooks' and the orphanage children. For Doris, riding to DeLand on Saturdays with Mr. and Mrs. Theodore Throop, who had the first Ford car in Enterprise, was a special treat. (The Throop's chicken farm, home to 50,000 chickens, and with its own cornfield for feed, was reputed to be the largest in the country.)

Holidays and birthdays were always special for Mrs. Brooks' children. One warm Thanksgiving featured a picnic with turkey and trimmings on the shores of Lake Monroe. The town and orphanage children came together for the Easter egg hunt following church services, when Mr. Throop gave the children eggs to color. Churchwomen brought colored eggs, cookies and goodies. Women guests at the nearby Brock House hotel bought the Easter baskets, and afterwards provided cake, ice cream and lemonade on the hotel porch. At Christmas, a hotel guest dressed up as Santa and other guests gave them candy and treats.

In a 1990 interview, Zona Faber McAlexander reminisced about an early Independence Day celebration in Enterprise, "famous at the time for its chickens and children." Doris, Euretta and Zona wore patriotic dresses and carried flags as the "Red, White and Blue Sisters." A parade followed, then singing, races, contests, and a picnic with homemade ice cream. The day ended with a speech and old-time singing at the historic All Saints Episcopal Church. She felt "the spirit of a young American" that day, Zona said.

Of course, there were chores and responsibilities, as in any family. Each child at Mrs. Brooks' had to make their bed, a process that included turning the mattress every day. Doris said that the older children helped the younger ones with this and other jobs like tending the garden and the animals.

As Doris tells it, when her father and uncle visited the girls for the first time, he sampled the water from Benson Springs (on the site of the former Enterprise power plant). Considered to be health-giving by the locals, it was "a combination of iron and other minerals" and tasted, she said, like rotten eggs smelt (sic). Mr. Faber told his daughters that if they didn't learn to drink the water, "I will take you away from here." So, they learned to drink it because "the threat of leaving Enterprise made us like it."

Religion was a major part of Doris' life from childhood until death. The same was true for her new mother, Hattie Brooks. Doris became a Methodist like Mrs. Brooks, and clearly found her new faith comforting in dealing with her new life in a new place. Religion was very much a part of everyday life at Mrs. Brooks' home. Doris recalled chilly evenings by a blazing fire, with Mrs. Brooks in a rocking chair, reading her Bible to the children sitting all around her, and Grandpa Greene, tall and stately, teaching them his favorite Psalms. The best learner got 25 cents to spend, as they liked. In those days, memorizing Bible verses was a routine childhood exercise. There was a Psalm and a prayer before breakfast.

For regular church services, Mrs. Brooks' children usually joined the Methodist children at the orphanage. Easter sunrise services were like ours today. But Doris paints an affecting picture of Vespers on moonlit summer evenings, when a "mixed group of children, guests, elderly and black" would often gather on the long Brock House dock to pray and sing hymns.

At one such service, after they sang the beloved hymn "Day is Dying in the West," a hotel guest told those on the dock the story of how the song came to be. Many years ago, near New York's Lake Chataqua, she told them, a young woman received a telegram that her fiancé was dead. In her grief, she ran to the lake, intending to drown herself. The dying sun's pink and gold rays were mirrored in the deep, darkening water, filling the wide evening sky with an angelic glow — the most glorious sunset she'd ever seen. She watched, transfixed, until dusk came, dim stars appeared and then, on the back of the telegram, she wrote the lyrics to what would become one of the world's favorite hymns:

> Day is dying in the west;
> Heav'n is touching earth with rest;
> Wait and worship while the night
> Sets the evening lamps alight
> Through all the sky.

"The story is mine," Brock House guest Mary Lathbury told the assembled crowd on the hotel pier. "I was that young woman."

Later in Doris' life, her relationship with a local beau ended badly when he married someone else. Doris often said "Day is Dying" meant more to her than any other hymn. Perhaps in a way she related to Mary Lathbury's sadness, and found solace from her own heartbreak in the "Heart of Love Enfolding All" (another verse from the same hymn).

Two other incidents from her childhood, as she recounted in "The Doris Story," help explain what made Doris Faber the person she was.

One Thanksgiving Day, Doris and others carried plates of food prepared by Mrs. Brooks to two elderly spinster sisters in Enterprise. The ladies' gratitude that they had not been forgotten, Doris said, made her own food that day taste better. All her life, she was known for her cooking and baking; it was one way she connected with people.

The second event occurred on her eighth birthday. She was hoping to receive a Bible as her gift; she would get to stay up half an hour past bedtime to read it, as that was the rule. Two days before her birthday, "one of the older girls" ruined the surprise by telling Doris she had seen her new Bible. She was still happy to get it, of course, but it made her a reliable keeper of secrets. Years later she said, "I love secrets to this day, but they are safe for I never want to have the joy spoiled like mine was."

One of many generous visitors to the orphans at Mrs. Brooks' home was Sara "Margaret" Wells of Johnstown, New York, and a winter resident of DeLand. Margaret, a single, middle-aged woman, was a judge's daughter who had been to far-off places like Scotland and Italy. "She'd entertain us for hours, telling about her travels and letting us look at pictures in her stereoscope," Doris recalled. Because she grew up without a mother, all her life Doris formed bonds with mother figures like Margaret Wells. Their connection, however, reached well beyond simple kindness shown to a young orphan girl. Meeting and getting to know Margaret Wells opened the door for Doris Faber to begin the journey that led to her full and happy life at Thornby.

Life-Changing Meetings

In 1916, armies were converging in Europe and the world was about to change forever. Much closer to home, two meetings in Enterprise that year would alter Doris Faber's world forever.

After Mrs. Brooks left her job as orphanage matron in 1909 to re-open her own children's shelter, the orphanage population continued to grow. By 1916, about 60 children lived there. While the Faber sisters were living contentedly (under the circumstances) nearby, in a homey setting under the close guidance of "Mother" Brooks, things at the orphanage were unsettled. Money for food, clothes and operating expenses was always hard to come by. Conflicts arose when some church officials tried, unsuccessfully, to relocate the orphanage to either Jacksonville or St. Augustine. But management turnover proved the most potent "source of demoralization." Six different superintendents had come and gone in the seven years since Hattie Brooks left. One of them, according to Doris Faber, was fired for misuse of church funds. Lack of stability was a problem, and the solution was literally right around the corner: bring back the excellent and well-loved Mrs. Brooks.

In a meeting that would prove life-changing for Doris and her sisters, Hattie Brooks agreed to return as orphanage superintendent, albeit with conditions. Mrs. Brooks said "she would take over the Home from the mess it was in," as Doris candidly put it years later, but insisted that the church committee buy the much more suitable "Smith place" on Lake Monroe, which came with an old, three-story farm house. Her "children" (the Faber sisters and four others she was raising) would come with her. She had been away from the orphanage for seven years; the trustees would probably have agreed to anything to bring her back. As reported in the *New Smyrna News* of September 8, 1916:

> .....A tract of 17 acres has been bought.....beautifully located on the banks of Lake Monroe. The newly-acquired land abuts that originally purchased for the orphanage site when it was established at Enterprise about six years ago. . . the dwelling on the property will be enlarged and improved. . . to make the orphanage an ideal home for children. . . with the natural advantages and beautiful surroundings this end will be obtained within a short time.

Doris, Euretta, Zona and Alma had no choice. When Mrs. Brooks went back to her former job as orphanage superintendent, they went with her. Doris was no complainer. She voiced no outright gripes about her new life, but one can infer that times had gotten a bit tougher. They ate "lots of grits and gravy and very good bread." Zona Faber recalled in the March 1928 *Orphans Friend* (the campus newsletter printed from 1926 to 1941): "The first meal in the orphanage I remember was a pitifully meager one. The dinner consisted of tomatoes. Yes, just that one thing. At first, we had to sit on boxes and eat out of tin cups." Boys slept on one side of a long sleeping porch, girls on the other, on cots separated by canvas curtains. There were two dressing rooms, one for girls and one for boys. Doris recalled Mrs. Brooks' father, whom the children called "Grandpa" Greene, chasing stray bats out of the sleeping rooms. After a couple of years, thankfully, accommodations improved.

Doris admitted that things at the orphanage got "critical at times" but "we used what we had and made the best of it," a philosophy that informed her whole life. Doris said in a 1984 interview that when she lived at the orphanage, it was financially supported, in large part, by many guests at Enterprise's renowned Brock House. If so, the rewards were mutual. In those days before radio and TV, hotel guests were entertained by local "players" from the Children's Home who recited poetry, sang and performed skits.

On Friday nights, the Home's girls dressed up and pretended to be visitors at the Brock House. "Here is where we got our first training at being hostess and welcoming guests," Doris said years later. For many years, then, pampered guests at Thornby would have had ample reason to be grateful to Mrs. Brooks' training, had they known where Miss Doris' aptitude for gracious hospitality had its start.

The Faber sisters, circa 1919, clockwise from top left - Doris, Euretta, Alma and Zona

The orphanage children had a work schedule for every month, and at the end of the month, they switched chores. Inside, Mrs. Brooks would test how well the orphanage children would clean by hiding dollar bills for them in places that might be easily overlooked. Outside, they kept cows, pigs and chickens. Wood for cooking and heating came from old railroad ties, pulled up by a horse and chain and "snaked" along the ground by the older boys. The acreage was used to grow vegetables like peppers, carrots, onions and cucumbers that were canned and preserved. During World War I, Doris said, "we had a large garden and canned and preserved everything we ate" — the output was later figured at 60,000 quarts. "The children did all the preparing of the fruit and vegetables. Everything had to be hand sealed and soldered, with an iron. We canned out of doors, under the oak tree, down by the flowing well," she said. It's no wonder that she learned to be frugal and not waste a thing. When she wrote a letter as an adult, her handwriting was squeezed on the page as if to scrimp on wasteful margins.

The same year, 14-year-old Doris met for the first time hotel guests Dr. and Mrs. James Glass, winter visitors from Utica, NY. The Brock House was almost a second home to Doris and the other orphanage children, and she already knew Mrs. Glass' sister, Margaret Wells, a regular seasonal visitor. Who could have then imagined that a simple introduction and a polite "how do you do?" would open the door to Doris' "life of interest and excitement" (her words) - and forge community ties so strong that friends and strangers alike would fight ferociously to preserve them — 75 years later.

By 1917, Charles Faber, the father who'd placed his daughters under Hattie Brooks' care seven years earlier, had fallen on hard times:

> ....through misfortune and loss of my property, I am not financially able to pay the amount agreed upon between Mrs. Brooks and myself, and I have not been able to pay the same for several years....

and signed a legal agreement to "release, remise and surrender to [Mrs. Brooks] the care, custody, and control of ...." Doris,15; Euretta, 14; Zona, 12 and Alma, 10. The Faber grocery business had failed; Charles and his relatives spent the next years struggling as small farmers in Brevard County. But Charles Faber, along with other family members, always had a role in his daughters' lives, and he made the long, dusty trip to visit them when he could. Doris was especially close to her paternal grandmother Barbara Faber, a tough "cracker" who lived to be 106 years old.

It was around this time that Doris began to call herself "Doris Brooks Faber." Her personal stationery was imprinted that way. Her social security card was issued to "Doris Brooks Faber." Her father had relinquished his parental rights; census and other sources refer to the Faber sisters as Hattie Brooks' "adopted daughters." Mrs. Brooks told a Methodist church publication in

1927 that of the nine children she'd adopted, four were grown, one married — a description that fits the Fabers to a "T." In a 1950s letter, Doris mentions her "adopted mother." Such evidence supports the conclusion that Mrs. Brooks legally adopted the Faber sisters; however, no official record of a Brooks-Faber adoption in the county archives has been located.

In the early 1920s, the orphanage population reached nearly 100 children, including the Faber sisters. New facilities were built on campus, the crops and animals were flourishing, and the residents' health was reportedly excellent, due in part to their "outdoor life . . . swimming and diving." At the head of it was Hattie Brooks, described by the Children's Home as "a dynamic and influential force during the formative years of the Orphanage." Doris later reminisced about one special Christmas around that time. Radio was just coming on the scene, and the orphans, instead of exchanging homemade gifts, saved every cent they could earn to buy a brand new Atwater Kent radio, which they gave to Mrs. Brooks for Christmas. Then they listened in awe as "Silent Night" and other carols floated across the airwaves, even after they went to bed. It was life lessons like this that taught Doris to give, to share, and to make the most of what you have.

In 1920, although Hattie Brooks "officially" resigned as orphanage superintendent for health reasons, she stayed on for three more years. According to the 100-year anniversary publication of the Florida United Methodist Children's Home, Mrs. Brooks served the orphans with "tremendous effectiveness." When she finally left in 1923, she moved just a few blocks away. Four years later, she had 18 children under her own roof, "not counting members of her own family." All nine of the children she had adopted were "making good," she said. Mrs. Brooks was planning a reunion of her 200 "children" and 20 "grandchildren," and "making provision for the continuation of the good work begun more than 20 years ago, after she passes away," according to The Orphans' Friend. "She is a woman of vision, consecration and courage," the newsletter said.

On Thanksgiving Day, 1929, Enterprise's Barnett Methodist Church was consecrated, after years of hard work that sprang from Hattie Brooks' $100 donation in 1914. Among special gifts to the new church that day were the pulpit Bible from the Faber sisters, and a piano donated by Hattie Brooks. Today, Barnett Methodist is still serving its Enterprise congregation from the same historic building.

At 67, Hattie Brooks was still caring for children. She was listed in the 1930 census as "manager-cook" of a "hotel" — or, more accurately, a foster home — in town. Seven of her "boarders" (Leola Dreggors, Jean Shaw, Frederick Poulson, Harold James, Eleanor and France Atwater, and A. B. Harris) were children under 14. Doris, Euretta, and Alma Faber lived there too; helping her care for the needy children in her charge, just as she'd once cared for them. They were listed as Mrs. Brooks' "adopted daughters."

Finally, at age 72, Mrs. Brooks retired. Although still living in Enterprise, for the first time in 30 years, she wasn't raising children.

The Faber sisters, of course, were no longer the little girls she had sheltered. Zona was the first to leave the nest. She attended high school and college in Alabama and returned to the orphanage to work as a dietician, where she married a fellow employee; they eventually had two daughters. Euretta became a teacher at the Enterprise Elementary School. Alma worked for the popular Morrison's Cafeteria chain for years.

Doris might never have left Florida had she not come down with malaria — a disease quite common in the state until the 1950s — as a young woman. A drier, cooler climate was recommended, and good friends came to her aid. "In 1923…Dr. and Mrs. Glass [took] me into their house at Trenton Falls, NY in order for me to get over it and have a change of climate. This changed my entire life."

Why did she feel that staying with the Glasses changed her life? She may have been referring to the bond that formed between the Glasses and herself. The ties between the cheerful, hard-working young woman and the childless older couple strengthened each year — ties that held firm until the end of their lives, very much like parents and daughter. According to Zona's memoir, Doris spent summers with Dr. and Mrs. Glass in New York in the late 1920s. Possibly, at least some of her trips were to recuperate from a medical condition she preferred to keep private. (In her diary, Doris mentioned having medical problems that led to major surgery, but she omitted dates and details.) The news was very frightening, she wrote, and she had no money for the operation. Once again, her powerful faith in God sustained her. Her prayers were answered, many friends contributed small amounts of money, sufficient to pay for everything, and "things worked out for I had no more trouble."

Kids were her Life

In 1933, 29-year old Doris Faber began work at the orphanage as housemother to the young boys in Brinkley Cottage. "I loved this service," she relates in her memoirs, "and my little family was a happy group. We had lots of parties and lots of fun." Being responsible for 20 or 30 little boys, 24 hours a day with one day off per month in the midst of the Depression couldn't have been *all* fun. Still, she had a sunny nature that delighted in children and treasured the chance to help them grow.

Depending on their age, every orphanage child had responsibilities. Boys did all the work with the chickens, pigs and sheep. Girls worked in the laundry. Enterprise resident Wilbur Bruce was one of the boys who lived at Brinkley.

Doris Faber and boys of Brinkley Cottage
Wilbur Bruce, bottom row, second from left

He remembers when a girl's arm was severed after being caught in a mangle. One of his jobs was laundry boy, meaning he was responsible for banking the steam boiler that heated water for the industrial-sized laundry that served the entire orphanage. In those stricter times, water too cold or too hot meant a whipping. At age 13, Wilbur had to milk six cows, twice a day (for 50 cents a month). However, as he told the *Daytona Beach News-Journal* in 2008, orphanage life also featured baseball games, bike riding, and swimming in the pond. Teenagers then were not much different than teenagers have always been. Wilbur relates how the older boys would slip off the grounds for late-night adventures that by today's standards might be considered rather tame, such as swimming in the springs on private property.

While Doris was housemother to the boys at Brinkley, her friendship with the Glasses that began a decade earlier, grew stronger. The Glasses took a special interest in the orphanage boys, and Doris must have valued the Glasses' kindness to the orphanage. In an undated letter, she described how, in 1921, the farm work and chopping wood didn't provide enough work to keep "44 big boys" busy. The older boys needed a new dormitory. Since Mrs. Brooks believed wholeheartedly in the idle hands = devil's workshop theory, they decided to build the dorm right there. With "brick making" equipment donated by Dr. Glass (more precisely, they were making concrete blocks) the boys, helped by the girls at times, went to work. The job took most of two summers. When Epworth Hall was completed, William Jennings Bryan was guest speaker at the dedication ceremony.

Doris tells that the boys in Brinkley Cottage enjoyed radio shows like "I Love a Mystery." With episodes titled "Murder, Hollywood Style" and "Temple of Vampires," it was no wonder. They also liked "The Grand Ole Opry." In addition, when the World Series was broadcast, she would set the radio on a windowsill so people outside could hear it, too.

The Depression years took their toll on the orphanage, as everywhere in the country. *The Orphans Friend* reported in 1931 that more than 3 million Octagon Soap coupons had been collected on campus. Not many people are alive today who remember Octagon Soap, but saving those coupons became a major part of Orphanage life. Soap coupons paid for a new truck, a kitchen range, and band uniforms for the residents when there was no money otherwise to buy them.

Another fund-raising vehicle was the Senior Choir, which Wilbur Bruce says was started in a desperate effort to help pay the Home's electric bill before the power company cut off service. Wilbur was one of the singers who, with their chaperone, toured the state in a church bus on weekends, singing for churches and civic groups. They did this for many years, and the donations they gathered went a long way toward keeping stomachs filled and lights on.

By cutting salaries and making other reductions, the orphanage kept its doors open for 130 children through the Depression. Still, some needy young ones had to be turned away for lack of funds. On Thanksgiving Day in 1934, the orphanage held its first homecoming. Maybe they were grateful that things weren't worse.

Discipline Back in the Day

A survey taken in the 1930s found that *more than 90 percent* of parents spanked their children. When Doris Faber was raised, authority figures like teachers were considered substitutes for parents when away from home. It comes as no surprise, then, that she believed that sparing the rod meant spoiling the child. Wilbur Bruce was one of her charges at Brinkley, and not all of his memories of those days are cheerful. "She was tough on boys," he says. Like Doris, Wilbur and his three brothers were "dependent half orphans," that is, children with a surviving parent who could not take care of them. He lived at the orphanage for 12 years, from age 6 to 18. It was a different day and a different way of life. "Everybody [who misbehaved] was struck," he recalls, relating how Miss Doris whacked him and another boy with a paddle while they were corralled in a bathtub. "If you got out of line some days, you'd go to bed without supper." His brother Howard, delayed on his paper route was paddled for feeding the animals late.

Some of the rules seem harsh by today's standards. For instance, church services at Barnett Methodist on Sunday were a must for every child, but Doris' insistence that church be followed by a one-hour nap meant that 6-year old Wilbur missed part of his father's Sunday visits when their dad bicycled from what is now DeBary to the orphanage. More than once, little Wilbur tried to follow his dad home by running after the bike, along the shell-and-clay road that's now Lakeshore Drive.

Wilbur's wife, Catherine Emanuel Bruce, grew up in Enterprise; she remembers that Doris once punished a wayward little boy by making him pick prickly sandspurs and then count them into piles. Wilbur, who lived with Doris Faber as his housemother for years, is quick to point out that she was "not a saint." Wilbur left the orphanage at 18, but came back to settle permanently in Enterprise in the 60s, eventually joining the board of Barnett Methodist Church, to which Doris Faber dedicated so much of her life. As he came to know her as an adult with kids of his own, any lingering resentment Wilbur held for her early tough treatment of him dissipated; in fact, his own two sons went to Miss Doris after school. "Our kids loved to go to Thornby," relates Catherine. "She'd cook and they got to see the animals. "To this day Joe can't forget the cookies."

The years have taken us far from the days when physical punishment of children was not only accepted, but also expected, and most people find it amiss to judge the past by modern standards. Doris Faber's ways of discipline were the ways of most people at the time, and those who knew her best accept that those ways grew out of her loving goal — growing children into the best adults they could be. Carolyn Langley sums it up this way: "Miss Doris had a reputation for keeping boys in line, and I know from personal observation how tough she could be. But, she was also very caring and loving and would help anyone in need."

What Once Was, Remains

In 1935, while Doris Faber was housemother to the little boys at the orphanage, "Mother" Hattie Brooks died while visiting relatives in San Antonio, Texas. A simple but substantial headstone in a quiet back corner of the Enterprise Evergreen Cemetery bears her name, and her death certificate states that her body was returned to DeLand, Florida. Although no burial records are available, it's safe to assume that she was laid to rest in Enterprise where she spent half her life caring for children in need. A few feet away lies her father, "Grandfather" Richard F. Greene, as well as the burial sites of two young girls from the Home who died more than 60 years ago. And under nearby pines, a plain white monument marked simply: "Florida Methodist Children's Home," stands sentinel like a mother watching over her children, day and night, year after year, decade after decade.

The Florida Methodist Orphanage, now called the Florida United Methodist Children's Home, has been a local landmark for more than 100 years, providing a home and other services, such as emergency shelter and counseling, to children from ages 5 through 18. It is a designated Florida Heritage Site. Most importantly, "It was a home," says former resident Larry Ivey. "We were all family and we are still family." Undoubtedly, his words would make Hattie Brooks and Doris Faber very proud.

> *The lives he literally saved through charity were many.*
>
> **James Glass' obituary**

CHAPTER THREE

To Live In Hearts We Leave Behind, Is Not To Die

Part I: A Charitable Man

Why do some people remain alive in our memory years after they die, while our memories of others fade?

Usually, families keep memories alive, either because they loved someone when they were living, or feel a bond with a relative they never knew. Or, like Elvis, some people were famous enough when alive to be part of everyone's memory. On the other hand, a person's name can be forever linked to an event, as Dr. Salk is to polio vaccine, or to a place, as Frank Lloyd Wright is to Fallingwater.

In the middle of New York State, on the famous Erie Canal, lies the town of Mohawk. It was a tiny village of 200 when James Henderson Glass, first child of Robert Glass and Emily Merrill Glass, was born there on June 15, 1854. His Canadian-born father was a wagon-maker, later a mechanic; his mother a farm girl with New York roots going back at least to the 1700s. Three younger brothers soon followed.

JAMES H. GLASS, M. D.
SURGEON IN CHARGE OF THE FAXTON HOSPITAL

What was life like for boys growing up in Civil War-era rural New York State? With its many waterways, the Mohawk Valley was a robust manufacturing center for textiles, furniture and other goods. The area likely reaped at least some benefits from a wartime economy, and no Civil War battles were fought in New York State. In the midst of a bustling commerce center, Mohawk had three churches, two hotels and a few other businesses. An old map of Mohawk shows the Glass family house just blocks from the Erie Canal and Mohawk River. James and his brothers probably played on the towpath, built rafts, and every chance they got, kept an eye on the boats and barges loading and unloading their cargo. In addition, "he was very fond of outdoor life and sports," his obituary recounted years later. "As a boy, he was one of the best baseball players in the county." They would have enjoyed the dense woods and fields on the village outskirts, too — playing soldiers, maybe. It seems apparent that Glass' lifelong love for wooded land, rivers and lakes, so evident in the Trenton Falls and Enterprise properties he bought later in life, grew from those early years in Mohawk.

The boys went to public school. In addition to youthful employment in a pharmacy, census records indicate that as a teenager, James Glass worked on a farm belonging to the Northrup Family in Onondaga County, New York. It wasn't uncommon in those times for teenaged or even younger children to leave home in order to help support the family. His arduous stint as a hired farm laborer may have helped shape the work ethic and stamina that stayed with him throughout his life.

We can only speculate about why James Glass, a small-town wagon maker's son, chose medicine as his profession. Did working at the pharmacy provoke an interest in medicine? Was he following in the footsteps of a yet-undiscovered doctor, a family or friend role model? Those would be the expected paths leading to medical training. Research suggests a tragically different possibility, however, because, of Robert and Emily Glass' four sons, James was the only one who reached adulthood.

Franklin Glass died at age 12, cause unknown. Harley Glass died much younger, cause also unknown. Federal census records report that Charles Glass, age 9, of Herkimer County, New York, died in 1869 of "hydrocephalus," or a closed head injury — typically, a result of trauma — a fall from a horse, for example. James was 15 years old when Charles died.

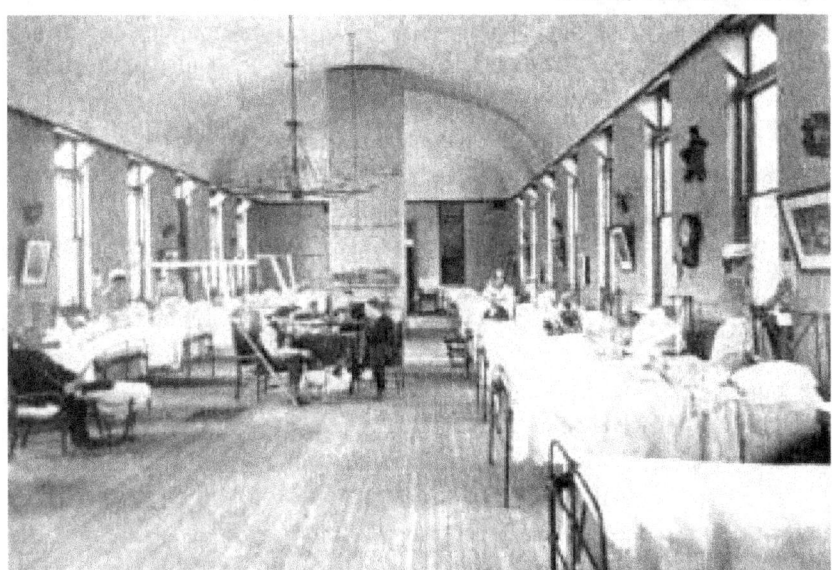
Bellevue Hospital, circa 1870

Did grief over his three brothers' deaths propel James to medical school? It was said of Dr. Glass as a surgeon that, "if a man had one chance in a hundred, he went for that chance."

During the 1800s, medical school was not four years followed by years of internships and residencies, all after four years of college, as it is now. After attending the University of Michigan at Ann Arbor for two years, in 1874 James Glass entered what was then Bellevue Medical School in New York City, living with an aunt each summer and "interning" with a physician in Oneida County, New York. After graduating in 1877, the new Dr. Glass stayed at Bellevue Hospital, doing "ambulance service and substitute work" for a couple of years.

Although his goal was to be a surgeon, he started in general practice, since in those days, that specialty was achieved through hard work and on-the-job training rather than formal education. He worked briefly in Watkins, New York, but the town suffered economic decline after the railroad changed routes. Seeking the opportunities a larger town could bring, he settled on Utica (pop. 33,000) because it was near his parents' home, and in 1880 he set up practice there. The young doctor soon got a very lucrative offer to partner with an established physician, but declined because he wanted to "stand on his own merits."

In only two years, Dr. James Glass became attending surgeon at St. Luke's Hospital, which means that he was already considered an expert in surgery. That same year (1882), he married Anna Wells in her hometown of Johnstown, New York. His career path took him to St. Elizabeth's Hospital, and then to the

Utica City Hospital. Finally, in 1893, he found a permanent home at Faxton Hospital in Utica, where he remained as surgeon in charge until his retirement almost 30 years later. Founded in 1875, Faxton Hospital, now Faxton/St. Luke's, is the largest health care provider in the Mohawk Valley.

As his fortunes improved, James moved his offices several times into larger spaces on Utica's busiest thoroughfare, Genesee Street. At 288 Genesee, office hours were unusual by today's standards: 12-1 pm; 4-5 pm, and 7-8 pm., but since his office was in his home, as was the case with most doctors then, it made sense. Mornings surely were filled with hospital rounds and surgeries. That he was making a good living is evident, since the Glasses had live-in help.

Over the next years, he built an extremely busy general practice, eventually phasing his work fully into surgery, as had been his dream. He carried a large caseload that only increased over the years. "He knew his anatomy as he did his alphabet," it was said in his obituary, and "he never lost a clean (non-infected) case," even though his referrals were often the worst cases that other doctors could not help. Along with his skills, his speed in the operating room won praise because in those pre-antibiotic days, the longer a patient's wound was open, the greater the risk of infection. At that time, being a surgeon meant being jack-of-all trades: he might set a broken leg in the morning and perform a Caesarian section in the afternoon. Dr. Glass was known as one of America's best surgeons, noted his obituary, yet he never recommended surgery unless there was no other option.

To get away from the pressures of the city and his home/office a few short blocks from the hospital, Dr. Glass bought a small weekend farm on the

Dr. Glass' former medical office and home as it looked in 2009

outskirts of Utica called Graffenburg Farm where he raised dogs, cattle, and chickens.

In about 1911, he sold the weekend place and began buying property on which to build a summer home in the Trenton Falls area of central New York State. At the time, Trenton Falls was akin to Niagara Falls or Saratoga Springs in its popularity with tourists. It's a geologic wonderland of waterfalls and rare limestone formations, valleys and ravines, and (like Enterprise) prized for years for its curative sulphur baths. Over the next 12 years, the Glasses bought 300 acres and remodeled the land's old farmhouse into a rambling white dwelling they called "The Mohawks." (Their actual address was Russia, New York, an Enterprise-sized hamlet near the Adirondack Mountains.) The property, situated on West Canada Creek, featured hills and woods and was "one of the most attractive places in this part of the state," according to a local newspaper. They farmed part of the land and built ponds and lush, terraced gardens that enhanced their dramatic view into the Trenton Falls. Trenton Falls was a popular enclave of summer residences for Utica physicians and their families to escape the city's heat and grime. There were picnics on the lawn, croquet matches, and hiking on scenic trails. The doctors' wives and children spent summers enjoying their wooded rural retreat, joined by their husbands and fathers on weekends.

Dr. and Mrs. Glass were known for opening their home to the community, and Trenton Falls was no exception. The couple did more than entertain and relax there. Dr. Glass had cottages built on his property that friends could use. Moreover, with his usual thoughtfulness, he invited nurses from Faxton Hospital to spend their few weeks' vacations as his family's guests at The Mohawks every summer. Likewise, the *Utica Herald-Dispatch* reported that "more than 50 women motored there" for a meeting of the Women's Missionary Society hosted by Mrs. Glass during the summer of 1919.

The Mohawks, Trenton Falls, NY, circa 1915

Professional recognition, honors and awards were heaped on Dr. Glass throughout his career. Consistently listed in *Who's Who in America*, he was president of his county's medical society, one of the *Notable Men of Central New York,* and was included in the *History of Oneida County,* which heralded him as "one of the foremost surgeons of the state." In 1897, he served as a delegate to the International Medical Congress in Moscow. His life-long quest to stay abreast of the latest techniques led him to observe surgeries in Europe and Asia, and in 1894, he authored a paper on "Original Transplantation of Entire Human Ovary." In a long career filled with significant contributions to medical science, though, one in 1891 stands out because it likely served (and saved) more people than anything else: in an era when infection probably killed as many patients as illness did, Dr. Glass started the practice of aseptic (sterile) surgery at Faxton Hospital.

In addition to operating up to five times a day (at two or three hospitals), Dr. Glass donated his surgical skills to the Utica Dispensary, a free clinic "for treatment of the sick poor." In fact, he was president of the clinic for years, staying on even after he retired. He was a lieutenant and surgeon in the National Guard, a trustee of Hamilton College in New York, and a member or officer of uncounted local, state and national professional societies, including the National Association of Railway Surgeons and the American College of Surgeons.

Professional achievements, however laudable, don't totally define a person. To know someone truly is to watch where their heart takes them, to see what they do for others and what they expect in return. By that measure, James Glass excelled in humanity in the same way he excelled in medicine. His obituary says he lived by the old principle of "do good and throw it into the sea." Today we might call it, "hiding your light under a bushel." He was rich, but he could have been richer. He'd perform surgery for a fair price, for part of it, or for nothing if the need was there. He gave away "very considerable" sums of money without expecting repayment, and no one ever knew about it unless the recipient told the story. "None will ever know the good he did for its own sake without a penny by way of recompense." (*Utica Daily Press,* Sept. 21, 1931). Health insurance was not generally available a hundred years ago, even if you had the money to buy it. We have to wonder today, if money that Dr. Glass' parents lacked to pay for medical care might have saved their sons from early deaths. He would make sure that other families didn't suffer the same fate.

Dr. Glass was dedicated, brilliant and successful, but he was not a back-in-the-day workaholic. With seemingly the same 24 hours in a day as the rest of us, he also managed to have a long and happy marriage; show prize-winning Irish setters and English beagles (as founder and president of the Central New

York Kennel Club); raise horses, and take hunting and fishing trips. For a time, he was an appointed "special game warden" in the Herkimer, New York area. And, there was his winter home at Thornby.

> The [property] which most pleased his fancy was Enterprise, at the head of the St. Johns River, and there he built a very handsome home where the river widens out and is known as Lake Monroe... He was exceptionally fond of his winter home and its environment... He kept himself busy... enjoying the outdoor life and the freedom from professional care. (*Utica Daily Press*, Aug. 5, 1931)

Throughout the early 1900s, Dr. Glass continued an intense schedule of surgeries, patient care, board meetings, education, philanthropy, and professional travel. Eventually, he suffered the effects of a chronic heart condition, no doubt exacerbated by his high-stress surgical career. In 1922, after nearly 30 years, he retired from his position as chief surgeon at Faxton Hospital. Even after retirement, he continued to support the Utica free clinic with his time and money, and helped to raise funds for a new building. However, every November through April, home was in Enterprise, at Thornby.

In Florida, Dr. Glass never took out an official license to practice medicine, although he is said to have helped people in emergencies, including victims of a local train accident in the late 1920s. His obituary explained that, to an experienced physician like Dr. Glass, the lack of a formal state license simply meant that he could more easily help people without concern about when, or if, they could pay. "He did, however, go in scores of humble homes" while in Enterprise, says his obituary, and "many a poor black man and many a poor white man received the benefit of his ministrations, and the only reward he would accept was their heartfelt thanks." Interestingly, the 1920 census shows that most of Thornby's neighbors were black. A white physician treating poor black people for free in the rural, segregated South of that time seems exceptionally enlightened. Maybe the reason Enterprise was a "happy little lakeside town" was because its citizens, both black and white, were truly neighbors.

The Glasses had a fair-share policy when it came to church fund-raising. The records of Utica's Westminster Presbyterian Church indicate that Dr. and Mrs. Glass donated $100 to its building fund in 1922, and records from Enterprise's historic Barnett Methodist Church show that Dr. Glass donated wiring and electrical fixtures for the new church building, dedicated on Thanksgiving Day, 1929.

> "He was a staunch friend, a good citizen, and in every sense, a manly man." (*Utica Daily Press*, September 21, 1931)

Although Thornby is a beloved landmark to people in Enterprise, the name of its owner, James Henderson Glass, is one that most today would not recognize. Dr. Glass had no children and his few descendants, gained through marriage, lived a thousand miles from Enterprise. He was famous, too, but not in a way that made headlines. When, with characteristic humility, he named his Enterprise home "Thornby" instead of "Glassby," it was virtually guaranteed that scant years after his death, very few would know the name of the man who once lived there, and fewer still would know anything about him. A handful of people interviewed for this narrative remember his wife, who survived him by many years, but none knew Dr. Glass. His home on Thornby no longer exists, and there are no signs or monuments on the land to commemorate who he was or what he did. The good things he did for Enterprise and its church, its orphans, its citizens of all colors, are lost in the jungle that covers his beloved property, lost like the Enterprise springs, the deer and bears that roamed the woods, the orange groves and corn fields, the steamboats on Lake Monroe, the famous Brock House. All that remains is the property called Thornby.

> 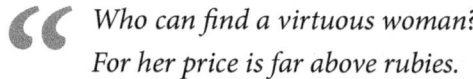 *Who can find a virtuous woman? For her price is far above rubies.*
>
> **– Proverbs 31:10**

Part II: One of the Loveliest Ladies I have ever Known

Anna Wells was born in 1860 into a prominent family in Johnstown, New York, a small town in the foothills of the Adirondack Mountains. She was the youngest of four children of Judge John Wells, a former state legislator, and his wife, Margaret. Her mother died when she was a child; her father remarried, then died when she was a teenager. After Judge Wells' death, Anna, her siblings, and her stepmother moved into the home of her paternal grandmother — and two servants. Overall, it was an upbringing considerably more privileged than that of her future husband.

How or when they met, no one now living knows, but James Henderson Glass, 27, and Anna Wells, 22, wed on May 31, 1882, in the bride's home town. They set up housekeeping in Utica, 60 miles away, where James Glass had started his own practice two years before. There, Mrs. Glass joined the Westminster Presbyterian Church.

When Carolyn Watson Langley, formerly of Enterprise, was a young girl, Mrs. Glass was in her 90's. Carolyn remembers her as a petite woman, quiet, and pleasant in nature. Carolyn regrets that she didn't ask more questions of Mrs. Glass to learn more about her life. Anna Glass was born before the Civil War and lived into the Sputnik era. Along the way, the small-town judge's

James and Anna Glass in Egypt, circa 1912

daughter who married a young doctor became the wife of one of the foremost surgeons of the day. She was a woman of her time. Her role as a prominent physician's wife would have been to love and support her husband, making their homes a warm respite from hospital pressures and the life-and-death decisions he made every day. She traveled the world with him, was an ardent church member and donor, and for years provided a gracious "home away from home" to visiting colleagues, family and friends, whether in Utica, Trenton Falls, or Enterprise.

According to passport records, in 1912, Dr. and Mrs. Glass spent six months traveling abroad. The following year, they sailed to Cuba and Hong Kong, returning to the United States via San Francisco. Carolyn Watson Langley vividly remembers Mrs. Glass' collection of beautiful china and glassware, brought back to Thornby from all over the world. One can imagine how their tales of adventure in far-flung places, brought back to tiny Enterprise, Florida, and shared on mild winter evenings on Thornby's big, welcoming front porch, delighted visitors, young and old alike.

The Glasses certainly enjoyed material success in the form of homes and properties, horses, servants, cars and foreign travel in a day when most people could only dream of visiting exotic places like Russia. They had a happy marriage, close family ties, and friends around the globe. James and Anna Glass seemed to have had everything they wanted except a family of their own. Perhaps an unfilled longing to be parents explains the Glass' lifelong dedication to children. Possibly the childhood deaths of Dr. Glass' brothers left a void that he filled by helping youngsters in need. Mrs. Glass' nieces and nephew, and their children, were always welcomed and treated as if they were the Glass' own children. One great-niece, Catherine Shotwell Clapp, was especially close. The granddaughter of one of Mrs. Glass' sisters, she and her family made regular trips from New Jersey to vacation at Thornby, over some 40 years.

After Dr. Glass retired, the couple continued to summer at The Mohawks and winter at Thornby. He was nearing 70, and would have known that his heart condition was incurable. In 1925, he wrote his will, leaving everything to his wife. His will stipulated that after she died, part of The Mohawks be transferred to five nearby property owners, who would become trustees and hold it forever "for a park or playground for the general public" or transfer the property to the New York State Park Commission. Today, although there are extensive scenic trails in the Trenton Falls area, there is no state park as he envisioned. Dr. Glass willed his other property, Thornby, directly to his wife without instructions or stipulations on what should become of it after her death. It seems reasonable to assume that he wanted Thornby to remain in the family.

Dr. Glass' will also provided that after Mrs. Glass died, any remaining money was to be given to worthy causes, including the funding of two scholarships for deserving students — one in biology and one in political science — at Hamilton College in Clinton, New York. Those scholarships are still awarded today. He willed money to the Utica Clinic and established two funds at Faxton Hospital: one for sick children, another to provide a "free room in the hospital for sick and indigent nurses."

For the 10-year period after Dr. Glass retired, records of the Glasses are practically non-existent. A peaceful life with family and friends, in the mountains of New York and on the river in Florida, enjoying their farm, gardens and animals, a chance to read, hunt and fish, and simply savor each other's company doesn't generate much official paperwork. No one could have wished them anything more.

On March 4, 1930, the *DeLand Sun* reported that Dr. J. H. Glass, who had been coming to Benson Springs (as Enterprise was then called) for 15 years, was critically ill. The physician who had saved so many lives was nearing the end of his. He died at age 77 at his home in Trenton Falls, with his wife, Anna Wells Glass, and Doris Faber at his side. Dr. Glass was cremated and his remains were interred in the Wells family plot in Johnstown, New York. He is also remembered with a headstone in the Mohawk Cemetery, alongside those of his parents and brothers.

 *A warm welcome will await those who enter its doors, their names and abiding places will be cherished.*

Anna Glass,
writing in Thornby guest book

CHAPTER FOUR

How Thornby Came to Be

On April 20, 1917, James Glass bought 80 acres in Enterprise from storekeeper William S. Thayer, his wife Julia A. Thayer and Bertha A. Sauls, reported the *New Smyrna Daily News*.

Nearly every square foot of the stunning property was covered with live oaks and southern magnolias that, even a century ago, astonished with their massive height — some so old and thick that two people with four outstretched arms could not surround their trunks. Slender, straight pines seemed to scrape the pale blue Florida sky. Native plants grew so dense in places that no one could see, let alone walk, through them. Wetland ponds covered about a quarter of the property, hosting visiting ducks; showy red bay trees spiced the air under nature's shady canopy. The rare sunny spot showcased wild ginger and jessamine. Utter silence reigned, except for the excitement of a red-shouldered hawk spying on his next mammal dinner.

A Thornby path

The land sloped very gently downward to the north shore of Lake Monroe. Relics of a wooden dock where oranges were loaded for transport before the 1890s freezes peeked through the clean, cypress-tinged water.

The property they bought was known as "Summerfield," once the site of Widow Summers' boarding house, one of numerous lodging places that flourished during Enterprise's prime tourist days. But its former name hardly matters now. Once it belonged to Dr. and Mrs. Glass, it became "Thornby," and "Thornby" it has remained.

How did the Glasses, who lived in Utica, New York, come to buy 80 lakefront acres in tiny Enterprise, Florida, back when you got to Enterprise by steamship via Jacksonville?

In Utica, their home and Dr. Glass' office was on Genesee Street, within walking distance from Faxton Hospital where he was chief of staff. For 20 years, as much of every summer as they could manage was spent at The Mohawks, their rambling white farmhouse on 300 hilly, wooded acres near Trenton Falls, New York.

When Dr. Glass' schedule allowed a getaway from Utica's seriously cold and snowy winters, they traveled to Florida. Although at first they stayed in the New Smyrna area, an oft-repeated tale has them climbing out windows in the dead of night to escape a hotel fire in 1912. It's a scary story, and if true, could explain why Enterprise replaced the beach as their Florida winter destination, and why Thornby became "the only spot in Florida that Mrs. Glass wanted to come to."

Mrs. Glass' older sister, Margaret Wells, was a yearly visitor to Florida from upstate New York. Reportedly, she owned a winter home in DeLand but often came to visit beautiful Enterprise and the well-known Brock House. With Margaret to introduce them to the local good life, the Glasses soon learned why Enterprise was a renowned tourist spot. In fact, so many travelers escaped to the Brock House from upstate New York's weather that they were known as "The Utica Colony." These turn-of-the-century snowbirds, like today's, filled weeks of warm, cloudless days with fishing, boating and picnics. Unlike today, they also shot alligators and soaked in the mineral springs. An entry in the Brock House's original "hunting log" tells us that in February 1916, Dr. Glass shot a 5½ foot alligator.

Because of the tight connection between the Brock House and the orphanage, it was inevitable that Dr. and Mrs. Glass would form a bond with the nearby orphans. They loved children, and spent a good deal of their time and money helping worthy causes. It probably didn't take much urging for them to join Mrs. Glass' sister Margaret when she called to see some of the orphanage children she'd gotten to know while spending time at the Brock House.

So it was, another story goes, that the Glasses found themselves in Enterprise in the spring of 1917, literally waiting for their ship to come in — in this case, a steamboat taking them from Enterprise to Jacksonville — when a short stroll eastward brought them face-to-face with 80 lovely acres on Lake Monroe in the St. Johns River. To winter-weary New York eyes on a Florida clear April day, it was a dreamy, bright green paradise of trees, vines and plants, with warm sun skimming the few unshaded spots, the river clean and sparkling, alive with boats chugging to and from the pretty town of Sanford, just visible across the water. Dr. Glass was 62 years old and thinking about retirement. In a 1984 interview, Doris Faber said that Mrs. Glass "persuaded" her husband to buy the property, which probably was not difficult. According to John Clapp, the man who would one day hold the key to Thornby's fate, they bought it right away for about $500. In today's dollars, the $500 Dr. Glass paid for 80 riverfront acres works out to about $8,300 — a little more than $100 per acre! The Florida land boom of the 1920s had yet to arrive. Indeed, waterfront land was not considered the prime spot it is today. Mosquitoes were armed and dangerous, and air conditioning was not an option.

Eventually, Dr. and Mrs. Glass put a stately winter home on their Enterprise property. The exact year it was built is unknown, although The Florida Division of Historic Preservation places it at around 1925, the pinnacle of Florida's housing boom. However, the 1920 United States Census says that James and Anna Glass were already living on their "farm" in Enterprise. Therefore, the Thornby house was probably built a few years earlier than state records suggest, one of a small number of homes built in the state in the World War I era.

The Thornby house was designed in the Colonial Revival style (although a better label might be "Colonial Revival, Southern Style.") Colonial Revival, which copied the look of 18th century New England buildings, was quite popular in the early 1900s, especially in the northern states. Thornby did have typical Colonial Revival features like symmetrical rooms and a central hallway, but its dominant porches are not commonly associated with Colonial Revival architecture. The generous, white-columned front porches on both floors evoked nothing so much as a pre-Civil War southern plantation. Constructed

Thornby house, early

of white-painted stucco over a wood frame, the house also had an attic dormer, a gable roof of dark asbestos shingles, two brick chimneys painted white, and two smaller side porches. No records identifying the home's architect or builder are known to exist.

Colonial Revival is a rare architectural style in Volusia County. In 1989, the county, in partnership with the state, commissioned a historic property survey of West Volusia. The survey focused on properties at least 50 years old that had "retained their architectural integrity to a large degree." Of 525 properties surveyed, less than two percent were built in the Colonial Revival style. Thornby was one of those.

Inside, the Thornby house was comfortably spacious, but not showy. There were two stories and an attic with lovely heart-of-pine floors throughout. On one side of the entry hall was the dining room. It had a fireplace, and on the walls were long wooden ledges. On them, the Glasses displayed plates collected on their trips: commemorative and souvenir plates that filled three sides of the room. Between the dining room and kitchen was a two-sided china cabinet, custom designed for Mrs. Glass' collection of dishes and china, more souvenirs from years of world travel. The kitchen, with wood-burning stove and ample pantry, was in the back. Dr. Glass' book-crammed library ("fantastic," as Carolyn Langley remembers it) and the sitting room combined into one large room. With a welcoming fireplace as its centerpiece, it filled half of the first floor. Long-time Enterprise resident Roxann Henderson Hardin remembers visiting Thornby as a child and being impressed by the staircase, which seemed gigantic to a little girl. Upstairs, the master bedroom had its own fireplace, bath, and a good-sized closet, unusual in the 1920s. Two smaller bedrooms on the other side of the central hallway shared a bath. Every front window provided a sweeping view of Lake Monroe, but the scene from the attic dormer windows was especially pleasing. Even so, the high, hot attic was used just for storage.

On the property then, as now, are flora and fauna that provide lessons about Florida's past — live oaks, slash pine, black gum, southern red cedar and southern magnolia trees, cabbage palm, wild blueberry, sparkleberry and more.

The Glasses built a thatched-roof, spring-fed pool in the shape of a keyhole, across the road and down by the lakeshore. The remains of the keyhole pool are still in place, but the bathhouse that served it has long since disappeared.

Dr. Glass used the pool for bathing (much to the chagrin of local upstanding ladies riding in carriages on the dirt road that became Lakeshore Drive). There was a duck pond not far from the house. Behind the house was a garage for the Glasses' shiny Chevrolet, and possibly a second spring-fed soaking pool. There were orange groves, grape arbors, prized gardens, and stables, too.

Thornby living room, year unknown

Padgett family (neighbors) at the Thornby keyhole pool, circa 1923

A young black couple named Walsten or Walstein worked for the Glasses and lived in a small house on the property with their pre-school daughter, Helen.

A very old, two-story "cottage" (possibly the former Summers' boarding house) was perched on the Thornby property when the Glasses bought it. According to the Watson siblings — Dwayne, Ernie and Carolyn — whose family lived and worked on the property 40 years later — the cottage at one time was occupied by an older couple, refugees from Russia. In the 1950s, in heavily accented English, they told young Dwayne how they fled the Revolution decades before to a new life in America. Unfortunately, their connection to Dr. and Mrs. Glass, and what became of them when they left Thornby, are unsolved puzzles.

A narrow-gauge railroad spur on Thornby may have used mules to transport citrus grown on the property, to and from groves that existed to the east and west of the property. Remains of the old rails can still be seen in the interior of the property, where they cross over a large, deep canal. The canal is most likely man-made, and may have served to drain the upland portion of the property into Lake Monroe in the days when that practice was the norm.

Remains of old railroad spur crossing ravine on Thornby property

Along the property's northeast border, the Enterprise Branch of the Florida East Coast Railroad ran from the main line at Benson Junction east to Enterprise and continuing to Titusville. Did the engineer blow the train whistle in greeting as he passed Thornby? When railroads in America took a deathblow in the 1960s, the rails were amputated. Now, several decades later, the old rail bed is the "East Coast Regional Rail Trail," a 51-mile, multi-use recreational trail.

Why was the Glass property named "Thornby"? Locally, the most oft-repeated story is that Dr. Glass named it for a female benefactor who helped pay his way through medical school. Another version, reported in a 1984 newspaper article, says Mrs. Glass inherited money from a friend in 1929 and "invested in building a house" across from Lake Monroe, which was named in the friend's honor. As decades passed, lives ended and memories faded, the real story slipped into obscurity.

How Thornby Got its Name

Her name was Jennie A. Thorn.

Jennie Thorn was born in New York State in about 1842. In the early 1900s, she and her husband were Utica friends of James and Anna Glass; the Thorn's opulent home was just a few blocks from the Glasses' home/office on Genesee Street.

Jennie's husband, Edwin Thorn, was a wealthy stockbroker and nephew of John W. Thorn. Although John Thorn's name may not be widely recognized today, he's known to historic railroad buffs as former president of the old Utica & Black River Railroad. With family interests in banking, manufacturing and railroads, John W. Thorn was on the right side of the tracks when it came to philanthropy. Before he died in 1895, he gave away a sum equivalent to more than $18 million in today's dollars to charities and individuals, and in his will bequeathed several million dollars more to Baptist associations, orphanages, and schools both in the U.S. and in England, his home country. Clearly, her husband's uncle set high standards of family generosity for Jennie Thorn to uphold.

In the 1870s, when Dr. Glass attended medical school in New York City, Jennie and Edwin Thorn lived in Chicago. The lack of proximity between James Glass and Jennie Thorn at this time casts doubt on the theory that she might have helped to pay for his schooling.

Sometime between 1882 and 1900, the Thorns moved from Chicago to Utica. Enormously wealthy, Jennie Thorn could easily have lived the life of a rich society woman, limiting her good works to hosting ladies' tea parties for charity, but that was not her style. Her way was to be heavily "hands on" as worker, management expert, and financial whiz.

The list of her personal accomplishments is impressive. She founded Utica's Home for Aged Men, later the Home for Aged Men and Couples (there was virtually no U.S. pension system at the time, and many older people became destitute) and did such a fine job as its treasurer that she held the post for more than 20 years. In a day when women couldn't even vote, she served as board member and then president of Faxton Hospital. (The duties of hospital presidents were apparently a bit different in 1907 than they are now. At Faxton's nursing class graduation that year, Dr. Glass gave the keynote speech and Mrs. Thorn presented every new nurse with an instrument bag.)

Jennie Thorn didn't only work for Faxton Hospital; she repeatedly opened her purse. The hospital's pathology laboratory was a gift from her. In recounting her many gifts to the hospital, Jennie's obituary says "At the close of the year, if there happened to be a deficit, it was always made good by her generous hand." When she wasn't keeping Faxton Hospital out of the red, she supported the Utica Clinic (one of Dr. Glass' own special causes) and gave her time and money to scores of other worthy endeavors like World War I relief and the Salvation Army. She was treasurer of a group that helped fund a memorial to Union Civil War soldiers in Utica. Among the causes closest to her heart, however, no medical schools or other educational institutions seem to be included — another hint that the story of a Thornby namesake who "paid for Dr. Glass' schooling" could be faulty.

Jennie Thorn and Anna Glass were good friends, close enough that they, along with Anna's niece Eleanor Shotwell, decided to take a lengthy car trip in July 1909. (Maybe they were inspired by Alice Ramsey, who, one month before, made national headlines when she and three others set off from New York City for California on "the first all-female, cross country road trip.") Without quite that much hoopla, the *Syracuse (NY) Herald* announced only that the "three women autoists" were taking a road trip from Utica to the West. Minus an account of that adventure, we can only presume that Jennie, Anna and Eleanor faced the same challenges that Alice & company did: learn the basics of car safety, wear hats and goggles, and cover their long dresses with dusters to protect themselves from dirt and dust. Not to mention the absence of real roads, the oceans of mud, and the lack of helpful road maps to accompany what could have been a months-long ordeal. Presumably, the three remained friends and on speaking terms, even after thousands of miles on the road.

Jennie Thorn's husband, Edwin Thorn, died in 1912 and left his wife their home, personal property, and securities valued at more than $3 million today. They had no children.

Dr. Glass and Jennie Thorn both left Faxton Hospital in 1921. In Dr. Glass' retirement speech, he said:

> I shall hope always to retain in some capacity my relation with the institution, which has been so closely identified with my life, friendship and work.

In the same speech, he praised hospital president Mrs. Jennie Thorn, whose resignation for health reasons was accepted with "great resignation and deep regret." Who better to appreciate the efforts of Jennie Thorn, the problem-solving, dynamic, extremely generous benefactor of Faxton Hospital, than the man who was its chief of surgery for almost 30 years? What better way to salute their Utica neighbor and great friend than for Dr. and Mrs. Glass to name "Thornby" in her honor? There is no record that Jennie Thorn ever visited Florida. Her name does not appear in the Thornby guest book. After leaving New York, she moved to California, dying there in 1928. Her will left $60,000 to Utica charities, including Faxton Hospital.

The highest compliment paid to Jennie may be in her obituary, which observed that, not only did she donate money to better the lives of the less fortunate, but also "she enjoyed more the personal service which made her so helpful in solving problems. . ." So, while the question of "why the name 'Thornby'?" may never be definitively answered, research points to Jennie A. Thorn of New York and California as the mysterious Thornby namesake. No evidence has been found that connects her to Dr. Glass' medical schooling. Rather, the "inheritance from a friend" story seems closer to what really happened. The Glasses could well have named their existing home "Thornby," both to recognize Jennie Thorn's bequest to Anna Glass, and to honor her years of giving to Faxton Hospital and Utica Clinic, both places dear to Dr. Glass' heart. Whatever the reason, Jennie A. Thorn would surely be proud to know that her good works and unselfishness yesterday, still remembered today, will live on tomorrow and forever in the name "Thornby."

> *Doris Faber's contributions to the community in which she spent her life helped form the community's foundation.*
>
> **The Volusian,**
> Dec. 13, 1989

CHAPTER FIVE

Train Up a Child In the Way He Should Go

The bottom seemed to drop out.

That's how Anna Glass said she felt when her husband died on August 4, 1931, a few months after their 49th anniversary. As close as any daughter, Doris Faber was with them at The Mohawks.

> *I Cannot Say, and I will not Say*
> *That he is Dead, he is just Away . . .*
>
>   * * *
>
> *With a Cheery Smile and a Wave of the Hand*
> *He Has Wandered into an Unknown Land*
>
>   **- from "Away" by James Whitcomb Riley.**

Mrs. Glass hand-wrote several verses in the Thornby guestbook.

Newly widowed Anna Glass was in her 70s and had never lived alone. She coped as best she could, comforted by support from her loved ones and many friends and bolstered by her strong religious convictions. Still, she must have felt rootless and lonely. She moved back to her hometown of Johnstown, NY for a few years, where she was surrounded by family. In 1934, she began selling off the Trenton Falls property until the last parcel was sold in 1940. In those Depression years, Dr. Glass' wish that the property become a state park might have been thwarted by the strangled economy.

Around 1935, Mrs. Glass moved to Enterprise permanently. She would have an unassuming, settled life at Thornby for her remaining years. The census that year recorded a hired companion with her at Thornby, 46-year-old Harriet Trumbull. In time, the house would have another occupant.

"Miss Doris Granted Leave of Absence from Home," announced *The Florida Methodist* newsletter in November 1941. After nine years on the orphanage staff, six as housemother at Brinkley Cottage, Doris Faber said her farewells under circumstances not entirely clear. Never one to air her feelings in public, her "official" explanation was that she wanted "a complete change of work for a while." While hinting that she might move to Orlando, in true volunteer form she promised that she would still work on the orphanage homecoming celebration. That she requested a leave of absence rather than resigning is puzzling. Although she did have surgery in Orlando in 1940, her stress may have been emotional, as well. (In an interview more than 30 years later, Doris implied that she had become unhappy with the home's management.) Wilbur Bruce suggests that old-fashioned paddling may have played a part in her decision. A new orphanage superintendent had been appointed that year, and the ways that Doris disciplined her charges — the ways she wholeheartedly believed were the best to raise children — might have fallen out of favor.

Scenes from Life at Thornby

In 1941, Mrs. Glass became briefly ill and needed help. "My dear friend Mrs. Glass came to see me and invited me to live in her home," Doris wrote in her diary. Just like that, a two-week stay became permanent. "I became companion, housekeeper and chauffeur," she wrote. In a 1978 newspaper interview, she joked about the move: "I guess I was like "The Man Who Came to Dinner." Until her last years, Doris stood ready to give care and comfort to people who needed her. "Mrs. Glass became my mother in the way I have been mother to those boys and girls of the Methodist Children's Home," she said.

Anna Glass was a grandmotherly sort who always seemed to find candy in her pockets. Catherine Bruce remembers, "She always had a good word." Wilbur Bruce says, "She was a nice lady." "She was always nice to us kids," agrees Dwayne Watson. "She was quiet," comments his brother Ernie. Their sister Carolyn remembers Anna Glass as petite and pleasant.

Doris Faber and Anna Glass shared an unshakeable religious faith. From its founding until her death, Doris belonged to Barnett Methodist Church, the church Hattie Brooks helped to start. Doris was "a very devoted, committed member of Barnett," church records tell us. She was children's Sunday school teacher and served as annual church conference secretary most of her life. For years, she was an officer of the Epworth League, a Methodist young adult organization. Always with more generosity than money, once when a beloved pastor died, she found a way to buy and donate a beautiful brass altar set. "She was a very Christian woman," says Dwayne Watson unhesitatingly. His brother Ernie agrees, adding, "She hauled a lot of kids to Sunday school."

For most of her adult life, Doris suffered from cataracts that were bad enough to require surgery — a much more complicated process in 1953 than today. Then, a patient was hospitalized for a week or more with sandbags straddling their head to limit movement. The outcome required very strong eyeglasses that distorted one's vision. She could not read for a year after her operation, she says, but she continued to teach Sunday school. Students could read for her, and she already knew chapter after chapter of scripture by heart. For that, she said, she was grateful for Mrs. Brooks' training, when as a child she had worked hard to memorize the Psalms.

Anna Glass was also a pillar of Barnett Methodist Church. She headed the Woman's Society of Christian Service. In 1949, when "nearly every man in town" helped re-roof the church building, Mrs. Glass provided a turkey dinner at Thornby for the workers. One newspaper story recounts yearly Thanksgiving dinners for the community that Anna Glass and Doris Faber hosted at Barnett Church. Mrs. Glass donated a dining room table to the pastor's residence in memory of her niece, Eleanor Carroll. Later, she presented the church with a new Hammond organ in memory of her husband "and to the glory of God for bringing them to such a beautiful place." That organ still graces Barnett Methodist Church.

Both Anna and Doris had an ardent love of nature and genuine affection for the plants, trees and animals at Trenton Falls and Thornby. Ernie Watson recalls, "Mrs. Glass wanted no trees cut and the place had to be spotless." Two men took care of the Thornby property for her. Isaiah Smith lived on the property with his wife, Annie, and two children. Wesley (last name unknown) was a day worker who lived in Enterprise. With Doris' power saw on wheels and two part-time workers, 40 acres of trees — but only the dead or dying ones — supplied enough wood for the stove and fireplaces. Former Enterprise resident Wise Hardin vividly remembers that saw: "The first one I ever saw," he says.

Anna, like Doris, lost her mother when she was very young. Both women loved children but had none of their own. Not given to bitterness or self-pity, "Aunt Annie" and "Miss Doris" were beloved family to their own kin and to many, many others fortunate enough to be part of their lives for years. Doris honored Hattie Brooks by introducing a new generation of children to the best parts of her early life in Enterprise. Anna Glass and Doris Faber opened their home at Thornby, as well as their hearts, to the people of Enterprise and beyond.

In keeping with Mrs. Brooks' custom from the days of Mr. Throop and his 50,000 chickens, Mrs. Glass and Doris continued the tradition of a Thornby Easter egg hunt. In 1956, the *Daytona Beach Morning Journal* reported that 60 children participated, vying for candy eggs. Marcus Nutt, from a long-time Enterprise family, was one of them. "There were two or three large goose eggs hidden among the chicken eggs, and if you found one, you would get a prize," he recalls.

When Mrs. Glass and Miss Doris lived at Thornby, "all the local kids swam in the keyhole pool there," says Wise Hardin. His wife, the former Roxann Henderson, also remembers how refreshing it felt on stifling summer days. They were allowed to play in the Thornby woods, too. Judy Connor of Enterprise was one of the kids who nicknamed the Thornby house "Miss Lily" because it seemed to glow starkly white against the dark woods.

Despite the loss of Thornby's "gracious host," the years when Anna Glass and Doris Faber lived at Thornby were golden ones. With Doris as her companion, helper and housekeeper in exchange for room and board, her church work, and frequent visits from family and friends, Anna Glass' last years at Thornby were as rich and satisfying as Doris' famous sugar cookies.

The Thornby Guestbook

Today, when people use the word "guestbook," they're probably referring to a website portal where computer users enter their comments. In connection with Thornby, however, "guestbook" has a more traditional meaning. The Thornby guestbook was a real book, in whose pages guests of the Glass family, and later Doris Faber, could write their comments about the place and their hosts. The whereabouts of the original book are now unknown, but thanks to the diligent efforts of former Enterprise resident Grace Stamile, a photocopy of every priceless page exists. Those pages — a passage both sentimental and intriguing into the vanished world of Thornby — were invaluable in helping to tell its story. A few of the pages are included at the end of this book.

"For years this book of dear names and remembrances has been locked... the book has traveled to Florida." So wrote Anna Glass on a fresh page of the Thornby guestbook, one memorable day in 1941. The cherished book, tucked away in mournful storage since Dr. Glass died and their Trenton Falls house was sold, thus began its new life at Thornby. Over the next 45 years, hundreds of those "dear names and remembrances" filled guestbook pages. The pages share glimpses of Thornby's past in a way that photographs and newspapers can't. Visitors' names and addresses provide interesting facts. Their comments and notes, echoing powerfully through the years, remind us that they, like Thornby, were once alive, vibrant and beloved.

A guestbook entry from August 13, 1942 tells us that a community vespers (evening prayer) service took place under Thornby's "big oak tree" followed by pineapple cake. In the midst of World War II, the prayers must have been for America and its armed forces. Another note that same year tells us that the 40 women attending the first meeting of the Enterprise Women's Club on October 19 enjoyed orange sherbet — likely made by Doris from Thornby's oranges.

In the 1800s, the Brock House highlighted the beauty and charm of Enterprise to presidents and other eminent folk who stayed there. Nearly 100 years later, with the hotel long gone, Thornby hosted its own parade of visitors. They weren't as famous as Brock House guests Ulysses Grant and the Prince of Wales, but they were just as enchanted with the sunshine, the trees and the lake. However, there *was* at least one visitor who qualified as well known. She was Margaret Clapp, a Pulitzer-Prize winning author, cultural attaché to India, and the second president of Wellesley College. She signed the Thornby guest book in 1960.

Most visitors to Thornby, though, were ordinary folks. They came from Enterprise, from all over Florida, and from 14 other states. In the 1940s, an Air Corps Major stationed in Leesburg signed the book. Doris' sisters, father and Grandmother Faber often came to call, as did Mrs. Glass' old friends from Utica and Trenton Falls. Some stayed for weeks, others a few hours. They shared their feelings: "always a wonderful time here;" others praised the "delicious food" and "beautiful flowers." Anna, Doris and their guests celebrated Christmas and New Years, Mothers Day, and Easter. On Thanksgiving, they feasted on Doris' 18-pound turkey, hand-raised at Thornby. More than 75 people — some from as far as California — attended an open house in April 1955, in honor of Anna Glass' 95th birthday.

Barbara Faber, Doris Faber and Anna Glass on Mrs. Glass' 95th birthday, 1955. She was the oldest citizen of Enterprise.

In the guestbook, some names return year after year: Clapp, Carroll, Shotwell and Argersinger. Theirs were weeks-long stays, often for holidays and mostly in the winter months. They wrote "Aunt Annie — loveliest time ever" and "there is only one Doris!" They were Anna Glass' relatives from New York and New Jersey. Family photos tucked among the pages make a pieced quilt of words and pictures, stitched together over generations. For them, Thornby was a feast for the senses, a respite from cold weather, and an array of Florida's charms that had nothing to do with theme parks or tourist attractions. In the 1940s began visits from Mrs. Glass' great-niece Catherine Clapp, her husband and four sons. The younger Clapp boys, Roger and John, were especially drawn to Thornby. They palled around with the Watson kids and with a local child, Frank Knight. Mrs. Clapp loved Thornby, maybe as much as did her great-aunt, Anna Glass. "Florida is for me the fountain of youth. One special spot, Thornby, is the center, and Doris is Queen," she wrote. "Have had a grand time on this wonderful place," wrote one of the Clapp boys in 1950. Two or three times a year, as the boys grew up, the Clapps, their cousins, and other family members stayed at Thornby. The notes they left behind are poignant or joyful, intimate bits of family life. "I left two teeth with you, Aunt Annie!" exclaimed one little boy.

J. Frank Knight's name first appears in the guestbook in 1945, in child's printing. In 1953, "Frank" and his father stayed at Thornby for several weeks. Frank wrote that Thornby "seems like home." He returned in 1955 and again in 1959. As an adult, Frank Knight would come to play a prominent role in what happened to Thornby.

Thornby Changes Hands

Anna Glass lived to be 99. In her final years, she experienced the frailties of extreme age, needing near-constant care. As a young boy, Ernie Watson slept on a cot in Thornby's upstairs hallway, so that he could help Mrs. Glass to the bathroom if she woke in the middle of the night. Doris was endlessly patient with Mrs. Glass' infirmities, no matter how trying things might get. Carolyn Watson Langley was a little girl when Miss Doris — with bad vision while wearing her thick glasses — drove Mrs. Glass to doctors' appointments in Orlando. There was no one else to do it, Carolyn says.

On the night Anna Glass died, Doris wrote these words:

> On June 29th, 1959, the hour of 11:30, closed out the life of the Mistress of Thornby, Mrs. Anna Wells Glass. She lived a full, useful, happy life and will be greatly missed by all who knew and loved her... She was like a mother to me, and all the care I gave her, I gave with a heart full of love and gratitude for my life with her here at Thornby.

The late June night was Florida muggy and still. Was Doris sitting at an open window, hoping for a breeze, a barred owl hooting in the distance? Was she thinking back to Hattie Brooks, who years before met four scared girls at the train, and became their "Mother?" Was she seeing the countless orphans she had helped raise as the only mother they knew? Was she reflecting on the grown-up girl who came to Thornby and began a new life as friend and companion to a childless widow? Doris would write later, "In her last years I made her life worth living, she told me many times." In the end, Doris cared for Mrs. Glass as Mrs. Brooks had cared for her.

Doris handled Anna Glass' final arrangements. The wake was in Thornby's living room. Seven-year-old Carolyn Watson, who had to climb on a chair to see, was impressed that so many people came to say good-bye. Anna Glass was buried with her husband, her parents, and other members of the Wells family in the Johnstown, New York cemetery.

What would happen to the Thornby property now that Anna Glass was gone? In 1952, Mrs. Glass first made a will leaving Thornby to her niece, Eleanor Carroll, but Eleanor died soon afterward. Two years later, Mrs. Glass signed a codicil that left the Thornby property, home and contents to Catherine Clapp of New Jersey, the grandniece so charmed with the house, trees, and flavor of life at Thornby that she and her family had been regular visitors for years.

Anna Glass' will left her "good friend, Doris Brooks Faber" $2,500 in cash, a car, and "approximately 8 to 10 acres" of land north of Old Taylor Road that adjoined property Doris owned. (According to Carolyn Watson Langley, part of the property Doris already owned was given to her by Dr. and Mrs. Glass. Records indicate that she bought two other small parcels from the state in 1946.)

Mrs. Glass' will also gave Doris the "guest cottage" (the old house in which the mysterious Russians once lived) on the Thornby property, and specifically authorized Doris to move the cottage to her own property, likely in deference to Thornby's new inheritor. Doris had the dwelling moved about a quarter-mile north to her own property, but she remained at Thornby and never lived in the cottage.

Doris wrote "my own house" on this undated photograph

Without Mrs. Glass at Thornby, Doris, then 57, was naturally concerned about her future, but the Clapps put her fears to rest. She would have a home for life at Thornby, they assured her. She could stay as general overseer to care for the property, keep the house the way Mrs. Glass left it, and have things the way the family wanted them when they came to visit.

More Children Than Anyone Could Imagine

The story of Thornby cannot properly be told without the children: "Miss Doris' kids."

Although Doris had a home at Thornby, her financial situation was fragile. To make ends meet, she sold eggs from her chickens, and rabbits she raised herself. She scooped Spanish moss from Thornby's oaks with a wire cage-type contraption on a long pole and sold the moss for furniture stuffing. But, most of her income came from providing day care for working parents and babysitting for neighborhood kids. In a 1973 interview, she said this began in 1945 (the year may be a misprint; it was more likely 1955) when several mothers asked if she would keep their children during the day and "Mrs. Glass did not object." Doris Faber had been surrounded by children all her life: as big sister, in Mrs. Brooks' home, at the orphanage, and as housemother at Brinkley. After Mrs. Glass' death, she probably increased the number of children she cared for, to pay for food and household expenses. Then, too, she must have relished the chance to share the fun and experiences of life at Thornby with a new generation. As Dwayne Watson explains, "She was always so interested in kids. That was her life."

Ask anyone who's lived in Enterprise most of their life about Miss Doris' kids, and they'll tell you all about them because, likely as not, they were one, too. They might have concocted Indian tepees from Jerusalem thorn branches in the dense "Glass woods." Maybe they chased fireflies on long summer nights, helped bake cookies in Thornby's venerated wood-burning stove, or were part of the chicken-feeding parade that started every time the little red wagon rumbled into view.

To Doris' kids, Thornby was part petting zoo, part nature study and part cooking class, with a big helping of responsibility. It was swimming parties and field trips. Parents who took their kids to Thornby so they could have "adults only" time might have wished they could stay behind with them. Kids lucky enough to enjoy Miss Doris' own special brand of no-nonsense-allowed-combined-with-love daycare while mom and dad worked, remembered that magical time for the rest of their lives.

Carolyn, Dwayne and Ernie Watson have a unique perspective on Thornby: they literally grew up on the property. From 1951 on, the Watson family lived first in one small house on the Thornby property, then in another. In exchange for these living arrangements, their father, Earnest Watson, a commercial fisherman, helped with heavy work on the property. He took over most of the maintenance work when long-time Thornby workers Isaiah and Wesley were let go by the Clapp family after Mrs. Glass died. The Watson boys helped clear the underbrush around the house with scythes, west about 800 feet to Broadway Avenue and north about 150 feet — a huge job. When Mrs. Glass was alive, Miss Doris helped her, and Carolyn helped Miss Doris. After Mrs. Glass died, 8-year-old Carolyn moved into the Thornby house with Doris Faber, and stayed until she left for college. She had slumber parties, teenage get-togethers, and her 1970 wedding reception at Thornby. "Thornby was a major part of my life," Carolyn says, her voice heavy with emotion. "Miss Doris was like a surrogate mother to me. She was an extraordinary person. She would do anything for anyone." To a fault, one might say. "She trusted people too much and they took advantage of her," Carolyn says, relating a story of home repairs trustingly paid for, but never received from a contractor who disappeared. Carolyn Watson (now Langley) and her brothers have graciously shared some of their strongest memories in these pages. This sketch is based on Ernie Watson's recollection of the Thornby property when he was growing up at Thornby in the 1950s and 1960s.

The Watson kids and Lani Friend were the first of "Miss Doris' Kids." Lani, who still lives in Enterprise, says Thornby was "every child's paradise," with stables and horses, a cow, pigs, chickens, turkeys, guineas, ducks and geese, a strawberry field and a grape arbor.

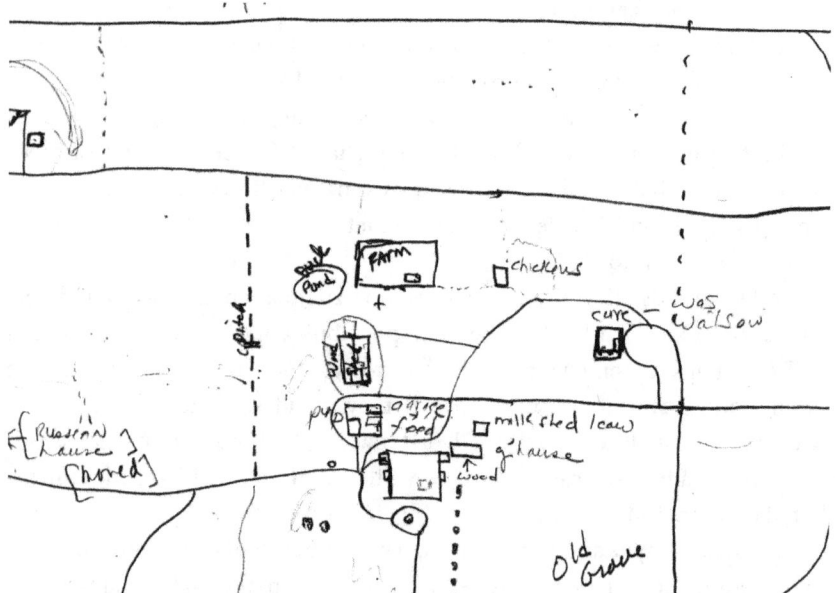

Ernie Watson's sketch of Thornby property as it looked, circa 1960

Behind the house was a two-acre garden where Doris grew and canned potatoes, peas, corn and beans, as she had done when she lived at the orphanage. "Everybody in town saved glass jars for Miss Doris," says Enterprise native Roxann Hardin.

Bob Bechir attended Enterprise Elementary School, in walking distance from Thornby. Sometimes he would go to Miss Doris' after school, and at times, spend the night there. "The land has some of the most beautiful oaks that I have ever seen," he marvels. "It was a wonderful experience to be able to climb them as a child growing up. In Deltona where I lived, there weren't trees like that." Long-time Enterprise resident Shirley Goodwin remembers the well-used tire swing on a strong oak branch, and how lovely the grounds looked when Doris lived at Thornby. "They were Florida natural and beautiful, with blooming hibiscus," she says. Thornby neighbor "Pa" Matheny helped keep the place looking nice.

The Thornby property shelters uncounted aged trees, including live oak, cypress and southern magnolia trees — most oversized, each beautiful, and all precious. Even in such rare company, one tree stands out.

For the kids who played at Thornby, it was a secret message drop, a meeting spot, and a safe-deposit box for valuables like turtle shells. The tree's "vault" has been squeezed shut by the passing years. What forgotten treasures of long-ago children remain sealed behind the bricks of the Thornby treasure tree, no one may ever know.

Thornby's "treasure tree"

Wise Hardin, who moved to Enterprise as a child, first met Miss Doris when he was a teenager and she yelled at him for shooting squirrels on the Thornby property. Every chance he got, Wise says, he would sneak into the Thornby "carriage house" just to peek at the carefully waxed, green, 1912-era Chevrolet that once belonged to the Glasses. Sadly for him, his boyhood dream of one day owning that car was crushed years later, when, just after he happened to spot it on a DeLand car lot, it disappeared forever.

Although Riley Nutt explains that his "Mom didn't work" and he and his brother Marcus could spend their days at home, they spent a lot of time at Thornby instead, "just to be there." In Doris' room, there was a little metal bed with painted lambs and a built-in nightlight for small children spending the night. Says Marcus: "We had a good time always. In elementary school and later, in junior high, I would stay with her. She didn't like to be alone much."

Once the chickens were fed and the other chores done, it was story and play time. Doris' real-life stories were ones that only she could tell. She had been "number 7 in the children's home," recounts Riley Nutt. "She would tell us she was lucky number 7 to be there."

Before the world had "tough love," it had Doris Faber. "She was a strict disciplinarian," remembers Carolyn Langley. "You were expected to do things or else." Doris' rule was to finish all your lunch, and then you get a glass of milk. Carolyn cleaned the hardwood floors, vacuumed and dusted every Saturday; occasionally, Doris would hide dollar bills under the furniture for her, as Mrs. Brooks had done for Doris. As befitted a Sunday school teacher and former housemother of the day, she believed that outdoor chores like raking and stacking wood for boys, gardening and egg gathering for girls, started children on a solid path to adulthood. The Thornby dining room, filled with the Glass family's antique furniture, was off limits to children. Anyway, to her, being outdoors was much better for kids than watching TV or listening to rock 'n' roll. Nor did she condone "drinking and doing things unbecoming to a Christian."

That didn't mean there weren't parties at Thornby. Doris, who really liked parties, did for "her children" what Mrs. Brooks had done for hers. There were home-baked treats for holidays, a special cake for birthdays. Even the cow got a party. Unfortunately, for Susie the cow, that party may have been her last. True to her rural roots, Doris Faber was all business when it came to raising animals for food. "Every year she had a butcher day," recalls Marcus Nutt. The Watson kids clearly remember when Miss Doris told them to, "say goodbye to Susie." Susie soon became hamburger, neatly wrapped and labeled ("Susie"), joining other cow-named packages in the freezer on Thornby's side porch. Carolyn says she never could eat beef at Thornby.

Suzie the Cow's birthday party, 1958
Left to right: Annette Watson, Carolyn Watson, Cheryl Argersinger, Susie, Lani Friend

If there's one overwhelming memory shared by those who knew Doris Faber, it's her cooking. It seems nobody ever had a bad meal, or even a so-so one, from her kitchen. She was famous for her pickles, relishes and coleslaw. When a guest complimented her New Year's Day "fresh pork" dinner (served with garden-grown mashed potatoes and black-eyed peas), they weren't just being polite. That pork roast was hand-raised in a pen just yards from the dinner table. She served favorite dishes like southern fried chicken and homemade pies, all concocted on Thornby's old iron stove. Doris made jelly from Thornby's grapes and neighbor Joe Brannon's guavas, heaping it on her home-baked bread for the kids' afternoon snack. Her tart grapefruit candy earned high marks, but melt-in-your-mouth sugar and spicy molasses cookies were her signatures. When the overworked wood-burning stove finally breathed its last in the 1970s, its replacement was not a gas or electric model, even though wood stoves weren't easy to find. Ernie Watson's father-in-law finally managed to locate one, and had it shipped to Doris in Florida — from Maine. Today, Ernie and his wife Emily remember her fixing such "down home" fare as squirrel and possum. They're only half joking when they tease that, "Miss Doris was famous for finding road kill that was still warm." When you grow up with very little, you learn unique skills. Not only did Doris cook turtle eggs that the kids would find, but if they found a "bulgy snake," she'd kill that as well, and if its egg was whole, it became food.

The Faber sisters had a flair for the kitchen arts. In addition to Doris' cooking prowess, Euretta was known for her fudge and candy making. Zona worked as a dietician at the orphanage. Alma had a career with the popular Morrison's Cafeteria chain, and her canning and cooking won ribbons at the county fair. Yet, as sometimes happens even when siblings are close as children, the Faber sisters didn't keep the same tight ties as adults. The sisters exchanged visits, especially on holidays, but they were not the "salt-of-the-earth type" Doris was, reflects Riley Nutt.

As a former orphanage "inmate," Doris knew how to make something out of practically nothing. That skill was even more impressive because her cataracts, not cured by the 1950s operation, got worse as she aged, making her eyes extremely sun-sensitive. It's the reason she is seen wearing an eye-shielding hat in most photos.

Doris Faber was known to people outside Enterprise, too. She volunteered for the Red Cross, attending meetings in Orange City. John Baker of DeBary visited Thornby with a friend in the 1970s. He remembers the horses and rabbits, the big Thornby oaks, and Miss Doris, who was, he says, "a nice old lady that all of the kids from in and around Enterprise knew and loved." Doris Faber, local resident Shirley Goodwin declares, was "a fixture in Enterprise."

By the time Carolyn and the other original "Miss Doris' Kids" were grown, Doris had mellowed with age on some subjects — TV, for instance. "Bonanza" became a favorite show.

In 1973, Doris was profiled in the *Sanford Herald* in an article titled, "Doris Faber is a Living Symbol of Love." The piece related how, after Anna Glass' death, Doris started a memorial fund at Barnett Methodist Church to honor her "dear friend and benefactor." With a goal of making $1,000, she collected unsold newspapers for resale to local fern growers. Growers used the folded papers to wrap bare-root ferns they shipped to northern markets, but first the color printing had to be removed and the newspapers folded "just so" before being neatly stacked in the hallway, screened porch or garage, according to Carolyn Watson Langley, who helped with the labor-intensive process. "Of course, when Mrs. Clapp was visiting, no newspapers were out," she says. The fern growers paid Doris 1 ½ cents per pound for the finished papers. It took more than 10 years for her to earn $1,000. Along the way, "whenever the church was in dire need of funds, Doris would lend them the money they asked for from this fund . . . but they always paid it back and she continued adding to the fund," the *Herald* reported. With her $1,000 donation to the church achieved, she said she did not intend to stop collecting and selling papers. Instead, she would use the earnings from future paper sales to buy "more food and groceries for the children."

Doris with newspapers, 1973

At Thornby, "work" was a special subject. On the one hand, as Dwayne Watson explains, "Miss Doris was so well known and so well liked that a lot of people would bring her stuff." Nevertheless, Ernie Watson is adamant. If a grown-up came with gifts or not, "Before you left the house you'd have a chore." You might be asked to move papers, gather eggs, put the chickens away, feed the rabbits, or any of the endless jobs that always needed doing on a small farm. Ernie's wife Emily concurs, as does this guestbook entry: "Just in time to fix car and garage door," wrote a 1979 visitor identified as "Mr. Gates." The same year, after inspecting citrus trees, Thornby heir John Clapp wrote in the guestbook: "Let's hope we keep on improving this property. Thanks to Miss Doris!"

So many local people, adults and kids, spent so much time at Thornby over the years that it was like a second home. However, for Catherine Clapp and her relatives, it *was* — literally — their second home. When "Aunt Annie" died, Catherine became family matriarch and Thornby heir. The Clapps and their extended family kept up their routine of at least twice-yearly vacations at Thornby. Catherine's appreciative comments fill the Thornby guestbook. "Real winter here," she wrote one cold January day, "but Doris keeps us warm and well fed, which gets her up at 5:30 a.m." Catherine's husband, Judge Alfred Clapp, was a leading figure in New Jersey and national politics. He visited Thornby, but didn't like it much. The Clapp boys did, though. They relished the same things local kids did: Thornby's animals, the woods, fishing, Doris' comforting care. Since the house had only three bedrooms, they got to sleep in the loft above the (by then unused) stable. Their words in the guestbook were thoughtful and polite. "Having a grand time, hope to come again soon," wrote a Clapp son.

Some people recount another aspect of the Clapp visits to Thornby. It's said that nothing could be changed in the house and grounds without the Clapp's permission. Doris' animals were OK, if they were kept far away from the house. Riley Nutt asserts the Thornby house was "perfect inside" down to the painted woodwork, but remembers when Doris made needed concrete repairs and worried that she had done it before getting approval. According to Riley, when the Clapp family was expected, Doris would "hustle" and make sure that things she had done were put away. Ernie Watson says Mrs. Clapp had "attitude." While Carolyn Langley says she never knew Catherine Clapp to behave badly toward Doris, getting ready for her visits was a "busy time" for everyone. All agree that Doris would get nervous when these visits, sometimes characterized in the nature of an "inspection," loomed. One of Carolyn's pre-visit jobs was to wash every antique figurine and piece of family china in Mrs. Glass' large china cabinet. Catherine Bruce, too, relates that the Clapp visits could be stressful. "Mrs. Clapp used to order Doris around. [Doris] was kind of afraid of [her]," she says.

The Clapps sometimes visited Thornby in the summer, but didn't stay there because the house was not air-conditioned. Marcus Nutt came to know Catherine Clapp, perhaps better than anyone else in Enterprise did. Looking back on his teenage years in the 1970s, Marcus relates: "She would come to Florida and stay a week or two, rent a car, and I would chauffeur her around. I don't think she could drive. We were good friends with the family. She was always very pleasant, and I enjoyed her company." He went to the beach with them, and to places like St. Augustine and Marineland. "I never saw anything negative," about Mrs. Clapp, says Marcus, "but everybody has different sides." Dwayne Watson says, "I always respected her. She was a first-class lady." Catherine Clapp loved to walk, he says; she would frequently stride along the lakeshore, up Broadway, and onto old Taylor Road behind Thornby. According to Dwayne, the Clapps "had money and influence, but you'd never know it."

Catherine's sons who grew up with memorable family times at Thornby were Alfred, Jr., Edward, Roger and John. Roger and John spent the most time at Thornby. "Miss Doris took them under her wing like sons," Dwayne relates. Alfred became an accountant and financial planner; Edward, a minister. Roger practiced law and after retirement, devoted his time to community and non-profit organizations. John Clapp became a real estate broker.

An interviewer once referred to Miss Doris' "indomitable spirit." It showed in her kind, open face, in her dealings with people, and in the way she made her Thornby home a place full of love, a home where all were family and anyone could find what they needed, whether it was food, fun, or friendship. If Anna Glass crowned Thornby as social hub of Enterprise, Doris Faber made it the family home. Perhaps Marcus Nutt puts it best: "She was not a friend. She was part of our families."

The Bruce and Watson families had second-generation Miss Doris kids. "Parents trusted her 100 percent," Ernie Watson says. "They knew she'd make those kids mind." Ernie, who once slept on a cot in the hall to help Mrs. Glass, now had Thornby kids of his own. "Our son hated going there because he had to work," he says with a broad wink. By 1981, a third generation of Clapp children was enjoying family trips to Thornby, as evidenced by a guestbook note that John Clapp's daughter "likes the baby rabbits."

Each year, Doris held a reunion and party for the children, now grown, she'd once known or cared for, at the orphanage or at Thornby, and for the people of Enterprise. Every Fourth of July, they came — from around the corner, from Florida, from all over — bringing spouses, children, and grandchildren, for an all-day, all-out, jamboree: eating, socializing, old-time games on the lawn, and guitar pickin' on the front porch. Doris was a meticulous person; the house and grounds had to be spruced up for the celebration. For weeks, she cooked on the wood-burning stove in the June heat, stockpiling

Thornby reunion, 1980

the pantry. Some guests brought food, but she did all the meat herself, loading up long tables with savory dishes like rabbit stew and rabbit BBQ. Riley Nutt comments that the food was "amazing," but more important was the setting. "The town was all connected then," he says. "Everybody played together, everybody went to school together." Doris proudly told a reporter that 67 people attended her Independence Day bash in 1977. Those reunions were her fun-filled labor of love, until, in her 80s, the large event finally became too much for her; her last was in 1984.

By the mid-1980s, she was surely slowing down. An interviewer wrote at Christmastime, 1984: ". . . she has five offers on how to spend her holiday. . . [until now] for so long she has been the hostess during the holiday season to friends and to the children for whom she cared at the Children's Home."

Every life's end has a story, but Doris Faber's story should have been different. Somehow, it would have seemed fitting if inevitable death came on a hot day from a heart attack while she chased a fat chicken for dinner, or if the ladder slipped while she energetically tackled an unyielding oak limb with a handsaw. But that was not to be.

Through the early 1980s, friends watched her slip slowly into the shadows of very old age. She kept caring for children when she probably shouldn't have. She still made cookies for her sisters' church because they asked her to. She still held the July 4 reunions, doing most of the work herself. To those who didn't see her often, she seemed OK. "We tried to tell them she really wasn't," says Catherine Bruce. Doris signed a power of attorney giving her sister Zona the right to make her important decisions. Now Doris, the woman who did the heaviest work, could barely get up the stairs. The fearless soul who had conquered every challenge now set traps for imaginary intruders. Riley Nutt remembers tearful phone calls. She didn't like to be alone; he would come and spend the night. She took to wandering. When Mrs. Watson sent over dinner and dessert, the dinner remained uneaten. Neighbors pitched in to do even more. Catherine and Wilbur Bruce helped with housecleaning. "A lot of people went there and did things for her," says Catherine. For a few years it was enough, but the time eventually came when she couldn't take care of herself.

She was 85 years old and her doctor said a nursing home was the only choice. No one had the heart to tell her. They tried to keep her at Thornby a while longer, but finally, the decision was made. They found a home for her dog. Zona handled the arrangements, but couldn't bring herself to be there when Doris left Thornby forever. That job fell to neighbor Catherine Bruce, who, even after all these years, finds it hard to talk about. She helped Doris pack a suitcase and lock the front door on a thousand memories. They met Zona at the doctor's office. The doctor advised Doris she needed to be in a hospital. Catherine alone took her to lunch, and then to the nursing home in DeLand. Later, Doris understood.

Dwayne Watson visited the woman who had lent him $25 to buy dress shoes for his eighth grade graduation. "It was pitiful," he said, shaking his head. She was crying; she wanted to go home. "Like a wild animal trapped in a cage," is how Carolyn Langley visualized Doris Faber in a nursing home. The Bruces visited regularly. "It was sad to see her," Marcus Nutt shared. "It's hard to take in, when someone is not the person you remember them to be."

Doris Faber died on October 15, 1989, one week before her 87th birthday. She hadn't wanted cremation, but her sisters decided: they didn't want a funeral. Maybe there was no money. Perhaps her sisters did not understand how important she was to the community. Instead of a church service, a graveside service was held for "very devoted" lifelong church member and Sunday school teacher Doris Brooks Faber.

Alice "Mickey" Nutt collected contributions for her headstone. She and Wise Hardin made sure everything was right. The burial day was warm for October, sun-filled and clear. Wilbur Bruce and another long-ago orphanage kid, Billy Finn, dug the grave where the urn would be interred. "She wanted to be near Mother Brooks," remembers Emily Watson, in a peaceful back corner of the old Enterprise Evergreen Cemetery. And so she is.

Most people who were there hold curiously few memories of the service or the reception afterward at the power plant. Some say a big crowd came; some say not that many. While the world went from poodle skirts to bellbottoms, from Eisenhower to Jimmy Carter, Miss Doris cared for, educated and entertained countless children at Thornby.

"She affected a lot of people's lives, but a lot came and went [over the years]," is how Ernie Watson explains it. Maybe the remembrances are too sad to retain. Maybe time has replaced sorrowful images of Doris Faber with joyful ones. Like the words engraved on her polished granite headstone:

> "Like an angel, she watched over her own each day"

PART TWO

With Rights Come Responsibilities

Found out that property is a gold mine, but am pessimistic as to what will be allowed.

John Clapp,
writing in Thornby
guest book, 1978

CHAPTER SIX

You Will Find That The Truth Is Often Unpopular

Advanced age and ill health had finally forced Doris Faber in 1987 to leave her beloved Thornby for a nursing home. After that, the heirs rented out the Thornby house for a few years, and then it sat vacant for the rest of its life. The once-cherished gardens ran wild like neglected children. The stately white house seemed frozen, an easy mark for vandals and thieves. With doors and windows missing, it squatted forlornly in its lonely green cocoon, visible to drivers on Lakeshore Drive and accessible to curfew-less teens looking for an illegal hangout. Graffiti defaced kitchen walls. The owners made no serious attempts to secure the house or reclaim the landscape.

"Demolition by neglect," as Ron Paradise, former county planner, calls it. Most of the outbuildings were sad, dilapidated eyesores. Ron says that Thornby local partner Frank Knight "always advocated sprucing up the Thornby house," but the Glass heirs were unwilling to spend the money. "It broke my heart," mourns Bob Bechir, who spent time there as a child. "The house was a fond memory that should have been preserved." As lifelong Enterprise resident Marcus Nutt puts it, "It was very hard for me to drive by there, to know somebody was renting it, to have no access. To all of us kids who grew up there, it was a second home."

Still, with a little imagination, as the 1990s ushered in the new millennium, you could picture Dr. and Mrs. Glass on warm winter evenings 70 years before, welcoming visitors from all over the world on the roomy front porch of their delightful home. Or, you might hear Miss Doris outside, speaking softly to the youngsters she so lovingly cared for, along with her menagerie, 40 years after that.

Inside, the house was in better shape than might be expected. The remodeled kitchen seemed out of place with the old fireplaces. The lovely original heart-of-pine floors were intact, and there was no sign of roof leaks. Stairs leading to the second floor and attic were still useable. Although full of junk and peppered with graffiti, the house seemed eminently restorable. Outside, Miss Doris' well-remembered chicken coop remained, along with predictable trash piles left from recent hard times and uncaring tenants.

In February 1989, Doris Faber was still alive. One month earlier, the Thornby owners' lawyer, Allen Watts, asked the Volusia County Planning Commission to re-zone the property for duplexes. County staff then asked for a 30-day delay "to allow the county's land acquisition committee and the Deltona Municipal Services District to consider joint purchase of the land for use as a park." Commission members said that a park would be the "ideal use" for Thornby, but the *DeLand Sun* reported that "the $2.5 million asking price stands in the way of any public use" and so the rezoning application went to public hearing.

At the hearing, Watts offered a carrot-and-stick deal: if you double our existing building rights, we'll build sewers. The commission turned him down unanimously, citing traffic problems on "scenic Lakeshore Drive" and "continuing land-use problems" (translation: flooding) at the neighboring condominiums. They suggested the owners find "less intensive uses" for the property than duplexes. This appears to be the owners' first attempt to intensify the allowed land use on the Thornby property. By respecting the land use they had (one residence per acre), taking into account the onsite wetlands and other constraints, the property could have accommodated at least 20 homes on good-sized lots. But, the owners did not consider that a viable option.

Thornby house, circa 2000

The 1989 sale proposal wasn't the first time the property was offered to Volusia County. Back in 1986, when Doris Faber was still at Thornby, the property was considered for acquisition under a new county $20 million bond program to buy park and conservation land. According to Volusia County Land Acquisition Manager Bill Gardner, the purchase "was never pursued as the asking price was too high."

Things Which Once Seemed Everlasting are Changing All the Time

Now, take a step back 27 years. The year was 1962.

Enterprise was peaceful, tree-filled and historic, much as it is today.

At Thornby, Doris Faber was contentedly caring for children of working parents, teaching Sunday school at Barnett Methodist, and managing her animals, the gardens and the house. That year, she hosted Thornby visitors from Montana, Washington and New York, and Thornby heirs Catherine and Alfred Clapp made another trip from New Jersey to Florida.

In 1962, Florida mega-developer Mackle Brothers bought 17,203 acres in west Volusia County, formed the Deltona Corporation, and began constructing what was originally called "Deltona Lakes."[1] Carolyn Watson Langley recalls that in the 1960s, the Mackles drove around West Volusia looking

---

1 The name "Deltona," a combination of "DeLand" and "Daytona," originally belonged to a small local nursery, says Wise Hardin.

for land to buy. Some say, however, that the Mackles' land-buying spree started a decade or so earlier when, in a foretelling of Disney-esque strategy, they quietly amassed desirable area properties. The land they bought included properties traditionally considered part of Enterprise, which, like many small Florida communities, did not have legal boundaries. In the next three years, 1,200 houses were built in Florida pine woods ironically known as the "Enterprise Scrub," home to gopher tortoises, scrub jays, and other native wildlife.

In 1961, two years after Anna Glass' death, Catherine Clapp sold the east half of Thornby's original 90-some acres to a Seminole County businessman, the late Irving Feinberg, for $27,500 (about $197,000 today). Ernie Watson says Feinberg agreed not to "flip" the property. Records show that Feinberg signed a mortgage allowing him to remove "only such individual trees as may be necessary for the clearing of one home site." Feinberg never built a home there, however. In 1971, he sold the property to the Mackle Corporation for about half a million in today's dollars. Two condominium complexes were eventually built on the site. Catherine Clapp was upset, Dwayne Watson says, when she saw that the huge, magnificent oak trees that once graced the property were no longer standing, and said she regretted having sold it. Enterprise resident Lani Friend put it bluntly, when she recalled in a 2004 email, "We were all appalled when the Clapps sold it… and it was leveled. No one knew what was happening until it was too late."

People who knew Catherine Clapp are adamant about one thing — she loved Thornby. At least twice a year for most of her life, she vacationed there with her husband, her children, and then her grandchildren. Her happy notes in the Thornby guestbook are some of the most heartfelt in its pages. "Such a perfectly lovely ten days of good times, eating dinners and picnics, learning about ducks, fine swims at Green Springs," reads one entry.

The Way We Were

On October 15, 1989, Doris Brooks Faber died, and, in many ways, an era ended. Government-regulated facilities had replaced special places like Thornby, where Doris Faber could let children bake cookies in a wood stove, feed the chickens and swim in the springs without fear of lawsuits. The Children's Home opened its own state-licensed daycare facility in one of the oldest buildings on campus. Some of the home's children now attended church in Deltona or DeBary instead of Enterprise. The home's children who once freely walked to town, and the town children who once casually visited playmates at the home, were now separated by state-mandated fences and gates. "I played with a lot of the kids from the Children's Home. There wasn't one fence when I was growing up," recalls Marcus Nutt. The world outside

Enterprise was changing, too, with Florida in the forefront. Everywhere, there was no-holds-barred destruction of wetlands and wildlife habitat. Thousands of treeless subdivisions, cleverly given names like "Tall Oaks" after the natural features they displaced, were hidden behind heavy brick walls as if their developers were ashamed of them.

Sleeping Giant Awakens

The behemoth-in-the-making, Deltona, grew so forcefully that in 30 years its original population of 180 had become 50,000. In the decade from 1970 to 1980, Deltona's growth rate was an astounding 223 percent. (By way of comparison, in the same period DeLand grew by 32 percent.) When Doris Faber was alive, she, too, saw the close-knit community of Enterprise in harm's way. In the early 1970s, she wrote that part of DeBary Avenue, named long ago for the legendary "Count" Frederick DeBary, whose citrus groves once included parts of Enterprise and employed many Enterprise residents, was now called Doyle Road, and "that should never be."

By 1990, "Deltona" was a Municipal Service District — a kind of governmental limbo in which residents lack self-governance. The Deltona MSD was 149 years newer and 25 times bigger than its neighbor Enterprise.

In 1993, Catherine Clapp died in New Jersey. Her husband had died five years before. Their four sons were now the absentee owners of the Thornby property. The stars were aligning over West Volusia, but they were dark stars for Thornby.

Deltona was originally marketed to senior citizens as a retirement haven, but over 20 years the average age of its residents had dropped from 62 to 35. Now, some Deltona residents were chafing under county rule: they wanted to incorporate as a city and set their own destiny. A loud, strong faction, however, remained strongly opposed to incorporation. The years from 1987 through 1995 brought not only rapid growth, but also intense conflict, controversy and contention, as Deltona's pro- and anti-incorporation forces locked horns through the newspapers, with county officials, and before the Florida Legislature. Those struggles were a preview of what was to follow: Deltona residents have often been agonizingly and publicly split on issues both significant and petty.

Of the many challenges that came with "to incorporate or not?" setting the new city's legal boundaries ranked at the top. In 1987, the citizens' Committee to Incorporate Deltona undertook the task of deciding where Deltona would begin and Enterprise would end. The issue had been simmering for years. Dwayne Watson says he was part of a group that drew up potential Enterprise boundaries as far back as the late 1960s and early 1970s. "We knew Deltona was going to take over," he says.

"They've been trying to reassure us that they don't want us," observed Valerie Grill. A kind of "Wild West" atmosphere prevailed, leaving much of the historic community up for grabs. In its 120-year history, Enterprise, like other tiny towns such as Cassadaga, had no official perimeters. "In the old days, boundaries of cities and unincorporated areas were fluid," says Tom Brooks, Volusia County planner, adding that whole communities could simply disappear due to diseases like yellow fever. It was "common practice for areas of the county not to be legally delineated, but what locals considered them to be," he explains.

Long-time Enterprise resident Alice "Mickey" Nutt was one of those who watched the boundary debate unfold. "We don't mind Deltona incorporating," she said. "We just don't want to be part of their city." Based on information from senior Enterprise residents, she sketched a map of the community's unofficial boundaries and presented it to the committee. Some joked that the plotted lines jogged so much that they looked like castles, but the resulting boundaries kept Enterprise separate and apart from Deltona. The committee's work was moot, however, because Deltona voters nixed the incorporation idea. A second ballot three years later yielded the same result. Then, in 1995, pro-incorporation forces re-grouped for a third bite of the apple.

Dark Stars

The Enterprise Evergreen Cemetery, established in 1841, shares a long and storied history with the Enterprise community. The cemetery land was donated by Enterprise pioneers with names like Padgett and Thayer. As president of the Enterprise Evergreen Cemetery Association, long-time resident Wise Hardin found himself enmeshed in Deltona incorporation maneuverings. From the beginning, he worked with the Committee to Incorporate Deltona on proposed city boundaries. He describes a give-and-take process, led by the late county council member Clyde Mann, much like a real-life Monopoly game: "We'll take that." "OK, we won't go there," resulting in borders acceptable to all. Those were the boundaries presented to Deltona voters for the first two unsuccessful incorporation votes.

As the third incorporation ballot approached, though, events took a dizzying twist. At a community meeting just days before the vote, organizers promised that the same proposed boundaries would apply. A break was called. Although most people left, Wise stayed. When the meeting reconvened, things had changed. Now Deltona's limits would include 25 homes on historic Braddock Road (the site of Taylor's original settlement and Polly Taylor's grave). To the west, the 1841 Enterprise Evergreen Cemetery would become part of Deltona.

Folks in the cemetery association didn't know their legal rights, and didn't have time to find out. Wise trudged door-to-door in Enterprise, collecting contributions to pay for this notice, which appeared in the *Orlando Sentinel* on Election Day, September 5, 1995:

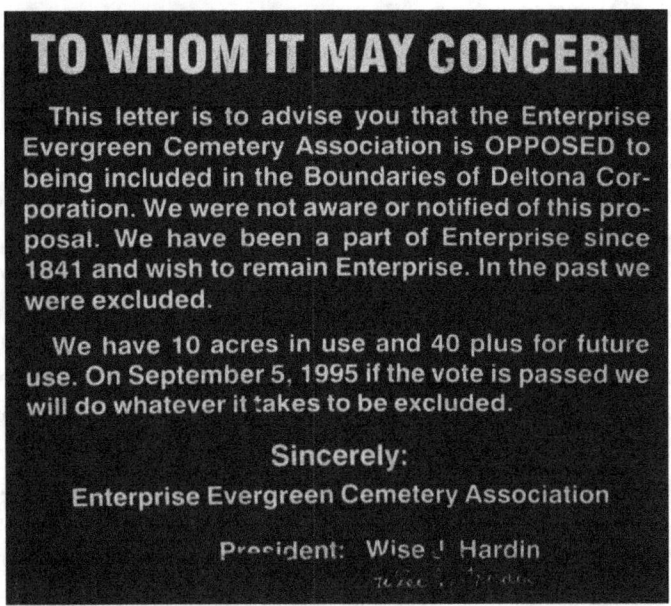

Notice printed in the Orlando Sentinel, September 5, 1995

On the third ballot, with a 54 percent majority voting for incorporation, Deltona became Volusia County's second-most populous city. Its boundaries were "as straight as possible," announced the committee chairman. Enterprise residents, of course, couldn't vote on either the incorporation or the boundaries. "No thought was given to [Enterprise's] history or community pride," lamented *Sentinel* columnist Bo Poertner on September 8, 1995.

In a portent of later Thornby controversies, the voting outcome didn't mollify city residents who opposed incorporation. Anti-incorporation forces immediately sought to undo the result. Likewise, Enterprise residents living on Braddock Road were disheartened. Caught by surprise when included in Deltona, they would have to try to de-annex from a city they hadn't wanted to be part of in the first place. However, they couldn't pursue the issue until Deltona elected its first slate of officials. "We want to keep our identity as part of historic Enterprise," said Bobbie Fortner. Unwilling to passively accept the carving up of her community, she did some research of her own. The echoes of what she found would reverberate from Enterprise, to Deltona, to DeLand, to Tallahassee, and back.

In researching the incorporation, Fortner found that the county elections office hadn't followed state law regarding publication of legal notice. The county admitted a mistake had been made, but labeled it a mere technicality. To Deltona's anti-incorporation forces, the slip-up was manna from heaven. They promptly filed a lawsuit to nullify the vote. It seemed that, between the conflicted boundaries and the irksome lawsuit, the incorporation had become something other than Florida sunny.

As the de-incorporation lawsuit made its way through the courts, Enterprise residents, led by Wise Hardin on behalf of the Cemetery Association, rallied. Hardin met with State Senator Locke Burt and State Representative Earl Ziebarth, assuring them that people in Enterprise wouldn't oppose Deltona's incorporation, but needed help to preserve their heritage. His plea went by certified mail to state legislators Evelyn Lynn and Stan Bainter, to Circuit Judge John Doyle, to Florida's attorney general, and to the local state attorney, detailing the fate that had befallen historic Enterprise. The letters carried a poignant message: "No one in Enterprise wants to be any part of Deltona, and if our deceased loved ones could speak, I know that they would second this statement." The state attorney replied that he couldn't find a criminal violation and "your only avenue would be to speak with the Volusia County Legislative Delegation." The Florida Legislature, meanwhile, was poised to use its legal authority to bypass the "technical error" and give its blessing to Deltona's incorporation. Volusia County Council Member Pat Northey told the Volusia Legislative Delegation on September 19, 1995, "We need to move forward and I ask you to ratify the election."

On September 23, 1995, the Enterprise Evergreen Cemetery Association published "An Open Letter to the People of Deltona," recounting the events that led to the unhappy state of affairs (opposite page).

Meanwhile, the new city was attending to business, albeit with a cloud over the elections. State Senator Lynn cleared the air. Immediately after receiving Hardin's letter, she invited him to put his case to the legislative delegation at an October 18, 1995 public hearing in Deltona. Hardin had one week to alert the people of Enterprise to the hearing, but he says, "I didn't need to tell them. There was a ruckus in town; everybody was upset." Three hundred people attended. Lawmakers listened as Hardin deplored what was happening: "It's as if the team at bat in the World Series could change the rules of the game to benefit themselves," he said. Acting as peacemaker, Senator Burt recommended that the Florida Legislature support Deltona's incorporation, and at the same time re-draw the boundaries to exclude rural residents in Enterprise and others near Lake Helen who found themselves clasped in the new city's unwanted embrace. Wise says legislators ultimately informed Deltona that the state wouldn't issue its city charter unless it removed the disputed areas from its city limits. After six months, those 44 property owners wiggled free from the city when its first commission de-annexed them "in order to show good faith to the Volusia County legislative delegation." It made "perfect sense" to de-annex the properties, says county planner Tom Brooks, "because they did not fit the overall density pattern of Deltona." Ten years later, when the Thornby property stuck out like a square peg in the round hole of Deltona's "overall density pattern," perfect sense wasn't so easy to find.

AN OPEN LETTER TO THE PEOPLE OF DELTONA FROM THE PEOPLE OF ENTERPRISE

We were shocked and dismayed to discover just days before the vote to Incorporate Deltona that the Committee To Incorporate Deltona had secretly changed the boundaries that had been agreed upon between Deltona and Enterprise and the Committee intended to confiscate large areas of historical Enterprise and to add insult to injury, take our 154 year old 42-acre Enterprise Evergreen Cemetery away from us.

Enterprise and its people have tried to be a good neighbor to Deltona. Is this what we get in return? Could it have been providence that someone at the country level made THE MISTAKE that will allow us to correct this miscarriage of justice before it's too late?

FACT: At the first try for Deltona to incorporate, a delegation from Enterprise attended the meeting in good faith with the leaders from Deltona and boundaries between the two communities were agreed upon and respected for that election.

FACT: On the second try for Deltona to incorporate these same boundaries were honored.

FACT: On the third try for Deltona to incorporate, at the meeting that a delegation from Enterprise attended, this delegation was assured by the leaders for incorporation that these same boundaries would be honored.

FACT: We in Enterprise were never notified in any way that these boundaries had been changed, and that Deltona intended to include large areas of Enterprise within the limits of Deltona.

FACT: Only days before the election was it discovered that the leadership in Deltona had gone back on their word and historical sections of Enterprise and our 154 year old 42-acre Enterprise Evergreen Cemetery were to be part of Deltona.

FACT: The residents in parts of Enterprise were notified by the election officials by U.S. Mail that they could not vote in the election on September 5, 1995, giving us no say in the losing of our cemetery.

FACT: The leadership in Deltona might claim that they included parts of Enterprise to avoid enclaves but in NO WAY CAN ENTERPRISE BE CONSIDERED AN ENCLAVE. WE WERE HERE FIRST!

FACT: The citizens of Enterprise feel that they have been the victim of the most dishonest kind of politics and will do whatever it takes to be removed from Deltona.

ENTERPRISE EVERGREEN CEMETERY ASSOC. 407-668-5108

Notice printed in the Orlando Sentinel, September 23, 1995

Dream Big

As of December 31, 1995, Deltona became Volusia County's newest and second largest city, with former postal supervisor John Masiarczyk as its first mayor. It was an exciting time. "Dream every dream you can dream," new-to-politics city officials were told. "Think big." Think big they did. Their stargazing included visions of a city police force within five years and Saturday hours at City Hall. But one oversized dream outshone them all.

"Mayor Pushes Public-Private Partnerships" proclaimed the *Daytona Beach News-Journal* on July 27, 1996. One of Masiarczyk's suggestions was that the city "partner with private investors for development of a commercial marina/restaurant/hotel on the vacant 38-acre Thornby property." I know these [ideas] may be controversial," he admitted. "This property is ideally suited for future economic development. This would show our interest in the lakeshore. There is only so much down there." "Down there," of course, was the community of Enterprise.

The new city soon had its own fire department. It also had its first planner — Bob Nix, a former Army artillery officer in his mid-50's with a master's degree in urban planning and a background in radio and TV broadcasting. However, Deltona didn't have a city hall. Commission meetings were held at the small, nondescript community center on Lakeshore Drive — not the most impressive place to conduct government business. The Thornby heirs, looking to get in on the ground floor, offered their property as a city hall site for a reported $1.2 million. If that number is accurate, they were asking the city for just half of the $2.5 million they asked from the county seven years before.

Dreaming Big at the Strip Center

On the night of August 4, 1997, as unwelcome as a sales call during dinner, Deltona dropped in on Enterprise. That's when the city commission voted to re-zone 12 wet, wooded acres across Providence Boulevard from Thornby into a 58,000-square-foot strip shopping center. At the first of two public hearings, a city staffer reported that the site was expensive to develop "due to the large number of trees" and asked the commission to give the developer "a significant waiver of tree replacement requirements." Mayor Masiarczyk asked about running a pipe through the property to funnel stormwater runoff[2] into Lake Monroe. The developer, they were told, had won many awards, and "all the final details" — like traffic — would be taken care of later. At the hearing, a nearby resident said he couldn't think of a more unsuitable place for a shopping center.

The vote in favor of a St. Petersburg developer was not noteworthy. Given the city's political climate, the result was not unexpected. Rather, the

---

2   Stormwater runoff contains pollutants like lawn chemicals and roadway oil.

circumstances of the vote remain bothersome. For the final vote, one commissioner was "out of the room." The result was a tie, 3-3, which meant defeat for the re-zoning/shopping center.

After the vote, "when it became apparent that Commissioner Donald Foss was not in the room," the mayor called a 10-minute break. When the meeting reconvened, the commission voted all over again. Two commissioners changed their votes, and this time, the re-zoning passed.

The required second re-zoning hearing on August 18 was attended by "more than 100 angry residents with environmental concerns." Along with others, Valerie Grill pointed out major problems with drainage, water retention and flooding. City Commissioner Wayne Gardner expressed concerns regarding the nearby bald eagle nest, impact from lighting to the surrounding residential area, effects on Green Spring, old oak trees three feet thick, and the possibility of a sinkhole on the property. As well, he voiced concerns about whether legal notice requirements had been followed. A majority of the commission decided they didn't have enough data to vote that night, so the hearing was postponed.

At the rescheduled hearing months later, the developer's attorney vouched for his client's "impeccable reputation." The 12 acres, he assured them, were "very difficult… to develop." The re-zoning was welcomed by Enterprise resident John Gray, who testified that he was developing 900 lots in DeBary and "those residents would drive to this location to shop."

Members of the public who spoke bolstered their concerns about drainage and flooding with models, technical information and maps. The attorney representing members of the public pointed out that the neighborhood was overwhelmingly residential and historical. She noted that the city staff report read as if it were recommending denial even though it recommended approval, and a resident agreed that "reading between the lines" of the report gave that impression. Nevertheless, Bob Nix, city development services director, referred to "several protective measures" in the development agreement, and nebulous "plans" to four-lane Providence Boulevard.

Commissioner Foss saw in his crystal ball that the Providence and Doyle intersection would be "two four-lane highways very shortly" [3] and that approving the shopping center would give the city "maximum control over how the property was developed."

Words like "inevitable" and "ultimately" were casually invoked, as if shopping centers are blessed in heaven, not at city hall. The vote was 5-2 in favor of strip shopping on Enterprise's border.

Three weeks later, the *News-Journal* reported that "enraged" residents complained that the shopping center site was being cleared without a permit.

---

3   The Providence and Doyle intersection has not become "two four-lane highways" as of this writing.

"There's nothing illegal going on," the city engineer shot back. "The developer isn't clearing the land." Four days later, the same newspaper reported that the developer with the "impeccable reputation" had been "warned not to *continue* preliminary site work without a permit."

Deal or No Deal

A couple of years later, in another *News-Journal* article profiling Thornby history, John Clapp raved about its "irreplaceable trees" being "the love of our family." He may have forgotten that two years before, he had tried to sell his "love" for a city hall. Interestingly, the fact that Thornby was not even in Deltona had not seemed to deter anyone in the city from planning its future.

Frank Knight was practically an Enterprise native. His father worked at the landmark Turner Power Plant for years, and he spent lots of time at Thornby. Like uncounted numbers of kids, he enjoyed the woods, the animals and Miss Doris' cooking. His name, in child's printing, first appears in the Thornby guest book in 1945, the first of many such entries. He was about the same age as John Clapp, and they became good friends, spending time together whenever the Clapps came to Florida. Knight became a business partner of the heirs, serving as their local contact with the lawyers and the city through the subsequent years of Thornby battles. Needless to say, this didn't win him any popularity contests with his Enterprise neighbors. Carolyn Watson Langley says that she heard jokes about Frank Knight being tarred and feathered. Marcus Nutt says he doesn't know why Frank "doesn't have a connection to the town." On the other hand, says former county planner Ron Paradise, "I knew Frank very well. I think he had an emotional tie to Thornby and Enterprise, but Thornby to him was ultimately an investment and he wanted a payoff." [4]

At a May 1999 Deltona City Commission meeting, Development Services Director Bob Nix, whose undergraduate degree was in history, proposed that the city submit a grant application seeking state funds to study possible restoration of the Thornby house. He told the city commission the property's asking price was $1.2 million and that the city was eligible for a grant of up to $2.2 million. Nix pointed out that the property had "some history of local significance" and that a restored Thornby house would promote ecotourism and area history. City officials dismissed the house as "dilapidated" and "of little value" but the mayor considered the property to be "prime waterfront property and one of only a few parcels left." Stonewalled on all sides by protests that Thornby was not in the city and the house had "no historical significance" and "no unique qualities," Nix's proposal didn't stand a chance. The Thornby owners were "most interested in selling the land to us for any public purpose

---

4 Frank Knight declined to be interviewed for this book.

and preserving the old Thornby house," he says today, but "the city commission could not see the wisdom of getting the city involved in this worthwhile project on the city border."

About this time, Deltona hired a consulting firm to help create its state-mandated comprehensive plan, guided by planner Todd Peetz. Now living in Ohio, Peetz clearly recalls "many conversations about the Enterprise area and how to be compatible with it," in the parts of Deltona that touched Enterprise. "It was decided that Enterprise had a lot of history, and that history and charm should be preserved," he adds. Bob Nix agrees. In fact, he says today, "I suggested that the [comp plan] visioning process should include our neighbors in Enterprise. I also suggested a joint planning area with them and the county. Neither suggestion was approved by the commission." (Nix points out that the commission's refusal to include Enterprise in the new city's planning efforts came on the heels of "intense lobbying of the Legislature by Enterprise residents who did not want to be incorporated into Deltona.")

Years later, Todd Peetz' first-hand experience with Deltona's comp plan would be a welcome boost to Thornby supporters, and would bring about one more Thornby coincidence.

Behind the Scenes

The notion of Deltona City Hall being situated on the Thornby property had been abandoned in favor of a city hall built on state-owned property in north-central Deltona. Even so, Thornby's owners still weren't about to settle for building at their allowed density of one unit per acre. "Development expected on Thornby land," announced the headline on the *News-Journal*'s December 6, 1999 article, predicting that Thornby would become "another casualty of encroaching development." The owners had ratcheted up their plans; instead of duplexes, they were now asking to build garden apartments and townhomes on the property. If you're outside the rules anyway, why not kick it up a notch?

In a different world with a more predictable process, this latest attempt to get the law changed would have met with the same response as the 1989 try — "No." However this is Florida, not Utopia. It was 1999, and elected officials were on the verge of a new millennium, where the answer to virtually every development plan was a resounding "Yes!"

The county council has the final say on changes to the "Future Land Use Map," the blueprint for "what goes where" on land within unincorporated areas. When someone applies to change the map, council members need to know how the proposed change would affect the surrounding area on such issues as traffic and drainage. Since they can't be familiar with every tract in every corner of the county, they generally rely on their staff, as well as the county planning commission, to do most, if not all, of the research.

The appointed members of the planning commission (now the Planning and Land Development Review Commission, or PLDRC) review applications to change the comp plan, and recommend to the council what its final vote should be.

> **Activist Lesson:** In some jurisdictions, an "in-house" review committee is the first stop for a land us change. Such groups often fly under activists' radar, as do advisory boards. To identify every step in the process, you can research applicable codes, ask staff members, and follow the jurisdiction's website for meetings and agendas. Ask the staff to put you on their list to receive copies of everything pertaining to the particular issue in which you are interested.

When Thornby came to the planning commission, member Mori Hosseini, one of the region's major builder/developers, justified his "thumbs up" on grounds that a future developer would still need approval from the St. Johns River Water Management District and Army Corps of Engineers, and both agencies would impose "stringent standards." He reached the bottom line: "… cities and counties… want higher densities… It's cheaper."

When someone wants a change to the land use map, county law requires the planning commission to consider, among other criteria, the proposed development's "impact upon the environment or natural resources." (*Volusia County Code of Ordinances 72-414(e)(2)*). Despite that mandate, planning commissioners voted unanimously to recommend that the county council approve a land use change allowing apartments on Thornby.

To take a general view of the land use change process, in proposing to amend the approved land use on his property, an owner and/or his attorney deals mainly with his county or city planning staff by phone or email. If the planned amendment is complex or massive, there will be in-person meetings, too. The county or city attorney may attend, as well as a council member — but only one. (That's because Florida's Sunshine Law prohibits two or more members of the same public board from discussing a matter that may later come before them for a vote, outside of a public meeting.) There may be several such private meetings, where plan details are refined and compromises made — for instance, how much total square footage will be allowed. These meetings are not advertised, nor are they open to the public. Other departments review the application, too, and weigh in with their own comments. In Thornby, the county's environmental management staff strongly recommended against changing its land use designation from one residence per acre. Two of the reasons cited were destruction of historic trees and polluted runoff into Lake Monroe.

Of course, the staff, or a council member, can discuss a proposed change to the comprehensive plan with members of the public. The hitch is that, at this stage, the public usually has no idea that a plan amendment is in the works, and so they have no reason to seek a meeting. The proposed change is not posted on any signs, printed on any agendas, or advertised in any fine-print notices until much later in the process.

> **Activist Lesson:** It's important to form good working relationships with staff planners, who can keep you abreast of the land use issues on which they are working. Don't hesitate to email or call them with your questions, whether you live in that city/county or not.

When all details of the proposal have been ironed out, the planning staff prepares its report, which carries a "yes" or "no" *recommendation* on approval. Then, the planning commission and/or the council can either follow or disregard what the staff says when either votes.

First Thornby Hearing: Volusia County

Volusia County's planning staff recommended approval of the land use change on Thornby, even though, as the *News-Journal* reported:

> ...they say there are difficulties in developing the site that has 7.5 acres of wetlands, an unknown number of specimen trees, a historic structure, high probability of archeological sites, 1,200 feet of shoreline and a nearby active eagle's nest.

Years later, county planner Ron Paradise explained the reasoning behind the staff's recommendation to approve condominiums on Thornby: from a planning standpoint, multi-family residences were logical on Thornby's 40 acres because there were condos on 40 adjacent acres. Of course, Thornby and its surroundings were the same in 1999 as they were in 1989 when county planners, concerned about traffic and flooding, reached the opposite conclusion and recommended *denying* Thornby duplexes. Veteran planner Doug Kelly explains the planning paradox this way: "You could look at the condos next door and say they are determinative of what goes on a property, or you could look across the street and see the lake, and say that is [determinative]." In other words, planning is informed by the prevailing political will.

Enterprise mega-activist Valerie Grill told the *News-Journal* "the proposals go along with what Deltona has brought down on us." The Baby Giant City was now pushing for a 7-Eleven on formerly residential, now re-zoned to commercial, property near Thornby at Doyle Road and Providence Boulevard.

When the Volusia County Council considered the Thornby land use change in February 2000, both county staff and the planning commission were recommending approval. The Thornby owners' lawyer, Mark Watts, reassured the council that the "many constraints on development" would be taken into account.

> **Activist Lesson:** This type of statement is not intended to provide facts, but just to sound good. Take notes of remarks you may want to follow up later. In this example, you would want to get details of the "many constraints on development" alluded to by the property owners' lawyer.

The meeting minutes reflect:

> Members of the public spoke against a higher density at this site, expressing concerns about the soil, flooding in the area during heavy rains, traffic flow, the impact it would have on schools in the area, environmental concerns and the historic nature of the site.

At the hearing, the county's historic preservation officer advised that the Thornby owners would need a permit before they could demolish the house.

With Deltona waiting in the wings, city annexation/control of Thornby was a very real possibility. "Council members said they were nervous about the prospect of the land annexing into Deltona," wrote the *News-Journal*. To allay their concerns, lawyer Mark Watts told the council that the owners

> ...do not have any plans of annexation at this time *or any time in the future.*

Council member Ann McFall told her colleagues about the previous year's attempt by Bob Nix that "this property, which abuts the city limits, be designated historic preservation property," but the Deltona City Commission had rejected his recommendation.

Councilwoman Pat Northey said she was confident that the county could "better protect" Thornby than Deltona and then moved to approve the land use change/density increase. It passed on a vote of 4-3.

> **Activist Lesson:** Were there really only two options: Hold Thornby in the county with a big density increase, or "give" it to Deltona? It's up to those opposing a land use change to explore and present alternatives to officials who may feel boxed in by the limited options presented to them.

"If the county denied the measure it would have opened the door for the owners to request annexation into Deltona," explained the *News-Journal*. Grace Stamile was one of the citizens who spoke that day. "We were horrified," she says.

IMPORTANT**IMPORTANT**IMPORTANT

March 22, 2000

Dear Stone Island Resident:

You may be aware of recent issues in the press which could have a *significant negative impact on the quality of life* in our Enterprise community that we on Stone Island love and appreciate.

These issues include, but are not limited to:

1. Possible annexation of Enterprise into Debary or Deltona.
2. City of Deltona's efforts to link all of Deltona's lakes with ditches that drain into Lake Monroe.
3. Volusia County's bid for a Comprehensive Plan Map Amendment to higher density—which would allow the construction of 350 apartments on the old Thornsby property at the corner of Lakeshore Drive and Providence.

The 3rd issue must be addressed immediately!

Please consider the intolerable traffic situation (a minimum of 700 additional cars) and the affront to the scenic beauty and sensitive environment of the historic canopied Lakeshore Drive/Enterprise Road.

Please visualize 350 apartments on that beautiful piece of land overlooking Lake Monroe—now visualize them in 10 years!

Please help to stop this damaging high-density development in our historic, land-sensitive community.

HOW CAN YOU HELP??

Simple. Just sign, date, and fill in your address on the attached letter.
(Or write your own letter with reasons and arguments)

Mail to: Senator Daniel Webster, 315 S. Dillard Street, Winter Garden FL 34787

PLEASE DO THIS TODAY!

For more details, call Valerie Grill 574-8484, Barbara Boalo 323-4696, or Carol Aymar 324-3766.

This flyer, a freshman effort by novice activists, refers to the property as "Thornsby" and solicits comments on three separate "issues." Two of the items are generalized concerns, and none of them is the bailiwick of a state senator.

Activist Lesson: Flyers should present one specific issue and convey a sense of urgency with dates, times and places when public opinion is needed. Include as many negative effects from the proposed change as space permits — e.g., traffic and schools and wildlife — to make the message resonate with more people. Not everyone has the same concerns.

Flooding on Lakeshore Drive/Thornby

It is worth noting that the Thornby core issues in 2000 were the same issues in place eight years later. For example, soil conditions on the property were documented by David Griffis, extension agent for the University of Florida, in a 1999 report that recorded most of Thornby's soil as either "somewhat poorly drained" or "poorly drained with excessive wetness." Likewise, the county's natural resources manager said, "an undetermined number of specimen and historic trees… would also be altered by a greater density of dwelling on the parcel." The same basic issues were presented to every official at every stop along the way. Some listened, but some chose a path of blissful deafness. Ten years later, former Volusia County Council Chairman Jim Ward, who voted against the land use change in 2000, reflected that the council's "yes" vote sending the plan on to the state might have been the easy way out. Yet, according to Ben Dyer, former county planning director, "There was not much opposition at that hearing." It was the last time that statement would ever be made with Thornby on the agenda.

Florida's Department of Community Affairs: The Way it Was

In Florida, in 2000, this was how the process worked:

Suppose you own land and want to make some money. Your land, like every piece of the county, is tagged with a "future land use" in the city or county comprehensive plan. This makes for predictable investing and building, and keeps Wal-Mart out of the wetlands (well, that's the theory, anyway).

*"Just Bought an Old Ranch Out by the County Line/
You See Wetlands, I See Dollar Signs."* [5]

Now suppose you suspect that, if you sell, your land under its sanctioned uses wouldn't be worth enough to support a carefree retirement in the Keys. What to do? If you're a well-connected landowner, (or can afford to hire a clever lawyer to be connected *for* you), you simply ask your local officials to *change* your land use to a more profitable one (i.e., more houses per acre). If they say "no," end of story. But if they say "sure," you're on your way to that oceanfront condo. Not so fast. There's another step, at the state level, and it's called "DCA," or the Florida Department of Community Affairs. That's where the Thornby plan amendment had to stop before finally passing go in Volusia County.

For example, when the Thornby plan landed at DCA, state staffers were not convinced that it complied with state rules. Their report, issued in May 2000, had more than a few things to say about community impacts; ecology; Thornby's relation to a designated Natural Resources Management Area; and that old favorite, flooding. Upon receipt of the objections, the county set up meetings between its staff and DCA and the Thornby owners' lawyer sent DCA a long letter saying not much more than "all your concerns will be addressed later if you'll just give us what we want" on every page.)

Now, Mr. or Ms. Unsatisfied Landowner, your wished-for change is pitched back to the county officials who green-lighted it in the first place, this time with a "caution" sign attached, for another whack. If the state has shown them the error of their approving ways, they now reject your change, and you're headed for Happy Acres Trailer/Retirement Park, taking with you, the allowed use that was on your land when you bought it — as you knew at the time, of course. But hey, can't blame a guy/gal for trying! However, if the locals are feeling ornery, they might just take on the state, sailing full speed ahead into lawyer-to-lawyer combat, tax dollars flying in their wake. Since comp plans should only be changed for the public's benefit — not Mr. or Ms. Private Landowner's — why would officials do that?

Second Thornby Hearing: Volusia County

Carol Aymar wrote to the county council. "Is anybody out there listening to the community of Enterprise?" she wondered. "It's obvious that Deltona's plan for a shopping center next to Thornby will fit nicely with the 350 apartments you approved there," she scolded, then beseeched the council to "acquire the Thornby estate property. Keep it out of the hands of the city of Deltona and high density developers." Council member Patricia Northey responded that she was "concerned for the long-term wellbeing of historic Enterprise."

---

5 Lyrics from "Developer's Stomp" copyright 2007 by Rog Lee,

She would look into a county purchase, but warned, "It requires a willing seller. I am not sure you have that."

After the state had its say, the Thornby owners' hope of leaping from one to eight housing units per acre came back to the county council in July 2000. The second time around, "it could have gone either way," says Ron Paradise in retrospect. "It wouldn't have surprised me if council had approved the change to apartments on Thornby." Enterprise folks were doing all they could to make sure that didn't happen. Carol Aymar and Valerie Grill met with Northey; Valerie and Chris Elmer met with Council member Ann McFall. "We believed," says Carol Aymar, "that if we had the passion and the community behind us, then [the] county council would listen to us."

That hearing marked the beginning of a strategy that would become the hallmark of the Enterprise community's presentations: Be ultra-organized, clear and focused. Passionate is OK, whiny is not. In addition, never make a statement you can't substantiate with fact. Ten years later, Ben Dyer, former county planning director, recalled: "We were really impressed with the number of people that showed up, and that level of involvement carried through the ensuing years."

> **Activist Lesson:** There **is** strength in numbers. Emails are good, but bodies at a hearing are better.

Says Dyer about the citizens who spoke, "Everybody was unified." Enterprise people drilled their points home, loud and clear. "It's ludicrous to think you would put high-density apartments on that strip of land," admonished Carol Aymar. Chris Elmer — determined, assertive, a born leader — informed them: "It is a gem, and you people are the only ones who can protect it." Wise Hardin says he didn't need to speak because "Chris did such a good job." Patrick Stamile affirms, "I think Chris really moved them." Suzanne Steiner calls him a "bulldozer." Five years later the same charisma would be displayed when city and county locked horns. Other speakers proffered facts about wetlands, trees, polluted runoff and buffers.

Thornby and its surroundings were exactly the same as they had been four months earlier when the county council said "hooray" to hundreds of apartments there. Why, then, the complete turnaround? Former council chair Jim Ward, in a 2010 interview, remembered it this way: "Credit should go to the Enterprise folks. They showed us the worth of the property." It was also the first public appearance of what coalesced into the Enterprise Preservation Society.

Convinced, council member Joe Jaynes said, "I'll take my chances at this point with Deltona. Maybe they'll take a hard look at what they're doing." "We [county planning staff] were cognizant of the fact that Deltona could annex the site," comments Ron Paradise. Dave Aymar remembers that while the council rejected the plan, its members gave the Thornby advocates a "stern warning." "They said our problems were just beginning if the owners annexed into Deltona," he says. "And they asked if we wanted to continue down that path."

In the end, council members said they wanted to take a strong stand against too much development at the site. In words that ought to be tattooed on the forehead of every official who votes on land use changes, Chairman Jim Ward said during the hearing, "I don't think we're responsible for providing housing at the expense of natural resources." He was responding to the lawyer's arguments that "the project should be approved because multi-family housing is desperately needed in West Volusia."

Ward says that after the vote, he talked to Frank Knight about county funds available through the Volusia Forever program, established to acquire and preserve environmentally significant land like Thornby.[6] Attorney Dennis Bayer remembers having a similar conversation with Knight's lawyer, Allen Watts. Bayer, an original Volusia Forever board member, recalls, "the asking price was astronomical. It was not going to go anywhere." He believes the Thornby owners were expecting to sell the 40 acres for $6 million.

The council's unanimous "no" vote on an eight-fold density increase on Thornby wasn't the only good thing to come from the meeting. When Councilwoman Ann McFall said she would nominate Chris Elmer to the Volusia Growth Management Commission (the county board with ultimate authority to approve or reject comprehensive plan amendments), it was understood that one day, he might play a role in Thornby's future. Years later, he did play a dramatic role — but not in the way anyone could have predicted.

In Enterprise, the lights were coming on. After the shopping center re-zoning, says Elmer, "the tide sort of turned in our favor because of all the attention it got." When the county council tentatively approved the land use change for apartments on Thornby, the community stirred in its sleep. A March town meeting to discuss Enterprise's future found it alert, with vital signs strong. Thornby had been the heart and soul of Enterprise for 80 years. On July 6, 2000, Enterprise, wide-awake and transformed, rallied to return the favor. No one then imagined that the cause would consume untold hours, thousands of dollars, and another 10 years.

---

6 In 1992, Volusia County became the first county in Florida to approve a dedicated source of funds to buy conservation land.

People in the small unincorporated area of Enterprise are known for their feistiness.

Pat Hatfield
in *The West Volusia Beacon*,
April 2, 2010

CHAPTER SEVEN

Enterprise Needs a Voice

By the time Volusia County officials had approved and then rejected multi-family land use on Thornby, no one could deny that Enterprise was under political siege. As Wise Hardin calls it, "Deltona kept wanting to take over Enterprise."

Suzanne Steiner moved to Enterprise in 1994. She knew the Thornby house only from driving by, but a 1999 news article about potential condos there got her attention. "It changed my life," she admits. "Now all my best friends are activists!" She soon connected with Enterprise leaders Carol Aymar and Valerie Grill. In those early days, she says, "We felt that if the whole community of Enterprise united, we could save this piece of property. We saw Thornby as the first step of the carving up of Enterprise."

Years before Thornby, though, Suzanne vividly remembers the day she visited the small block building known as the Deltona Arts & Historical Center, begun by then-mayor John Masiarczyk who happened to be onsite. Along with a brochure about historic Enterprise, she got a mini-lecture on what was best for the community. "They'd be so much better off under our stewardship," she says he admonished her. "We could protect them better than the county."

As for Suzanne, she felt rather pleased that her new home town was so special that "everyone wanted us."

Valerie Grill

"She was a great leader of the cause." — **Chris Elmer**

"She's incredibly effective." — **Suzanne Steiner**

A few years ago, Valerie Grill "retired" from West Volusia activism and returned to her farm in eastern Tennessee. Some speculated she was burned out from years of high-profile, often-frustrating activism. Some guessed that she ran afoul of one too many powerful developers, and in the process came close to personal misfortune. The real reason is more elemental: Valerie and her husband always considered their Tennessee farm as home. That fact doesn't diminish her hard-earned legacy to Enterprise. Her intense love for Enterprise and willingness to put it before self, exemplified the legacy of those who came before.

In 1985, Valerie founded the non-profit West Volusia Conservancy — the godmother, in many ways, to the Enterprise Preservation Society. Over the years, the Conservancy, with Valerie as president, varied from 25 to 60 members, gaining a reputation for collecting hard-hitting facts and clearing the political/bureaucratic jungle. Its biggest achievement was protecting Enterprise's rare Green Spring, now a Volusia County park and one of the few remaining pure springs feeding the St. Johns River, from death-by-development. The group lobbied to establish the 3,000-acre Kratzert Conservation Tract and spacious Mariners Cove Park, both on the river, and started the county on its path to a 50-mile recreational trail from Enterprise to Titusville.

At public meetings, Chris Elmer says, "Valerie was fearless when it came to standing up to the developers and their lawyers. She was completely dedicated; she attended and spoke at every meeting that I can remember." As Carol Aymar puts it, "Valerie was our 'clean-up batter' in front of city and county councils. She would quietly stroll up to the podium and sum up all the issues, logically and thoroughly, in such a convincing manner that only the most developer-friendly official could scoff at our arguments."

Valerie insists that credit be shared, citing Janet McFarlane, Pat Beeker, her Braddock Road neighbors, the Volusia-Flagler Environmental Council, and "so many people and organizations that were there for us." The Children's Home provided meeting space. "It was always about *us*," she stresses. Valerie was one of the first to challenge Deltona Mayor John Masiarczyk's fast-growth agenda. She soon found out that Enterprise and its residents were, as Chris Elmer puts it, "just an obstacle to his ambitions" for Deltona.

There were crushing defeats. In 1987, Valerie organized a boat protest in DeBary Bayou, gaining TV and newspaper coverage of attempts to demonstrate the permanent damage that would be caused by a plan to build boat docks on the shallow bayou. Ultimately, that project was pushed through.

Another was the shopping center plopped onto 12 wet, wooded acres at Doyle Road and Providence Boulevard.

Their successes, nonetheless, were sweet. "It never ceases to amaze me each time I visit to see the changes and a dream take shape," she declares. Her can-do spirit is still at work, as she writes grants to provide affordable housing for the elderly on behalf of a Tennessee college.

Even though she was a formidable opponent, "Power was not what I was looking for," Valerie says now, looking back all those years ago. "My reward is seeing everything that I worked for come into being. It was always about community, a sense of place, and a healthy, sustainable environment."

We in Enterprise might not be as skilled as we should be at connecting our nearly-unspoiled surroundings to the fact that those areas are there because of other peoples' difficult work. Had it not been for a group of citizens, including early members of the West Volusia Conservancy and the founders of the Enterprise Preservation Society, our green parks and quiet trails might now be cul-de-sacs and Taco Bells. This book is a tribute to their legacy. They truly "unpaved the way" for us, giving us the foundation for saving Enterprise, and Thornby as well.

The Times They Are A-Changin'

After Deltona changed residential land at Doyle and Providence to commercial, what was left of the wet, thickly wooded property hunkered next to a high concrete wall behind a supermarket, liquor store, video store, etc. The re-zoning that made it possible festered like an abscess under the skin of close-by residents of Deltona and Enterprise. In early 2000, after council's initial approval of the land use change for apartments on Thornby, they felt helpless, invisible and ignored by elected officials who seemed to hold all the power. Enterprise residents felt betrayed when county officials blessed a density increase on Thornby, sending it up the ladder to the state.

Making matters worse, as reported in at least seven *Orlando Sentinel* articles in early 2000, were the contentious relations between Enterprise and its neighbor Deltona over development. One such article drew a sharp retort from Deltona's mayor, who challenged the paper's statement that the city had no regard for Enterprise history. To prove otherwise, he pointed out that Deltona had donated more than $6,000 to the Deltona Arts and Historical Center, which displayed memorabilia from the city's earliest days.

As bad as things were, worse was coming. The vision of door-to-door apartments on Thornby — chain-link-fences surrounding sterile retention ponds, asphalt parking lots baking in the sun, and green-painted dumpsters supplanting 40 acres of trees and 80 years of history — was the catalyst for

Enterprise's drive for self-preservation. "I just couldn't sit back and let it happen," says Carol Aymar.

One month after the Volusia County Council approved a land use change on Thornby, a revival-like gathering to explore possible ways to save Enterprise took place at Enterprise's old First Baptist Church. More than a hundred people attended. Grace Stamile remembers, "All the old-timers from Enterprise were there."

There was no clear consensus on what path the community should take. "Enterprise likely will be best served by annexing into DeBary," said Bob Bernosky, whose wife's family members were early settlers in the area. Mark Matzinger, on the other hand, favored the incorporation avenue that would bring autonomy to Enterprise. After all, he reasoned, "If Enterprise annexed into DeBary, then it wouldn't be Enterprise anymore." The *Sentinel* reported, "Residents are a long way from agreeing on how to save the community from being swallowed bit by bit, but they have… agreed that all of their options need to be examined."

Carol Aymar, a founder and director of the Enterprise Preservation Society (EPS) vividly remembers that evening:

> In March 2000, we had only lived in Enterprise for about a year when my husband and I found ourselves among a large group of concerned Enterprise residents gathered at the old Baptist church to hear a plea for the western part of Enterprise to be annexed into DeBary. Three or four speakers made a compelling case about how our little community would soon be gobbled up by Deltona, and we could "save" the more historic part with their proposal. Suddenly, a woman sitting quietly in the back spoke up, as though she could no longer contain herself. She told us that the very first, most urgent issue was not the DeBary annexation. It was the county's approval of townhouses on the Thornby property. She spoke with such authority and conviction that I remember thinking how ignorant I was of what was really going on, and how I could learn volumes from her.

After that, Aymar disseminated a "Resource list for Thornby and other issues impacting Enterprise" to give residents contact information for county and state officials. She and Valerie get the credit for igniting the "save Thornby" fire in Enterprise by showing residents what could be lost

The Enterprise Preservation Society

After the county council made a U-turn at the second hearing and denied the Thornby land use change, residents held a town meeting in August to explore available options to preserve their community. Ultimately, neither annexation nor incorporation would be the answer to Enterprise's problems. The DeBary annexation option eventually died for lack of community support, and the incorporation process was too complex and uncertain. The most direct way to protect the environment and the way of life that Enterprise residents valued was to organize a Florida non-profit corporation. Such a group could speak with one voice for Enterprise residents.

In late 2000, the Enterprise Preservation Society was officially chartered, with Mark Matzinger, Wise Hardin and Valerie Grill among its initial directors. Its mission was to preserve the identity, history, and rural character of the community of Enterprise, Florida, founded in 1841. Key concerns:

- Lack of representation with local governments
- Runaway development, annexations and rezoning
- Continuing loss of identity as a community
- Preservation of the history, environment and culture that makes Enterprise unique

On behalf of the newly formed EPS, Carol Aymar, Chris Elmer and Valerie Grill formulated "Speak Out on Enterprise," a survey the organization mailed to residents of Enterprise and surrounding areas. "It gives us the information we need to speak for the community as a whole," said Valerie Grill. The one-page survey gave about 1,000 folks a chance to weigh in on topics such as historic buildings, commercial development and tree protection. Ninety-two percent of those responding said the Enterprise Preservation Society should represent Enterprise before local governments. Many offered comments such as, "We need to save the town of Enterprise" and "Deltona should not be allowed to re-zone wherever it pleases."

Can't We All Just get Along?

Chris Elmer and Valerie Grill sat down with Deltona City Manager Fritz Behring and Development Services Director Bob Nix to discuss their worries about inappropriate development encroaching into Enterprise. Behring admitted, "EPS' concerns would fall on deaf ears" at City Hall. As for Nix, "He seemed set in his thoughts," recalls Chris. "Though he listened, he was not open to our position."

"Deltona's reputation has been taking some hits lately," opined the *Sentinel*. Mayor John Masiarczyk said he "would like to put the rumors to rest" that Deltona would "disrupt their [Enterprise] community." The paper praised his plan to attend the August Enterprise community meeting, but Masiarczyk didn't show. Perhaps he was preoccupied with another Enterprise-area cataclysm.

On August 7, 2000, the city commission voted to re-zone eight acres on Thornby's north border (across from the new Publix at the Doyle and Providence intersection) in order to plop an all-night convenience store with 12 gas pumps half a block from Lakeshore Drive and Lake Monroe.

The property owner's lawyer boasted it would be "a very unusual convenience store." If by that he meant that the property was unusually beautiful, wet, and tree-covered before it was blanketed with asphalt and gas pumps, he was right. With Lawyer Allen Watts representing the developer, concerns for the nearby eagle nest and onsite wetlands were dismissed, despite the fact that Watts stated that the "dam from the [old] railroad bed keeps the property wet." Commissioner Doug Horn offered, "With proper management, the property could be made into something better than it is," and said he had walked the property looking for wildlife [but] the only thing he noticed were lots and lots of spiders. Enterprise and Deltona residents again adamantly protested any more drastic upheaval on the "border," to no avail. "Your decision tonight will affect Enterprise far more than it will affect your own city," Mark Matzinger told Deltona officials. That statement came true in a way he couldn't have expected. Healthy wetlands adjacent to Thornby were soon smothered under pea-green, stagnant water and construction debris. After residents complained to the St. Johns River Water Management District, the property was posted:

Posted wetlands next to "7-Eleven in a hole"

In the future, the sign would be a potent rebuttal to the city's unceasing claims that Thornby was "surrounded by urban."

A few weeks after approving the "7-Eleven-In-A-Hole" (a nickname coined by Carol Aymar because of its sinkhole-like site), Deltona officials boarded a bus for a road trip to "locations within the city of Deltona." The minutes relate that:

> While traveling through the Enterprise area, Mayor Masiarczyk stated the city commission needed to talk about what it wants to see in the areas bordering Enterprise... Mayor Masiarczyk stated the commission needs to ... direct staff on how to proceed in this area.... [The city manager] expressed concern that if the city set up a development board it might appear as a takeover method and the city at this time did not have anyone in Enterprise to negotiate with... Commissioner Ken Runge stated that the commission needed to discuss such issues as a group. Discussion continued regarding the Enterprise situation and the areas bordering Deltona's boundaries.

Dr. Gisela Oeffen, a Deltona resident with a background in business planning, was the first from her city to speak out in print against officials' overreaching land use policies she termed "megalomania." "Residents in Enterprise and surrounding small communities are not paranoid," she said. "Development is put on the fast track. Reason has fallen by the wayside. The threat is real and relief is not in sight."

By now, Deltona didn't need Thornby for a city hall. It needed Thornby for taxes generated by the stores and offices to be built there. Why? In the three years from 1999 to 2001, the city pipelined eight separate annexations of mostly residential land. The city was on what Deltonan Jack Hoyt called an "annexation binge," ingesting more land to be used for more houses for more people who had few places in the city to work or shop.

Bo Poertner, in a 2000 *Sentinel* story about Central Florida ghost towns, wondered if in the next 100 years Enterprise would fall by the wayside, just another "used to be" place. That was because, like many vulnerable communities, Enterprise faced uncaring annexations and "just because we can" re-zonings that altered the quality of life its residents treasured. Lake Helen Mayor Mark Shuttleworth, in the midst of his own city's battles with Deltona over encroaching roads, advised EPS to "work around Deltona and get to the owners who are annexing" — an approach that proved unfruitful. When EPS directors approached Volusia County about legal protection, they learned the facts of life: available remedies were depressingly limited. Lawful annexations usually can't be stopped, and re-zonings are difficult to oppose. County officials agreed to explore other possibilities, such as creating a historic district that might guarantee Enterprise a more protected future.

Performance stage at the first EPS Festival

First Old Florida Festival

Not since the years of Doris Faber and her Fourth of July parties had Enterprise seen an outpouring of community spirit like the one under a blessedly mild, cloudless sky on November 4, 2000. It all sprang from Chris Elmer's enthusiasm. Months earlier, he spearheaded a community meeting at the Enterprise firehouse where he and 30 others — from Enterprise old-timers to brand-new Stone Island residents — brainstormed ideas for the first Enterprise Old Florida Festival. The results were nothing short of euphoric.

"We are celebrating the community of Enterprise, old and new," said Chris, the festival chair, to an overflowing crowd. More than 100 volunteers helped stage an unforgettable, all-day bash at Lakeshore Drive's Mariners Cove Park, funded by community donations and loans from EPS members. Five or six hundred people were hopefully expected. By the end of the festivities, 1,200 folks — about as many as live in Enterprise — had munched, relaxed and socialized their way through more than 900 meals. They stayed all day for the lively bluegrass music, kettle corn, hot dogs, square dancing, apple bobbing and all things Old Florida. Ricky Godwin's fresh-caught, fried catfish was hugely popular, as was the Enterprise history exhibit — tall, flat, heavy boards loaded with Enterprise memorabilia, a moving museum of old photos, letters, steamship timetables, and antique maps. On loan from the West Volusia Historical Society was the Brock House's hunting logbook, which so impressed the organizers of the Deltona Spring Festival that they asked to display it at their own event. Over 250 "Speak Out on Enterprise" surveys were completed and turned in.

Carol Aymar co-chaired the entertainment committee. "We wanted the community to be in awe of Enterprise and what a treasure they had," she relates. She credits Chris with much of that day's stunning success. He was "fired up and very dynamic." By any measure, the first-class event was a remarkable achievement. At festival's end, the overjoyed organizers had taken in enough money to repay their backers, with some left over to fund EPS operating expenses for a while. "I remember practically 'floating' around the park that day," Carol says, of her elation that they'd pulled it off. She adds, "I saw John Masiarczyk and a couple of Deltona commissioners standing in front of the stage during a performance and looking — I can only say — impressed." Most meaningful was the resurgence of small town atmosphere, and the feeling of "we're all in this together" that the day reawakened. "A lot of people who came had not seen old friends and neighbors in years," said Chris. That night, the tired and happy organizers celebrated at his home, already planning next year's festival.

The Enterprise Preservation Society has hosted its Old Florida Festival every year since 2000. Events, size, and locations have changed and changed again. New folks have come on board and others have moved away. Vendors, food and ideas have expanded as the festival grows and flourishes, still a winner every year. But, as with love, the first time is memorable and very special, just because of its newness.

Speak Out on Enterprise

With results from more than 350 EPS surveys in hand, on January 18, 2001 Carol Aymar, Chris Elmer, Valerie Grill, Dale Hansen, Wise Hardin and Mark Matzinger represented Enterprise in front of the Volusia County Council. Mark explained that residents "want to save Enterprise from annexation and development." Chris thanked them for their pro-Thornby vote the year before and got down to business. Our community and our lifestyle are threatened by development, annexations and re-zonings, he told them. The "Speak Out on Enterprise" responses leave no doubt that residents overwhelmingly support preservation of the environment, quality of life and history. We want Lakeshore Drive, home of Thornby, to remain a tree-lined, scenic drive, he told them. He asked that the county develop a growth management plan for Enterprise, and said Enterprise would work with Deltona "after the plan is in place." Valerie echoed the plea for a growth plan for Enterprise. Lakeshore Drive residents Patrick Stamile, Dan Trimmer and Philip Reilly spoke in support of EPS.

Although their words were well received, no specific results were achieved. Council member Pat Northey expressed support for EPS, but said Deltona should be involved in any management plan for Enterprise. Council member Jim Ward commented, "There are so few pristine areas like Enterprise" but made no commitment. "We weren't expecting them to roll out the red carpet for us" was Elmer's after-the-fact assessment. The *Sentinel* put it plainly: "The Enterprise Preservation Society has passion and a mission. What it doesn't have is power." If EPS members had hoped that the council would definitively address development in Enterprise, they were disappointed. Others, though, were more than willing to jump into the gap. "Someday we'll need to address how Enterprise is to develop," said the mayor of Deltona.

On February 1, 2001, having resigned his seat on the EPS Board, Enterprise stalwart Chris Elmer took another one. This seat was on the Volusia Growth Management Commission — the agency with final say on plan amendments like Thornby.

EPS Attempts to Buy Thornby

To forestall high-density development on Thornby, EPS needed to buy it. Ron Paradise told Valerie Grill that such a purchase was "very doable," but finding the money while Thornby was still under county jurisdiction was key. If annexed into Deltona, the property's value would skyrocket from the expected building density increase, putting it off limits to anyone but a flush developer. Grill connected with the Florida Trust for Public Land (TPL), an arm of a nationwide organization that helps structure land transactions to create protected rural areas. After researching the property, TPL considered Thornby an ideal match with its conservation mission. But government doesn't turn on a dime, and grants don't fall like cash from an ATM. Putting a deal together would take time.

Annexation

The long-dreaded event finally arrived: the "A" word was now front and center. Because Volusia County refused to allow a change to higher-density housing on Thornby, the owners decided to find a government that would. On January 30, 2001, they applied to the city of Deltona to annex the property.

Four days later, the mayor of Deltona, at his instigation, met with EPS board members Carol Aymar, Dale Hansen and Mark Matzinger. The mayor was "cordial and friendly" during the four-hour meeting in which the board asked him for a one-year hold on city annexations in Enterprise. A year would buy enough time to design a community plan for Enterprise and maybe work out a way to buy Thornby, they explained. Masiarczyk told them he "strongly agreed" with protecting Lakeshore Drive from commercialization. "We sat at a table with a map," recalls Aymar, while the mayor talked of the city's population swelling to 150,000 or even 200,000. "Our residents want access to Lake Monroe," he said, while at the same time, says Aymar, "he told us there was currently no activity regarding the Thornby property." In fact, they had no way of knowing that the city's annexation process had already started.

At the meeting, the mayor said he wanted to build a bridge between Deltona and Enterprise, and promised to notify the society if a Thornby annexation application came in. He stressed, "The enemy is not Deltona. Nothing will stop landowners from annexing when money is the motivator."

> **Activist Lesson:** It's true that virtually every annexation is motivated by money — money that flows to the landowner from land use changes and rezoning after the annexation. Money would cease to be a motivator if officials weren't so eager to award land use changes and rezoning.

He said he would agree to suspend Enterprise annexations, but couldn't speak for the rest of the commission; he suggested they bring their request to the city commission on March 5.

On February 14, Matzinger received that promised call from the mayor, who told him he just heard that the Thornby owners had applied for annexation. The vote will be on March 5, said the mayor.

Longtime Thornby connection Frank Knight lived in a comfortable brick home on tree-lined Lakeshore Drive, with very few neighbors and a quiet view of Lake Monroe. Next to him was the one-lane road whimsically named Broadway Avenue. On the other side of the crumbling road was Old Florida at its best: Thornby. Surely, Frank wouldn't want multi-family housing next door. Surely, as a long-time resident, *he* would want EPS to buy Thornby — not see Enterprise split like a log, erasing a big part of its history, its roots lost to indifference and greed. After all, Frank and his boyhood chum John Clapp were once practically at home on Thornby. If anyone knew the property from end to end, savoring its beauty and uniqueness from childhood, it was Frank. EPS directors Carol Aymar, Chris Elmer, Valerie Grill, Dale Hansen, Mark Matzinger and Wise Hardin met with Knight at the Enterprise firehouse on February 21. He was cool to their request that the owners withdraw or delay their application, but said he'd consider it if EPS submitted a letter outlining purchase price, sales terms, and plans for the property before the March 5 hearing. As they started a mad dash to try to comply with Knight's request within the two-week window, a letter from Thornby attorney Mark Watts quashed any remaining hopes. The hearing will not be postponed, it said.

On March 1, Mayor Masiarczyk told the *Daytona Beach News-Journal* that he had not learned of the Thornby annexation application until after he met with the Enterprise Preservation Society. He also said, "I think we can do a better job of protecting the [Thornby] property than the county" and that he did not support a suspension of Enterprise annexations. "I'm all for protecting and preserving Enterprise and the [Thornby] annexation is in the best interests of Deltona," he said.

> **Activist Lesson:** Unsupported opinions are too often presented as fact. Hold them accountable for their words. The press rarely does.

"Looking back on this period of high anxiety and emotion, I remember feeling that our board was manipulated, skillfully, by John Masiarczyk. When he expressed a desire to meet with us to 'build a bridge,' I think he was really trying to slide this annexation through with the least political fallout for him," says Carol Aymar today.

By law, annexations require two separate commission "readings," or hearings. Although Deltona has a planning and zoning board (P&Z), the Thornby annexation application did not go before that board, but directly to the city commission, over protest by P&Z member Jack Hoyt, who says: "It was done purposely to keep the public from knowing about the annexation." Mark Matzinger says that the mayor told him that there would be no planning board meeting "because this is a straight annexation without zoning changes."

> **Activist Lesson:** When a question arises about whether required government procedures are being followed, with time of the essence, Attorney Tanner Andrews says, "It is probably best to talk to an attorney." He notes that, "You may need to recruit someone who is directly injured." In the example above, that could be a by-passed planning board member.

On March 5, the first item of business before the Deltona City Commission was a presentation by the Enterprise Preservation Society. Chris Elmer took the floor and asked that the city simply acknowledge that EPS represented the residents of Enterprise. Appealing to Deltona's sense of community as neighbors, he made a formal request for a one-year pause in city annexations. Referring to the "Speak Out on Enterprise" survey results, Elmer appealed for Deltona's help in preserving Enterprise's identity. "Mayor Masiarczyk thanked Mr. Elmer for his presentation," the minutes show, and then moved on to the next item:

> **"Ordinance No. 04-2001, Providing for the voluntary annexation into the City Limits of 39.44 acres of property located at the northwest corner of Providence Blvd. and Lakeshore Drive, for first reading; Applicant — Frank Knight."**

The public hearing was open.

Chris Elmer asked whether the EPS presentation would be discussed. The mayor cut him off with orders: "only speak regarding the proposed annexation."

The word on Thornby had trickled out to Deltona residents like Carole Archambeault and Gisela Oeffen, who spoke against the annexation. Grace Stamile, Patrick Stamile, Dan Trimmer, Kevin Carney, Dale Hansen, Carol Aymar, Dave Aymar, Robert Pacetelli, and Wise Hardin also spoke, but their words were not included in the meeting's typed minutes.

Lawyer Watts' words *were* recorded, however. He called EPS' request for a moratorium "meaningless," and helpfully added that he "has spoken with Enterprise residents about joining with Deltona or DeBary because Enterprise is too small." C. Allen Watts was a major player in the Volusia County land use game. He had a penchant for invoking the U.S. Constitution during trials, as well as quoting poetry, particularly by Robert Frost. His 30-year resume was packed with clients like the Volusia Home Builders Association, and he'd been attorney for four different Volusia cities. No one doubted his message that hooking up with Deltona was "in the best interests of the property owner."

As to the mayor's desired "lines of communication?" As Dr. Oeffen saw it, "... city commissioners have developed a direct line-auditory connection from one ear to the other — sound enters one ear and bypasses the brain."

It was time for the commissioners to speak. Commissioner Ken Runge set the tone: "Enterprise has been around for approximately 160 years and has had plenty of time to plan regarding the subject property... no one is being 'steamrolled'. .. [unnamed Deltona] residents... have requested more commercialization to help the tax base... it behooves Deltona to move ahead." (Runge's comments were the first public hint of a marriage between "commercial" and "Thornby".)

Commissioner Carl Carey waxed plaintive: "... Deltona is asking for trust from Enterprise. Deltona has development regulations that are more stringent than the county."

> **Activist Lesson:** A statement like this made at a public hearing by an elected official calls for a written follow-up. Ask the official for a list of the regulations he referred to.

No one has stated the property would be zoned commercial," he said. True enough — no one *had* said it. However, his words might have been more convincing had not Commissioner Bill Harvey missed the hint, offering that the commission would still have to approve commercial, anyway.

> **Activist Lesson:** This is a variation on "This is just the first step," a ploy used routinely to deflect attention from the fact that the first step is, in fact, the most critical. Like falling dominoes, each approval along the way makes the next one likelier — a fact that bears repeating long and loud.

Commissioner Doug Horn sounded mechanical. "Deltona can help to preserve land by having it under the city's jurisdiction. Deltona needs to develop lake view property." Harvey chimed in: "it would be better if Deltona has some control over the property."

The lawyer said wistfully that Frank Knight "wishes to become a part of Deltona," and Harvey echoed his sentiments. Horn asked what could be built on the property with its current county zoning (he meant land use).

Watts stated one unit per acre — a fact that would prove very inconvenient in the future, when the city repeatedly stood on its bureaucratic head to contend otherwise.

Commissioner Harvey reminded the room that "on several occasions" he had expressed empathy for the Enterprise residents, and, after all, "this is only an annexation and not a rezoning."

> **Activist Lesson:** The words are offered to deflect attention from the rezoning that everyone knows is coming, whether it happens at the same hearing or at a later date.

Then Watts made everyone feel better by admonishing that the whole thing "would take months to accomplish."

> **Activist Lesson:** Officials hate to be accused of rushing into things, probably because they often do. Point out that they can't absolve themselves of responsibility for starting the process, no matter how long it takes to finish.

In the pre-orchestrated circus, one voice of reason rose above the din. Commissioner Joe Perez stated that Deltona needs to stop looking at Enterprise as an "all you can eat buffet." He said the Enterprise Preservation Society is trying to preserve their homes, and that Deltona should "look within its own borders instead of devouring somebody else's." He said Enterprise needed to be protected. At this, Harvey accused Perez of "grandstanding."

Near the end, someone had the guts to say it: *To put commercial development on Thornby is the only reason for this annexation.* That person was Joe Perez. Today, his take is just as fearless: "I didn't see any signs that the commission was well-intentioned. It was a developer-driven interest. I suspect that developers were lobbying certain members of the commission to gain their support."

Motion of the City of Deltona to annex the Thornby property passed, 6-1, on first reading

Before that night, EPS had hoped mightily to "bypass" the mayor's pro-annexation views and appeal to the city commission; however, it became obvious that a majority of the commission was in lockstep with the mayor. A speeding train was barreling from Deltona, with Thornby tied to the tracks.

Still, was the notion of an Enterprise-hungry Deltona realistic, or was it paranoia? Not everyone was convinced that annexation would ruin Thornby. "Becoming part of Deltona doesn't necessarily spell doom for the Thornby Estate," chided the *News-Journal*. In the same paper, lawyer Mark Watts predicted coldly: "We see that Enterprise is surrounded and will someday be slowly absorbed into DeBary or Deltona." His words appeared in an article titled "Enterprise Moves a Step Closer to Annihilation."

Between the two hearings, Kevin Mooney of The Trust for Public Land wrote to John Clapp: "We would be most interested in discussing with you your family's willingness to sell..." Later, Mooney said that Clapp "was pleasant and suggested I stay in touch." Carol Aymar phoned John Clapp, who "seemed annoyed," to hear from her she says, and informed her there would be no delays. "I've been trying to sell it to the county since 1986," she says he said. "I'm not going to delay 16 people." [Thornby heirs]

Fourth Thornby Hearing: Deltona City Commission

The second annexation hearing was March 19, 2001. Before things got started, the commission took time to chastise members of the public about the "degrading and distracting" audience behavior at the first hearing, although Grace Stamile, a veteran of every Thornby hearing, says she doesn't recall disruptive behavior at either one. Nevertheless, at least one brash remark prompted Commissioner Lucille Wheatley to announce that she was "offended by the Enterprise people." Stamile says, "If the audience did anything, it might have been laughter or a groan at some absurd thing [the city or Allen] Watts said."

Public meetings must be controlled and orderly, but where is the line between rude behavior and honest emotion? Stuck in a hard seat for hours, you have to swallow self-serving fiction served up as fact without refuting a word — your three minutes was used up hours ago. There's no way to halt the runaway train. Frustration leads to anger, and unchecked words spur "out of order" gavels. You can do nothing but sit in the audience and listen, while up front your world spins out of focus. Far too often, this is the pattern at public hearings. Deltona hearings were no exception.

At the second annexation hearing, several speakers brought up a possible acquisition of Thornby through the Trust for Public Land. Valerie Grill, Suzanne Steiner and Grace Stamile again asked the city to put a hold on the Thornby annexation. Valerie presented a letter of support for EPS from Volusia County. But public purchase was out of the question, city officials said, unless Deltona controlled Thornby's fate.

Volusia County did not offer any money, Commissioner Runge was quick to point out. No one has offered to buy it, Watts said. (It is unknown if he knew that John Clapp had just declined a purchase overture from the Trust for Public Land.)

Dale Hansen, Chris Elmer, and Patrick Stamile asked to work with Deltona, explaining that Enterprise was trying to save itself. Thornby is a valuable resource, Patrick reminded them. Its value is measured not in dollars, but in the region's, even the state's, future.

Jack Hoyt lived in Deltona. He was a former member of Deltona's planning and zoning board, and he knew city codes. Directly, he informed his city commission that the Thornby annexation did not follow city law, which requires planning board review of all land use changes. The petition for Thornby annexation had wrongly gone straight to the city commission, Jack said. The mayor argued with him. Janet Deyette was a planning board member when the Thornby owners applied for annexation. "All of us on P&Z were upset that the annexation didn't come through the P&Z Board," she says.

"No one on the commission is thinking about more taxes for the city," said Commissioner Carl Carey. "Regardless of the vote," he said, "the commission is sensitive to the residents of Enterprise." (Any audience laughter at this remark was not recorded in the minutes)

On the other hand, Commissioner Harvey, who usually focused on finances, fussed that "the [county's] support is not monetary." The "highest and best use" for Thornby is what he was after. (Translation: Thornby + Deltona = commercial development = tax dollars)

Then it was the mayor's turn. He was on cruise control, heading straight for Annexationville. He informed everyone that he'd spoken about Thornby with (unnamed) members of the county council. Kevin Finn well remembers Masiarczyk's leading question: "What makes you think we can't protect Thornby better than the county?"

The mayor griped that Thornby's fate "is only an issue because the annexation involves Deltona." In a final shot, he claimed to have received calls from (unidentified) people who just happened to want to annex into Deltona, "but are concerned with backlash from the society [EPS]." He did not speculate on what kind of "backlash" might come from a handful of small-town, middle-aged, working people with families.

"The property is valuable," Masiarczyk intoned, like a father concerned for his daughter's virtue, "and one day someone is going to want to develop it and it is better to have the development controlled by Deltona."

Motion of the City of Deltona to annex the Thornby property passed, 6-1, on second reading, March 19, 2001.

"It's a shame," sighed the *News-Journal*, "but ... there's probably little that Enterprise residents can do about it."

> *Never doubt that a small group of thoughtful people can change the world. Indeed, it's the only thing that ever has.*
>
> **Margaret Mead**

CHAPTER EIGHT

Around the Kitchen Table: Friends of Thornby

Thornby was now in Deltona, and John Clapp told the Trust for Public Land that he "wasn't ready" to sell.

Valerie Grill didn't accept losing Thornby to Deltona easily. After the annexation slid through the city apparatus like a gator slipping into Lake Monroe, she sought legal help, hoping to find a way to undo it. Local land use attorney Dennis Bayer, who would reappear in the Thornby saga years later, says that his research didn't discover any grounds for reversing the annexation. "Annexation is governed by state law, and it's pretty much cut and dried," he explains. The bottom line is that, generally, anyone in Florida whose property adjoins a city can ask to annex into it, whatever their reason. And with the siren song of pumped-up tax revenues echoing in their ears, cities seldom, if ever, say "no."

Making its Mark

In the summer and fall of 2001, the Enterprise Preservation Society was working to get off the ground, convince people that it was worth their support, and eventually obtain IRS non-profit status. At an EPS-hosted community meeting in May 2001, organizers asked for support for two "resolutions." One requested that the county form the Enterprise Municipal Services District (the same organizational structure used in Deltona before incorporation). The other resolution asked Deltona to forego "zoning changes along the southern city limits" that would affect Enterprise. The resolutions garnered 19 pages of signatures.

EPS was building a sound, respected organization and earning recognition from Volusia County; after reversing its position on the Thornby land use change, the county had become an important ally. At the instigation of council member Ann McFall, who represented Enterprise, Deltona and DeBary, a town meeting was called on September 19, 2001 to determine whether Enterprise should pursue becoming a municipal services district (MSD).

Impressively, five of seven county council members attended the spirited forum, as did the county's growth and resources management director. The 200+ residents in attendance were in accord. "We don't want any new services," one attendee emphasized. "We just want to be left alone and to keep Deltona from annexing individual properties and re-zoning them for commercial."

> **Activist Lesson:** See Chapter 7 and comments about annexation. There is little that citizens can do to stop legal annexations. The key is for elected officials not to "reward" annexations with land use changes and upzonings.

That evening, however, marked the death of any notion that forming an Enterprise MSD would resolve the biggest problems: annexation and inappropriate development. An MSD isn't the answer to property owners (like Thornby's) who want to annex into Deltona, and it won't stop unwanted commercialization of Enterprise either, county bigwigs stressed. Okay, the crowd responded, what will? The best scenario, they were told, would be a "joint planning agreement" between Deltona and the county, acting on behalf of Enterprise. Another idea: form an Enterprise Historic District with development codes to protect the District's character. Yet another option was to establish scenic corridor standards for Lakeshore Drive. "There are a lot of things that we could have done years ago and we're hearing now that should be done," said a county planner. Enterprise is not the only place in Volusia County trying to protect itself, she noted. The *Daytona Beach News-Journal* reported that a "female voice" in the crowd called out, "We want it to happen and we want it now!" to rowdy applause. Although she wasn't credited, the voice belonged to spunky Stone Island resident Suzanne Adair. At last,

THE STORY OF THORNBY • CHAPTER EIGHT   131

residents' pleas were echoing in the right places. That night, those in charge at the county delivered a firm commitment to begin crafting an Enterprise Local Plan. "We hear them, and I will bring the issues up at the council meeting," promised McFall.

In a letter to the editor a few days later, EPS chairman Mark Matzinger lauded the September 19 forum as "effective, responsive government" and predicted "future generations will be assured that areas such as Enterprise will not perish." Besides, he added, "We just celebrated our 160th birthday, and we want to be around to celebrate 160 more."

Says Ron Paradise about that night: "It was a big meeting. And Thornby was what served as the impetus or sparkplug for the county's efforts to save Enterprise."

ENTERPRISE:

DON'T LET THE COUNTY

OR <u>OTHER</u> CITIES

DECIDE OUR DESTINY !!

<u>SHOW UP OR SIT BACK</u> . .
<u>YOUR DECISION.</u>

Hosted by Ann McFall, our County Council District 5 Rep.
Wed. Sept. 19th at 7:00 p.m.
Methodist Children's Home Gym

Message by the Enterprise Preservation Society, Inc.

Flyer for town meeting

The County Keeps its Promise

The first step on the road to protection was to measure residents' commitment to preserving Enterprise's rural and historic character. With EPS input, county planners Tom Brooks, Ron Paradise and Iris Schiff developed a 35-question survey that was sent to more than 800 property owners in Enterprise and on the borders of Deltona, DeBary and Osteen. Brooks had a Master's Degree in Public Administration and extensive experience in preparing and analyzing surveys and statistics. Expanding on the earlier EPS questionnaire, the county's survey covered everything from trees to apartments, and from green space to roadways in the community.

Brooks, who interpreted the returned surveys, called the 42 percent response rate "phenomenal." The results confirmed what Enterprise residents had been saying: We want a sense of community, history, trees and green space. We don't want large-scale commercial development or annexations. Eighty-five percent of those responding thought Deltona was putting too much pressure on Enterprise to develop. As to the proposed Thornby project, the answer was loud and clear: apartments and townhouses, especially in a high-density development, do not fit the character of our community. In summary, county staff said, "The residents who responded to the survey want an old rural Florida lifestyle, which they appear to have found by moving to Enterprise."

Building on the survey results, county staff, under the direction of Director of Planning and Development Services Montye Beamer, worked up a five-point planning initiative for Enterprise that included the options outlined at the September 19 meeting. As part of their research, staffers prepared an inventory of land uses, soils, zoning and resources for a 7,000-acre Enterprise study area extending from Maple Avenue on the west to Courtland Boulevard and Lake Bethel on the east. The Enterprise Plan would be the most encompassing of several such plans in Volusia County.

To allow time to complete the ambitious Enterprise preservation plan, Volusia County aimed to accomplish what the Enterprise Preservation Society had been unable to do: get Deltona to agree to a one-year hold on annexations in the Enterprise area. Enterprise's other neighbor, the City of DeBary, was asked to join in. When push came to shove, Beamer says, Deltona's mayor refused to bring the proposed agreement up for a city vote unless the Enterprise Plan area was reduced.

In January 2002, county council member Ann McFall, accompanied by EPS Chairman Mark Matzinger, asked the Deltona City Commission to agree to an interim joint planning agreement and a one-year moratorium on annexations. She was rebuffed by a vote of 4-3. Later, on the advice of its attorney, Deltona agreed only that it would not *actively seek* annexations for a year.

DeBary followed Deltona's lead, although it was unclear how relevant the agreement was to that city, since it had not aggressively pursued Enterprise annexations, anyway. DeBary mayor Carmen Rosamonda affirmed his city's support for Enterprise in a letter to EPS. As for Deltona, Thornby seemed to be the only Enterprise property that Mayor Masiarczyk was interested in. And it was already Deltona's.

With a temporary moratorium on annexations in place, "that year gave us the chance to get a plan for Enterprise into the county's comprehensive plan," Beamer says. On June 11, 2002, County Planning Manager Ben Dyer presented a draft of the Enterprise Local Plan for Enterprise, Deltona and DeBary's review. These words seemed to adumbrate Thornby troubles that lay ahead:

> The proposed multi-family and commercial use of the property has the potential to conflict with the goals of the Enterprise management plan.

Activists Are Made, Not Born

In Deltona: Seven people elected to public office. Seven people sit on a dais. Seven agendas.

In Enterprise: Thirteen people around a table. Thirteen backgrounds. One agenda.

In Limbo: Historic Thornby ripped from the fabric of Enterprise and pasted on Deltona's sleeve. Forty acres of riverfront majesty and an 80-year old historic home poised for sacrifice as one more "Plywood in the Pines" development

Thus, Friends of Thornby was born. Who were they?

- **Carol Aymar**, a founder of the Enterprise Preservation Society, who opened her home to Friends of Thornby;
- **Kevin Finn**, a Deltona resident and serious history buff;
- **Lani Friend**, a local historian, one of "Miss Doris' kids" who almost grew up on the property, moved away, and returned years later to stave off dangerous development that threatened Enterprise's Green Spring;
- **Sandy Lou Gallagher**, a self-taught eagle expert. She started out unwilling to speak in public, and ended up running for public office.
- **Jack Hoyt**, a never-say-die senior citizen who delighted in prodding Deltona's power structure;
- **Mark Matzinger**, a burly, redheaded volunteer fireman and "Old Enterprise" resident;
- **Dr. Gisela Oeffen**, a retired executive from Germany by way of Los Angeles, with built-in savvy and loads of business smarts;

- **Debra Richardson**, a stay-at-home mom, new to the area; she took on the issue of overcrowded schools like Mama Grizzly protecting her young;
- **Bob Sayre**, a/k/a "Whiskey Bob" (named for his job, not his habits), a laid-back sales rep who made sense of often- incomprehensible traffic jargon and numbers;
- **Grace and Patrick Stamile**, a couple willing to tap their life savings if it meant preserving Thornby;
- **Rich Vail**, a developer with a conscience — and friend of the planner who worked for the Thornby owners;
- Me — **Sandy Walters**, a born-again activist, originally from Pittsburgh, a 30-year Florida resident who came to Enterprise by way of Pensacola, Miami, St. Petersburg and Orlando.

Most were from Enterprise, some were Deltonans. All refused to stand by passively while Thornby's legally allowed land use was sacrificed on the altar of "the public be damned." Some were part of the group from day one, some joined along the way, but all were dedicated and determined.

Of course, the Enterprise Preservation Society would have been the first responder to the Thornby emergency. The Society was steadily gaining respect and influence in the community and with county officials; however, EPS had applied for non-profit status with the IRS. With its activities restricted by IRS rules, its directors were uncomfortable tackling political activity or lobbying. So, the Aymars' kitchen table became ground zero for a fresh mix of EPS members and new faces, united behind one cause: "Save Thornby."

The preliminary item of business was, of course, a name. At the time, a grassroots group calling itself "Friends of the Loop" was making news for its efforts to save a well-loved bicycle route on the county's east side, skirting the Tomoka River. We thought that our group, working to save a well-loved historic property on the west side on the St. Johns River, should be "Friends of Thornby." We met in the evenings, because almost everyone worked during the day.

Main item of business: the Thornby comp plan amendment would go before the Deltona Planning & Zoning Board in a couple of months. Even though P&Z's findings were only advisory, a "no" recommendation would send a potent message to city officials. Officially, at least, we would focus strictly on the land use/density issue. The owners had a legal right to build one unit per acre; our goal was to hold that line. (That didn't mean we couldn't hold the dream of a someday park, of course. After all, the park idea had been kicked around by county and city since as far back as 1986 — long before the Friends of Thornby existed.)

To persuade the P&Z board to recommend against a density increase on Thornby, we would first need to identify the core issues. Each person would focus on an issue, learn about it, and squeeze weeks of research into an effective three-minute presentation. The plan sounded simple, but its execution was not. In effect, we were starting the Academy of Thornby Activism, with the Friends of Thornby as faculty and students.

> **Activist Lesson:** When citizens become involved in land use, salesmen, teachers, secretaries, and construction workers must become instant experts on complicated, unfamiliar, and often baffling issues. That is, if they can manage to decode just what those issues might be. There's always a deadline, and the final exam is a public hearing. This higher learning happens around their job, family responsibilities, and personal chores. At the same time, a veritable army of lawyers, engineers, consultants, economists, technicians, hydrologists, biologists, traffic experts, planners, environmental specialists, statisticians, graphic artists, is on the payroll of developers, governments, and various professional groups and agencies. Since they are paid to make projects happen, they have all the time, resources, skills, knowledge, staff support and connections needed to build their case. When it comes to citizens participating in land use issues, the playing field is not level, and never can be. That's the first bitter lesson.

The second lesson takes longer to learn: having the facts on your side doesn't guarantee success.

There was one more step: We needed to see Thornby for ourselves. A few of us had already ventured into the house; others had wandered further on the grounds; however, no one other than Lani knew the whole Thornby story. Her affection for Doris Faber and her happy memories of life at Thornby made us anxious to see it from her perspective.

On a glorious June day, we fumbled through heavy brush to the just-right-sized house, stately in its magnificent oak setting despite some smashed windows. From his engineer's viewpoint, Roy Walters recounts: "I was amazed at the good condition of the structure. The roof did not leak. We saw no termite damage inside. Obviously, the house was built of heart of pine lumber." Vandals' scars on lath-and-plaster walls testified to the house's naked vulnerability. Two red brick fireplaces conjured thoughts of cozy winter fires in chilly weather that must have still felt good to the Glasses, compared with upstate New York winters.

We climbed to the second and third stories on still-sturdy wood stairs. From the front room windows, Lake Monroe shimmered over the treetops.

Outside, we trekked through nature's bounty. In just a few yards, we were soon enveloped by wilderness like tribe members on "Survivor." Though not isolated by distance from civilization, we were wrapped in thick, green silence.

As we stood among old trees so tall and densely grown that they seemed as crowds of living giants, a primal detachment settled upon us, replacing modern concerns with the sounds, sights and smells of an ancient, living world. Crowns of bright sunlight, clear, soft air, fist-sized, delicate spider webs, shimmering emerald foliage springing from the loamy-fresh, black dirt of centuries — these were powerful reminders of our individual connection to the natural world and our collective purpose to preserve Thornby.

There were leftovers from farm life — a chicken coop here, a metal roof there, decaying remnants of Thornby's past lives already half-buried under decades of Florida jungle. We found the path on Thornby's border called Old Taylor Road in homage to Cornelius Taylor — at one time an Indian trail, then a main road to Florida's east coast. It had never been paved, but the dirt was still compacted from years of travel. With its towering tree canopy, it was like a tunnel to the past.

We found the old duck pond, replete with swimming "quackers." In low, marshy spots, we pushed on through heavy flora toward the lake, our shoes in constant threat of being sucked into waist-high, Jurassic-like ferns resting in the thick, dark mud. To our surprise, there was a canal, about 12 feet deep and 25 feet wide. Walking in the trench was easier, so we inched down its banks and kept going and spotted railroad tracks that spanned the deep ditch. There was a trestle with vertical concrete supports on each end and metal rails across the ditch, but the ties had long ago rotted away. Looking westward, the old rail bed was treeless and visible.

Going farther, we discovered traces of another road. Very near stood an immense cypress, notable even in this mob of trees for its four-foot girth, too thick for even four outstretched arms to surround.[1]

Friends of Thornby field trip

Fighting our way toward the lake through tough, snaky vines and wild, resisting underbrush, we saw more and more huge oaks. Lani showed us the small, keyhole-shaped spring-fed pool on the other side of Lakeshore Drive, built by Dr. Glass in the 1920s, with its steps for access still in place. Cement structures along the lakeshore seemed to have once supported a dock. Lani pointed out, too, shells protruding from the soil along the road — visible remnants of the state-documented Thornby Midden.

With that few hours' journey began the work of many years. We had the rare privilege to see and feel what Florida once was — not on a PBS special, but as part of our everyday world. After that, Thornby was wrapped around our hearts as tightly as the thick, brown vines that embrace Florida's aged trees. This place had to be saved, not drained and leveled.

---

1   Cypress trees are closely related to California's giant sequoia trees.

The Friends of Thornby

Carol Aymar

The Aymars' kitchen table was not round, but it fostered as much camaraderie and solidarity as King Arthur's table ever did.

Like many others, Carol Aymar came to Stone Island in Enterprise from somewhere-else Florida. A third-generation Floridian, she grew up in the tiny fishing village of Port Salerno on the state's east coast.

Her husband Dave grew up in Arizona far removed from swamps, wetlands and towering cypress trees. Nevertheless, his love of the water meant he was thrilled when his company transferred him to Florida. Life for the Aymars BE (Before Enterprise) was in Longwood, a suburb of too many comfortable homes. Carol, Dave and daughters Kathryn and Jenna craved more space and a more rural lifestyle. They scoured Central Florida for their dream place — south to Osceola County, west to Apopka, north to Sanford, east to Chuluota but "We kept coming back to Lakeshore Drive and the north bank of Lake Monroe. We were in love with the look and the feel of Enterprise and it brought back memories of growing up on the water in South Florida— before all the condos, traffic circles, and parking lots," Carol says. Simply put, Enterprise seeped into their bones.

Carol is a retired teacher and a tree-hugger in the best sense of the word, with a practical mind and no history BE (Before Enterprise) of political involvement. At the church meeting, Valerie Grill's vision of what could be lost was her epiphany. After that, the Aymars opened their front door to neighbors who shared their commitment to preserving Enterprise, including Valerie, Mark Matzinger, and others. From there, the Enterprise Preservation Society was born. Make no mistake: Carol Aymar is the Founding Mother of EPS.

Those gatherings led to the kitchen table meetings where Friends of Thornby got its start. The Aymars' door stayed open for years of planning and strategy sessions, with Thornby's fate swinging in the political winds. Always, she explains, "I bounced ideas off my logical, engineer husband — my sounding board and most reliable advisor for all of my important decisions in the battle to save Thornby." Dave admits, "I was never involved in any form of activism before moving to Enterprise, and my livelihood depends on growth. [But] my wife and the Friends of Thornby opened my eyes to the enormous amount of time and effort it takes for ordinary citizens to fight city hall."

As for Carol, she has been a director of the Enterprise Preservation Society for all but one year of its existence. What accomplishment is she proudest of? In 2000 EPS held its first, resoundingly successful Old Florida Festival. Carol helped to shape the vision that gave the festival a theme, look and feel that set it apart from similar events. She wanted it to be a family-friendly event, with bluegrass music, square dancing, a fish fry and old-time games like a pie-eating contest, all evoking a simpler time. "We wanted to raise awareness of what a treasure they [people in Enterprise] had," she says. Every year since, she's poured her heart and soul into the festival, with no detail too small to overlook. Every year the festival's gotten bigger and, more importantly, better.

"There's a group of us here in this live-oaked wetland paradise that sure think we have something special," she wrote in 2010. And Dave adds, "This experience has made me realize how important it is to get your children involved in learning about local issues and how they can make a positive difference in their community." For the Aymars, those are words to live by.

Kevin Finn

Kevin Finn could be the last guy you'd expect to have a zest for history. He lived in Deltona, not Enterprise. He was a sizeable guy who worked as an estimator in the construction industry. Yet, he had collected enough old, rare letters, books, photos and memorabilia on local history to make a small museum jealous. Searching for such finds on eBay was almost his second job; his wife, Kathy, was part owner of an antique store. Their home happily overflowed with lovingly displayed bits of the past.

Like his next-door neighbor Sandy Gallagher, Kevin came to Florida from Ohio. He moved to Volusia County in 1983, a young single man who just wanted a change of scene, with no interest in the past like most twenty-somethings. He found work in the construction industry and in 1998, bought a home in Deltona. Then bad luck arrived in the form of a serious health problem, surgery and a long recuperation. Facing routine days filled with tedious TV, he looked around for a hobby he might enjoy. He found metal detecting and started scouting on eBay for old maps and other bits of Enterprise's past. From there, it was a natural step to the first Old Enterprise Festival where the ever-gregarious Kevin chatted about local history with EPS' Dale Hansen and showed Board members some of his already-considerable collection. "It got their attention," he allows. "And I was hooked."

"History to me is fascinating. The first time I went on the Thornby property, it was amazing," he says, raving about the experience as if seeing Old Taylor Road and the timeworn railroad trestle today, for the first time.

Kevin went to both county meetings when the Thornby plan amendment was debated, but he didn't speak. He hadn't yet evolved into the natural public speaker that he became after so many hours around the Aymars' kitchen table. When Friends of Thornby would "divvy up" the issues at meetings, Kevin generally wouldn't commit to one subject. We never knew what he planned to say at hearings, but we knew it would be expressive. "Before I speak at a hearing,

I think about it for three or four days," he says. "For Thornby, I took my cues from the opposition and tried to make valid points by showing how what they said was wrong." He gave enough speeches over the years to fill a file folder, but there's one he calls especially personal: the night he told Deltona's planning board how, as he labored over his Thornby "homework," his wife and daughter questioned the effort. "Why are you doing all this?" they challenged him. "It's futile. Nothing is going to happen from all this work." His answer: "I never would give up."

Although he worked hard on every presentation, Kevin always came across like Average Guy, which was a very good thing. In this case, "average" meant average Deltona citizen, begging the question of whether people from Enterprise were the only ones loudly opposing the notion of multi-housing on Thornby. Ears perked up when he'd calmly begin, "My name is Kevin Finn and I live *in the City of Deltona*" at Thornby hearings. His words were conversational without being cute, respectful without pleading.

For three years, Kevin Finn from Deltona served as chairman of the Enterprise Preservation Society. "I believe in the EPS cause," he says. "We got kicked in the teeth a lot of times, like when Thornby was annexed." Llike die-hard fans of a college football team, he loves having something to root for, a sense of belonging and dedication. He explains, "You don't get that in many communities."

Lani Friend

Lani Friend was known locally and statewide as a historian. More importantly for Thornby, however, she was one of "Miss Doris' kids." Thornby was a large part of her life for years; she and her family were living in the house where she'd been raised, half a mile or so away. She knew every foot of the property, she'd known Frank Knight and John Clapp from childhood, and she was determined that seven people with no understanding of its history would not ruin this part of Enterprise and her own history.

It was Lani who opened our eyes to Thornby so that it became even more than the fascinating, puzzling treasure we saw while driving by. Her stories of Doris Faber put things into context. She was the catalyst who conveyed the real meaning of Thornby to the rest of us, and why its history was unshakably entwined with Enterprise. When Lani shared her Thornby memories, sharp curiosity became overwhelming comprehension. What our eyes saw, and our ears heard, entered our hearts. We understood that there was nowhere else like Thornby.

Sandy Lou Gallagher

"Mr. and Mrs. Eagle" get most of the credit for Sandy's activism. Known to the State of Florida by their official names of VO1 and VO2, the eagle pair's love nest was in a tall slash pine on the condo property formerly owned by Catherine Clapp. Since 1978, the nest hatched two chicks every year except one. The neighbors were quite proud of "their" eagles, keeping an "eagle eye" as the birds became parents, raised their eaglets, and expanded the nest every fall.

When 12 wooded acres at Doyle Road and Providence Boulevard were rezoned for a grocery store and strip shopping center, Florida's Fish & Wildlife Commission extracted conditions from the developer to protect — at least in theory — the nearby eagle parents and fledglings from construction noise, light and disturbance. Deltona resident Sandy Gallagher had a special interest in our national symbol. "I had seen the eagles flying around since I moved here in 1990," she explains. "That is when I learned where the nest was located. When the [Publix building] started, I got really concerned for their wellbeing." Concerned enough to do something about it, she applied and was accepted as a state-designated "eagle watcher," volunteering her free time to monitor the eagles in Volusia Nest #12.

Credit also goes to Valerie Grill. "I was introduced to Thornby by Valerie Grill," recalls Sandy. "We met at the Enterprise Post Office and became friends. I told her that I was keeping watch on the eagles, and she asked if I knew whether there was a nest on the Thornby property across the street. She asked if I'd been to the Thornby house, and told me about Dr. Glass and how Enterprise was once a very busy port on Lake Monroe."

In the struggles to save Thornby, bald eagles and their nests became heated points of contention, whether on the land itself or on adjacent land. From the beginning, Friends of Thornby knew that we needed more than pure "green" speakers and dire emotional pleas, to counter the city's claims that a hefty density increase on Thornby wouldn't destroy the property's ecological worth and natural systems. Until Sandy told us, most in the group didn't even know about the active bald eagles' nest near Thornby. Some of us knew that federal and Florida laws slapped protection zones on construction near eagles' nests, but those rules, like so many other species-protection laws, were unendingly subject to the dreaded "C" word: compromise. Likewise, we had no idea if, or how, the nests would affect development on Thornby, and vice versa. Nor did we know what a developer could or couldn't do to the eagles, or their nest. Eagles are prone to abandon even long-term nests for "alternate nests" nearby, and then return to the original nest. Thornby was inside the protection zone of the VO12 nest. If the fight to save Thornby was uncharted territory, with every unexplored side trail needing its own captain, who better to lead the eagle campaign than someone whose email address was "Eaglesandy"?

Sandy, originally from Ohio, was an engineering technician for a construction-consulting firm, which gave her added expertise in land use issues. She had never been involved in anything resembling activism or politics, but she wanted to save Thornby and safeguard the eagles, an endangered species since 1967. She would meet with us around the kitchen table and work hard on the issues, but someone else would have to speak at hearings, she said. She had never done it, couldn't do it, would never do it. After a few meetings, it was obvious we had more issues to cover than people to cover them. Little sideways glances were routinely sent Sandy's way. Finally, like a reluctant gladiator about to face hungry lions, she could see what was coming. "Why do I need to talk about the eagles?" she asked dolefully. "Because they can't talk about themselves," was the answer that trumped her stomach-burning aversion to public speaking. Many people share her distaste, but few meet it head-on. Fewer still make a U-turn, re-routing their life in the process. Thornby transformed shy Sandy Gallagher into a motivated activist: first as a Deltona Planning and Zoning Board member, secretary, and vice-chair; then as a candidate for city commission; and finally as Deltona's representative to the Volusia Growth Management Commission. It all started at one nerve-wracking hearing, when she spoke up for the eagles who couldn't speak for themselves. "And I would do it all over, and over again," she says.

Jack Hoyt

Jack Hoyt had a file folder. Actually, he had many file folders — boxes of them — but one in particular was special. Inside, he had carefully printed the names and phone numbers of four women. It wasn't extra-marital flirting that accounted for the list; Jack was devoted to his wife, Annie. Rather, the women he named: Sandy Walters, Carol Aymar, Suzanne Steiner and Lani Friend, were four of the "awfully nice people" he decided to help "protect their environment and Enterprise."

Almost as much as he loved his wife, Jack loved catching officials in some civic hanky-panky, and then coming down hard. "I'd been watching Thornby," says Jack. "I was so interested in what the city was doing and I was dead set against the city annexing it." To say that Jack Hoyt was "interested" in what his city did is like saying that the IRS is "interested" in your income.

He had first challenged the city, years before, on a specific, technical, point in his own Deltona subdivision: The city was allowing a developer to include water areas when figuring a property's allowable housing "net density," although this practice was contrary to city ordinance. "It was very clear they had violated their own city statutes," he recalls. The resulting lawsuit and win, he says, "started me on, 'what the hell's going on in Deltona'?" The same issue would later hit him full force with Thornby.

Jack was appointed to Deltona's first planning board in April 1999, and served until the month before Thornby's annexation, never missing a meeting. Time after time, he raised neglected issues when plans came before the board: What about the scrub jays? Where are the sidewalks? Who protects the wetlands? Sometimes his questions filled pages. In 1999, he voted against the disastrous 7-Eleven at Providence and Doyle, declaring that both people and land use would be "severely impacted."

With a resume that reads like a long-running episode of "Star Wars," hands-on everything from Minuteman ICBMs to moon landers, this Purdue graduate probably never sang "Kumbaya" around a campfire. When he turned his analytical mind toward his city's business, and saw things going on that didn't meet spec, they must have thought an Apollo missile had hit city hall. As Jack explains, "When I take something on, I will keep at it and do everything I can." If that meant writing to Florida's governor to complain about the latest city disregard for its own laws, he wrote. If it meant meeting with the city attorney about violating city ordinances, he'd meet — or try to. Through it all, Jack never lost his sense of humor, and never stopped saying, "I like the mayor personally." "I like the guy, I just don't agree with him," he would invariably say when he clashed with a commissioner. No matter what he wrote to the city, and no matter how many votes he protested, he always kept it civil.

Jack attends few city meetings these days, but his eyes dance like moonbeams when he recalls how the mayor once proposed what he calls a "gag order" against him on grounds that, as a planning board member, he couldn't speak as a private citizen. It was all just practice for Thornby.

Someone — he doesn't remember who — invited Jack to the Aymar's kitchen table. "I was a stranger to all of you," he says, but he was no stranger to fighting city hall. "If I thought we didn't have a chance, I wouldn't have done it," he adds, no matter how things ended.

Mark Matzinger

Mark, another Ohio native (what's with these Ohioans? Is the Ohio River pumped full of activist juices?), moved to Florida in 1969. A professional firefighter until he was disabled by a serious heart condition, Mark re-trained as a draftsman. In 1993, he moved to Enterprise with his wife and children. He was recovering from a heart transplant just about the time things got cooking in Enterprise. "I was on a reduced work schedule," he explains, "and when I found out about the meeting at the church, I thought, why not help my community?" For Mark the meeting in March 2000 at the Baptist church was a lightning strike, kindling in him a fire to make sure that Enterprise didn't smolder away. Even while working full-time and serving as a volunteer fireman at Enterprise's Indian Mound fire station, he became the first chairman

of the newly-fledged Enterprise Preservation Society. He then took on the job of obtaining IRS non-profit status for the society — a necessary but exacting task that took months of diligent effort.

Mark's profession as construction administrator for a structural engineering firm gave his Thornby technical presentations a sound foundation. With his calm demeanor and an even-handed style, as chairman of EPS he was an always-effective voice for Enterprise. His presentation to the DeBary City Council, with Vice-Chair Carol Aymar, resulted in the city's "strong message of support" for Enterprise. That influential letter became part of every pre-hearing packet of information that we provided to officials.

Mark remained on the EPS board for ten years. He's worked up the plans, and built the stage, for every festival, as well as shouldering much of the heavy lifting — literally — of chairs, tables, history boards and tents. On top of everything else, he's shepherded the Enterprise Heritage Center project from its first days, providing expertise and resources to turn a vintage school building into an Enterprise centerpiece.

Gisela Oeffen

Gisela always seemed to look at "Thornby" issues a little differently. Maybe being a native of Germany gave her a different perspective, or perhaps her life's work as an executive afforded a broader view. To Gisela, Deltona's plan to put multi-family housing on Thornby was, at its core, simply a bad business decision.

She had worked in health care management on two continents, earning a Ph.D. in business administration and government. While living in Germany, she bought property in Deltona sight unseen, not knowing that a few years later she would be hired to turn around a chain of Florida bankrupt nursing homes. Before that, she lived in Los Angeles, Baltimore, Seattle, and on an Eskimo reservation in Alaska, after leaving Germany because "there was a big wide world out there." However, for retirement she picked Deltona, whose sandy soil, pine trees and lakes reminded her of her hometown, Berlin.

When she talks about the political process, Gisela uses words like "bureaucrat" and "power hungry" — natural, perhaps for someone who grew up in World War II Germany. "Because of my education, travels, and living in different places, I saw the problem as bigger than Thornby. It was officials using politics and government to get power, taking over, changing the environment, changing the comp plan." When the Thornby issue came along, Gisela was working to get a medical clinic started in Deltona, as well as watching and commenting as the city's first comprehensive plan took shape. "I was new in town and the city commission was my entertainment," she jokes; at every meeting, she sat in the front row. As for the Thornby hearings? "They were always quite lively," she grins. With a keen interest in archeology, even before getting involved with Thornby she'd amassed stacks of information about the earliest inhabitants of the St. Johns River basin.

"I have always admired the people in Enterprise, how they stuck to it," she says. "They were serious, they wanted to preserve their community, and it was up to them." As to the Thornby development, "The (developers) were going to put up all these houses. Nothing was really planned." In Gisela's view, poor planning was the worst of it. "Bureaucrats do what they are supposed to do. It's not wrong; there's just no common sense," she asserts.

As a dedicated government watcher and student of Deltona's comprehensive plan, Gisela helped keep the Friends of Thornby's presentations businesslike and on target.

Debra Richardson

Debra grew up in upstate New York, and moved to Enterprise in 2002.

Before that, she lived in Palm Beach County and worked for The Advertising Council. "South Florida had become so built up, with so many people. There were so many changes in the county," she explains. "The reason we moved to Enterprise was that it was a rural area, and I loved the beauty and natural ambiance of Lakeshore Drive."

Debra was a stay-at-home mom of daughter Arika, an activist-in-training. "We marched after the 2000 election," she says proudly. Her work experience and volunteering in schools and for school events made it natural for her to focus on school overcrowding, a very pressing issue in 2005. "I remember calling the school board and researching student population numbers. Because my daughter would soon be attending one of the much overcrowded high schools, I truly felt that [proposed high density on Thornby] would not be beneficial to our community." She notes that today, as a substitute teacher, she sees the results of bad planning that changes local comprehensive plans, increasing or allowing houses where none existed before. Example: masses of portable classrooms.

A Stone Island neighbor, Carol Aymar, introduced her to the Enterprise Preservation Society. Debra chaired the annual Old Florida Festival for a couple of years. Why did she join EPS? "I didn't believe that Enterprise should be part of Deltona. Sometimes growth takes over and important places lose their heritage and culture."

Debra learned about Thornby from Lani Friend, who, she says, "told me all about it. She showed me the ravine; it was so beautiful." She found the plan to change land uses distressing because "Increasing the density on such a large piece of property, along a scenic roadway, in a historic area, without regard to the protests of other residents, was not a wise decision." (In other words, it's not always right to do something just because you can.) With that in mind, teacher Debra joined Friends of Thornby in its campaign to halt the eightfold density increase that would add hundreds of extra students to, and subtract prime natural resources from, the Enterprise community.

Bob Sayre

Of the original Friends of Thornby, Bob Sayre lived in Enterprise the longest — more than 10 years. Widely known as "Whiskey Bob" in homage to his long-time career as sales rep for a large distillery, he was the only one with lots of pre-Thornby activism experience.

Raised in Columbus, he attended college in Athens, Ohio, in the Appalachian foothills. "That's when I fell in love with the natural beauty that is all around us, once we get out of the noise and bustle of the city," he says.

After college, he helped run a friend's successful campaign for the Ohio State Senate that resulted in defeat for a lobbyist/entrenched member of the local "good old boy network." When Bob and his wife, Linda Poff, moved to Florida, they wanted to live in a place surrounded by nature, and "that's how we sought out and found Enterprise," he says. "I wanted to save Thornby because it was the last little patch of pristine Old Florida left on the lakefront and was home to many critters. They've got to live, too."

The critters he focused on for Friends of Thornby, however, were the kind with engines — cars that sped along Enterprise-Osteen Road (extension of Lakeshore Drive) behind his house, cars that flew past in no-passing zones on tricky blind curves, and the motorcycles revving their "loud pipes" that echoed through the rural quiet. The increased traffic from a major density increase on Thornby would massively overload the two-lane, winding, scenic road all the way from DeBary to Osteen through the heart of Enterprise.

Bob wasn't in the first couple of Friends of Thornby meetings, but found out about the group quickly. He pored over traffic reports and met with county traffic engineers, learning along the way. Eventually, he became so adept at deciphering jargon like "Level of Service" and "Pass-by Trips" that he could spot bogus numbers several car-lengths away — or at least, raise serious questions about them — a skill that stood us in good stead during the ensuing struggles.

Bob believed that Thornby's "beauty should be preserved for future generations, so they can see what life used to be like here many years ago." He keeps in touch with the Ohio senator, now retired. "He taught me well," Bob says. "Never give up and never back down, even in the face of long odds. Every time he visits Enterprise, he applauds what we have already accomplished and cheers us on for the next struggles."

Grace and Patrick Stamile

Over a hundred years ago, Enterprise had hotels and saloons, banks and stores, and even, for a time, its own newspaper. Today, about the only prominent entrepreneurs you'll find in Enterprise grow colorful, premium hybrid daylilies for wholesale markets worldwide.

"Floyd Cove," 30 acres of beautiful Old Florida, home to both bald eagles and hummingbirds, was also home to Grace and Pat Stamile, owners of a thriving wholesale daylily business. They have since retired to California, but the business still operates under new owners.

Former teachers and Long Island natives, they came to Enterprise by way of Sanford in 1996. Growing literally thousands of seedlings per year, they specialized in creating new daylily varieties, garnering numerous medals, awards and honors from the likes of The American Horticultural Society and

international organizations. Both traveled the world from their Enterprise base as speakers and experts in the rarified world of flower hybridizing. In addition to daylilies, the Stamiles grew a myriad of other plants, shrubs, vines and vegetables.

A short distance away was the Thornby property, whose gardens and landscaping had been shoved aside by unruly natives. Like anthropologists, Pat and Grace climbed over logs and slogged through muck to spot these undisturbed plants, some rare. They learned about Thornby's plants in much the same way that Sandy Gallagher learned about its eagles and Kevin Finn learned about its history: curiosity led to absorption, absorption to fervor.

When a "For Sale by Owner" sign appeared on the Thornby property around 1997, it piqued their interest. "We understood the land use was one [house] per acre," says Grace, and having once lived in a historic home, she believed the Thornby house could be restored. They didn't get the chance to learn more, however, because the sign disappeared just days after it was posted. The papers reported that the owners had offered the historic property to Deltona as a city hall site for $1.2 million (see Chapter 6). Rumors swirled that the asking price was too high for the new city's budget.

Like others, the Stamiles were relieved to see Thornby stay intact. Then it was 1999, and the county was poised to approve duplexes there. They understood that intensive development meant sure death to most of Thornby's 40 acres of native trees and plants. Developers are not required to protect plants, even endangered ones, and even trees older than Florida statehood don't live when bulldozers come calling. The notion of elected officials increasing lawful densities simply to benefit private interests bothered the Stamiles as much as the loss of Thornby's plants and trees would have. "We felt [the land use change] was wrong and still do," says Patrick. "It was wrong for the community," he says. "The owners weren't entitled to have it changed just because they wanted it."

Grace and Patrick were at the hearing when the county council voted for multi-housing on Thornby, and when the same council reversed itself they helped make it happen. When the Aymar's kitchen table became the nerve center for saving Thornby, they were there, too.

Richard Vail

Although just shy of 30, Rich Vail could claim several distinctions among the Friends of Thornby. He was the youngest member, and he lived closest to the property. He is a land developer. Something else made him unique: his friendship with Bruce Andersen, the consultant hired by the Thornby owners to cook up a development that would go down easy.

Originally from Minnesota (where land use laws are enforced rather than changed, he says), Rich moved to Enterprise from South Florida in 2000. He came to cherish the wildlife he saw on Thornby: red foxes, raccoons, deer, otters, quail, and wild hogs. And, of course, the eagles. "I'm a fisherman," explains Rich, as to why he worries about Florida's natural resources and the effects of over-development. Startling to hear those words from a developer? "Developers can't have every piece of property," he retorts. He also relates an intriguing story of a neighbor whose property backed up to Thornby: "She had a dream about a bear attacking her house, and an Indian boy saving her and her house. When I started to dig into the history of the property and found that at one time Indians (and bears) lived there, my hair stood up."

When he saw the orange hearing notices go up on Thornby, Rich thought he was on his own. "I didn't know there was any group," he admits. Poring over the Thornby file at Deltona city hall, he saw Carol Aymar's name, and got in touch with her. Because he was, and is, active in the property business as an investor, consultant and developer, he already knew Sanford architect Bruce Andersen. "We had a very professional relationship," recounts Rich. "I mentioned to him that we needed help on the Thornby property, and that's when he informed me that he represented the Estate and Mr. Knight. I could read between the lines that his clients were bullheaded and did not want to compromise. I perceived from him that most of the family were [from out of state and] had elitist mentality." At the time, Andersen was working in the background, advising the Thornby owners. By the time he came to play a very public role in the Thornby plans, Rich had moved away from Enterprise.

Rich admits to a genuine case of nerves every time he went up against the city. He says, "I had faith that we could succeed in the short term. But in the long term, because of how the laws are [written], and the sometimes lack of ethics, I didn't think we would." Still, as a principled player in the often-shady game of land development, he decided to join up with the "other side."

St. Johns Ain't what it Used to be—I Guess that No Place is/ But it's Still a Lovely, Peaceful Place to be[2]

To save the Thornby property from becoming one more mind-numbing, crowded and paved byproduct of Florida development gone wild, was always the goal of those who fought to save it. Thornby was 40+ densely wooded acres fronting Lake Monroe, part of the St. Johns River, Florida's only American Heritage River. Of those acres, 7-1/2 were wetlands. The property served as both drainage and storage for the Floridian Aquifer. The presence of archeological remnants from a Second Seminole War fort, as well as other historic artifacts, was a very real but never-investigated possibility. A protected bald eagle nest was close enough to influence any building done on Thornby. A rare 1920s spring-fed pool remained, as did a century-old railroad spur once used to carry citrus from upland areas to waiting steamboats. The hefty oak and magnolia trees, big even for those massive species, likely were growing there before Florida statehood. The Thornby house was a state-listed historic structure. Each reason was important on its own. Collectively, they were strong enough to bring strangers together, to draw a line in the sand, to organize, educate and "just say no" to plans to change the public law for private benefit. One reason outshone all the others — Enterprise itself, one of the oldest towns in Central Florida. Enterprise had a long and vital history. Thornby was its center, literally and emotionally.

2 Lyrics from "St. Johns Lullaby," copyright 2007 by Rog Lee

Moreover, if Thornby was the heart of Enterprise, Doris Faber was the soul of Thornby. It was her home for nearly 50 years. She was like a daughter to Thornby's owners, Dr. and Mrs. Glass. She helped widowed Mrs. Glass keep Thornby going. With lots of love, and discipline when needed, she helped raise other people's children at Thornby. Thanks to her hard work, Thornby hosted holiday celebrations and reunions. People went to her for food, a loan, or a helping hand, and she gave it even when she had very little to give.

Most who fought to save Thornby grew up somewhere else. Many had moved from crowded spots elsewhere in Florida — places too late to save. They wanted to sustain the rural community they'd adopted as home, whether for environmental, historic, community or political reasons. But for folks raised in Enterprise who'd known Doris Faber for most of their lives, the struggle was more personal. To them, annihilating Thornby would be like spitting on her grave.

> *It's just a piece of real estate.*
>
> Former Deltona city commissioner
> **Lucille Wheatley**

CHAPTER NINE

Behind the Woodshed

Fifth Thornby Hearing: Deltona Planning and Zoning Board

Deltona aborted its August 21, 2002 planning board hearing before the board had a chance to vote on the Thornby amendment. The fizzled-out hearing proved notable for two reasons. First, the mask was off. City Commissioner Carl Carey's unctuous defense when the property was annexed a year before — "No one has stated the property would be zoned commercial" — had been a non sequitur. From beneath the bureaucratic veneer emerged the real plan to develop Thornby:

220 apartments
+ 35,000 sq. ft. shopping center
+ 65,000 sq. ft. "library-type space" [1]

The second reason the hearing was significant? It laid the foundation for years of Deltona's disingenuousness regarding Thornby.

---

1 Permitted uses under this category include libraries and wastewater treatment plants.

The city's planning board, like most such boards, is composed of volunteers. Most serve from a sense of civic duty. Most are committed to fairness, but the very fact that they are ordinary citizens means they may be unfamiliar with issues that come before them. Often, they simply don't know what questions to ask; they rely, to a great degree, on the professional staff's report. Expecting transparency, they tend to assume that what they're told is factual. The city staff's report on Thornby recommended approval of the development plan and asserted, "The development of the property will not change the appearance and character of the area."

> **Activist Lesson:** Maps, enlarged photos, video, PowerPoint are effective ways to introduce the property and its surroundings to decision-makers unfamiliar with the area.

There is no rule against members of boards and commissions visiting property they will vote on. If they do, they simply have to disclose it before they vote. It's not an announcement you hear often, even though, as former Volusia County Council Chairman Jim Ward says, "I don't think you can do the kind of job you need to do [as a voting official] without seeing things for yourself." No board members said they had set foot on the Thornby property, although at least one, Janet Deyette, said she drove by. As the hearing unfolded, the images of the Thornby property that were conjured up by the city and the owners were very different from the reality.

> **Activist Lesson:** If possible, arrange for decision-makers to visit the property. At the hearing, ask how many have seen the property in person.

The 22-page staff report seemed uncoordinated with the proposed project. "According to information from Frank Knight, there is no canal on the property," it said, and then went on to describe the "large, deep canal" documented by the county in 1999. Further, "the city is willing to work with the property owner to explore feasible ways … by which the house may be conserved," it said, while recommending adoption of land uses that virtually guaranteed its demise.

At the hearing, Bob Nix, Deltona Director of Planning and Development said:

> Thornby is surrounded on three sides by urban development and on one side by water.

Walter Geiger, Deltona Planning Manager said:

> I walked the site. There was talk of a canal but I don't believe one exists. Many trees in the center of the site are dead. The majority of the trees are dead. The house is in a dangerous condition and children could get hurt. There are few wetlands.

Mark Watts, lawyer for the owners, said:

> This is a significant piece of property for Deltona. We have to change the land use.[2] The owners plan a quality gathering place with protection of environmental features and 18 acres of houses.

Planning board member Daniel Warren said:

> It's all developed all around it.

No one inquired about the long, 12' deep canal that bisects the property north to south. Board members did not question how many pine trees out of thousands were dead. No one asked if a structural engineer had assessed that the house was "about to fall down." Nobody mentioned that the "few wetlands" covered more than seven acres. No one inquired how a person could "walk" acres of luxuriant Florida woods in the summer without a machete.

Debra Richardson walking in the Thornby canal

---

2 Annexation does not trigger a requirement to change land use. Chapter 171, Florida Statutes.

Watts recounted for the board the attempts to change the land use when Thornby was still in the county. Calling the Department of Community Affairs review process a "transfer," he was not required to tell the board that the Florida Department of Community Affairs had found the county's former Thornby plan not in compliance with state law. He was not asked about what happened last year. The *Orlando Sentinel* had already interviewed him about Deltona's new Thornby plan. "I don't think anybody needs to be scared of it," Watts condescended.

As Deltona's Director of Development Services, Bob Nix's job was to present a thorough and impartial picture of the effects of commercial and hundreds of apartments on 40 heavily-treed lakefront acres, 7.5 of them wetlands, on a two-lane, constrained road in a small community. He recommended that the planning board approve the project without citing any negative effects that might result. According to former Deltona commissioner Joe Perez, "the city's planning department buckled under commission pressure."

Bob Nix:

- Opined that the existing county Natural Resources Management Area (NRMA) on the property "was not attuned to small areas."[3]
- Stated that under the current (county) Low Impact Urban (LIU) land use "affordable housing" on Thornby would bring five residences per acre.
- Told his Board that commercial, business and industrial uses were *already allowed* on Thornby under the county's existing land use. This was a crucial point, kicked back and forth like a soccer ball between county and city for years.

As Ron Paradise explained at the time:

> While the LIU does potentially allow non-residential uses, the chances of a non-residential use at this site are remote because of the lack of suitable traffic infrastructure. The land use incompatibility issue makes a non-residential urban use at this site inconsistent with the criteria of the LIU.

Volunteer board members do not normally research land use issues on their own. Rather, they rely on the city staff to provide the information they need.

---

3 NRMA provides extra protection for environmentally sensitive land that has "remained relatively unfragmented," with no restriction as to size.

Before public comment began, would-be speakers had to deal with planning board chair Rafael Valle, who, with 18 names on the sign-up sheet, was concerned about the meeting running long. He said that if a husband and wife both wanted to speak, they had to pick one mouth between them. (The following day, I faxed a protest on this point to the mayor. He did not respond.) Valle then announced that speakers would have two minutes instead of the usual three. An "uproar of displeasure" from the audience changed his mind.

First up was Chris Draper, an attorney representing residents of the nearby Edgewater Condominiums, who drew applause when he compared the Thornby process to "judge shopping," pointing out the obvious — that the public's comprehensive plan was being changed to accommodate a developer.

Other speakers, including Kevin Finn, Suzanne Steiner, Stephen Wiechert, Gisela Oeffen, Patrick Stamile, Delmari Howell, Lee Perry and Jack Hoyt addressed issues of school overcrowding, traffic, the county scenic corridor, centuries-old tree cover, and more. "I remember Nix pushing for that commercial property on Lakeshore Drive," Kevin recalls. I quoted from newspaper articles detailing how the county had rejected multi-housing on Thornby, and read a *Sentinel* item titled "Volusia's Version of David and Goliath," written by none other than Joe Perez when he was Deltona's vice mayor. In it, he praised not only Enterprise's "old oaks and its old-Florida look," but also "those activists who are desperately trying to save it from the bulldozers." The audience was in an applauding mood. Carol Aymar asked: if the county's land use category is so liberal that it would allow anything on Thornby from a sewer plant to a gas station, as Nix claimed, then why was the county expressing deep concerns over what Deltona would do to it? To verify this, she produced a letter from the county. Lani Friend earned an ovation worthy of a ninth inning home run, when she suggested that the board apply a land use designation that would turn Thornby into a showplace and nature preserve that would be a model for the county and provide a tourist attraction. Former Deltona city commissioner Wayne Gardner spoke on behalf of the Barnett Methodist Church — the church so deeply connected with Hattie Brooks and Doris Faber. Through his work as youth pastor, he had known Doris Faber well. Contacted in 2010, Gardner said, "I would have loved to see the house restored. I didn't want to see the memories, and the good things Doris did, get wiped out." At the hearing, he questioned the impacts of increased traffic, especially on the Methodist Children's Home. It may have been Gardner who mentioned the fact that the county's traffic engineer projected 5,600 car trips to be generated every weekday by the development, a figure not included in the meeting minutes.

Gardner's concerns must have set off an alarm. After hours of testimony and city staff's glowing picture of commercial and hundreds of apartments on Thornby, Nix suddenly announced that he needed to take a "closer look at the storm water study." He also said that vital traffic data was missing. This hearing should be postponed, Nix advised. It was, but not before P&Z member Janet Deyette spoke up. Deyette, who served on the board for six years before being elected to the city commission in 2005, appreciated Thornby's significance from the beginning. She expressed concern about the county's support letter and its plan for Enterprise, and wanted to know "how we could give them time to do it." Nix responded, "We'll address that next time."

> **Activist Lesson:** It will serve you well to find out the mechanics of meeting agendas: how, when and by whom they are set.

Two days after the terminated hearing, the *Sentinel* reported that to preserve Thornby, Enterprise residents Grace and Patrick Stamile had offered $1.2 million to buy it. Mark Watts said the owners "would consider any offers." In a 2010 interview, the Stamiles confirmed that they made the offer to Watts. He "had no interest in it," they said. "He never responded."

How to Prepare

After that, the Thornby Spin Machine revved up:

Thornby-Speak	Translation
"The city's land use needs to be **updated**"	Thornby's land use needs to be **drastically urbanized**
"Industrial use is out of the picture"	Industrial use was never realistically **in** the picture
"Will help the city meet demands for new houses"	Will help the city **increase its tax base**
"Commercial will be a distinct upgrade from the strip-mall mentality. A quality gathering place for the people of Deltona"	There are no guarantees.

Meanwhile, Deltona's Mayor Masiarczyk assured *Sentinel* readers that he thought the city would "attempt" to get something "aesthetically pleasing" on the property (presumably, he meant something more aesthetically pleasing than the thousands of trees already there.) At the same time, a *Daytona Beach News-Journal* report on Deltona flooding quoted Masiarczyk's annoyance with what he called "bugs-and-bunnies" people.

Musicians know this basic truth about their art: the most important part of music is the space between the notes. In the same way, one could say that the most important part of activism is the space between the hearings. When a poker-faced official listens to a series of three-minute speeches aimed at influencing their decision without asking a single question, it seems an exercise in hopelessness. Hard-hitting activism happens *before*, rather than during, a public hearing — well before, although that's not always doable. As described in Chapter 6, the land use process is not crafted to alert members of the public to a pending land use change before public notice signs pop up on the property. Still, the word sometimes slips out in other ways. Friendly staff members can "leak" details (it's perfectly legal for the public to have this often-obscure information). A curious reporter may dig up an impending amendment. A public records request will yield helpful documents, once you know there's a reason to look.

When Friends of Thornby asked The Trust for Public Land's Kevin Mooney for an update on its purchase efforts, he said that John Clapp was "quite courteous and though not interested in pursuing a sale… indicated that TPL should stay in touch."

In late summer and fall 2002, it was tough for Volusia County residents to be uninformed about Thornby. The local papers carried 12 Thornby-related stories, including sentimental interviews with former Thornby kid Lani Friend, details of the attempted land use changes, several doses of Enterprise history, and a photo of Mayor Masiarczyk at the Deltona Historical Center, examining "an outdated map of the city." The only people busier than the reporters were the Friends of Thornby. We were preparing for a second trip to the city's planning board.

Roy Walters shot a three-minute video of the long, commuter-time traffic backups snaking through Enterprise. Before the hearing, he was denied permission to show the tape. His formal request that the city attorney provide the legal basis for denial went unanswered.

> **Activist Lesson:** If you plan to use a visual aid at a public hearing, make arrangements beforehand, usually with someone from the city/county manager's office. If permission is denied, bring the item to the hearing and "put it on the record," [i.e., during public comment, describe the item that you are not using]).

Rich Vail sent out a press release alerting local TV and radio stations to the upcoming Thornby hearing. It sparked the interest of the late Keith Altiero, award-winning broadcaster at WDBO-AM in Orlando, who contacted him and then visited the property. (Keith attended the September 18 planning board hearing, and featured a couple of Thornby segments on his radio talk show.) Rich also researched the numbers on available commercial and multi-family properties in Deltona. Carol Aymar got a strong grasp of the nearly complete Enterprise Plan by talking to county staffers. She also tackled Deltona's comprehensive plan, focusing on its requirements for intergovernmental cooperation. Mark Matzinger reviewed county wetland and soil maps, where he discovered "stark differences from what the city was claiming" about Thornby's soils. Jack Hoyt boned up on the objections to Thornby development that the state enumerated in 2000. Lani Friend re-connected with the Trust for Public Land and learned they were still interested in buying Thornby — if the owners would sell. Sandy Gallagher networked with John White of the Florida Fish and Wildlife Commission, arming herself with up-to-the-minute eagle nest data. Suzanne Steiner's photographs of the places that best depicted Enterprise's rural nature were enlarged for impact. I talked with state and county planners who helped me understand the relationship between annexations and land use changes. When I called Mark Watts, attorney for the Thornby owners, with a question about the amendment, he was quite friendly, assuring me that commercial development on Thornby would be "the gem of Enterprise." That he was badly underestimating the Friends of Thornby is perhaps understandable.

Since officials rely on staff reports, and staff reports are written by planners, we needed to learn Planner-ese. I spent untold hours calling planning firms in three counties, hoping to find an angel willing to help a citizens group. At the height of the building boom, planning firms had all the work they could handle and then some. It was "sorry, no" all the way — until we found a pro-bono angel, Chris Bowley, a 30-something, soft-spoken, highly experienced planner with Canin Associates in Orlando. Chris had a generous nature and a kind heart for grassroots groups. (When we met, I learned he was a friend of the Orlando attorney I was then working for. A Thornby Coincidence for sure — but not the only one involving Chris Bowley.) Over lunch, Chris heard the story of Thornby, and at a pizza party, he met the group and agreed to advise us on the plan approval process. Along the way, he taught us about the physical conditions onsite, the proposed densities, and the carrying capacity of the land. He explained that the underlying soils precluded development as proposed. He became, and remains, a true Friend of Thornby, never too busy to answer a question or decode a baffling sentence. Chris had a family connection to Utica, New York — another Chris Bowley Thornby Coincidence (a third would surface much later). While Chris was guiding us through the land use process like an instructor readying shaky students for the driving exam, help came from an unexpected source. Her name is Esther Dobens, but I just called her "The Mole."

Flyers Distributed In Area .9/02

LOCAL RESIDENTS

THIS IS WHAT DEVELOPERS AND DELTONA ARE TRYING TO DO TO LAKE MONROE

252 New Housing Units on Site

Man-made Lakes for Lake-front Housing

Traffic Congestion

Schools already Overcrowded

Commercial Development & Parking Lots on Lake Monroe

100-Year Old Oaks Bulldozed on Scenic Roadway

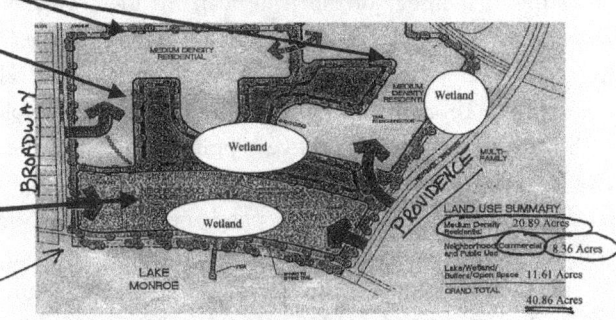

IS THIS WHAT YOU WANT?

CALL:

John Masiarczyk, Mayor	386-561-2100
Bob Nix, Development Services	386-561-2200
Walter Geiger, Planning Manager	386-561-2200
J. Frank Knight, Property Owner	386-668-6429

OR ATTEND THE ZONING HEARING:

Wed. Sept. 18, 7:00 p.m.
Deltona City Hall
2345 Providence Blvd.

■ BECAUSE ON SEPT. 19 IT WILL BE TOO LATE ■

Flyer for first Deltona Planning and Zoning Board meeting

The Spy Who Loved Me

Esther Dobens, a native New Englander, had lived in Deltona from its earliest days. She'd worked for city incorporation in 1995 and supported John Masiarczyk's election and re-election as mayor.

She says, "When we came here in 1976, the Mackle Brothers' Realtor gave us a tour of the area. She drove us to Enterprise, pointed out the historical sites, the huge magnolias, all the plant life. What impressed me about the area was the quietness. I was here before it was overloaded with people. You could ride a bike in Deltona then. My husband and I used to ride our bikes to Enterprise, around Stone Island." As a staunch Methodist, Esther was "averse to any growth that would injure the Children's Home."

Esther, a member of the American Business Women's Association, met Janet Deyette when Deyette received an ABWA college scholarship for working women. Deyette, like Jack Hoyt, was a member of Deltona's first planning board. Then Thornby came along. That's where "The Mole" came in.

Esther was in her 70s and very politically aware. She didn't like what the city had planned for the Thornby property. "There wasn't a city park conducive to older people. I wanted a passive park, a green place for picnics, with trails," she says firmly.

Of Mayor Masiarczyk, she says, "I'd known him from his post office days. I thought the power had gone to his head." In a 2010 interview, she told the author, "Thornby was an inspiration to me to get out there and do even more." She continued, "I went to every hearing, although I didn't speak. You didn't know who I was. I was so impressed that you and Roy were busy people working so hard that you would give so much time to your passion. I saw your name in the papers talking about the eagle nest and called your house one evening. Roy said you were at a Friends of Thornby meeting. I left my number but didn't want to use my name." She was calling to offer her help to Friends of Thornby. Information that her friend Jan Deyette might obtain as a planning board member, although it was public record, wouldn't necessarily be available to the public in time to do us much good. For example, in the days before meeting agendas were posted online, phone calls and trips to city hall were the only ways to be sure what and when a particular issue would be heard. Even then, last-minute changes, an all-too-common occurrence, would tie the whole ball of carefully-wound strategic yarn — witnesses, supporters, documents — into a panicky knot. Esther came to the rescue by keeping us in the city's loop with dates, times, agenda items and issues as they were added, changed or eliminated. She saw a problem and reached out to solve it, proving how important one person's efforts can be.

Sixth Thornby Hearing: Deltona Planning and Zoning Board

September 18, 2002 was a typical late-summer Florida evening, with temperatures in the humid 80s. Long before the 7 p.m. hearing start, cars began to enter the big, open parking lot. Friends spotted friends, gabbing in small groups, making their way together into the windowless commission room on the first floor of the square, colorless City Hall perched above Providence Boulevard. In the lobby, a slow line backed up to enter the meeting room. An even slower line waited to sign the yellow "speaker cards" that would give each person exactly 180 seconds to exercise their First Amendment rights. Inside, overworked air conditioners struggled mightily to cool the bright, jam-packed room. After every chair was filled, someone found extras, and when those were used, folks leaned on the back wall. Channel 9-TV Orlando showed up. Noise levels swelled as raised voices collided with hard floors and walls. Lawyers were polished and prepared. In the audience, John Clapp and Frank Knight waited expectantly. For the Friends of Thornby, it felt like giving a concert at Carnegie Hall or facing a firing squad. As an advisory group, the planning board wasn't the final decision-maker, but we were as psyched as if the Supreme Court had convened in Deltona.

That morning, the *Sentinel*'s front page screamed "County Tries to Save Land" along with "then and now" photos of the Thornby house. Hoping for no more than a respectable turnout, we watched incredulously as hundreds of friends and strangers poured through the doors. The chairman disclosed that an "enormous amount of correspondence from the public" had bombarded city offices. Weary hours spent composing, printing, copying and distributing hundreds of flyers had paid off. The upwelling of support was as unexpected, and just as welcome, as a bright rainbow *before* a storm.

The official meeting summary is 11 pages long. At three minutes each, it took two hours and five minutes to hear from all 30 people in opposition; no one spoke in favor. (Fortunately, for interesting reading, *Sentinel* columnist Bo Poertner quoted some of the more colorful comments, because most speakers' exact words are absent from the printed meeting minutes.)

Late that night, amid the throng, the lights, the noise, the disruptions and charged-up emotions, the Deltona Planning Board rejected the whole idea. What convinced four of six (one was absent) board members to ignore the advice of their city staff and the best arguments of a seasoned land use attorney? Actually, there were plenty of compelling reasons.

To make the development pill easier to swallow, the staff concocted their version of a "bad cop, good cop" land use scenario. Bad Cop was their version of "potential" county land uses on Thornby and Good Cop was the city's intended, intense land uses. My worn copy of the staff's memo was striped with yellow highlights as I struggled to find the key to planning logic.

As ordinary citizens, we assumed that planning is a science, like chemistry. Not so, says Ron Paradise, who believes that "planning shouldn't be the domain of lawyers and planners." That viewpoint, if it ever prevailed in Florida, was trampled long ago. In today's stampeding bureaucracies, "planning" too often means simply lining up rationale to support the prevailing political will. As another seasoned planner, Doug Kelly, bluntly puts it, "Planning in Florida is such a political process."

At this "do-over" hearing, the city relied on its consultant's testimony that the eagles had abandoned the "tennis court nest" near Thornby. (This was important because that nest's "protection zone" extended onto Thornby property.) According to the minutes, the crowd "erupted with their disagreement." The nearby condo manager said he'd seen the eagle flying from Thornby to Lake Monroe. Twenty-year Audubon eagle monitor Barbara Samler said she'd personally observed a nest on Thornby. Sandy Gallagher introduced evidence on identified Volusia County nests. The last feather — oops, straw — came when Attorney Alex Costopoulos, representing the condo association, showed photos of the "tennis court nest" complete with eaglets. After so much confusing testimony, Bob Nix, in view of 200 startled people, escorted the blonde-haired, mini-skirted consultant from the hearing room. It was Kevin Finn who declared that Nix "took her out behind the woodshed," a phrase that still brings grins of remembrance when we reminisce about that night. One thing was sure, Nix said: The city needed to find the eagle nest.

Nix told the board that the issues of wet soils and poor drainage had been "re-evaluated." In response, Mark Matzinger, with a solid construction background, showed a "Destruction Plan" of the environmental consequences that would result from the onsite work required to drain, fill and conquer the property's saturated soils. He "added fuel to the fire," pointing out that although a county report identified four wetland areas on the property, the city reported only one.

Lack of traffic numbers was the rationale given for stopping the August hearing. After that, the city hired a traffic consultant, who used words like "variables" and "estimate" to support her conclusion that — what? Commissioner Janet Deyette tried to determine if the existing roads were *already* "deficient." (In traffic jargon, "deficient" is a term linked to "levels of service," not to common sense.) Although her query brought audience cheers, the traffic guru happily attested that her "original" *estimate* of 6,439 daily trips to be generated by the Thornby plan had slid downward to a mere 2,986 daily trips. This is because the city would "now limit" the commercial part to 35,000 square feet. Keeping things loose, she reminded the board that 2,986 was only a "preliminary estimate" anyway. After Vice Chairman Dale Barberi joined Deyette in questioning the numbers game, Nix jumped in, informing them that city policy allowed extra traffic, anyway.

> **Activist Lesson:** It's always preferable to hire a traffic engineer to make sense of and/or dispute highly technical traffic testimony. You might encounter the "we are allowed to make a bad situation worse" scenario. That's where the rules allow more car "trips" to be added to already-clogged roads. In that case, a picture of backed-up traffic is worth 1,000 words.

During public comment, Roy Walters described for the Board the video he was not permitted to show them of the blocks-long, twice-a-day, traffic back-ups through Enterprise, from (mostly) Deltonans commuting to Interstate 4.

The minutes summary breezily recounts that a "few questions from the board" about matters like access and industrial use were "easily addressed" by Nix. He let them know that state law provided no protection for endangered or listed plants. That remark may have backfired when Grace Stamile of the Florida Native Plant Society produced color photos of some of the property's rarest plants. Patrick Stamile said, "This is not an urban corridor. This is a pristine piece of Old Florida that you should treasure and preserve."

Since the city's own report confirmed that Thornby was in an "archeologically sensitive area," Dale Barberi voiced concerns about the historical implications of the site. Nix responded that it was not a county-designated historical site, without mentioning that he'd once informed the city about Thornby's "history of local significance." Barberi kept hammering. He wanted to know about possible archeological resources that might be damaged during "clearing." He, too, was applauded. "We have processes in place to deal with that," Nix replied.

> **Activist Lesson:** Board members don't usually press for specifics when statements like this are made. That's where activists come in. Ask for details on what processes are in place, how they are triggered, and what happens afterward. Research the applicable procedures to verify what you are told and/or to fill in any gaps.

In my turn at bat, I produced three letters spanning 1996-2001 sent by the Director of Florida's Division of Historical Resources to the City of Deltona. Although each one related to a different comp plan amendment, their messages, highlighted in yellow for fast reading in limited time, were right on point for Thornby. They said that, since Deltona has never assessed its possible historic resources, unidentified archeological sites might exist. In one of the letters, the division called attention to this policy in the city's comprehensive plan:

> Prior to 2008, the City of Deltona shall adopt and implement measures to preserve and protect significant historical and archeological resources under public and private ownership.

But, *"This seems to be a long time to implement measures to protect significant cultural resources. At current development rates, there is the possibility that many significant sites could be destroyed by then,"* wrote the director in 1999, as if he was having a Thornby premonition. The letters were quoted in the *News Journal*'s report of the hearing.

> **Activist Lesson:** I didn't know the letters existed until a helpful state staffer mentioned them in general conversation about historic preservation, proving that luck can play a part in any activist cause, too.

I further told the board that state and county planners had explained to me that Thornby's current land use could stay as it was, unless the city wanted to increase its development potential. Therefore, the "we need to change the land use" argument was misleading. In response, Nix conceded, *"We do not have to change the land use at any particular time."* It was an important point, since board members might naturally feel pressured to recommend approval based on a false sense of urgency.

At the failed August hearing, Nix had slipped in a casual reference to "affordable housing credits" on the property that was now resurrected as a threat. He inferred that the plague of "affordable housing" was lurking just outside Deltona's limits, waiting to infect the Thornby property if they didn't back the project. Because the phrase "affordable housing" evokes strong images of run-down, crime-ridden dwellings, it can be a potent scare tactic. Nix announced authoritatively that a countywide density credit for affordable housing would result in between 160 and 175 affordable (government-subsidized for low-income persons) units on Thornby. Friends of Thornby didn't know any more than board members did about the rules for affordable housing (in other words, nothing). Taking Nix's words as fact, we realized we had to bone up on the subject before Thornby went to the city commission.

Mark Watts didn't say much, except to rehash "the property is surrounded by urban development." We were prepared for this. Ferd Reinlieb, with a 25-year background in land development, urged the board to think about what's best for the community. Suzanne Adair gave a briefing on the county's Lakeshore Drive Scenic Corridor (which Deltona simply did not acknowledge). Suzanne Steiner nearly brought down the house. "I'm confused," she said in a soft, puzzled voice, "when I hear that Thornby is 'surrounded by urban.'" She displayed poster-sized blow-ups: skinny Lakeshore Drive curving through moss-shrouded oaks; the Children's Home's historic red brick buildings dotting its 70-acre, tree-filled campus; one-lane Broadway Avenue dead-ending at glistening Lake Monroe. City highways like Deltona Boulevard and Saxon Boulevard are urban and Enterprise is urban, too? "I don't understand," she said, innocent as a lamb.

Thornby property on both sides of Lakeshore Drive

It was important to prove that there was a canal on the property for a couple of reasons. One, it showed that Friends of Thornby had our facts straight while the city did not. Two, a drainage canal, even if man-made, proves there is something to drain. It bolstered arguments that the property was both (a) wet and (b) an aquifer discharge area. I produced photos of the canal as well as of huge, healthy pine trees.

Referring to city staff comments about the "huge, dead pine trees," Dan Trimmer thundered: "I walked that property just the other day. Either city officials are lying or my eyes are lying. A false record has been created here."

Jack Hoyt took on the issue of state DCA review. Although the minutes summary doesn't reflect it, no doubt he mentioned his past service on the planning board. (He had served with four of the current members.) He informed them of the state's objections when the county attempted to change Thornby land uses in 2000 — objections that the city staff was now ignoring.

Kevin Finn noted the environmental "mess" that resulted when the 7-Eleven was built on swampy land next to Thornby. (See Chapter 7)

Approaching things from an economic standpoint, Rich Vail introduced statistics on vacant land in Deltona with both residential and commercial potential. He specifically referred to the city's "Activity Center," 900 areas of undeveloped commercial and industrial promise near Interstate 4.

While the county was knee-deep in drafting a plan to protect Enterprise, Deltona kept its head officially in the sand. Although a finished plan was still a long way off, the first part, consisting of goals, policies and objectives, was poised to become part of the county's comp plan. Since Deltona's planning board wouldn't learn about it from their city, Carol Aymar alerted them to the plan's first goal:

> Maintain the natural historical, cultural and scenic values associated with the Enterprise community within a framework which will allow for growth compatible with the *established development pattern and current land use policies.*
>
> **(Volusia County Comprehensive Plan, Ch. 1, Sec. F, ENT 1)**

Even in John Clapp's wildest dreams, multi-family wasn't part of Enterprise's "established development pattern." Therefore, apartments on Deltona's Thornby wouldn't fit with neighbor Enterprise land uses. A planner might say that adjacent land uses are *inconsistent* — a word that would one day play a starring role in Thornby's fate. However, that was far in the future.

Carol reminded the Board that Deltona's comp plan required it to cooperate with the county when planning for lands on its Enterprise border, as follows:

> The city of Deltona *shall* coordinate with adjacent local governments to ensure consistency in land planning for those lands adjacent to an unincorporated area or an adjacent city to reduce potential negative impacts of development.
>
> **(Deltona Comprehensive Plan, Sec. 7.3, Policy 1(d))**

> **Activist Lesson:** Describing local officials' reluctance to adhere to the provisions of comprehensive plans, Norm Erickson, former Vice Mayor of the City of DeBary, says "Comprehensive plans mandated by the state for cities to follow are ignored... even rules mandated and set forth in state statutes are not tolerated if they take precedence over the personal agendas of elected officials."

After thanking board members Barberi and Deyette for their support, Carol asked Nix whether the city commission would have access to the minutes from this meeting. Nix's response was that it "depended on how quickly his staff produced them."

Deltona residents Adele Saxe, Lily Higgins, Gisela Oeffen, Lee Perry, and Laura Hardesty implored their city's Planning Board to recommend denial of the plan. Enterprise residents Jane Trimmer and Steven Wiechert shared their objections. For 30 years, the Wiecherts had lived in the closest house to Thornby's western boundary. Sierra Club member Betty O'Laughlin from Lake Helen registered her opposition to the plan because it contravened the property's existing land uses.

In a way, it was a reunion. Former Deltona Vice Mayor Joe Perez was there, getting deserved credit for his memorable "Enterprise = all you can eat buffet" comparison, reminding the board why poor planning makes poor cities. And Carolyn Watson (now Langley), now living in Ormond Beach, came "home" with an emotional plea to spare the Thornby house and property that still meant so much to her. (After the hearing, she asked her old friend John Clapp how he could do this, knowing how much his mother, Catherine Clapp, had loved the property. She says he told her he needed the money for his children's inheritance.)

Bob Nix, off balance from the eagle fiasco, promised to get the answers he didn't have, and claimed that he "had not said anything in favor of this amendment."

Dale Barberi moved to recommend denial of the 12 residences-per-acre plan. Janet Deyette seconded the motion to deny, stressing that she wanted to be "good neighbors" with Enterprise. She was concerned about the nesting bald eagles, as well. Board member Q. L. Snook seemed confused. He first asked about a "compromise" to retain part of the property as a "historical section," but that wasn't the plan in front of them. Discussion. Snook next tried to abstain from voting. More discussion. Then he brought up a "compromise" where the owners "would get a small percentage." That idea hit the room like a tsunami. The back-and-forth was nerve-wracking and confusing. What was going on? Snook said he was voting against it. The crowd applauded, too soon. Barberi asked Snook if he voted "yes or no for the motion," and then Valle asked Snook if he "voted against the motion." Stomachs went into overdrive. "Mr. Snook said since he could not abstain he will vote 'no' and then quickly said 'yes' to the amendment," report the minutes. At this point, heads were bursting. Barberi explained the motion to Snook: "Yes is to deny and no to not deny." Snook said, "Whatever it's yes or no… I think there should be a compromise; if there can't be a compromise then I am against it." But they weren't done yet. The chair asked Snook for a "yes" or "no." Snook said "no." Further discussion "because Mr. Snook seemed unsure of what the yes or no meant." The chairman explained that "no" meant he was voting against the motion. The city attorney jumped into the snake pit, asking Snook if he was in favor or opposed to the application. We stopped breathing. "If I can't abstain or add a condition, then it should just be dead," he replied. Please, God. Then, mercifully, the city attorney asked simply, "Would your vote be to deny the application?" Just as simply, Snook answered, "yes." The room exploded. Board chair Rafael Valle joined with Barberi, Deyette and Snook in a 4-2 majority, defeating the application. Later, Valle said he was "swayed by the crowd and its passion."

"The audience applauded and made noises at the outcome of the vote," the minutes relate. The audience hugged, cried, did the happy dance, and hugged some more. The wrung-out chairman called a recess. Q. L. Snook, like Elvis, had left the building; Jan Deyette later explained that he had recently had surgery. After the hearing, thank-you notes from Friends of Thornby went to Barberi, Deyette, Valle and Snook.

As the board moved on to other business, Thornby supporters left the building, too, but it took a while for us to re-enter earth's orbit. When we did, we could re-live it. Sandy Gallagher remembers: "When I got home and turned on the TV, the news was starting, and there was Kevin and me."

In his long newspaper career, *Sentinel* columnist Bo Poertner witnessed his share of political battles. You'd expect him to be jaded, yet he was openly impressed with our achievement, calling it a, "powerful, passionate and successful display of community will." "Anyone who gives a tinker's dam about Florida's dwindling natural and historical resources had to be moved by the parade of speakers Wednesday night who argued against development of the historic Thornby property on Lake Monroe," he marveled.

In the days, months and years to come, there would be lots of Thornby decisions and hearings in many different settings. September 18, 2002 was a milestone. Before that night, Friends of Thornby was just a bunch of p-o'd people in someone's kitchen. In a system stacked against the public, we took on the second biggest city in the county, a powerful mayor and the county's premier land use attorney. Ferd Reinleib comments: "I believe we all thought that defeating the city was going to be an exercise in futility, but we decided to give it a try." Public testimony was "firm and loud," recalls Roy Walters. "We were going to go down fighting," vows Patrick Stamile, adding with a smile, "We were all so nervous!" Carol Aymar pointed out that "We sent a strong message." Kevin Finn glows with pride: "We crushed them!" It didn't matter that the P&Z was "only" advisory. We had proven that you needn't be a lawyer, planner, or consultant in order to deliver an important lesson in citizen engagement.

When the *News-Journal's* report, "Preservationists Win Round in Land-Use Battle" appeared, the mayor was quoted as saying he "wouldn't be surprised if the owners reconsider their request." Was he psychic or just savvy?

> *My intent is to find the right buyer for the whole property and not have it chopped up for houses.*
>
> **John Clapp,**
> quoted in the *Daytona Beach News-Journal*, February 11, 1998

CHAPTER TEN

Once It's Gone, It's Gone

Exploding opposition at the Deltona Planning Board kicked off a PR campaign from the Thornby heirs. In a September 29, 2002 guest editorial in the *Orlando Sentinel*, Lawyer Allen Watts accused "a community, by sheer force of numbers" of picking on his clients to "ease their own guilt" and implying that people expected Thornby to become a "donated natural museum." He drew seductive word pictures of a "public plaza, pier, green space, public promenade, pastry shop, ice cream shop, bicycle rental" on the lake, even as the city's own report said: "The actual property uses and building square footages that may be built on the property are unknown."

> **Activist Lesson:** Until a final development order is issued, almost everything is subject to change. Less-experienced board members should be made aware of this.

Such a diatribe couldn't go unanswered. In the *Sentinel*, Roy Walters rebutted the implication that we were fighting all development on the property, and punctured the inference that Volusia County would have approved industrial uses on Thornby after rejecting apartments there.

Watts' piece prompted a personal appeal from EPS Director Kevin Finn to John Clapp. In his letter, Kevin — a Deltona resident, as he informed Clapp — pointed out that no one expected anything to be "donated." Trust for Public Land was still very interested in Thornby, and Kevin entreated the owners to work with them on a sale at a fair price. He described the "very dedicated and organized group of citizens working day and night to see that the land is protected." He even mentioned the possibility of a Clapp family legacy through a museum if the Thornby house were restored. Clapp did not respond.

The Enterprise Plan: Closer to Reality

The Enterprise Preservation Plan was in final draft stage. DeBary was on board, but Deltona was squawking. The mayor said the plan was "one-sided." Memos gleaned from Deltona files show that city staff had an objection to nearly every sentence. The new planning manager, Gary Schindler, said that limiting commercial to those areas planned for it could result in urban sprawl. Bob Nix called the county's Enterprise survey "biased" and said he didn't feel that it met valid scientific criteria. Nix objected to the sequence of the questions and the size of the Enterprise boundaries. He protested the survey's use of the word "Enterprise." He suggested that commercial use along the north shore of Lake Monroe would be "in keeping with the community's history as a busy port in the 19th century." (Of course, in keeping with the 19th century, Deltona would not have existed).

Deltona's planning staff was given an opportunity to review the draft survey, but "really did not make any meaningful input," according to former county planner Ron Paradise. County planner Tom Brooks says, " my memory is that we held up the survey for a couple of weeks to give [Deltona] a little extra time before it was sent out," but "Deltona did not send their comments critical of the survey until after we had mailed it out and got the surveys back in." Nix claimed that Deltona "had no opportunity to participate in the survey" but did not pursue the charge. A few years later, though, the complaint resurfaced and this time, it was the main event in a city-county head-butt over Thornby.

Brooks remembers the survey process differently than Bob Nix did. The county sent the survey to Deltona for review, he says, but the city waited so long to submit its comments that the (state's) deadline couldn't have been met if those comments were included. Brooks points out, as well, "Survey preparers went out of their way to ensure that the results were fair by not including any criticism of Deltona." Planner Ron Paradise remembers Nix arguing with now-retired Volusia Director of Growth and Resource Management Montye Beamer over the survey's content. "It got testy," he says, "then we calmed them down and they agreed to disagree." About her meeting with Nix, Beamer recalls, "I'd have chewed on him a little more if I had the chance."

In November, Carol Aymar got an encouraging email from Deltona City Commissioner Michele McFall, who wrote: "Right now, I am on your side … I envision that area to be some sort of park, or area that would not greatly impact the area like condos or a strip mall would."

On December 10, 2002, the county's Planning and Land Development Review Commission (PLDRC) voted unanimously to recommend adoption of the Enterprise Local Area Plan's goals, objectives and policies into the county's comprehensive land use plan. Several EPS members attended the public hearing. It was holiday time, and Carol Aymar's December 15 guest editorial in the *Sentinel* set a yuletide tone:

> Our neighbor, the city of DeBary, has expressed unanimous support for this plan. Where does our other neighbor, the city of Deltona, stand?... The lights are off, the window shades are down, and there are no glowing embers in the fireplace. Deltona ... said "no" to the idea that Enterprise deserves any special protection... Enterprise needs four-lane roads, high-density subdivisions, and 7-Elevens, Deltona said.

She explained that:

> The Enterprise Local Area Plan is a citizen-driven initiative and powerful proof that when neighborhoods band together in one voice, government must step back and listen.

In Enterprise, 2003 started as a banner year on a wave of county good will. In March, the county council voted to add the Enterprise goals, objectives, and policies to the county's comprehensive plan (*Volusia County Comprehensive Plan, Ch. 1, FLUE*). The plan's fundamental goal was:

> To maintain the natural, historic, cultural and scenic values associated with the Enterprise Community within a framework which will allow for growth compatible with the established development pattern and current land use policies.

Although it was an encouraging step, it was just the first step. Three pages of feel-good generalities needed to be shaped into land development regulations that would protect Enterprise's low densities and natural resources. If it received state approval, the plan would be final the following year, county officials told us.

Yet another reason for Enterprise to be hopeful: the county hired TEI Engineers and Planners to structure a Lake Monroe Corridor Protection Plan — the initial stage toward winning state scenic corridor designation for Lakeshore Drive/Enterprise-Osteen Road. Project manager Sue Pederson-Stahl was well-qualified and kind, with a quiet demeanor.

Then, too, there was the "Bypass Road project." As Deltona's population had increased over the years, so had commuter traffic through Enterprise. Since at least 2001, Volusia County planned to return "downtown" Enterprise to its quiet roots by building a new road to relieve blocks-long driver backups to and from Interstate 4. Construction was slated to begin in 2003.

The Meaning of "Sweat Equity"

On May 17, 2003, the Enterprise Preservation Society happily joined the St. Johns River Alliance's first annual Riverfest celebration of history and culture along the St. Johns. It was a full Saturday of EPS-sponsored live music, Enterprise history displays, tours of All Saints Church (listed on the National Register of Historic Places), and a slide presentation of central Florida's past. The unquestioned highlight was the amazingly popular trolley tour of Enterprise's noteworthy buildings and fascinating spots. All day, hundreds of folks stood patiently in line, waiting their turn to hop aboard the little, open-air tram we had rented from the county. As it chugged through Enterprise, history-loving passengers hung on Kevin Finn's informative and fun narration of the Enterprise story, from Indians to the Brock House to the Children's Home to Thornby. By the end of the day, he was hoarse, exhausted, and, like the rest of us, jubilant.

Maybe it was last year's rebuff by Deltona's planning board, or possibly because of Kevin's letter to John Clapp. Whatever the reason, members of the Enterprise Preservation Society were ecstatic to learn in early 2003 that the owners had contracted to sell Thornby to Trust for Public Land (TPL) for $2.5 million. TPL would hold title as a stopgap while the society worked to secure grant funds from its funding arm, Florida Communities Trust (FCT), a state land acquisition program. The society would ultimately own and manage the property. Like a critical patient, Thornby was getting CPR — (call it "Community Purchase Resolve"). "We'll try to breathe in and out as we wait for your next phone call," Carol Aymar emailed TPL's Kevin Mooney, as final details were ironed out between Clapp and TPL.

To be eligible for a grant, EPS had a short time to prove "solvency" in the form of a $100,000 "bond." With the society's bank balance holding at around $5,000, Grace and Pat Stamile came to the rescue by offering an interest-free loan of $100,000, to be repaid from fund-raising efforts over three years.

Thornby's fate would hinge on earning a high score from FCT. The 18-page grant application called for a load of information, including a complete financial analysis of the organization and a detailed Thornby conceptual site plan. To help, TPL graciously lent EPS the services of Tallahassee-based grant writer Suzanne Woodcock. Hosted by the Aymars while in Enterprise, she spent several days trekking the property, meeting with board members and volunteers — and with Bob Nix — while reviewing maps and charts, inspecting photos and reading reports. She concurred that the Thornby house was a worthy candidate for restoration. Suzanne helped brainstorm individual ideas into the "Thornby Historical Park and Nature Reserve," a passive park focusing on open space and low-level, site-appropriate activities. The plan called for a restored Thornby house reborn as the "Thornby House Historical Museum" and community-gathering place. Amenities would follow, as funds were available. The spacious grounds would be accented by a small environmental learning space, an Old Florida garden, and a compact picnic area with a kids' play spot. (While everyone felt that the Doris Faber-model of nature-based play for kids was more fitting, Suzanne explained that including a small play area would boost our ranking.) A serene nature trail would wind through the heavily wooded property, linking the canal, Doris' duck pond, and the house. Along the lakeshore would be a raised walkway. Parking space and access roads would be adequate but minimally invasive.

The application required creation of a seven-year Thornby management plan. The community responded whole-heartedly. Nineteen local experts in such areas as historic restoration and wildlife helped to put the grant package together; those Good Samaritans volunteered to donate their time and talents, as well. Among them were Bonnie Cary, Volusia County naturalist; Chris Bowley, environmental planner; and John Harper, Volusia County Parks Director. Organizations like the West Volusia Historical Society wrote support letters. EPS Directors signed on to contribute their individual expertise to the undertaking; scores of residents pledged to donate their time and sweat toward restoring the historic home.

Brian Schieck was a young biologist who heard about Thornby shortly after moving to Deltona. He wanted to learn more. He recalls that when he turned up at the Aymars' kitchen table, "a lot of questions" were asked, "about how I heard about the meeting." He grins that there were "concerns that I might be a spy for the owner or developer." Fortunately for everyone, the grilling was short-lived, Brian's sense of humor stayed intact, and he became a valued Friend of Thornby. As required by one section of the FCT grant application, Brian and a couple of botanist friends walked the property with owner permission, documenting the flora and fauna — the first time such a project had been accomplished.

At the Enterprise Preservation Society's annual meeting on May 7, 2003, hundreds applauded as EPS directors presented a PowerPoint describing the grant process and the proposed plan to bring Thornby back under EPS ownership, as the heart of Enterprise, even though it was now legally in Deltona.

The final grant application, including 150 pages of supporting data, was completed, copied, assembled, indexed and tabbed in four binders, each stuffed nearly two inches thick. Suzanne Woodcock assured us that our submission would merit a high ranking. She said the property's imposing trees, wetlands, plant communities, and historical echoes combined to make it an exceptionally strong entry and virtually guaranteed that we'd receive funding.

On June 4, after nearly three months of community hard labor, the grant package was bundled off to Florida Communities Trust. When applications

Town meeting flyer

were rated in October, we'd know whether a community's dream would turn into reality. On June 6, TPL's Doug Hattaway told the *Sentinel*, "We have strong community support and have confidence that we could secure grant funding."

A Very Bad Time

Five days later the sale, and the dream, were DOA.

"I'm sure there's a developer or someone out there who will think the land is worth a lot more than that weak appraisal," said John Clapp, referring to the just-completed property appraisal that set its value at $2 million. At the 11th hour, he called off the sale. The *News-Journal* reported that the asking price was now nearly twice that amount. It was pure agony for all who had labored for months to perfect the grant application, but there was no choice: EPS had to unplug the grant process. Unmoored from potential funding, Thornby drifted further from the safe harbor of public ownership.

In shock, and calling it "a devastating blow," EPS tried to re-group. Aymar told the *News-Journal* she was bitterly disappointed. "We've worked so hard on this. It's not every day a community gets to preserve a magnificent piece of property. We won't give up." The reporter noted that, "Structurally, the house is sound, with only minor damage to interior walls and frame." Lani Friend assessed minimal defects "that Bob Vila could fix in a weekend." Floors and stairs were intact. Aymar told the *Sentinel* that the most serious problems were rain damage and vandalism. She said the society would ask permission to board up the house or put a tarp on it. Clapp refused. "I don't want those people on my property," he said.

Kevin Finn opined, "We're extremely lucky that some idiot hasn't thrown a lit cigarette butt and torched the whole thing." John Clapp told the reporter. "We're going to do whatever we can do to sell the property."

"A" for Effort

"We came with an 'olive branch," Carol Aymar wrote to Bob Nix, but "we are miles and miles apart." She and Mark Matzinger had hoped at least to open a dialogue with Deltona about the Enterprise Local Area Plan, now approved by the Florida Department of Community Affairs. "The whole [Enterprise Plan] process shows the power of the people to effect change," says planner Doug Kelly. Unfortunately, the September 2003 meeting between Enterprise and Deltona changed nothing. Nix called the Plan "very flawed" and "completely unrealistic." He was intractable in his support for condos on Thornby. Furthermore, he informed them, he didn't see "how Deltona will have a significant impact on Enterprise borders." "We regret that we could not achieve *any* common ground with the city," Carol's letter concluded. Instead of building a bridge, they had hit a wall.

Grief and Sorrow

On an ordinary, football-watching night on a sweltering September Sunday, the Thornby house that would have required a county permit to destroy was burned to the ground.

That evening, the flames rose — high enough to be seen from the lake's far shore. "When the Thornby house burned, I got a call, and I was on the second floor in my office overlooking Lake Monroe. I looked at the boat dock at the water's edge, and beyond that, I saw the flames of the burning house rising above the treed horizon." — Carol Aymar.

The flames didn't just destroy a piece of local history. They also incinerated one of the most compelling arguments for preservation. When daylight came, four questions smoldered in the ashes. Reporters asked the first question on everyone's mind: Was there insurance? The answer was unclear. The second question was: how did it happen? Fire investigators found evidence of gasoline spread in the upstairs bedroom where Dr. and Mrs. Glass used to sleep. The third question: Who did it? was resolved within days. Afterward, only the fourth question remained: why?

Out of the Ashes, Townhouses

To the hard workers, gutsy activists, friendly neighbors and statewide partners trying to preserve Thornby, losing the house was a knockout punch. A house, like the people who lived in it, can "die," bringing numbness as cold as stone, and regret as sharp as broken glass. When the death was deliberate, it's even more devastating. At Thornby, a once-stately reminder of bygone lives was

Thornby house, September 15, 2003

now a tangled heap of scorched rubbish. Scores of people had invested years, hearts, souls and dollars to save what they left us, so that someday everyone could say, "this place belongs to me." Moreover, since the irreplaceable home was the natural centerpiece of any future park or historical project, attracting purchase money would be doubly hard — even if we had a willing seller. On the grief-stricken morning after the fire, we had nothing.

Nothing, that is, except fervent determination and shreds of hope. The *News-Journal* quoted me as EPS Director, a few days after the fire: "For us, this is not the end. We still want to save the property." We still had Trust for Public Land as a willing partner. Although the owners' "expectation of value exceeded the present market value of the property..." wrote TPL's Kevin Mooney one month after the fire, "... we will do everything we can to revisit our participation... so that the legacy — and the memory — of the estate would be preserved for future generations."

From his home in New Jersey, John Clapp commiserated. He was sorry for the loss of the house, too, he said. He spent many happy childhood winters and springs there, he reminded the *News-Journal*. Nevertheless, he was moving forward with development plans, "probably some type of townhome project."

Three for the Road

The Deltona Fire and Rescue Department's multi-page report analyzed both the technical and human aspects of the arson. One category listed 26 "Suspected Motivation Factors." In that box, the fire marshal checked: "Thrills." Quick investigative work by the department and the Volusia County Sheriff, combined with a couple of Crime Stoppers tips and a $1,000 reward, nearly brought justice. On September 17, officials arrested three Deltona residents — Michael Higbee, Holly May Burman and a 17-year-old juvenile — charging them with felony arson. The arrests were satisfying, but nothing could bring back the 85-year old Thornby house. "We considered Thornby the centerpiece... of our community," Carol Aymar told Mike Lafferty of the *Sentinel*. She continued, "The historical significance for Volusia County is extremely important, and now it's gone."

Deltona Fire Marshal Chris Nabicht's narrative report untangled the circumstances that culminated in three aimless locals, on one of many nights spent hanging out on the Thornby property, driving, ironically, to the "7-Eleven In a Hole" to buy the gasoline that cremated what to them was nothing more than a useless wreck.

Standing next to Thornby's ruins with *Sentinel* columnist Lafferty a week after the fire, Aymar told him that "she and a corps of dedicated preservationists" would redouble their fight to save the 40-acre site and its treasures, though the vault of a community's memories and promises was now just an empty, cinder-covered spot ringed by trees. Lafferty was no Pollyanna. While they talked, he literally heard "from a distant construction site" the sound of hammers. To him, it was a metaphor for the grim reality of Florida's ceaseless extermination of "trees, critters and fragments of partially buried history."

"How could Mayor John Masiarczyk, who runs a Deltona history and cultural center from a 1960s-era home, justify failing to protect the oldest structure in his city?" Lafferty asked his readers. "When Deltona annexed the property… it agreed to assume not only legal jurisdiction but also moral responsibility," he scolded. Acknowledging the community's continued optimism in the face of heartbreaking loss, he wished them luck in a tone that was anything but hopeful. The "impossibly large" trees, the keyhole pool, the old trail and the potential fort site all still merited preservation, but he noted, "Politically speaking, trees are much easier to remove than are historic homes."

Tangled Up In the Justice System

Since 2000, members of EPS and Friends of Thornby had been learning about Florida's land use system by "on-the-job-training," never imagining we would be shoved into the world of criminal law, too. We found ourselves strangers in one more unfamiliar universe, this one populated by pleas, sentencing and criminal lawyers.

When interviewed by Fire Marshal Nabicht and State Fire Marshal Detective Greg Kunkle the day after the fire, Burman admitted her involvement. Higbee requested a lawyer. His green Honda, used to transport the gas to burn Thornby, was impounded. His left arm, singed by the flames, healed.

Both were jailed and released after they posted bond. The juvenile denied involvement, but when his story didn't ring true, he, too, was arrested. Bit by bit, the miserable story came out. "They went out and ended up going to the house and just decided to burn the place," Deltona Deputy Fire Chief Robert Rogers said. The 17-year-old juvenile was "upset" because his girlfriend broke up with him. Some pre-burn vandalism, a gallon of gas and a lighter were all it took to "lose something so precious over nothing," as I told the *News-Journal*. Seven years later, I chanced to meet Lt. Mike Maples, one of the firefighters on the scene that night. "We couldn't save the old house," he told me, shaking his head. "All we could do was keep the fire from spreading through the woods."

All three defendants pled innocent to second-degree arson. The challenge was to convince the prosecuting attorneys that this wasn't just "routine" arson. Notoriously overworked and underpaid, their days were filled with murderers, child abusers, violence and victims. They had never heard of Thornby. To them, an old, vacant house was torched. Nobody got hurt. Two of the defendants were first offenders. The property owners wanted nothing but restitution for demolition costs. In criminal parlance, it spelled "slap on the wrist."

I tried to meet with the assistant state attorneys, but they were busy. EPS and Friends of Thornby wrote to the assigned judges and attorneys, enclosing newspaper clippings and documents from our years of preservation struggles, to show that "the people of Enterprise have been irreparably and permanently harmed by the wanton and vicious acts of these defendants in destroying the structure that came to symbolize our community and its restoration efforts." The documents explained the arduous grant process we had gone through, the Stamile's $100,000 loan offer, and how hundreds of residents had come together in support of this cause in the past three years. We asked for the maximum sentences, and that any community service imposed would be performed in Enterprise.

Paula and Tom Lewis; Kevin Finn; Chuck Blystone; Autumn Justice; Pat Stamile; and Michael Sack were among many who contacted the Court. "… Please don't take this lightly…" urged Paula. "Actions like this express contempt for the community we live in." Autumn Justice wrote, "Besides destroying a piece of property, these arsonists destroyed a central part of the Enterprise community's heritage."

In the weeks following the crime Jill Fitzgerald, the attorney prosecuting the juvenile, was helpful and understanding of what the destruction of the Thornby house meant to the community. Her efforts were a major factor in the strong sentence meted out by Judge Hubert Grimes, a pleasant but nononsense man. At the juvenile's October trial, I was allowed to testify to the historical and future damage to Enterprise caused when the house went up in smoke. He pled guilty to second-degree arson and was sentenced to 18-36 months in a maximum risk commitment center for juveniles. Upon release, he was to serve 1,000 hours of community service in Enterprise. (Painfully, newspapers reported it would be served "in Deltona.")

All lawyers weren't on the same page, though. Higbee and Burman pled not guilty. Assistant state attorney Colleen Taylor indicated that a plea agreement might be in the works and, furthermore, an Enterprise representative wouldn't be permitted to testify when their sentences were imposed. The possibility that the adults might get off with a more lenient sentence than the juvenile's was infuriating. We sought help from county councilman Bill Long, a former law enforcement officer and a friend of state attorney John Tanner. Long was kind enough to contact Tanner and stress that the Enterprise community was looking for strong prosecution of both adult defendants. Deltona City Commissioner Diane Obremski went to bat for us, too.

In February 2004, arson ringleader Michael Higbee, 21, changed his plea to guilty and hired a local criminal attorney to keep him out of jail. Our efforts paid off: Paula and I were allowed to testify at his sentencing. We depicted for Judge James Foxman the three-year community effort to save the property.

We testified that we still hoped to turn it into a solid asset to the area, but that obtaining grant funding would be infinitely more difficult without the house. With a demeanor that shifted between outrage and disdain, Higbee's lawyer argued that his client torched an old, empty house. There were no injuries. Jail time would be cruel and excessive, he complained, but Judge Foxman wasn't swayed by his lawyerly grandstanding. Paula recalls: "I liked the Judge; he seemed to take to heart what we were saying. It gave him a different view to hear how much Thornby meant to us." Higbee was sentenced to a year in jail followed by five years' probation, 300 hours of community service, payment of restitution and costs, and ordered to write letters of apology.

On May 5, 2004, Holly Burman came before Judge Foxman. She was a slightly built, worn-looking girl who worked as a cashier at Kmart. Like Higbee, she'd dropped out of high school. She testified that Higbee and the juvenile picked her up from work that Sunday night and they all rode to the "haunted house." The males did the burning while she acted as lookout. Her parents described a daughter who had made a one-time mistake, a portrayal slightly marred by the fact that, a few weeks after the fire, she was arrested for shoplifting at Bealls in Orange City. Judge Foxman, silver-haired and distinguished, made no bones about the fact that at 18, Holly Burman was on the fast track to ruin unless she turned her life around, pronto. She shed copious tears and agreed. Sparing her a jail stay, the judge placed her on community control for two years, followed by two years' probation and 100 hours of community service with the Enterprise Preservation Society.

The post-conviction worlds of Higbee and Burman featured more antisocial acts; over the next few years, both were charged with probation violations and other offenses.

Give the People What They Want

Sixty-one days after the oldest structure in Deltona was consumed by fire, John Clapp, described as being "… consistently closemouthed about his plans," opened up. His plans were for townhouses — 227 of them, he told the *News-Journal*. "We've been talking to a lot of people down there," he said in a phone interview from New Jersey, "This seems to be what they want." The same article reported that the project's architect would be meeting with the community. "We want to know exactly what our opposition will be on this," said Mark Watts. After two off-the-mark planning board hearings, he aimed for no more missteps.

Silence is Golden

I met Holly Burman on a Saturday, months after the fire. She was in Enterprise because a judge ordered her to be there. She was part of the EPS Adopt-a-Road crew working on Lakeshore Drive, already sweating under the hot morning sun. She wasn't belligerent or hostile. She was just quiet. As we pulled fast-food wrappers from bushes and retrieved beer bottles tossed from car windows, I looked her in the eye, sounding like an actress in a 1930s gangster movie. "Holly," I asked her, "Will you tell me what happened the night of the fire? Why did Michael burn the house down? If you tell me, I swear I'll do whatever I can to convince the judge to lighten your sentence. Please tell me how it really came down." Under the blue sky, Holly Burman lowered her head and stared at her dusty sandals. I waited, but a silent teardrop was her only reply.

The Enterprise Historic District

If 2003 was Thornby's watershed year, 2004 started at rock bottom. Although the *News-Journal* editorialized that the Thornby disaster "must be a reminder to elected officials that they, more than anyone, can determine whether an area's heritage is preserved or lost," the only reminder on Deltona officials' radar screens was that Thornby would be back to the planning board. "It really was like killing Dracula. It just wouldn't stay dead!" says Bob Sayre in exasperation.

In the fire's aftermath, some things remained uncharred. In February 2004, the county brought in GAI Consultants, Inc., a national firm with offices in Orlando, to work with county planners Ben Dyer and Ron Paradise to create an Enterprise Historic District as part of the Enterprise Plan. With nearly 20 years' planning experience, GAI's Doug Kelly was project manager. Like the Lakeshore Drive Scenic Corridor consultant, Sue Pederson-Stahl, Doug was an instant kindred spirit — knowledgeable, professional and simpatico with Enterprise's core values — a pleasure to work with, always willing to go above and beyond. Doug and Sue were more than consultants; they became Enterprise's cohorts, as well. When his company was hired, says Doug, "It was conveyed that the Enterprise Preservation Society was a friend of the county, and GAI should make sure we had a good ear toward them. The county's mantra was: the squeaky wheel gets the grease," he chuckles. Enterprise was now a very loud squeaker.

Doug and colleagues Dennis Smeltz and David Dunne got to work, collaborating with community volunteers to identify and analyze 28 historic Enterprise structures. Volunteers included Carol Aymar, Debra Blanchard, Kevin Finn, Lani Friend, Mark Matzinger, Riley Nutt, Gisela Oeffen, Susan Reed, Ferd Reinlieb, Bob Sayre, Marvin Titus, Jeanie Wilby and me.

As Jeanie says, "I remember Doug Kelly searching for what makes Enterprise unique and how to keep the rural integrity of the area." In the spring of 2004, GAI held a workshop in Enterprise to focus on consensus-building for rural policies. More than 80 participants identified key issues, such as protecting the views of Lake Monroe and maintaining rural community character, and then brainstormed ways to translate their vision into reality.

The Little White Schoolhouse

"When one door closes, another one usually opens," Mark Matzinger philosophized in the *Sentinel*. In Enterprise, that door opened into a historic school building.

Soon after flames consumed the Thornby house, the Volusia County School Board made the Enterprise Preservation Society an offer it didn't want to refuse — the 1936-era, two-story Enterprise Elementary School building. No longer used for classes, "We knew that we couldn't tear it down because of its historic value, but its location within the school campus combined with [other factors] created a very expensive dilemma," says Saralee Morrissey, then Director of Facilities Services for the Volusia County School Board. Although EPS and the school board had been exploring the building's possibilities for some time, after the Thornby house was destroyed, the notion of a historic schoolhouse museum rising like a phoenix from its ashes won instant acclaim from EPS, community members and the papers. In his column about the project, the *Sentinel*'s Mike Lafferty called EPS "a very dedicated group of people determined to save what is left of the historic community."

In March 2004, the school board generously transferred title to "Building 8" to the Enterprise Preservation Society. "Saving the schoolhouse ended up being a win-win for both the community and school district," Morrissey remarked, explaining that the school district was able to assist in the relocation of the building and then proceed with much-needed improvements at the current school campus.

Ahead lay years of more (and harder) work than anyone envisioned — fund-raising, grant applications, more fund-raising, moving the building, and more fund-raising. Through it all, pride of ownership, combined with dreams of a future community-centered museum and meeting space, re-created period classroom, research/archive facility, and an EPS office kept the community's sunken spirits lifted, all the while the future of the Thornby property was hanging by a political thread.

I've been working on this since 1978; do you think I'm going to give up now?

John Clapp
quoted in the *Daytona Beach News-Journal*, October 23, 2004

CHAPTER ELEVEN

This Is No Time to Make New Enemies

In October 2003, Deltona Planning Director Bob Nix gave the city P&Z Board the word: A development plan for Thornby is coming back. The bad news was that Bruce Andersen was along for the ride. The good news? Bruce Andersen was along for the ride. Andersen, a licensed architect and Florida Real Estate Broker, had been working for the Thornby heirs.

In November, Deltona added the "Enterprise Overlay District" to its comprehensive plan, officially acknowledging, "Enterprise has recognized historical significance." While the sentiments were appreciated, the "Overlay District" was nothing more than design and architectural guidelines for whatever would be built on Thornby.

Two months and one day after the house was burned, J. Frank Knight, on behalf of Thornby Partnership, presented the city with a complete traffic study and other documents in support of their application to cover most of Thornby with a "PUD" (Planned Unit Development). The commercial "gem" on Lakeshore Drive that caused such uproar was gone. In its place was a plan for more than 200 townhouses sandwiched side-by-side like Lego blocks, their 20-foot strips of front lawns edging three new roads that would circle the property. The Thornby home site would become a swimming pool. Leftover wetlands — those that had not been filled — would now be retention ponds, lending "waterfront" distinction to some units.

In a December 2003 letter, Andersen addressed county concerns about potential historic and archeological sites on Thornby: Don't worry, he soothed the county's historic preservation officer: if bulldozers dig up anything important, "there is still even more time and review before we get to the final plat and engineering."

> **Activist Lesson:** A stark example of "this is just the first step," a gambit to quiet the concerns of officials who feel uneasy about voting for approval.

To diffuse the opposition buzzing like irate wasps, members of Thornby's development team needed community buy-in. They offered a friendly public meeting. At Enterprise's Indian Mound fire station, residents would get their first glimpse of the brand new, bouncing baby development plan. It was nicknamed "Thornby Oaks" but its full name was "Thornby Oaks, a Planned Residential Community *in Enterprise, Florida.*" The brochure/birth announcement featured a photo of Lakeshore Drive, imaginatively re-named "Lake Shore Drive Natural Preserve."

Bruce Andersen was prepared for the happy event. His easel was fresh, his color drawings were lovely, and his answers were primed to explain and diffuse all of the crowd's questions, concerns and objections. There was just one problem. Friends of Thornby had no intension of giving our case away. Grace Stamile recalls gleefully, "We had all agreed before not to say anything; we had talked before he got there. We were poker faced," she says chuckling, as "they told how people will walk everywhere, it would be low impact, with no kids." Kevin Finn elaborates. "This is typical. They want to iron out all your arguments before they get to the city commission."

> **Activist Lesson:** Developer-requested "community meetings" are a potential minefield. In the guise of "listening," such meetings allow the opposition to discover and prepare for the public's objections early in the game. Don't give your case away; save your arguments for the decision-makers.

THE STORY OF THORNBY • *CHAPTER ELEVEN* 189

Volusia County wetlands map of Thornby property

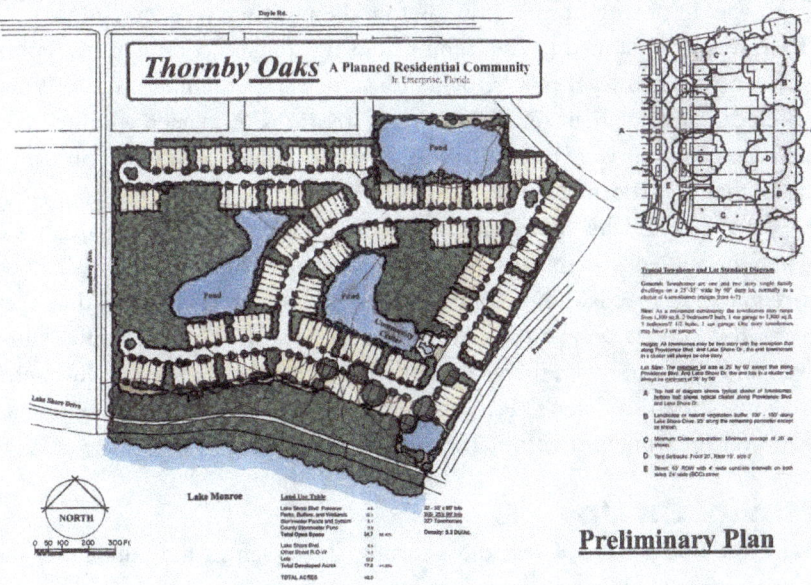

Thornby Oaks plan

Thornby Oaks conceptual drawing

View of Typical Homes

At that point, it was tough to be stoic. Merriment swept the room at Andersen's drawing of a bicycle-riding child pedaling happily through the streets of Thornby Oaks. The warm and fuzzy scene would have been more convincing it if he hadn't already told us that his grand community would cater to seniors. (He must have intended to deaden fears of traffic congestion, but got carried away as he described elderly residents loaded with grocery bags, walking home from Publix.) Before the meeting, we'd learned that the Thornby team planned to use "senior housing" to gain community support, so we researched legal requirements for age-restricted communities. When specifically asked about senior housing restrictions, Andersen admitted that no such restraints were planned, sending the "over 55" snow job up in flames faster than the Thornby house.

For the rest of his presentation, Grace says the architect "was in shock" when the audience simply listened politely, as mildly interested as visitors on a required science lab tour. Andersen and Watts seemed perplexed as they pressed the crowd: "Any questions? No questions at all?" In our folding chairs, we looked at each other, then back at them. "Gee, I don't have any questions, do you?" "No, I sure don't." Perhaps they thought their listeners were tongue-tied over the wonderfulness of Thornby Oaks.

Movin' On Up

With the house torched and the Thornby Oaks plan in the public eye, the battlefront shifted. For five years, the skirmish had been small, local and relatively insular, but that was about to change. It looked like Thornby was finally going before the city commission.

As the papers kept Thornby in the news, it was crystal clear that not everyone recognized why its land use should not be altered. A small but aggressive group of Deltona residents (seemingly philosophically aligned with the Flat Earth Society) formed in cyberspace, their *raison d'État* epitomized by a posting on March 30, 2004: "Why should anyone listen to the Enterprise people? They don't live here they don't pay taxes here." (sic)

Larry French was a long-time Deltona resident, Civil War buff, naturalist and senior science textbook editor. A city commission vote to sell off parkland where their daughters had played (it became a CVS pharmacy) didn't sit well with Larry and his wife, Robin. Much like with Sandy Gallagher, a local land issue lured him away from the sidelines and into the game. When he learned about Thornby, he investigated the property and concluded that, "Just like Dupont Lakes [the former park now partly commercial], none of the intrinsic values and sense of place that this unique piece of land had, was being told." Larry became a regular blogger, always with a calm, logical voice. "Why can't we (city) change the direction this thing is going in, and work with the EPS in getting the additional money?" he queried Commissioner Doug Horn.

Motivated by the chance to provide Deltona residents with information they weren't getting, I joined in the blogs. I believed that, once people understood the property's history, attributes and potential, they would value what Thornby could mean to their city. Nevertheless, month after month, the Thornby online threads thickened, swollen with innuendoes, misstatements and fear.

More than ever, Friends of Thornby needed allies in the struggle. No idea was too far-fetched, no contact too remote. Anything might lead to a way to enlarge the groundswell to save Thornby from Death by Density. To that end, I contacted the Seminole Indians (possible Native American graves on Thornby); the Florida Department of Environmental Protection and the Army Corps of Engineers (wetlands regulations); the Nature Conservancy (property too small for their programs); 1000 Friends of Florida (same); local archeologists; and two authors of books about the Seminole Wars (Fort Kingsbury). I researched past commission minutes to find Deltona residents who might support Friends of Thornby (how I met Larry French). In the days before unlimited calling plans, my cell phone bill for one month was $500. Others also reached out to anyone who could lead us to grassroots salvation — e-mailing questions, calling experts, networking, fact-finding, attending meetings, gathering information and forging in-person contacts with government officials, staff members, groups and individuals who "got it" on Thornby. As before, flyers were distributed on windshields at the formerly-wetlands shopping center and posted at the nearby condo mailboxes. The efforts were Herculean; the results, priceless.

This flyer (even with spelling error) gives hearing details and contact options

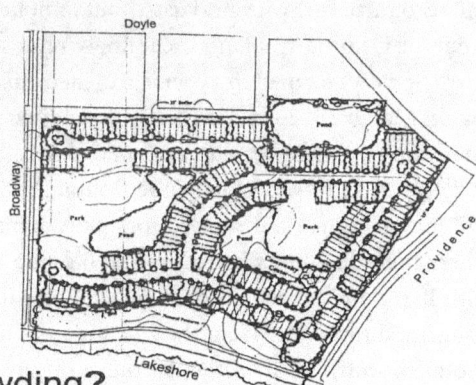

THORNBY OWNERS TRY AGAIN

DO **YOU** WANT:

* More school crowding?
* 227 townhouses on Thornby property?
* City traffic on scenic roads?
* 200+ yr. old oaks destroyed?
* Wetlands turned into retention ponds?
* Our water supply pollutted?
* A gated, high-density community in the heart of historic Enterprise?

ATTEND: Public Hearing at City Hall
Wednesday Feb.18, 7:00 pm
2345 Providence Blvd.

Call: Mayor Masiarczyk or Bob Nix (386) 561-2100
email: jmasiarczyk@ci.deltona.fl.us

Through local archeology experts, I connected with David Butler, a Registered Professional Archeologist who taught at the University of Central Florida. Although David and I never met, in a letter to the planning board he expressed his ardent hope that an archeological assessment would be performed. "There is a possibility … that the remains of Fort Kingsbury (a Second Seminole War fort) are within the confines of this parcel," he wrote.

The Volusia County Historic Preservation Board voted unanimously to "strongly encourage" that soil samplings be taken for unidentified archeological deposits, as outlined in a letter from board chair Bruce Piatek to Bob Nix. Without authority over city property, the county board could do no more.

Biologist Brian Schieck's field report of Thornby flora and fauna, originally prepared for the ill-fated EPS grant application, was presented to the city's planning board in affidavit form.

Riverkeeper is a nationwide organization dedicated to preserving rivers and their watersheds. In February 2004, the St. Johns Riverkeeper, Neil Armingeon from Jacksonville, met me at Thornby to see for himself the unquestioned environmental impacts of such a drastic land use change. Neil's letter to the planning board outlined why "this land type is hardly conducive to a high-density development such as the one being proposed." The reasons included habitat destruction; preponderance of wet soils; polluted runoff into Lake Monroe and adjacent posted wetlands of concern.

Volusia County Forester Joe Waller notified Deltona that he "could not support approval of the conceptual plan" until the issues of wetlands, drainage, buffers, historic trees and eagles were addressed. Moreover, he reminded the city that Thornby is within the county's Natural Resource Management Area overlay, which carries special restrictions; therefore, the project needed to be "modified accordingly."

University of Florida expert David Griffis, who had analyzed Thornby soils for the county five years before, was asked by the city to re-analyze them. His report said that soils in wetland areas had potential for flooding, standing water, low soil strength and excessive wetness.

Deltona resident Jane Rogers criticized the proposed plan in a three-page letter to her city officials. She pointed out its incompatibility with "our neighboring community, Enterprise" and urged them to "protect the citizens of Deltona from environmentally destructive, costly, inappropriately dense development."

Another major issue was school capacity. At this writing, overcrowded schools seem a distant memory. For years, however, Florida had more students per school than any other state, and Volusia was no exception to intense overcrowding. Saralee Morrissey, by then Director of Site Acquisition and Intergovernmental Coordination for the Volusia County School Board, worked with local governments on development issues. She supplied us with statistics establishing that the three schools to which Thornby would send students were already 29 percent to 62 percent over capacity.

Buoyed by expanding local and regional support and riding a wave of expert opinion, yet chilled to the bone by relentless efforts to produce a high-density tsunami, Thornby supporters headed to city hall for the third time.

Seventh Thornby Hearing: Deltona Planning and Zoning Board

The planning board had changed a bit since 2002. Rafael Valle was still chairman, with Jan Deyette as vice-chair. Dale Barberi was gone, as was Q. L. Snook. Of three new names, one was familiar to us: Sandy Gallagher. "I applied for appointment to the planning and zoning board in 2003 because of my concern with the eagles near or on the Thornby property. If appointed, I could have a say when it came to endangered species on properties that the city might annex or develop," explains the no-longer-shy Ms. Gallagher.

If planning board hearings had a theme, then the September 2002 theme would have been "Happy Days." The theme of the February 18, 2004 hearing, however, might have been "Leave it to Bruce."

The Thornby owners' expert, Bruce Andersen, implied that Deltona was attempting to save the property from a fate worse than death — keeping the county's land use category on what was now city land.[1] Lawyer Mark Watts buzzed that when the county council turned down Thornby apartments in 2000, "a suggestion was made that perhaps the property would be best suited in Deltona and could be reviewed by the city of Deltona." (No one interviewed for this book who was present at the county hearing remembers such a suggestion, nor do the minutes reflect that such a suggestion was made.)

The staff report stated that at the planning board hearing in September 2002, there was a "recommendation to the commission that a residential low density would be more appropriate." (In other words, since commercial was now off the table, maybe a six-fold residential increase wouldn't be so bad.)

Andersen spoke for half an hour. He presented a PowerPoint on Thornby Oaks and gushed that Deltona is now "ready for this kind of luxury development" (though his brochure labeled it as being in *Enterprise*). We promise to save six acres of trees! We *want to* be compatible with the neighbors! We will leave about 55 percent open space! (City regulations required 60 percent). We'll preserve the interior wetlands! (as retention ponds, but he didn't say that). We'll do what has the least negative impact on the community! Acknowledging that Deltona had a school overcrowding problem, he labeled the plan an "adult community" (the strategy that flopped at the Enterprise community meeting), then made a U-turn, telling board member Wesley Kihlmire that the development was not an adult community, but it would be "upscale and children would not live there." Although new to the board, Kihlmire wasn't naïve. He correctly challenged Andersen that, by law, children can't be excluded unless it's an official over-55 community.

Sandy Gallagher's homegrown example of construction on filled wetlands and wet soils was the notorious "7-Eleven in a Hole." When she confronted

---

1 Had the city chosen this option, the NRMA designation would have remained on the property.

Andersen with technical details, he tried to dismiss her input. The soil and hydrology won't be changed, he said, blinking. Sandy, who worked in the construction field, shot back: "You're going to take out a lot of the natural vegetation on that site." Andersen's response (omitted from the transcribed minutes) was: "You're correct. Where the townhomes and streets will be built is going to be altered. It won't look like the way it does today." Meanwhile, city planner Carol Bowden maintained that the land use change was simply a "map notation" to "complete the annexation process."

> **Activist Lesson:** Beware of the staff when they are on a mission defined by superiors.

Kihlmire and Gallagher weren't the only wide-awake board members. Janet Deyette questioned how high density on Thornby would fit with the Enterprise Historic Overlay and the Lake Monroe Scenic Corridor. With so much technical help from the board, it may have seemed that Friends of Thornby could just pack up and go home, but things could never be that easy. The city's staff report was recommending approval. More than 20 people spoke, and every one of them opposed the plan.

Before testimony began, a legal kink had the potential to stop the hearing before it started. We had agreed that Riley Nutt would speak first about hearing notices posted on Thornby that didn't follow city code. Riley presented photos and diagrams that indicated discrepancies in the number of posted signs and the required distances between them. Watts retorted that he, Frank Knight and Bruce Andersen had placed the signs. City attorney Roland Blossom said it wasn't an issue the board could resolve. (Later, Blossom was taken to task by another resident, who complained that his office had given her erroneous information about the nature of the hearing). The hearing continued, with the public providing straightforward, fact-based testimony.

Professionals reinforced the arguments we "civilians" had been making for years. GAI's Doug Kelly showed an aerial photo of Enterprise boundaries. He explained the county's ongoing work to establish a rural protection overlay to maintain its rural character.

Sue Pederson-Stahl of TEI reported on the Lake Monroe Corridor Management Plan, slated for county approval. One of its goals, she told the board, was to negotiate a county-city planning agreement for Lakeshore Drive. Sue's presentation led to a courtroom-style "cross examination" by Lawyer Allen Watts. Demure and self-effacing by nature, Sue was caught unaware. She tried gamely to defend her facts against Watts' prodding, while board members watched in silence. The audience soon rose to her defense: "Sue, you don't have to justify your opinions to him." "He's out of line." "This is not a trial!" Shaken, she finally sat down, probably wishing she had never heard of any of us.

Planner Todd Peetz was the first expert hired by the Friends of Thornby. Because Todd had been a primary consultant on Deltona's original comprehensive plan, Doug Kelly referred him to us. Todd testified that, when he had worked with Bob Nix on the comp plan, "the idea was that new development adjacent to the Enterprise area would be consistent with Deltona's Enterprise Overlay District." The high-density plan in front of you turns the equation on its head by making Thornby's density like Deltona's, instead of the other way around, he pointed out. It's "the wrong message to send" when your comp plan says you want to be compatible with Enterprise.

To know why traffic was a major issue, imagine a development of 650 people which had only one driveway onto a two-lane road that ended at a narrow, policy-constrained (i.e., it could not be widened), two-lane road along a lake with a 30 mph speed limit. Bob Sayre had the bases covered, using startling statistics from a county traffic study of speeding drivers on Enterprise roads, "primarily Deltona drivers trying to get to work." Later, he affirmed that he had studied the records "so I knew what I was talking about." "As far as I know the numbers were all correct," he says. "Traffic counts are kind of hard to dispute." Numbers or not, the city was still using the "phantom" future four-laning of Providence Boulevard (see Chapter 6) in attempting to justify 250 townhouses. As further rationalization, city traffic consultants, in deciding there would be no real traffic problems from such a colossal density increase, admitted that their conclusion was based, at least in part, on the "bypass road" being finished on schedule.

We were on track and well prepared, even though Sierra's Betty O'Laughlin, who felt fine earlier, began having flu-like symptoms that rapidly worsened. She left her seat, half-collapsing into a chair near the door. Several people, including Deltona Commissioner Diane Obremski, who was in the audience, offered her a ride home. "No, thanks," said Betty. "As long as I can still get to the front of the room, I'll stay and put Sierra's words on the record."

My husband, Roy Walters, a Florida Registered Professional Engineer, followed up on board member Kihlmire's concerns about the supposed senior community. "Unless the project is registered as an 'over 55 community' with the state, the developer would be breaking the law by refusing to sell to anyone who wanted to buy, and that includes any age and number of children," he said. He called the city's "industrial use would be okay on Thornby under county rules" argument a "total mischaracterization."

Marvin Titus called on board members not to approve the plan. As a former developer, he knew that higher density translates into higher profits for the developer, but he also knew that it was not "in keeping with the rural setting" that the residents of Enterprise were trying to protect.

Tillandsia fasciuculata on Thornby (endangered)

Carol Aymar had plenty of time to fume after hearing Mark Watts say that four years before, a suggestion was made that Thornby would be better off in Deltona. (Neither she nor anyone else interviewed for this book heard such a suggestion at the county council hearing.) Carol told the P&Z Board that she heard the council say they "*feared* if they denied this proposal that the owners would annex into Deltona. " She continued that the proposal for town houses was not compatible with the character of the surrounding community, and she distributed photos of Enterprise as well as a "Petition Against the Thornby Development" with pages of signatures. When Deltona annexed the property, Carol reminded them, city commissioners said they could protect it better than the county. "Is this the definition of 'protection'?" she wanted to know.

Patrick Stamile told them that the property is a "horticultural paradise;" Grace Stamile brought photos of Thornby's more exotic plants, such as spider orchids.

Suzanne Steiner used her three minutes to read the Riverkeeper's letter into the record. Mirroring the flooding concerns repeatedly voiced by the public, the report from the city's own environmental consultants said the proposed development "may sever the flow" of water that drained the property to Lake Monroe and that "a regional analysis of the local watershed may be required to provide assurance of no-negative impacts to upstream properties."

As promised, under-the-weather Betty O'Laughlin stuck around long enough to warn the board that destruction and disruption of natural systems on the property would result in wildlife habitat fragmentation, before "very carefully" driving herself home to Lake Helen.

New voices — Helen Williams, Linda Chaffee, and Deltonans Timothy Haynes and Sharon Blough — joined the chorus urging the board to once again recommend denial.

Deltona resident Kevin Finn urged his city to recognize the impact of its actions on surrounding communities, and to preserve Thornby as a resource for the city and its residents of all ages. The meeting agenda, he says, "assumed a foregone conclusion for development. But how do you convince someone not to destroy something priceless in three minutes?" His carefully worded statement said that Thornby is one of a kind, and urged his elected representatives to explore non-development options.

In the years that we had been fighting the Thornby land use change, I had learned a head-aching lot about comp plans. I used my time to convey to the board what I regarded then, and still do, as the heart of the issue: When someone wants to amend the comprehensive plan, the law presumes that the change will not be granted *unless it benefits the public.*

> **Activist Lesson:** Put another way, nobody is **entitled** to a comprehensive land use plan change. The principle is absurdly simple, but mostly overlooked in the haze of distractions, jargon, and political posturing that often accompanies plan amendments.

Thornby's Superman, Jack Hoyt, didn't fool around. He told board members they were there because of the "aggressive approach and policy of Deltona towards annexation." He said the public's presentation had been "outstanding," and said he wanted to see "100 percent rejection" of the project.

Fittingly, Sandy Gallagher made the motion to deny, and Jan Deyette seconded. We did get rejection, although it was not 100 percent. Still, the 4-3 vote brought "overwhelming applause from the public."

Board Chair Rafael Valle was one of three votes favoring the land use change. Two years before, he'd voted the opposite way; at the time, he said he'd been "swayed" by the crowd's passion. Now, he suggested that board members were approaching the issue "from an emotional standpoint." Why the switch? He may have been influenced by the city's claims that "this use is better than those the county would allow."

Wesley Kihlmire was one of four votes opposing the change. Later, he explained: "Deltona was messing where we shouldn't be. Developing Thornby wasn't the right thing to do. I'm always sympathetic with an owner who wants to make best use of their property, but this was for the greater good of the community of Enterprise."

Sandy's poem written after the 2004 planning board hearing

Optimism is not a Condition, It's a Duty
    By Sandra Walters

To **Riley**, who stood out in the cold
Waving signs on Main St., in a move so bold
To **Debra**, you didn't get to talk
Save it, girl, when you do, you will rock
To **Carol**, moral support, brains, encouraging words
Without your help we'd all just be nerds
To **Betty**, you were so sick but just wouldn't go
You knew you were needed as part of the show
To **Patrick**, you told 'em to leave it all green
To **Grace**, beautiful plant lady, what a team!
To **Kevin**, they got the message from us –
When you described your kid riding the bus
To **Bob**, no traffic guy was needed
Because you got up there and succeeded
To **Suzanne**, you love our river and it shows
A perfect reading of some awesome prose
To **Lani**, as usual you set them straight
A win in Deltona because you are great
To **Michele**, I want to thank you for being a friend
And hope we can count on you until the end
To **Marvin**, you worked in the rain and worked in the cold
The flyers got out and the people were told
To **Roy**, with almost no notice you came through
Not just a good job, but a fine one, too
Linda, there when you were needed
EPS has a friend in you indeeded (?)
Jane, Diane, our FOT pals
Stay with us, we really need you gals

FRIENDSHIP, BONDING, HOPE AND CARING
THEY KEEP US GOING & KEEP US DARING
NO MATTER WHAT HAPPENS AS WE KEEP UP THE FIGHT
AS PEOPLE AND FRIENDS, EACH OF YOU IS JUST RIGHT

I'm proud to be your friend
Sandy

For Larry French, the evening was pivotal. "It was encouraging to hear so many people who valued the land more naturally, than transformed by concrete," he recalls. "The zoning board listened. Surely *this one* [unlike the city park that partly became a store] is going to be handled in the right way, I thought as I drove home. Little did I know then how many more times I would be speaking and writing about Thornby." "It was a beautiful night for us," says Bob Sayre, who called it "truly democracy in action" and remembers that several folks had a celebratory drink afterward. "The Founding Fathers would be happy to have seen such a feisty display," he smiled. Suzanne Steiner called the win "heady and encouraging." Patrick and Grace Stamile said in an email, "We are so proud to be a part of such a fine and committed group." Lani Friend praised, "Such a great group of citizens exemplifying what it truly means to be an American." County council member Pat Northey offered kudos: "You are this little band of determined community activists fighting for all that is good and right, taking on the challenges of the big guys all around you. You are making a difference in your community. Keep up the good work."

For Friends of Thornby's planner Todd Peetz, it was also a fateful night. "I have been involved with many grassroots projects," says the planner. "I thought the group did their homework and really laid out an excellent case not to approve the development. The presentation was well-organized and I think it made a big impact." As welcome as Todd's compliments are, it took more than a winning vote to put a gleam in his eye. "When I arrived," he explains, "you (Sandy) were surrounded by your neighbors. There was a little blond in the front row so that is where I sat. Kirsten was working as a consultant for the city. We exchanged business cards, e-mailed a couple of times and met for lunch about a week later and have been married for five years now." Might they name their first child "Thornby?" He grins, "Well… maybe as a middle name." Somewhere, Dr. Glass must be smiling at this happy Thornby coincidence.

Up Close and Personal

"CITY MUST RISE TO CHALLENGE" — As if the *Orlando Sentinel*'s editorial board was yelling at city hall from a sound truck parked outside, its March 2004 editorial was harsh. "The planning and zoning board has twice heeded pleas to keep density in check, agreeing that the property's wetlands and massive trees are worth preserving," the editorial persisted. The Thornby tract "represents a chance for Deltona's city commission to show it is more than just a rubber stamp for development interests."

With Thornby on the April commission agenda, the chance was right around the corner. It was time to get personal, and so Friends of Thornby added "lobbyist" to our ever-growing activist resumes. We considered the mayor a hopeless cause, but his vote was just one of seven. By meeting individually with the others, absent the pressure of a public hearing, maybe we could open their eyes to why intense development on this fragile piece of land would be a multi-pronged disaster.

> **Activist Lesson:** Face-to-face meetings with officials are usually better than written communications — the earlier the better. "Don't make personal attacks. Think cooperation, not criticism. Portray commitment, not complaining. Be logical — don't be emotional or uninformed. Don't get confrontational or defensive. Demonstrate that you're considering the entire community." Excerpted from the *Jackson Hole Conservation Alliance News*, Fall 2010.

Commissioner Lucille Wheatley didn't respond to our request to meet. Commissioner Michele McFall encouragingly told Carol that she recognized Thornby as a special place and wanted to protect its history. When Carol and Grace met with Commissioner Doug Horn, a licensed Florida Realtor, he was unwilling to budge from his support of the development. Commissioner Bill Harvey was courtly when Gisela and I asked him to oppose hundreds of townhouses on this rural, scenic spot on the St. Johns River, but offered no hint as to how he would vote.

Welcome to the VGMC

The Volusia Growth Management Commission (VGMC) is an appointed group of 21 citizens. Little-known but extremely powerful, the group was created in 1986 when well-meaning voters must have envisioned it as a way to "manage" growth. Volusia is the only Florida county with such a group. In Volusia, neither the county nor the cities can change their comprehensive plan without VGMC certification. If one government objects to another's amendment, VGMC is the final decision-making body. The key word is *"consistency."* VGMC has to find consistency between plans in order to certify an amendment.

Whether voters actually got what they wanted is a debate for a different forum, but for the first many years of its existence, the VGMC had a near-perfect record of finding that every plan amendment was, or could be, *"made to be"* consistent. That is, its rate of approving comp plan amendments stood upwards of 99 percent in 2001, when Enterprise's Chris Elmer joined the commission. (See Chapter 6)

In March 2004, Deltona applied for VGMC certification of the Thornby comp plan amendment even though it had not yet gone to the city commission. The county promptly objected to the amendment on the ground that high density on Thornby "represents a land use that is *inconsistent* with the Enterprise Local Plan," said county planner Ben Dyer.

When a Volusia local government objects to another government's proposed comp plan amendment, most such disputes are negotiated between the VGMC staff and the arguing local governments without the involvement of individual commissioners. If the issue can't be resolved — like the controversy between Volusia County and Deltona over the Thornby plan amendment — a hearing ensues. In Thornby, the county wanted a hearing on its objections to Deltona's plan. As a government, it had "standing" (i.e., full rights to participate in the case). Friends of Thornby needed standing, too. Without it, we'd be limited to a parade of short speeches as at other hearings; we could not appeal a vote against us. However, standing at the VGMC was not automatic for the public. The commission would vote on whether to give us standing.

Carol and I made sure that Friends of Thornby submitted a correct and timely petition for standing to VGMC. If it didn't follow the rules precisely, we would never get our "day in court." Once again, Doug Kelly was Enterprise's Best Friend. Having experience with VGMC, he walked and talked us through the process, explaining the "whys" and "hows," what to do, and what to expect. VGMC administrator Lynn LaRue helped us through nerve-wracking weeks of faxes, emails, phone calls and questions. Friends of Thornby's petition was filed on March 30, signed by Carol Aymar, Kevin Finn Lani Friend, Jack Hoyt, Gisela Oeffen, Debra Richardson, Robert Sayre, Grace Stamile, Patrick Stamile, and me. In addition, we provided 29 documents, (including Deltona's own consultant's report) in support of our position that "Thornby Oaks" was inconsistent with the city's own comp plan.

I also submitted five pages of annotated comments pointing out discrepancies in Deltona's initial VGMC application. Maybe it was overkill. Still, those of us who had been connected with Thornby for years couldn't sit silently while Deltona told the new-to-Thornby VGMC that its plan for Thornby was preferable to the "industrial uses" the county would allow there.

Can You Hear Me Now?

At the same time we were working against the VGMC deadline, we had to ready our case for the city commission hearing set for March 15, 2004.

We asked The Trust for Public Land to document its past efforts to buy Thornby. Doug Hattaway wrote that TPL had worked with EPS on a grant application to Florida Communities Trust in 2003, but the owners terminated the option contract. He noted, "The landowners believe the property is worth more than the determined value," and repeated that TPL would be happy to reestablish negotiations if the owners wished.

Also at our request, Todd Peetz wrote a fact-filled letter to the "Honorable Deltona City Commission." He stated flatly that "Industrial or commercial use is not currently permitted under county zoning" and it was "gross exaggeration" to imply otherwise. He noted the plan didn't have enough open space to comply with city law. He said traffic levels were recorded as failing. As a consultant on the city's original comp plan, he informed them that the plan was intended "to have this area of Deltona be more like Enterprise and not the other way around." Finally, the bottom line: *"What is the public benefit of increasing the density six times what is currently permitted?"*

Seminole Audubon and West Volusia Audubon joined the groundswell of voices urging Deltona to maintain existing land uses on Thornby as more appropriate for the property than high-density development. John Baker, president of the Environmental Council of Volusia/Flagler, referred to Thornby's many majestic trees, listed plant and animal species, isolated and connected wetlands, nearby trail site, potential effect on the eagles' nest, adjacent lakeshore and scenic Lakeshore Drive, traffic management, and the Enterprise Plan. He cited four specific elements of Deltona's comprehensive plan that would be violated if high densities were approved.

Michele Moen of Osteen was familiar with Deltona's comprehensive plan from fighting her own land use battles against the city. She had done the math, and found that the city came up short on parks by a minimum of 60 acres of the comp plan's goal of four acres of park per 1,000 residents. Moreover, there was only one passive park for its 77,000 residents. A passive park, she wrote, provides "relief from the pressures of urban life" and recreation activities that are "based on and conserve the natural resources of the park site."

Deltona continued to claim that county rules would allow industrial uses on Thornby. After the planning board hearing, the county's Montye Beamer wrote a letter to the city spelling out that, under county zoning, uses on Thornby must be low impact and "consistent with the natural resources safeguard-oriented provisions of the Natural Resource Management Area (NRMA)." (The city's plan would strip Thornby of NRMA protection.) Her letter didn't sit well with Bob Nix, whose terse email to county planner Ron Paradise forecast bitter weather ahead between Volusia County and Deltona. One month later, Beamer followed up with a more detailed letter, pointing out that the property contains natural resources of merit including wetlands, riparian flood plains, forested uplands, habitat for wildlife "and is associated with cultural/historical resources."

Before city commissioners voted, we made certain they had the facts. Carol emailed the mayor and commissioners, calling their attention to the most critical issues from the last P&Z meeting:

- The scare tactic of "county would allow commercial or industrial use on this property." If this were true, she asked, then "why on earth would the property owners have annexed into the city to get a land use change?"
- Bruce Andersen's stated density of 5.5 units per acre was not calculated in accordance with city rules.
- Andersen said "Deltona is ready for this kind of luxury development," but his project is named "Thornby Oaks of Enterprise."
- Andersen's admission that the site "won't look the same" after large-scale land removal and fill dirt was omitted from the typed minutes.
- Todd Peetz, who worked on Deltona's original comp plan, said that the city's Enterprise Overlay wasn't intended to make Thornby development compatible with high density.
- The Riverkeeper's letter explained high-density development impacts to the river.
- Andersen's statement that under current county land uses, there would be no open space or wetlands is untrue.
- The owners have a right to ask for a density increase, but the city has no obligation to grant one.

Carol concluded by urging the commission to heed their constituents and neighbors, rather than the "primary landowner who ... does not drive on our congested streets, does not enjoy the beauty of Lakeshore Drive on a daily basis, does not suffer the consequences of flooding from poor development decisions."

Online, Kevin Finn tried to rally Deltonans to the commission meeting. Citing Mayor Masiarczyk's call that residents "not be swayed by the comments and concerns of outsiders," Kevin felt compelled to remind everyone that most of the Thornby owners lived in New Jersey.

Emails were sent, letters prepared, research completed, witnesses contacted, flyers out, calls made, schedules arranged. Then, a day or so before the hearing, the city postponed the hearing due to Allen Watts' "scheduling conflict." Our work was wasted and everything had to be redone the following month.

Activist Lesson: Do governments ever instigate last-minute changes as a way to keep the public off-balance and hold down attendance at hearings?

Eighth Thornby Hearing: Deltona City Commission

I wish I had been wrong.

In the *News-Journal*, I exuded optimism: "We can only hope that the commission takes into account the public interest like the [planning] board did and denies this." Privately, I likened Friends of Thornby's chances of prevailing at the city commission to those of a runaway slave in an Alabama courtroom.

It was April 5, 2004. Allen Watts stepped in for his son to represent the Thornby property owners. The staff report supported the proposed amendment, and commission chambers carried the suspicion, though unproved, of preordained outcomes. Opposing the change, Carol Aymar, Gisela Oeffen, Jack Hoyt, Debra Richardson, Betty O'Laughlin, Ellen Williams, Eric Blythe, Suzanne Steiner, Monica Luedecke, Kevin Finn, Ida Hart, Susan Collins, Riley Nutt, Lani Friend, Grace Stamile, Pat Stamile, Suzanne Adair, Jane Trimmer, Dan Trimmer, Roy Walters and I did our underdog best. Not one person spoke in favor.

After 21 people voiced their objections, it was time to inflict a land change from one house per acre to six houses per acre on Thornby. The motion was made by Commissioner Michele McFall (who two years before said she was "very familiar with the history of the area" and "this is one of those areas we need to be careful of") and seconded by Commissioner David Santiago, a licensed Florida real estate agent. The Deltona City Commission voted unanimously to approve the comp plan amendment, with Commissioner Diane Obremski absent due to illness. Later, she wrote that she was "really hoping that at least one of my fellow commissioners would … listen to the people … I don't know why we have a planning and zoning advisory board when their decisions aren't even taken into consideration."

To accompany Thornby's new land use, the city commission next voted on re-zoning the property. Bruce Andersen said the property is "Eighty-three percent developable" and gave assurance that "there will be plenty of opportunity to assess the site for its historic value." In a city where the average home cost $91,000, Andersen's boast of condos selling for up to $500,000 dazzled officials. The motion to re-zone Thornby for up to six residences per acre was made by David Santiago and seconded by Doug Horn. The vote was unanimous in favor. After the hearing, John Masiarczyk, Doug Horn and David Santiago lamented loudly and publicly that they didn't hear anything legal enough or legitimate enough or factual enough to make them say no to greenlighting a subdivision on Thornby.

Reaction was swift and visceral. *Sentinel* columnist Mike Lafferty called the city commission a "doormat for development" and a "poster child" for Florida Hometown Democracy (the proposed state constitutional amendment that would give voters a say on comp plan amendments in their communities). Lafferty quoted Santiago, who had said in relation to another project that: "We should be a good partner to the school board and not overburden them by adding more and more children to the area." But "Didn't Santiago vote for the Thornby project in April, and won't that burden schools?" Mike asked. Ronald Williamson of the *News-Journal* praised Thornby's beauty and charm as "symbol of a lost past, growth and an uncertain future. No other place is quite like it." His column was titled "Last Hope for Thornby Estate Beauty Fades."

Lawyer Allen Watts was quoted in *The Informed Volusian*, characterizing "insistence of the will of the majority" as a "disturbing trend" when it infringed on "rights and liberties."

> **Activist Lesson:** There is no legally protected "right" to a land use change.

Deltona Speaks

In Deltona at a routine P&Z meeting, Bob Nix read to board members from Deltona's Vision Statement: "The lasting image that Deltona will leave on visitors and residents will be unique neighborhoods, extensive natural landscaped right-of-ways (sic), public parks and natural areas."

Around the same time, Deltona resident Larry French emailed Bob Nix, asking that he try to turn the park idea into reality. In a three-page response, Nix told French that in the late 1990s he'd proposed a city-county partnership to rehabilitate the Thornby house, but the city commission "did not want to direct staff resources to a site outside city limits." He said that in 2003 when the Enterprise Preservation Society tried to buy Thornby "I offered the Trust for Public Lands' (sic) representative the assistance of my agency's resources in preparing the grant application ... Our offer of assistance was refused." ("I can only say that I would not have refused the city's assistance with the application and I doubt Suzanne [Woodcock] would have, either," says Doug Hattaway of The Trust for Public Land. It "probably was a misunderstanding," he adds.)

Further, Nix told French that he didn't think that Deltona had "$2 million or more" to match a grant, but "if the county is willing to provide the local match" it would go a long way toward public purchase. "I am confident that the owners would be willing to sell the property to the public, if their attitudes have not been changed by the opposition to their three applications for plan amendments and/or rezoning," he said, and asked, "How would the over 77,000 citizens of Deltona benefit from the acquisition of this property?" French replied with a suggestion that Deltona partner with EPS to approach the county about providing funding to buy Thornby. Nix answered that "no coalition is necessary" and that a possible solution would be "for the county to step up to the table with matching funds and [park] management services." Larry persisted, asking if "we can get the county, EPS and you to talk more about these possibilities." The last email in the chain quashed French's hopes. "Thank you, but no," said Nix. "I have no interest at this time in discussing this issue with the county or EPS." He added, "My capacity in this issue is to act as an umpire, however unpopular that may be, not a participant in the land use game that has evolved concerning this property."

Frustrated, French wrote: "He [Nix] says he'd like to see it as a park, but he will only go whichever way the commission directs. Yet the information and recommendations he supplies the commissioners does not offer them any of these alternatives to direct him to do otherwise. A process seemingly operating in isolation from the public it's supposed to serve."

Government at its Most Contrary

Although Friends of Thornby's petition gave us entry into the world of the Volusia Growth Management Commission, we weren't exactly welcomed like long-lost friends. It didn't take long to realize that the VGMC had been sliding along its comfortable track for nearly 20 years, with the public's station somewhere north of West Nowhere. The VGMC, while funded by Volusia County, is essentially autonomous — a good thing, you're thinking. It *would* be good, except for the fact that virtually all its real work is done by the VGMC staff of Orlando lawyers and planners whose firms have been firmly ensconced in their jobs since the first days of the commission's existence. "Staff" is defined as one who assists, but over the years, the relationship between the VGMC commissioners and their staff has become skewed. When one jurisdiction objects to another's plan amendment, VGMC staff meets with city or county representatives, but not with the public. The commissioners (other than the chair, at times) are not part of negotiations or behind-the-scenes meetings with government or landowner representatives. The VGMC staff makes recommendations to the commission on how a plan amendment could be "made to be consistent," and commissioners usually follow them. The staff attorney takes an active role in commission meetings, rather than a more advisory role. Perhaps Allen Watts described VGMC best when he admitted in 2004, "Political give and take is the name of the game."

Friends of Thornby was in a Catch-22 with the VGMC. In order to participate fully in the hearing, we needed standing, and we couldn't get standing without a VGMC vote. But they wouldn't vote on standing until the hearing! Meanwhile, since we weren't officially part of the case, we had to ask to see the back-and-forth correspondence between Deltona, VGMC, and the county as they prepared for the hearing. This sometimes meant making a trip to VGMC's Daytona Beach office during its limited operating hours. At least one document we requested wasn't received for a month.

As described earlier, since the VGMC settles most plan conflicts without a public hearing, Thornby was a rare case. Neither the county nor Deltona were backing down over the intense density increase. The county's Ron Paradise was endlessly patient with questions and helpful with uncertainties. His support made him, like Doug Kelly, a genuine Thornby Hero during that hot, stressful summer of 2004. Ron kept us in the loop while VGMC and the county pressed the city for missing details on critical issues like compatibility with the Enterprise Plan, wetlands protection, eagle nests, historic trees, archeological features, utilities, traffic impacts, and more. They were the same issues we'd been spotlighting for four years. As is the government way, the wheel was being reinvented.

At the annual meeting of the Enterprise Preservation Society in May 2004, Chairman Mark Matzinger brought the large crowd up to speed on the remarkable number of issues then facing Enterprise and West Volusia, issues such as Deltona's attempts to annex the 5,000-acre Leffler property in Osteen (later ruled illegal); the status of the Enterprise Local Plan and the Lakeshore Drive Scenic Corridor; the Enterprise schoolhouse project; and, of course Thornby. I took the microphone. With Mark holding up my poster boards, I explained that Thornby was at a crossroads. The Deltona's City Commission approval had bumped it to the next steps: another review at state level, then on to the Volusia Growth Management Commission, the final arbiter. We can't do this alone, was my message: we need your support every step of the way.

Things Get Tougher

If you've read Chapter 6, you know the next step. On July 29, Deltona submitted a small tree's worth of paperwork to the Florida Department of Community Affairs (DCA), seeking to change Thornby's land use to accommodate the new zoning already put in place by the city commission. DCA had 90 days to decide if the amendment was "in compliance" with state law. We were green about state procedures, but had to monitor the case, learn DCA's rules — especially crucial time deadlines — and figure out how to provide meaningful input to state planners, all from 300 miles away. Thankfully, GAI planner Doug Kelly was always willing to answer questions and walk us through the process.

Closer to home, Bob Nix, fed up with what he called the county's "contentious" objections to Thornby development, told the VGMC to go ahead and set its hearing. We're not answering any more questions from you *or* the county, he told them. VGMC scheduled a September 22 hearing. At that, Friends of Thornby found ourselves sparring in two arenas at once.

Visitors

"What's in a name?" asked William Shakespeare. The answer is, "plenty," when the names are part of history. James Glass built Thornby. Doris Faber renewed it. In 2004, Charley, Frances and Jeanne (no last names) may have saved everything.

> *God has cared for these trees, saved them from drought, disease, hurricanes, tempests and floods. But even He cannot save them from fools.*
> **Paraphrasing John Muir**

CHAPTER TWELVE

The Credit Belongs to Those in the Arena

"On humanitarian grounds, I ask that you extend to us the courtesy of re-scheduling the Sept. 22 public hearing on the Thornby comp plan use change."

It was September 9, 2004. With electricity restored for the second time in three weeks, I emailed the Volusia Growth Management Commission the rescheduling request, noting that "... we were without power for five days after Hurricane Charley and five days after Hurricane Frances... we have homes, families, jobs, damage, property and claims issues to deal with... and a third hurricane is looming." My email didn't give more details, but they weren't needed.

For three weeks, Central Florida residents had endured various combinations of flooding, contaminated water, road closings, sandbagging, disrupted mail, questionable sewers and cancelled garbage pickup, missing roofs, overwhelming debris, and sporadic phone service, while existing without air-conditioning in sweltering temperatures. My husband and I kept food in an ice chest, but the nearest ice was two counties away. Gas was scarce. Water levels were rising. The occasional alligator swam down our street. From a tiny TV connected to a car battery, we learned that hurricane number three of that season was on its way.

Volusia County joined Friends of Thornby in requesting a continuance of the VGMC hearing. Montye Beamer wrote that, "… some impacts associated with these storms have yet to be assessed and addressed. The County of Volusia has reprioritized resources and personnel to respond to the hurricane-related challenges." She noted that VGMC rules permit cancellations due to natural disasters, and asked that the chair reschedule the hearing. Friends of Thornby had to "reprioritize resources," too. Even without other problems, we couldn't email without electric power, talk to staff who weren't on the job, or do research in the dark.

VGMC said they would vote on the requested postponement at their September 22 hearing. If they denied it, as Deltona was asking, the hearing would start then and there, which meant we had to be ready. Bombarded by storms and flooding, and now this, I wondered if Dr. Glass was still smiling down on us.

People vs. Staff

In patches and pieces, we prepared for a VGMC hearing that might not happen. The St. Johns River Water Management District asked the city for information not included in the staff report. Doug Kelly explained to us that probably: "… all the VGMC has is what the city submitted and Megan Wimer's (VGMC planner) report." We wondered: what happened to the 29 documents submitted by Friends of Thornby?

The VGMC staff report was as devastating as any that ever came out of Deltona. While recognizing that the Thornby plan was ineligible for certification because it was inconsistent with VGMC criteria, the planners had concocted a way to "make it consistent." If the city would submit (1) another environmental analysis, and (2) a historic survey (either of which *might* lead to "an additional public hearing)," Thornby Oaks would obtain VGMC certification.

Between hurricanes two and three, Friends of Thornby challenged the report in a long letter containing hard facts on 15 issues, from overcrowded schools to Deltona Planning Board denials to the validity of the Enterprise Survey. On the day of the "maybe/maybe not hearing," we submitted yet another response — an analytical *tour de force*, if we say so ourselves — seven pages citing specific sections of Deltona's comprehensive plan and Volusia County's comprehensive plan, demonstrating how they weren't consistent with each other. We corrected misstatements made by the city, and concluded that: "The applicants have failed to produce even one shred of evidence as to any benefit that would inure to the public from this requested change." After that, there was no more to say.

Saved by the Storms

Although we had sent rebuttal documents and followed the VGMC rules, we were unprepared for a hearing. The VGMC venue and format were new to us. Issues were controlled by unfamiliar county ordinances. Their planner's report was pockmarked with errors and questionable assertions. (For example, it echoed Lawyer Mark Watts' words that at the 2000 county council meeting, "a suggestion was made that the property would be best suited in Deltona" — a suggestion that no one interviewed for this book remembers hearing.) Hurricane-related problems focused supporters' energies elsewhere. The county was pinched for time and staffing. On September 22, at the hearing chambers in DeLand, Deltona hoped to get a vote in favor of high-density housing on Thornby. Instead, the VGMC voted unanimously to postpone until October. Everyone (except Bob Nix) breathed a sigh of relief and went home.

At the State Level

Pretty much by luck, we happened to discover that the Thornby land use amendment was parked on a desk in Tallahassee, awaiting a green light. It seems that Nix, who formerly worked for the Florida Department of Community Affairs, had visited the state capital to lobby his former employer. (It was not uncommon for cities to send their taxpayer-paid staffers to meet with DCA with a big comp plan amendment in the works.) We were told by DCA planner Anoch Lahn that Deltona was requesting that the Thornby amendment be "fast tracked," implying there was no opposition. The plan nearly worked until we got wind of it. Our task then was to derail the bureaucratic machinery set to bless the plan amendment with little scrutiny. DCA normally considers applications it receives to be accurate. Its staff handles thousands of plan amendments every year, and most are boilerplate. In Florida's inflated development boom, the agency was overloaded with plan amendments that sought to pile more intense uses and density increases on top of what was already approved.

After streams of phone calls and emails from our team, DCA seemed convinced that we weren't just a group of local crackpots, tree huggers or troublemakers, but deeply involved citizens with verifiable data on traffic, wetlands, historical significance, and environmental resources. Both Carol Aymar and I recall a phone conversation with Lahn when we let her know that the city's submittals weren't necessarily accurate, and "fast tracking" was not appropriate for the Thornby plan amendment. Before making a decision, DCA staff needed to scrutinize the information we would send them, we insisted.

In DCA's defense, as we came to realize, it was uncommon for ordinary citizens to become entwined in their process. The agency didn't know what to expect or what was about to hit them. One thing that hit them was my fax machine. In between natural disasters and power outages, I sent documents they did not get from Deltona, such as Montye Beamer's letters. I sent the US Weather Service's flood warning for Lake Monroe, to show that the property was susceptible to flooding. In total, I pummeled them with nine faxes — enough information that they probably wished they had never come across the name "Thornby."

On September 13, 2004, the DCA informed Deltona Mayor John Masiarczyk that, "… We have determined that the proposed plan amendment should be formally reviewed…." On a purple sticky note still affixed to my copy of that letter, I wrote: "Because we called, wrote and badgered them!"

The decision to review was a relief, yet, "It seems that every time we answered one of her comments, she came up with something new," reads one of my notes from that time. "She" was planner Anoch Lahn, and she was relying on incorrect information (for instance, that the county would allow five housing units per acre) and possibly wasn't referring to the information we'd sent. The DCA would issue its report in weeks. We were frustrated and needed help.

By way of Gwen Straub of the Environmental Council, I was lucky to find Terrell Arline, a Tallahassee land use attorney who had years of experience working with the DCA. Since Friends of Thornby was a grassroots group, he agreed to represent us for a reduced rate.

> **Activist Lesson:** Those who are new to civic activism may think that free legal help is available to fight an especially egregious or high-profile land use issue. The fact is that finding an attorney who will help a citizens' group for free is even rarer than finding an elected official who will deny a plan amendment.

In the local comprehensive plan amendment game, the DCA's job is different from the VGMC's. The VGMC's role is to decide whether plan amendments are consistent with each other, while the DCA's is to determine whether a plan amendment is *internally* consistent with the plan itself. Our goal, then, was to show the DCA that the Thornby amendment was inconsistent with Deltona's *own* comp plan. To use just one example, Deltona's comprehensive plan calls for minimum disturbance to wetlands, but the Thornby plan would destroy wetlands. (Thornby's soil was so wet in places that building hundreds of units would require massive onsite re-engineering, i.e., filling wetlands.)

Terrell knew the people at the DCA, what questions they would ask, and what documents would inform their decision. After several conversations and a good look at the mounds of documents, he was up to speed. I remember his comment that anyone relying on the city's descriptions would think that Thornby was surrounded by Miami. He lost that mindset as soon as he saw Lani Friend's Enterprise PowerPoint and an EPS calendar featuring month-by-month scenes like Lakeshore Drive and Thornby's majestic oaks — all very un-Miami-like. Terrell laid out our case in a letter to DCA attorney Charles Gauthier. "… Don't just rely on Deltona's staff report. Understand the very real, special place affected by the amendment. Note the lack of data and analysis in the file…" he advocated, and asked for a meeting with DCA staff.

When the Florida Division of Historical Resources reviewed the plan, it cautioned, "Because of [Thornby's] location on the lake, evidence of prehistoric occupation would be expected." Deltona should survey its historical resources, the state said for the umpteenth time.

If any state agency should have spotted warning flags from the Thornby plan, one would expect it to be the Department of Environmental Protection. The DEP's lily-livered report made Friends of Thornby see red. It ignored potential impacts from hundreds of condos by not evaluating the effects of dense development on the 7.5 acres of Thornby wetlands, drainage into the imperiled St. Johns River, the six-fold density increase, historic and specimen trees and endangered plants on the property. In response to our request, supporters e-mailed the DEP, expressing their dismay. I reminded the DEP reviewer that the Thornby developer's agreement would allow paving 24 of Thornby's acres and destruction of 85 percent of its trees. Instead of providing meaningful technical review, the report disrespectfully talked about Thornby being a "pretty property" and residents being "hurt" by possible development.

> **Activist Lesson:** When faced with a technical report that glosses over the facts or side-steps critical issues, question it. Provide the report writer with data that might have been overlooked.

On October 7, 2004, Carol and I met Terrell at DCA offices in Tallahassee. Recognizing my passion for Thornby and my tendency to get agitated, Terrell cautioned me not to appear angry when I talked to DCA folks. He knew how badly I wanted to make them understand the "specialness" of this property they would never see. "You catch more flies with honey than with vinegar," was the core of his lawyerly advice.

Around the DCA's large conference table, Terrell laid out his case, describing for planner Anoch Lahn and supervisor Marina Pennington why the Thornby amendment was inconsistent with both Deltona's comprehensive plan and state law. The lawyer showed pictures of the rural character of Enterprise, including aerials provided by Doug Kelly. They saw photos of the river cresting Lakeshore Drive and profuse storm water runoff from the property onto the road. Documents we provided included a hydrology report expressing concerns that Thornby development would sever the drainage canal's flow — a report I found in the city's files. Terrell reminded them that the VGMC, the local decision-maker, had yet to weigh in on the plan.

DCA staff was professional and friendly. Carol recalls, "They treated us with respect and not like we were just a bunch of tree-huggers." They opposed the small strip on Lake Monroe being designated "City Public/Semi-Public/Conservation," but questioned whether development on Thornby had to be compatible with the Enterprise Plan, as we contended. "I remember Marina conveying the uphill battle we faced," Carol says, "But we felt there was hope."

In our thank-you letter to the DCA, we reiterated the issues of overcrowded schools and Enterprise's historical features. We made sure they knew that Trust for Public Land was willing to fund public purchase in conjunction with EPS — just so they would know the depth of community support that existed. As well, now that I'd met with their staff, I followed up with more than 20 technical and relevant documents that I realized the DCA had not seen.

> **Activist Lesson:** Send a follow-up email thanking government staffers for their time in listening to your concerns. Copy their supervisor.

Florida's Department of Community Affairs

When the state issued its report, we knew that the DCA staff had paid attention, after all. "Not enough analysis of natural resources such as wetlands, vegetation and wildlife habitat, historical and archeological resources on the site," it said. Other objections focused on utility services and a "reduction in naturally vegetated open space."

"It seems they didn't read the amendment," snapped Bob Nix in reaction to the state's criticism of the Thornby amendment. However, he warned, "It doesn't change our thinking."

"We are pleased but not surprised," I told the *Daytona Beach News-Journal*, on behalf of Friends of Thornby. "This plan is not in keeping with the rural character of the Enterprise community, nor is it in the public's best interest."

The reporter reached John Clapp. "It's interesting to hear them [the state of Florida] talk about preserving trees when they don't preserve any of theirs," sniped the Thornby heir, munching on sour grapes in New Jersey. The state report he dismissed as "just another step."

Fast Track Derailed

Dear Mr. Brandon (wrote Bob Nix to the VGMC Chairman):

> "....indefinite postponement... wish to have additional time ... may be significant changes ... postpone the hearing until we can resolve the ORC Report issues..."

Thank you, Charley, Frances and Jeanne. And Terrell.

Looking for the Ballot Box

The reprieve was temporary and elastic. Like death and taxes, a revived Thornby plan was a sure thing. This time though, it wouldn't zoom along quite so fast. The city had other fish to fry.

What Jack Hoyt aptly called Deltona's "annexation binge" was in full swing. The 5,000-acre Leffler property, as well as other properties totaling 800+ acres, promised to bulge city borders. The *Orlando Sentinel* reported that residents in rural Volusia were "watching Volusia County's largest city as it pushes east, annexing timberland and pastures by the hundreds of acres." At the county level, 71 percent of voters had just approved keeping urban sprawl in check by putting clear urban service boundaries into the county's comprehensive plan (a referendum ultimately blocked by the VGMC and later voided by a circuit court judge who objected to its semantics.) Deltona publicly opposed the boundaries, legally using tax dollars to educate its residents on the issue.

In November 2004, the *Sentinel* reported on the "scuffle" between Enterprise and Deltona over Thornby, noting, "In mid-October the state Department of Community Affairs rejected the city's plans to pack the land with town homes." Focusing on the 2005 elections, Carol Aymar observed, "We're expecting continued challenges until there is a change in power in Deltona."

Back to the Planning Board

"These objections are correct and based on truth," Riley Nutt told the *News-Journal* in March 2005, referring to the state's objections to the Thornby amendment. Bob Nix did not agree. "The objections stemmed from a misunderstanding of the approval process," he said. John Clapp's response? "We just have to keep trying."

With Thornby back to the planning board for the fourth time, threats of "affordable housing" still darkened the horizon. By talking to members of county staff, I learned that in the program's 10-year history, not one builder had applied for affordable housing certification, which carried with it stringent criteria that such a development on the Thornby property would not be able to meet (for instance, easily accessible public transportation and hospitals).

To imagine subsidized housing on the highest-priced land in the city was quite a stretch. A county official told me, "This is being blown out of proportion. It's a scare tactic." Nevertheless, the city persisted, and the nearby condo residents were easy targets. In 2002, they had turned out in large numbers to oppose high density on Thornby. After that, the city started to talk about "affordable housing" on Thornby and now, the rumors of low-cost housing across the way made them nervous. Mostly retirees, many snowbirds, few attended city meetings. (At the time, commission meetings were not televised.) Some assumed that fancy digs on Thornby would boost their own property values. Property managers dreamed of commissions from sales of "upscale" condos. Most residents cherished their peaceful surroundings and knew that their quiet lives would be changed by the massive traffic increases that Thornby development would bring. Before every hearing, depending on who was in charge there, Friends of Thornby might (or might not) be allowed to post flyers on the mailboxes of the people who would be most affected by Thornby building. One association president helped me distribute flyers, but was worried about the "affordable housing" rumors spreading like a virus. (In a three-page letter, I explained to him why this far-fetched threat was unreasonable.) Knocking on residents' doors was prohibited. Security guards thwarted flyers on windshields (I tried). There were hundreds of residents, but virtually no way to give them the facts they needed to make an informed decision.

Still, the thorniest issue was the bald eagles' nest. At the memorable 2002 P&Z hearing (see Chapter 9), public testimony of a possible eagle nest on Thornby prompted an out-of-earshot chat between Bob Nix and the city's consultant. An eagle nest was never found on the property, although city consultants searched on the ground, by small plane and by helicopter. Likewise, John White of Florida Fish & Wildlife performed annual flyovers for the state and never saw a nest there. He did spot the VO12 nest pair at the nearby condo "tennis court nest" every year. That nest's "protection zone" spilled over onto Thornby boundaries.

In April 2005, a ringing cell phone usually meant a problem, or an urgent "who will say what?" decision for the next hearing. This time, however, it wasn't Carol or Lani calling me. Instead, it was John White, and he had startling news. On his latest flyover, he had spotted an active eagle nest in a tall pine almost dead-center *on the Thornby property*. White speculated that the VO 12 nesting pair had relocated to Thornby because of Hurricane Charley (or Frances or Jeanne). He had already notified Audubon Eagle Watch.

John's heads-up was important. From talking to state and federal eagle experts, I knew that official guidelines *could* require a no-build zone of up to 750 feet around an active nest, with varying distances for "primary" and

Bald eagle nest on Thornby, 2005

"secondary" zones — but not necessarily. Eagle protection zones, they told me, were often "negotiated" with developers and landowners.

Lynda White (no relation to John) was Audubon's eagle watch coordinator, and she wasn't afraid to step on official toes if it meant protecting our national emblem. She knew a Deltona planning board hearing was coming up. On April 19, she faxed the new nest's coordinates to the city, advising that, "It would be in the best interests of the eagle and the citizens of Deltona if a substantial conservation area around the nest were created."

As well, I wrote guest editorials about the realities of Thornby. My *News-Journal* piece informed readers that Deltona High School was 80 percent over capacity; that "upscale condos" was a marketing tool; that 75 percent of soils on the property were hydric (wet); and that neither senior nor affordable housing were viable options. "Our goal is to keep the current land use on the property so that three-story apartments on zero lot lines won't stick out like a sore thumb in our historic community," I explained. In the *Sentinel*, I took a more esoteric approach, pointing out that the concept of "property rights" does not include using government machinery and taxpayer money to get one's land use changed.

As the hearing approached, Lani Friend told the *News-Journal* that, "Deltona needs to come to the realization of what a historical and environmental gem it has in the Thornby property." In the *Sentinel,* Jo Tanner of Enterprise feared for scenic Lakeshore Drive, where first-time visitors always remark about the beauty of the road's tree canopy. Meanwhile, Bob Nix was confident. "I don't see anything that should stand in the way of getting this through," he predicted.

Ninth Thornby Hearing: Deltona Planning and Zoning Board: Eaglegate

On April 21, 2005, performer Will Smith had a Top Ten hit called "Switch." The Deltona Planning & Zoning Board switched, too. Thornby was switched to a special meeting. The law firm representing the owners made a switch in who would speak for them at that meeting — from Mark Watts (who had twice failed to convert the board to the faith of Thornby upped densities) to his father, Allen, a senior partner at the Cobb and Cole law firm. Bruce Andersen switched to a backseat role. A new member replaced Janet Deyette on the planning board. The hearing tone switched, too. Words were sharper, demeanor less genial.

When the DCA pronounced "Thornby Oaks" a loser, the city promised "significant changes." Like an actress changing clothes behind a screen, Thornby/Thornby Oaks switched, too. Its stage name became "Thornby Special Area Plan."

> **Activist Lesson:** Other feel-good terms like "village" and "hamlet" often pop up in an attempt to put lipstick on the proverbial pig.

City employee Sung-Man Kim churned out maps faster than McDonald's makes fries. Bright-colored maps covered with tiny shapes of densities reaching west to I-4 and north to crowded Deltona subdivisions five miles away, pastel contour maps streaked with wavy lines — 19 maps in all, designed to impress, overwhelm and divert attention from where it belonged: the criteria in the city code that the planning board must consider. One criterion was, "impacts to environmentally sensitive lands."

The "Special Area Plan" had "special" features intended to allay some of the more prominent objections. It required a 100-foot "landscaping" (not "natural") buffer on the Lakeshore Drive Scenic Corridor. It required completion of a historical resources survey (but did not specify how historic resources would be preserved). Under the Plan, Allen Watts said, the canal that drained upland areas during heavy rains would become "conservation" — but only if it were later "determined to be a wetland." (The city finally acknowledged that the canal Frank Knight said in 2001 did not exist, really did.) Likewise, the

"Special Area Plan" would preserve the eagle nest *protection zone* — unless Fish & Wildlife said preservation wasn't needed (through "negotiation"). Jack Hoyt called it "just the same old development plan that has the name conservation to make it sound good, particularly when they're trying to get it approved by the Department of Community Affairs... Vote against it!" he urged the board. He gave them copies of his 2004 letter to the mayor naming specific city codes that were violated by Deltona's way of calculating allowable densities. The mayor never answered me, Jack told them.

Diligent readers won't be surprised at statements made: (By Watts): "... prior to there being any actual site development all of the necessary studies will be done." (By Andersen): "There is no doubt that the [bypass] road would be in place and well used before this project is built." (By Nix): "This is a more restrictive use category than the [county] one that applies now."

Roy Walters, permission granted this time, used the city's numbers and graphics in a PowerPoint, with eye-popping results.

Carol Watral of Deltona characterized the property as "irreplaceable."

Kevin Finn reviewed attempts since 2000 to change the land use, and questioned the use of his city's taxpayer dollars to fund "study after study and report after report from city staff."

Doug Kelly spoke at the county's request, but he had the same three minutes as everyone else (except Allen Watts and Bob Nix). Doug narrated the origins, purpose and content of the Enterprise Plan. One of the Plan's elements is joint planning between governments, he said. Another is the protection plan for Lakeshore Drive. Another will designate a historic district that abuts the Thornby property on the west. The community of Enterprise abuts the property on the north and west and, "That is why the county is concerned to ensure that this project and any future projects would be consistent with the Enterprise Local Area Plan," he explained.

Carol Aymar echoed the importance of compatibility with the Enterprise Plan. "The citizens have worked for years to get this plan in place to preserve what is special and unique about Enterprise. It seems that Deltona doesn't care about the cultural, environmental and historical value of the area. It seems that Deltona wants to ruin what we have. The city refuses to enter into a joint planning agreement to protect the Enterprise borders. Twice before, the planning and zoning board rejected density increases, you went up against the Deltona city development machine and you were heroes. Do you have the courage to be heroes tonight?"

Eleanor Slyker, West Volusia Audubon's conservation vice president, had written to the planning board about Lake Monroe's impaired water quality. Now, she said that county wetland maps and soil reports clearly demonstrate that a density increase had "nothing positive about it whatsoever."

Debra Richardson quoted the city code requiring that the board consider adequacy of public schools in making a decision. School board data relevant to Thornby supported her presentation.

Bob Sayre reported that the proposed Thornby subdivision would add 1,465 vehicle trips per day, further stressing an already-failing roadway. County traffic engineer statistics backed him up.

Gwen Straub, president of the Environmental Council of Volusia-Flagler, disputed how the city calculates densities. (The issue of "gross" versus "net" densities in Deltona was what Jack Hoyt had been fighting for years.) In the county, unbuildable areas like wetlands, buffers and rights-of-way are deducted *before* calculating allowable densities. The city, on the other hand, awarded densities purely based on the overall property size, even if part was not buildable. Said Gwen, "This idea of figuring density based on gross acreage of the site is a gift to the developer, but it's a slap in the face to the citizens of Enterprise."

Suzanne Adair called the board's attention to Lakeshore Drive. Any road improvement will cause the loss of large trees, wetlands and impact drainage, she told them, adding a personal plea: "We hope you're listening to us, because we care."

Gisela Oeffen, a resident of the condos near Thornby, wearily brought up the flooding issue. "This is flood plain and this area should not be further developed. I'm terribly disappointed by the way this government works. Policies have been changed, ordinances have been changed and criteria have been changed. The opinions of the citizens of this area are absolutely ignored."

Dave Aymar was blunt. "We all should know what is going to happen to that property if it's developed. According to the soil report there is very little appropriate soil for development." The University of Florida soil report supported his testimony.

Dustin Johns, a developer, remarked that, "the city hasn't taken good advantage of the money they should have received for impact fees and doing roads… for all of the [prior city] developments. The sole reason for this [plan amendment] is money."

Larry French rooted for a city park. "You know that no form of development is going to be appropriate for Thornby," he told the board. "Vote this down and get our city to look at this park proposal."

Betty O'Laughlin, speaking for the local Sierra Club, suggested that a park would be a "feather in the city's cap."

Janet Deyette had opposed the Thornby amendment when she was on the planning board. She told her former colleagues about attending a workshop on the benefits of historic areas, but "Our leaders in Deltona weren't there. They continue to overlook the piece of history right on our doorstep. I feel it would be a terrible mistake for Deltona to develop this area." Instead of condos, she visualized "trails, raised wooden walkways for sensitive areas… a museum." She challenged board members to "send the recommendation to the city commission to find a way to purchase this irreplaceable site." Knowing that Nix had once pushed the city to apply for grant funding, she urged that the board "challenge [the commission] to put Bob Nix to work on this project." She begged, "Don't let this rich historic area get away from us."

Eaglegate Part I

I brought to the hearing a copy of a fax sent two days earlier from Audubon to the city, confirming the coordinates of the newly-identified Thornby eagles' nest. All evening, I'd been waiting for Nix or another staffer to mention the nest. Nobody did. It seemed inconceivable that the planning board would vote on a land use plan without knowing that a protected eagle nest was sitting practically in the middle of the property, but that's the way things were headed.

The information gap meant I had a lot to cover in three minutes. I rushed through the issues I'd planned to present: (discrepancy in wetland areas; lack of tree survey and destruction of vegetation along Lakeshore.) Then I put Audubon's letter on the overhead projector so that the board could read it. I told them that the nest was 500 feet inside Thornby's southeast corner, and that city code required they must "take into consideration impacts on public schools, traffic and environmentally sensitive lands."

Eaglegate Part II

Calling the nest location "new information," Nix promised to have a biologist research it, and suggested the eagle nest might actually be an osprey nest (a comment not included in the officially adopted minutes).

Although it's not in the minutes either, the *News-Journal* reported Allen Watts' snipe about those who spoke: "I've never heard so much misinformation in a single space in my life." Reporter Jeannine Gage noted, "That comment and several others by Watts and Nix were met with groans and boos from the audience."

When it was time to vote, board members, apparently tangled in a web of undirected goals and confused motivations, simply approved what was in front of them. A new member said she had to follow the "facts" the city presented. (She did not say why the facts the public presented didn't merit the same attention.) Wesley Kihlmire (who voted against Thornby Oaks in 2004) declared that the board was "by no means approving the development plan," then voted to recommend approval of a land use change that would allow the kind of development he didn't want.

Drawing by Larry French, 2005

See How They Run...

> **Activist Lesson:** "It's all about the entitlements," says planner Ron Paradise. Once entitled to a land use change, the horse is out of the barn. Board members won't hear that from the staff; they must hear it from you.

Sandy Gallagher and Ross Culver were the minority in a 5-2 vote that recommended approving a "Special" version of the "same old development plan."

One question is unanswerable: If Planning Board members had learned of Thornby's eagle nest from the city instead of from me, would the outcome have been different? A few days later, the *News-Journal* commented that, "A pair of bald eagles showed more sense of appropriate development than the Deltona Planning and Zoning Board."

Eaglegate Part III

The next day, Lynda White got a call from the city. "They are really upset with these pesky eagles," she joked in an email to me. She and John White were interviewed in the *News-Journal*. Channel 13-TV ran the story all day. Deltona's biologist found the Thornby nest where the experts said it was. Lynda wrote Nix: "I have been told that you stated this [nest] was new information when, in fact, you were informed of the nest in a letter from me faxed to you on April 19."[1] Bob Nix labeled charges of a cover-up "ridiculous." Later, Lynda emailed, "I have encountered some really arrogant public officials in my dealings with eagle issues, and Nix is one of the worst."

---

1 The fax transmittal sheet from Audubon to the city is stamped "04-19-05 PO4:03 RCVD"

Bob Nix

Janet Deyette probably knew the enigmatic Bob Nix as well as anyone at city hall did. "He could be exasperating at times," she sighs, "but maybe he was just trying to do his job." She elaborates, "When I sat on the planning board, we had numerous discussions in his office, sometimes after hours. I would discuss the pros of saving Thornby, and he would argue that the commission was more interested in developing it. He told me he once suggested to the commission that Deltona annex Enterprise and do a historic overlay to protect the whole area." She says he complained to her that, "The Enterprise people don't trust Deltona." "Can you blame them?" she asked. "EPS doesn't trust me, either," he retorted. She shot back, "That's because you don't have the last word — the commission does."

Thornby = Everywhere

In Deltona, Larry French, recently appointed to Deltona's Parks and Recreation Advisory Committee, told the <u>Sentinel</u> that, "The problem here is a process devoid of communication and viable alternatives." His copy of the planning board agenda is jotted with terse comments like, "Watts started out by rebutting that there's lots of misinformation — right, Allen, who's putting it out?" Larry's optimism that Thornby would be handled "in the right way" had faded like bright colors in the Florida sun.

Dustin Johns' letter to the *Sentinel* protested that, "the only ones benefitting from this approval are the landowners and the city's tax base." In a *News-Journal* guest column, Carol Aymar described the hearing "fiasco," where only two board members asked intelligent questions and one "did not even know the reason for the hearing." Deltona needs a change of leadership, she wrote and urged residents to "get off of the couch, step away from the TV, and attend a city hearing." Residents, including Pam and Rudy Baumann of Enterprise, emailed the city commission that the new Thornby "Special Plan" did not correct the state's objections.

Tenth Thornby Hearing: Deltona City Commission

The travesty that was the city commission meeting took place on May 16, 2005. There was no need to marshal the facts and no reason to prepare, although three determined souls — Kevin Finn, Cliff Foster and Jack Hoyt — went through the motions. Kevin reminded his commission that it was an election year.

Eaglegate Part IV

Bob Nix told the commission that the Thornby eagle's nest "was discovered too late to be discussed at the recent planning and zoning meeting."

The evening's menu featured the usual political doublespeak — the "threat" of affordable housing; land use changes presented as "property rights," and that old bug-a-boo, "this is just the first step." When the last tale was told — "The people in the Enterprise area have had plenty of chances to buy that property" — it was time to vote.

Unanimous vote to approve the Thornby Special Area Plan and transmit to the Volusia Growth Management Commission and the Florida Department of Community Affairs.

> *Instead of thinking of this as a commodity, they should think of Florida as a treasure…*
>
> **Former Florida Governor Bob Graham**

CHAPTER THIRTEEN

To Everything There is a Season… And Then Another…

Like Bill Murray's cynical TV weatherman in the movie "Groundhog Day," Thornby was stuck in a time loop by the summer of 2005. Twice before, in 2000 and 2004, Florida's Department of Community Affairs (DCA) got a whiff of high-density proposals for Thornby; both times the agency turned up its nose. Nevertheless, with the amendment reworked for the third time, state law called for another review.

In 2004 at DCA, we had been like late-arriving moviegoers fumbling for seats in the dark. This time, we would be settled in when the film started. Before Deltona had even sent the latest Thornby plan to the state, we asked for all correspondence between the DCA and Deltona in the last six months, and that's how we learned that Bob Nix and Allen Watts had been to DCA offices to try to resolve the agency's concerns about the new "Thornby Special Area Plan." "DCA made no promises, and the city and applicant's attorney made no promises on any items or issues," DCA staff told us. So far, so good.

With the DCA reviewing the current Thornby proposal, we re-started the prior year's barrage of politely persistent fact bombs. We couldn't assume that the busy new DCA planner, Chris Edmonston, would have a handle on Thornby files that dated back to 2000. Eighteen mostly technical documents, like Deltona's environmental report, and a three-page letter pushed my fax machine into overdrive. I also sent articles and photos about Enterprise history as well as information about our school restoration project, figuring it couldn't hurt.

Edmonston, now a transportation planner for a private Tallahassee firm, later offered his perspective in an email to me:

> At the time I received the City of Deltona's Comprehensive Plan Amendment pertaining to the Thornby property, I was already balancing somewhere between 10 and 15 different reviews from both Volusia and Osceola Counties. As usual, I was not given any indication as to the magnitude of this proposed change, or the history behind it. It wasn't even a week since the file hit my desk that I began receiving an extraordinary amount of mail from concerned citizens. Needless to say, I quickly figured out that this review would be anything but simple.

Friends of Thornby re-hired Attorney Terrell Arline to advocate for us at the DCA. Carol Aymar and I didn't need to go to Tallahassee because Terrell was now fluent in Thornby-ese. He deemed the latest Thornby plan, seemingly designed to allow construction of a marina/boat facility on Lake Monroe, "confusing at best." Another feature of the "Thornby Special Area Plan" was indeed special: it could permit the city to automatically expand density without further review by the state or another agency — truly a gift to keep on giving.

In 2004, DCA blasted the "insufficient analysis of historical and archeological resources" on Thornby (as we had been saying for years). In response, the owners hired Southeastern Archeological Resources, Inc. (SEARCH), a firm described by state archeologist Ryan Wheeler as "a company which researches sites for developers," to dig on Thornby. SEARCH agreed to review our background material on the property before poking shovels in the ground. Lani Friend furnished details of Enterprise's early history. I sent information on Dr. Glass. EPS Chair Mark Matzinger wrote to SEARCH, explaining that local residents had been working with the county to save the property for five years. He urged them to "... intensify the search for the fort and artifacts with all due respect to Enterprise, Central Florida, and Florida history in general."

Indian Mound Verified

In the summer of 2005, an interested neighbor got word from SEARCH workers that they had located an Indian mound on Thornby. Workers reported the find to the state, as required by law. We requested state records; the find was confirmed by Department of Historic Preservation archeologist Ryan Wheeler. From our "Eaglegate" experience, we knew that it was essential to shine light on this discovery so it couldn't be locked in a political closet. Bill Dreggors, executive director of the West Volusia Historical Society, called the find "significant." In the newspaper, Bob Nix shrugged that "it would have very little effect on the project,"[1] and then claimed to be "deeply concerned" about the site, implying that if it were vandalized, it would be our fault. "Every time we go to a public meeting, someone invents something else," he sniped. Allen Watts sounded dyspeptic: "They've claimed there was an eagle and a fort. Now there is a midden, apparently." He added, "We know that the fort is not there." We were told that SEARCH's report of its findings would be private. Unless the owners authorized it, no one — not the state, not the newspapers, and certainly not the public — could see it. The owners' archeological report was kept private. It would be five years before I had the report in hand.

Florida Department of Community Affairs 2005

Deltona persisted in claiming that commercial land use on Thornby would have been okay if the land was still under county jurisdiction. That contention would make it easier to justify even high-density residential now that it was in the city. At our request, Volusia County's Ben Dyer schooled DCA planners on Volusia County's guidelines for commercial development. According to the rules, commercial should be on "thoroughfare roadways," and Dyer explained, "The Thornby parcel is bordered by narrow, 2-lane roads with... Lakeshore Drive identified ... as a [county] scenic road. There are no major roads serving the site, no plans to expand existing roads... its use as commercial would be inconsistent with this guideline," he wrote in an effort to put the city's weak allegations to bed, once and for all. Unfortunately, it was a claim that would soon re-emerge — this time in the high-stakes drama at the VGMC.

---

1 Middens on private property in Florida that do not contain human remains are not legally protected from development.

During state review, the Volusia Soil & Water Conservation District conveyed to the DCA its concerns that the Thornby project would be "deleterious to both soil and water quality in the Lake Monroe basin, watershed area and wetlands." The Florida Department of Environmental Protection said the city's new "conservation" land use category was vague and ambiguous. Because it could allow non-residential uses on the Thornby property, it didn't provide assurance that resources would be protected, warned state environmental specialist Suzanne Ray.

Around that time, then-Governor Jeb Bush declared that Florida must improve its growth management policies. Thornby supporters echoed his words in letters to the DCA, requesting that Thornby high-density development be found "not in compliance" with state law. Among individuals who wrote were Jane Rourke, Donald Phaneuf, and Herb Hiller; groups included The Enterprise Preservation Society; The Florida Bicycle Association and The Volusia-Flagler Environmental Action Committee.

On August 29, 2005, for the third time, the DCA issued a reproachful Objections, Recommendations and Comments (ORC) report on Thornby (it was one of eight properties totaling 820 acres annexed into Deltona for land use changes, calling to mind Jack Hoyt's half-joking comment that city annexations "seemed to happen over the weekend.") The state's report found each change "not in compliance" with state law. Thornby's issues were inadequate school facilities and lack of protection for natural resources. The DCA said that Deltona's custom-tailored "conservation" category allowing intensive non-residential uses on Thornby's environmentally sensitive land was not consistent with the city's own comp plan.

One item the state's report didn't address was traffic, since the DCA considered it a local issue. Chris Edmonston predicted, "The VGMC will have plenty to say about the impacts to the local roads," and added that he "appreciated all of the work done on this amendment." His gracious words, the only time a government agency publicly acknowledged Friends of Thornby's efforts, were almost as pleasing as his report. What he prophesized with respect to VGMC and traffic didn't happen.

Readers might logically assume that the DCA's fault-finding report was the death blow for Thornby jacked-up densities, but that was not the case. Because the state agency lacked the power to pull the plug on even the most harmful comprehensive plan amendments, it could only make "recommendations." Therefore, the ball was back in Deltona's court. Under state procedures then in effect, the city could revise the Thornby plan; drop it entirely; or pass it anyway. In Volusia County, though, the amendment process has a second head: the Volusia Growth Management Commission. No matter what the state's report says about an amendment, no Volusia city (nor the county itself) can change its comprehensive plan without VGMC certification. If the Growth Management Commission certified Thornby, the state's objections would be negotiated into nothingness, shrunk like a bargain shirt in a hot dryer. The 21-member VGMC was a local force, complicated and largely unknown. Depending on your viewpoint, it could be either the Equalizer or the Terminator.

Volusia's Charter Review Commission

While the state was assessing the latest Thornby plan, a heavyweight commission was taking shape locally. Every 10 years, the county convenes a charter review commission (CRC), a group of citizens who meet for months to consider, discuss and recommend changes to the Volusia County Charter. At its meetings, the CRC takes testimony on charter-related issues from experts and from members of the public. The commission can't change the county charter on its own, but its recommended changes, if approved by the county council, appear on the next countywide ballot. I applied for appointment to the CRC, but quickly realized that the group's makeup was way over my head. Although anyone could apply, only true Volusia "movers and shakers"— a prominent land use attorney, a Daytona Speedway executive, a chamber of commerce bigwig — were chosen. Of 15 members, only two were women, both named Patricia: Patricia Drago, Executive Director of Facilities for the school board, and Patricia Northey, a former county councilwoman. Northey made sure CRC meeting schedules were convenient for the public.

What did this have to do with Thornby? Since the VGMC existed under the county charter, the CRC had the power to recommend its dissolution. It seemed auspicious that a charter review commission would be in session just when Friends of Thornby was — for the second time — in the midst of the VGMC process. When we encountered the VGMC in 2004, the experience left us filled with frustration, bewilderment and anger. Our overall impression was of a voter-created commission that was largely managed by its staff, instead of the other way around. I didn't comprehend at the time that the VGMC had always been Volusia County's version of Henry VIII. By that I mean, it could be loved, hated, feared, or all three at the same time, depending on which way political winds were blowing.

In an interview she gave during the ongoing charter review process, Pat Northey said the CRC wanted to replace the VGMC. Even if that happened at the next county election, it would be too late to help us — Thornby would be back to the VGMC before then. Still, I very much wanted to help change the powerful VGMC, which to me was an obscure, sewn-up system laced with cronyism and, to quote Doris Faber, "That should never be."

When the charter review commission took public comment on August 22, 2005, the minutes reflect:

> Sandra Walters distributed a handout concerning the Volusia Growth Management Commission. She stated she had often been disappointed in and frustrated by the VGMC process, and listed several reasons why. Her opinion was that the VGMC was a failed experiment and should be abolished. Ms. Walters stated the commission should find a successful working model and pattern Volusia County's structure upon it. Ms. Walters felt it would be possible to reform the VGMC only if an extremely thorough change were implemented on several levels. She felt the charter review commission should also explore options for restructuring.

I addressed the CRC about problems with the Volusia Growth Management Commission at a "public listening session" like a crusading witness testifying to Congress. It was dawning on me that few people, including the ones I was addressing, knew much about the VGMC's inner workings. How would they, unless they had ventured onto VGMC's turf, as we had for Thornby? In the 20 years since its creation, very few citizens had. I used my allotted three minutes to explain to the members how the system discouraged public input and seemed structured to cater to the interests of governments and landowners over those of affected residents. I had handouts showing examples of VGMC's distance from the public, such as its hours: its Daytona Beach office was open from 9 a.m.–2 p.m., Monday through Thursday.

Of several people who provided public comment to the CRC that evening, the last one to speak was a familiar face in the Thornby wars: Deltona Commissioner David Santiago. Taking verbal aim at my VGMC remarks, he ominously warned the CRC about listening to "organized groups with particular agendas." His words sparked images of Tony Soprano, the Mafia, and a group even more sinister than the Corleones: the Friends of Thornby.

New Faces on the VGMC

While the charter review commission debated its fate, the Volusia Growth Management Commission conducted business as usual, but big changes were afoot. Chris Elmer resigned after four years of service, leaving behind ample reserves of good will and an empty seat. Another of five county-allotted seats was vacant at the same time. Nominations for both seats would be made by newly-elected county council member Joie Alexander. I had supported Joie's campaign platform favoring countywide growth boundaries to protect agricultural lands and water supplies. When she asked me for suggested VGMC nominations, I almost couldn't get the names "Suzanne Steiner" and "Tony Cole" out fast enough.

Tony Cole says that, like most Volusia residents, he "knew very little about the VGMC" when he was appointed. When I asked him if he would like to seek nomination by Alexander, he researched the VGMC process. When he understood that the commission had real authority — they could approve or deny comprehensive plan amendments — he got interested. Though he had heard that the VGMC had turned into a rubber stamp agency over the years, he thought it "might actually be used to stop some of the rampant, irresponsible growth if the VGMC had enough members who were willing to vote to deny."

Before Suzanne Steiner was appointed to the VGMC, she knew it only from her neighbor, Chris Elmer. "He believed that to save Thornby, we needed to convince the VGMC members to deny the request to put condos on the property," she says. "I thought nothing about the appointment or being on the commission until another Enterprise friend, Sandy Walters, asked if I would like to be nominated and recommended me to Joie Alexander. At that time, the VGMC had great power, but they approved almost all comp plan changes that came before them. The county council members did not pay much attention to who was appointed. In my opinion, it was because most of what the council asked for, the council got."

Pat Northey saw things differently. She said, to the contrary, county council was unhappy over the VGMC's "rubber-stamping of applications that the [individual] board [members] never got to see or weigh in on." On the November 2006 ballot, county voters had the chance to dissolve the Volusia Growth Management Commission and replace it with a mediation-type "Growth Management Dispute Resolution Commission." The proposal was defeated by a 63 percent majority.

In July 2005, Enterprise residents Tony Cole and Suzanne Steiner were unanimously appointed by the county council to the Volusia Growth Management Commission.

Preparing for the VGMC

The 2004 hurricane chaos was the reason the Volusia Growth Management Commission cancelled Thornby's certification process. Now, in 2005, the VGMC was gearing up to restart the interrupted process, review the latest plan, write a staff report, hold a public hearing, and vote.

Getting our hands — and eyes — on the information stream flowing between the VGMC and Deltona was a top priority. It was the only way we could adequately prepare for the coming hearing. We needed to know if the updated staff report would track last year's work, introduce new issues, or both. I spent lots of mornings cozied up with Thornby public records in the VGMC's Daytona Beach office, assisted by its gracious new coordinator, the whimsically named Merry Chris Smith. There I learned, for instance, that VGMC planners were delving into the issue of Thornby's wetlands and VGMC lawyers were researching citizen "standing." In one memo, the lead VGMC planner predicted that the Thornby amendment would generate an "extremely intense public hearing."

The VGMC office wasn't the only official spot taking up my spare time. I also haunted Deltona City Hall, where busy staffer Marlene Brown would set up a chair and a table that wouldn't collapse under the weight of bulging brown folders that seemed to breed between visits. "I well remember those standing-room-only Thornby hearings," says Marlene today, "and the passion of the Enterprise folks about the Thornby estate. Those meetings had everyone's attention." (I was such a familiar figure that the city started to send me notices of hearing by certified mail, even though it was not legally required.) Over the years, I had already seen almost everything in the files, but now and then, new finds would emerge from the stacks of folders.

One new document in city files was an environmental report confirming the existence of the Thornby eagle nest. It talked about a bald eagle management plan for both the onsite nest and the nearby "condo nest," while referring off-handedly to an "incidental take permit."[2]

The files revealed that Frank Knight was fretful. "Is the Thornby property in the 'in basket' of the VGMC yet?" he emailed Bob Nix. The next day, he wondered in another email to Nix: "Now how about the DCA? Is it on the way? I worry that hurricanes or late responses will run us out of time like last year." Nix consoled him: "I am meeting with the new DCA staff in Tallahassee."

Further research in city files turned up an email I sent to Deltona Planning Board member Frank Dragoun in 2004. After Dragoun recommended approval of high density on Thornby (an especially perplexing vote coming from a hydrological engineer), I sent him a detailed analysis of adverse effects from Thornby high-density development — everything from schools to traffic to wetlands. How did my email get into Deltona's files? Dragoun forwarded it to Frank Knight, who forwarded it to Bob Nix.

> **Activist Lesson:** Don't assume you are in the loop for all communications about the contested issue — or that others outside the loop aren't privy to your conversations.

Although the state planner had confidence in the VGMC's traffic expertise, we weren't inclined to entrust the future of Enterprise's roads to the VGMC planner in downtown Orlando who had likely never even seen

---

2 An "incidental take permit" under the Federal *Endangered Species Act* gives a pass to private entities undertaking projects that might result in the "take" of an *endangered* or threatened species. "Take" means to harass, harm, pursue, hunt, shoot, wound, kill, trap, capture or collect any threatened or endangered species.

Lakeshore Drive. I scouted for a local traffic expert. The search proved futile; in Volusia, good engineers tend to work for developers. Jacksonville, home of Buckholz Traffic Engineering, was close enough. Dr. Jeffrey Buckholz, a nationally recognized transportation expert with more than 25 years' experience, was a Professional Engineer licensed in six states, a former University professor with advanced degrees in civil engineering and an MBA in Finance. He had written three traffic-training manuals and consulted for clients such as the Florida Department of Transportation, Flagler County, and Wal-Mart. "I've worked for developers, government agencies, and citizen groups, and I try to approach the project in essentially the same way," he explained in a 2011 e-mail. He sees his job as giving decision-makers the "straight technical scoop." In Jeff, we had the star atop the traffic expert Christmas tree.

Ducks in a Row

In the summer of 2005, Thornby was on lips and minds at the DCA, the VGMC, and the charter review commission. It was the same at Deltona City Hall, where the planning board's July agenda was light. Bob Nix scheduled a "training session" to generally discuss state and local procedures for amending comprehensive plans. With Nix as engineer, however, the information train soon jumped the track as the session devolved into a one-man Thornby slugfest. Working up a full head of steam over the thought that "opposition groups" might "attempt to stymie the hearing process," he talked lawyers and lawsuits. Anticipating that planning board member Sandy Gallagher would carry his message to Friends of Thornby, Nix looked her in the eye. "Now we're going to play hardball with this," he said. "We've had enough of hardball from the other side and trying to be nice and it's over."

Thanks to the generosity of Enterprise entrepreneur Pam Cook, we had a potent new way to mobilize residents. Pam's Voice Broadcast Messaging service made automatic phone calls to hundreds of EPS members, telling them the date, time and place of the VGMC hearing and letting them know how much we needed their in-person support.

Anxious over the upcoming VGMC hearing, I worried that county officials might lose their resolve. If for some reason the county had a change of heart, Friends of Thornby would be left to shoulder the burden of objecting to Deltona's comp plan amendment at the VGMC. Being proactive, I squeezed five years' work into a three-page letter to county officials and built the case for saving Thornby brick by brick. "How Will This Project Adversely Affect Volusia County?" my letter asked, answering its own question with 13 detailed examples — from the lost NRMA designation to the aquifer recharge to the crowded schools. In case they wanted to know "What Should Volusia County Do?" I had the solution: they should keep objecting.

> **Activist Lesson:** If you have support from a local government concerning another jurisdiction's land use issue, let officials know you are counting on them. Remember, however, that government policies can shift, seemingly overnight, and conflicts between jurisdictions can be negotiated away, leaving only public opposition to carry the day.

Looking back, my letter seems a bit nervy, but I sent it to the county manager, county council, and county staffers Beamer, Dyer, and Paradise, with copies to Doug Kelly, Friends of Thornby, and a couple of reporters for good measure. The letter might not have made a difference, but we were heartened to see the county, with Ron Paradise as "point man," carrying on with preparations to challenge Volusia's largest city at a public hearing before the Volusia Growth Management Commission.

A Popular Government without popular information or the means of acquiring it is but a Prologue to a Farce or a Tragedy, or perhaps both.
James Madison

CHAPTER FOURTEEN

Politics as Unusual

Through the years, wars have been fought on multiple fronts. Napoleon's armies campaigned against British, Spanish and Russian soldiers at the same time. In 2005, on a less massive scale, Friends of Thornby was running multiple battles at once: at the Deltona Planning and Zoning Board, the Deltona City Commission, the Volusia Growth Management Commission, the Florida Department of Community Affairs and — possibly the toughest arena of all — in Deltona city elections.

The published notice of the April 2005 "Eaglegate" planning board hearing had listed the start time as 6:00 p.m. instead of 7:00 p.m. Attorney Tony Cole helped Thornby neighbor Stephen Wiechert and me file an appeal with the city commission, contending that the published error made the hearing invalid. The city attorney said the printed error made no practical difference. Our appeal was ignored and never put on the city agenda. At that point, with so many other "irons in the fire," we reluctantly dropped the issue.

Things Get Hopeful, Then Ugly

I've forgotten most of my first conversation with Dennis Mulder. What I do recall is that it gave me a faint glimpse of a distant star called Hope.

In November 2005, Deltona would elect a new mayor. John Masiarczyk, the city's first and only mayor, was term limited. During his ten-year reign, he had ignored, challenged and belittled Enterprise residents who had tried to open up a dialogue with Deltona and refused the Enterprise Preservation Society's 2001 request for a one-year mandatory suspension of annexations that would have given them time to try to put together a public purchase of Thornby, and/or a community plan for Enterprise. The Thornby owners' lawyer had called the request "meaningless." Masiarczyk said it would take too long.

Masiarczyk ran meetings in a "gavel-heavy" style that left little opportunity for citizens to participate meaningfully. He would sometimes instruct citizens who expressed a complaint to go home and write a letter about their concerns. A repressive atmosphere at city hall meant that, "at the end of his tenure, hardly anyone attended commission meetings," according to Deltona activist Jack Hoyt. A majority of the commission seemed to lack imagination and flexibility. The city was financially sound (city hall was built without debt) but had paid scant attention to aesthetics such as landscaping of public areas. Recreational trails were virtually non-existent in what was now Volusia's most populous city. Road improvements were bypassed although money was available for the work. Worst of all, the city's policy of continually annexing county lands and building thousands of new homes only intensified its problems. The lack of a town center, coupled with virtually no local businesses, gave Deltona the aura of a suburb disguised as a city, and did nothing to encourage a feeling of community in most residents. At the same time, Deltona's relations with Volusia County were downright contentious, fueled by the city's annexation of the 5,000- acre Leffler property near Osteen.

Entrenched city commissioner Doug Horn was the obvious Masiarczyk successor for mayor. He said things like, "The only way to control what's going on around us is for 'around us' to be part of us."

Horn's opponent was Dennis Mulder, a 27-year old political unknown. (A third candidate dropped out of the race early on.) Despite years of media coverage, Mulder knew only the basics about Thornby: waterfront property + development = fight. He agreed that, despite all the newspaper articles and TV coverage, most Deltonans were in the same boat. Some residents weren't aware that their city included thousands of feet on Lake Monroe's shoreline. Others didn't know that Lake Monroe is part of the St. Johns River. In addition, some folks' opinions on Thornby were colored by noise from a tiny core group who loudly opposed efforts to preserve it, much less put it into city ownership.

As Mulder's campaign picked up steam, Friends of Thornby and others brought him up to speed on why Thornby would do more for Deltona intact than bulldozed. He went public with his support, telling the *Orlando Sentinel* that he wanted to bring businesses and better jobs to the city, but not at the expense of historical properties such as the Thornby estate. Although he "never set out to be an environmentalist," reported the *Sentinel*, Mulder had "the support of some local environmentalists who say he is the only candidate who listens to them about their communities' needs." His call for slower growth and redevelopment of worn areas fell on Deltona residents like a shower on parched summer streets. As for current city officials, "They stopped listening to the people of Deltona a long, long time ago, and it's evident. You can call them, you can write them, you can have *30 people stand up in a meeting* and they don't listen," he said. The reference to Thornby was obvious.

Deltona's first 10 years after incorporation were stuffed with annexations and single-family home building in a city that offered little else to its residents. Originally envisioned as a retirement haven for Northerners, its infrastructure had been stretched to the breaking point by waves of a younger population in need of schools and inexpensive houses. Most of the city's residents endured a grinding commute to Orlando or environs, arriving home late and tired, in no frame of mind to follow politics. Masiarczyk, the two-term mayor, told an interviewer, "In order to offer our residents the services they desire… we have to expand our boundaries" without addressing other avenues like inner-city redevelopment or the Interstate 4-based "Activity Center" as a site for businesses and entertainment. For voters suffering from overloaded roads and schools, "business as usual" wasn't on their menu. If Deltona was a café, "Today's Special" was always the same: Annexation with a side order of Upzoning. Worse, it had become stale.

Doug Horn told the *Sentinel* that he wanted to keep the city going in the same direction. In fact, "I would just like to see things going more quickly," he said. Mulder, on the other hand, said that "… residents and those who live in rural communities near the city [Enterprise and Osteen] are frustrated because commissioners are dismissing their concerns about annexations… ."

The mayor's race wasn't the only flashpoint for change. Former P&Z Board member Jan Deyette, who had fought for years for recognition of Thornby as a city treasure, was vying for a city commission seat. During her campaign, she said, "Deltona's approval of a condo development on the Thornby property is an example of the commission's lack of concern for wetlands near Lake Monroe." In another commission race, Friends of Thornby member Sandy Gallagher sought to replace Michelle McFall, who had voted for multi-family land use on Thornby. Sandy, who had once avoided public speaking like an open manhole, was now determined to "really have a say" in city affairs.

Mayoral campaign collage of newspaper headlines

Deltona's new 'village' is same old thing
— SENTINEL April 2005

Lake Helen's formal objection to Deltona's extension of its water service boundary is not "off the deep end," as one Deltona commissioner suggested. The "deep end" is the cavalier manner in which Deltona's mayor dismissed Lake Helen's interest in the larger city's aggressive move. — NEWS-JOURNAL June 2005

Deltona flexes to add 5,000 acres
Volusia County likely will sue if city takes in sensitive land
— ORLANDO SENTINEL Mar. 2004

Deltona High School is a D school — JOURNAL June 2005

Deltona must end the sprawl
— SENTINEL Nov. 2004

Dated policies result in Deltona flooding
— SENTINEL Nov. 2002

Commissioners have heads in the swamp
— SENTINEL Feb. 2004

I had never set foot in a campaign office, but I was soon part of strategy meetings and began my "on-the-job training" in subjects like: "Knocking on Doors 101" and "Advanced Sign Waving." Campaigning, I learned, is hot, exhausting work, not for the thin-skinned or the semi-committed. It's sometimes exhilarating and often frustrating. Thornby's fate was tied to the 2005 city elections like "do" is tied to "or die." We needed four Deltona officials empowered enough to "just say no" to urban-type development on property brought into the city for just that purpose. If we didn't get them, the last large, undeveloped tract on Lake Monroe would likely go the same, shriveled-up way as much of Florida. And with it would go the very fabric of Enterprise history, from Cornelius Taylor to Dr. Glass to Doris Faber, taking with it the shining, peaceful lake shore, buried bits of history, and most of what makes Enterprise a "happy little lakeside town."

The *Daytona Beach News-Journal* ran a couple of pieces that featured Thornby as part of the larger, regional picture. In July, Debra Richardson, Osteen activist Michele Moen and I met with the late Kay Semion, associate editor of the *News Journal's* editorial pages. Kay's extensive "Rural Communities are Worth Preserving" column quoted our opinion that the biggest threats facing unincorporated Volusia were annexations, expanded water/sewer service boundaries and increased traffic. In September, an article headlined "Deltona Land Changes May Alter Cityscape," highlighted Thornby as one of eight pending city land use changes that could add more than 62,000 car trips per day to Deltona's roads. (The city's rationale was that the amendments could bring "new and interesting" residential development.) At about the same time, Carol and I, along with other Volusia activists, met with the Sentinel's editorial board at its request to discuss Thornby and other West Volusia land use issues like Deltona's annexation and planned development of the rural "D-Ranch" property into a subdivision and shopping center.

> **Activist Lesson:** To persuade a paper's editorial board to meet with you, "be able to show how your issue impacts the local community. If appropriate, show that your issue is part of a bigger trend. Local papers are often looking for stories to tie their community to a national trend." Excerpted with permission from *www.boatus.com*

On both sides of the aisle, those following the Thornby saga were keenly aware that the coming elections would probably decide its fate once and for all. In the bitterly contentious mayor's race of 2005, Thornby was arguably the most divisive campaign theme. Nowhere was the controversy more evident than on the blogs, where Doug Horn posted fictional tidbits such as:

> The [Thornby] owners agreed to give to EPS the portion of the property on which the home sat. They also offered to assist with $$$ in the restoration of the property. EPS refused to discuss the offer. The Thornby developer wanted to close Lakeshore Drive to all but walkers and cyclists, and the Enterprise people turned it down.

The most poisonous blog-venom was reserved for Mulder/Thornby supporters, who were routinely mocked and harassed online. An ongoing exchange among Kevin Finn, Larry French and their city Commissioner Doug Horn proved frustrating. Kevin urged fellow Deltonans to see Thornby for themselves. "Welcome to real Florida, our home," he posted. Larry refuted bogus claims that only Enterprise people wanted to save Thornby. "There are people in Deltona as well as the county who would like to see the area remain as pristine as possible," he corrected. Both Larry and Kevin waded through Horn's apparently limitless supply of misstatements. For instance, Horn also wrongly claimed that a city meeting was postponed because "the Enterprise Preservation folks" had a "scheduling conflict."

The T-shirt that made the papers

At the same time, the barbs moved from the Web to people's chests. Cheap white T-shirts proclaiming "Sandy Walters Doesn't Live Here But I Do" in bright red letters were printed up for anti-Thornby bloggers. I found out about the shirts when the late Rick Paine, friend, neighbor and vociferous Enterprise online advocate, happily infiltrated a gathering of bloggers and smuggled one out for me. I tucked "my" shirt away for the day when it might be useful.

No matter the fallout, Thornby supporters were determined to keep putting the facts online. Why bother? "I wanted to refute the lies and stop the misinformation," Kevin asserts. Deltona resident Mike MacHardy says it was "discouraging" that bloggers "didn't want to share" city or county tax dollars to buy Thornby. Larry tried dispassionate dialogue, but relates, "After a while, anything I posted was immediately set upon by circular critiques and segues to repeated statements of misinformation." His repeated pleas for a public forum on Thornby were hijacked and credited to someone else. On another blog, he says, "I found excerpts and sound bites taken of my comments at public meetings and in print, were clipped and taken out of context to make me appear ridiculous." Kevin Finn's personal tax and property information, taken from public records, was paraded for blogger comment. My property information was posted, and my caricatured face graced at least one rude cartoon. My name was mangled for laughs. Personal animosity, neighborhood divisiveness and fiction paraded as fact were now the costs of taking a public role in the fight to stop a Thornby land use change, but like schoolchildren targeted by bullies, we tried to pretend it didn't hurt. None of us had anticipated the depth of acrimony aimed by some at Thornby, Friends of Thornby, Enterprise and Stone Island. Maybe most revealing was an anonymous poster's grudging blog: "... *perhaps we should have left the property in Enterprise. Don't forget the first step in this process was for Deltona to annex this problem.*"

Although most bloggers were rabidly anti-Mulder (and anti-Thornby by association), it was evident that a majority of Deltonans craved a shift in the city's direction. They wanted more attention put on the needs of existing city residents, and less on building more subdivisions.

Maybe the best part of campaigning is connecting with like-minded people. Deltona's Kevin Davidson was one of about 20 on the Mulder campaign trail, often accompanied by his 6-year-old daughter, Leeanne. Kevin and I talked about Thornby while canvassing city streets and afterwards at Wendy's. When he saw the property for himself, he realized on the spot that he wanted to save it — not just for now, but for his child and her someday kids. Beyond his appreciation of Thornby's history and beauty, there was a special connection for Kevin: he and his wife, Diane, had adopted their blonde, pig-tailed cutie from the Methodist Children's Home. Other Deltona campaigners who became Friends of Thornby include the late Pat Bonaparte, George and Joanne Gehring, Veronica and Johnathan Kenny, Michael Kiepert and Bill Tavernier, and, of course, Esther Dobens, a/k/a "The Mole." When Esther worked on Mulder's campaign, I finally got to meet the woman on the other end of the phone.

The St. Johns:
Florida's Only American Heritage River

A *Sentinel* article in October 2005 profiled the St. Johns Riverkeeper, Neil Armingeon, and his role in the grassroots struggle to save Thornby:

> During a trip to Central Florida last year, Armingeon met with Walters to scrutinize the controversial Thornby property in Deltona. Armingeon identified property adjacent to the Thornby property as "wetlands of special concern," then wrote a letter to the city explaining how denser development would harm the river.

In the article, I explained that one of Neil's jobs was to guide citizens through complex issues within the St. Johns watershed. "It's technical things like this that are important," I said.

May the Best Man Win

Despite a long-standing editorial position strongly favoring Thornby preservation, the *News-Journal* endorsed Doug Horn for mayor, reasoning that a politician who had been around the block would make a better leader for Volusia's most populous city than a political virgin would. The *Sentinel*, on the other hand, wrote, "Deltona needs Mulder's vitality and focus to help redirect the city." In city commission races, the paper recommended Janet Deyette and Mike Carmolingo; however, it picked Michelle McFall over Sandy Gallagher, even while calling McFall a "disappointment in her support of the Thornby project."

Recalling the campaign, Mulder evokes some of the election slime flung his way: "I spent a great deal of time explaining away lies like 'Sandy Walters bought the commission.' And why Thornby wouldn't cost $30 million." He seemed to be everywhere, running a high-profile campaign with a plethora of volunteers. At rush hours, a tightly packed schedule (not common to all campaigns, I've since learned) organized "waving" on main roadways. Drivers who pulled over were surprised when the candidate raced to their car to shake hands. In the evenings and on Saturdays, he joined in neighborhood door-to-door visits. On weekdays, a campaign team would stop at Deltona businesses to say hello and distribute brochures. When anyone inside expressed an interest in the candidate, we would ask if they wanted to meet him. They would hesitantly answer "well, okay," not realizing he was right outside the door. Once he saw he wasn't intruding, he would step inside, introduce himself and listen to their opinions about the city. Many folks were incredulous: "I've been here 10 years and no candidate ever came to meet me before." I was new to all this, but even I could smell a winner.

Decisive Election Results

The election results are (mostly) happy history. We celebrated for the new mayor, as well as District 5 Commissioner Jan Deyette, and District 6 Commissioner Mike Carmolingo, but our hopes for a pro-Thornby commission majority were crushed when Sandy Gallagher missed toppling incumbent Michelle McFall by a mere 37 votes. Michelle's anti-Thornby preservation votes in 2004 and 2005 were made even more hurtful by the fact that, as a teacher at Enterprise Elementary School, she spent her days close (in distance, at least) to Thornby. If her viewpoint prevailed, a new generation of local kids, unlike "Miss Doris' kids," would never know Thornby's wonders at all. Jack Hoyt says he never could understand "the schoolteacher's" failure to support preservation of this historic property. He was well satisfied when the defeat of Masiarczyk's cohort, perennial Thornby opponent Doug Horn, ended what he calls the former mayor's "dynasty."

On election night 2005, "Congratulations Mayor Mulder" bounced jubilant red letters over Interstate 4 from the treetop-tall electronic sign at the Deltona Inn. Inside, I posed for photos next to the new mayor in my "Sandy Walters Doesn't Live Here" T-shirt. No, I didn't live there. But Thornby did.

Though the election results were gratifying, the outlook was one seat short of rosy. Still, driving home late after the post-election bash, I couldn't resist tooting the horn as I passed Frank Knight's house next to Thornby on tree-lined Lakeshore Drive. I imagined him on the phone, giving John Clapp the bad news of Doug Horn's loss. For a while, those old trees were safe. I thought, tonight is good, almost perfect. Tonight, there is hope.

> *Keep in mind that neither success nor failure is ever final.*
>
> **Roger Ward Babson**

CHAPTER FIFTEEN

Why Can't We Just Say We Aren't Accepting It?

Eleventh Thornby Hearing: Volusia Growth Management Commission

The Volusia County Administration Building is a 1970's, plain-Jane stucco structure that fills a small block in downtown DeLand. The final round in the Thornby fight would play out in that building, in the city that ousted Enterprise as county seat more than a century before.

At dusk on a muggy Wednesday in early November 2005,[1] rush-hour commuters had deserted DeLand's now-quiet streets. The Volusia Growth Management Commission convened in the large, windowless chamber used for county council meetings. No TV crew was in sight. If asked to cover a

---

1 The VGMC hearing was held two days before the Deltona elections (see Chapter 14).

VGMC meeting, local news crews would have probably responded laconically, "Film *what*, now?" Leftover pencils, stray papers and nameplates confirmed it as borrowed space and added to the sense of "officialness," as did the large American flag in a corner. In rows of matching black frames, photographs of former county officials smiled for posterity. Behind the dais, straight chairs were temporarily wedged among dark, cushy leather ones as commissioners jostled for seats, where, squeezed knee-to-knee, they would share microphones for the duration. From the raised platform, they peered at the government-green chairs filling with bodies. The room hummed with loud voices, wired nerves, and fluorescent lights. I took my place up front. On the dais, I saw Suzanne Steiner and Tony Cole. Behind me was a roomful of Friends of Thornby, faithful as sunrise. Next to me was our lawyer, Scott Selis. Jeff Buckholz, our traffic expert, was there, as was the Riverkeeper, Neil Armingeon; Audubon's Lynda White; Thornby neighbor Steve Wiechert; Roy Walters, and Carol Aymar. But, someone was missing as the Thornby team took its place. He was tucked out of sight, waiting.

Scott Selis

"The city of Deltona is trying to place a square peg into a round hole."
— **Scott Selis**

Scott Selis was not a land use lawyer. Land-use lawyers are hard to find. Personal injury, divorce and bankruptcy lawyers abound like tree frogs after a hard rain, vastly outnumbering those who practice land use or environmental law by at least two to one. The few land use lawyers in captivity can generally be spotted working hard for interests that run more to paving than saving. This scarcity is a tough truth that civic and environmental activists face, once they come to realize that they are, in effect, soldiers fighting a war, and wars need generals. In a prizefight, it's called "ring generalship," and it's all about taking command.

Scott was a very tall, dark-haired fellow in his late 30s who had lately downsized his Daytona Beach workers compensation and insurance defense practice after being diagnosed with a serious kidney condition. Just about then, the Friends of Thornby came knocking. Scott was sincere, very bright, and pugnacious when he had to be, with an "affinity for historic preservation." As a former Ormond Beach city commissioner, he came with a bonus — political know-how. I liked him right away; however, we've gotten a bit ahead of the story.

When the Deltona City Commission blessed the "Thornby Special Area Plan" in May 2005, it re-started the comp plan amendment process interrupted by hurricanes in 2004. This time, however, helpful Acts of God wouldn't save us. At the city level, we had climbed about as far as citizens could go alone.

For the next stage — the Volusia Growth Management Commission — we needed a lawyer like a mountain climber needs a pickaxe.

Thornby would be Scott's first land use case in a while. He came in cold as a Minnesota winter: Like most Volusians, he had barely heard of the Volusia Growth Management Commission, didn't know how it operated or the rules of the game. He would face Allen Watts or his son. Mark Watts had a softer edge than his dad did, but no matter who it was, Scott would oppose a prominent land-use lawyer with plenty of Thornby experience. He acknowledged up front the steep learning curve ahead. Yet, he was "really excited to represent Friends of Thornby," Scott said years later. "My heart was in it. I realized that developing that property would not be such an important, significant contribution to the area that it was worth sacrificing the historic and environmental benefits it brought to Enterprise and the St. Johns River."

Soon after our initial meeting, Friends of Thornby sent to Scott's office chunky cartons overflowing with enough paper to choke a Tyrannosaurus — five years' worth of memos, notes, letters, emails, photos, maps, minutes, agendas, and staff reports from six public hearings; a year's worth of VGMC with reports and letters; bulky folders crammed with DCA's and Tallahassee attorney Arline's files. The "Thornby contacts" list alone covered three pages. A few weeks later, Scott gave us a list of tasks to be accomplished before the hearing. Some were already finished (get updated school enrollments); some would be completed in time (reconfirm the Soil and Water District's opposition), and some were wishful thinking (demonstrate that there is a fort on the property). "All of this needs to be done scientifically," he emphasized. "I've reviewed everything now and all I can say is WOW! You've had your hands full."

The Most Powerful Appointed Board in Volusia County

Before a job change led him to the planning firm that contracted with Volusia County to draft the Enterprise Plan, Doug Kelly spent four years working for the firm that supplied VGMC staff planners. Doug asserts, "The development community had absolutely no power/influence over the commission." His words ring true, since VGMC members are appointed, not elected. Yet, "The feeling I got as a new member was that most members let the staff take the lead and only asked a question if someone came before them to rock the boat, something that hardly ever happened," says Suzanne Steiner. The 300+ page Thornby staff report was mailed to VGMC members six days before the hearing, but her copy had only arrived that day. No matter what she already knew about Thornby, she says, she felt obliged to study the VGMC staff's position "as best I could." When she announced at the meeting's start that she hadn't had time to do research, two long-time VGMC members reacted almost simultaneously: "Research? That's why we have staff!" Her request that the hearing be postponed until she had time to study the report was defeated.

The Thornby amendment was the third item on the VGMC's agenda. The commission took it up at 8:40 pm. At the microphone, the VGMC's long-time lawyer, Paul Chipok, explained the voting ground rules. Although each Volusia city had one appointed VGMC representative, it wasn't a case of one-person-one-vote. Rather, when voting on plan amendments, each member's vote was "weighted" according to their city's population: the bigger the city, the bigger its piece of the voting pie. The county's voting share was split equally among its five appointees.

Added to this bureaucratic brew was what Scott Selis later called VGMC's "wacky voting rules." For instance, when the commission voted on a plan amendment, an absent commissioner's vote was counted as "no." An unappointed seat voted "no" as well. Thus, even with Daytona Beach's VGMC spot vacant, the city's voting share (the second highest percentage on the panel) on a determining vote would be tallied as "no." Further, the attorney explained, the rules had been "consistently... interpreted" to mean that more than 50 percent of VGMC's *total weighted vote*—not just those present and voting — was needed to make a decision. The result: empty commission seats had as much power as filled ones when a vote was taken.

The commission chairman queried members: "Does everybody understand?" but, from the questions that followed, it seemed that some commissioners would have failed a pop quiz on their own voting rules. It wasn't that they were inattentive — it was just that, for them, voting on comp plan amendments was a rare event. Few amendments ever ended up where Thornby had — at a consistency hearing — because the VGMC considered plan amendments "consistent" if nobody objected to them. Even if another government objected, such conflicts were routinely "conditioned away" by VGMC staff and approved by its chairman without the members' involvement. Doug Kelly alludes to the "unwritten rule" that meant a local government would not challenge another government's application. As for the public, it was virtually unheard — of for citizens to tackle the VGMC, file a formal objection, and maybe hire a lawyer. But that was BT — Before Thornby. (One VGMC rule, however, was clear to everyone: If an amendment failed to win VGMC approval, it was eligible for another try in one year.)

That night, as commissioners settled in, they focused on the lively audience, the suit-wearing lawyers and unfamiliar experts, the ready-to-go PowerPoints, and their fellow citizens, dressed up and watching them intently from the first few rows. In the Thornby amendment, they were facing probably the most highly charged, and surely the most well publicized, issue in the commission's nearly 20-year existence.

Standing

Before Hurricane Charley, and before Scott Selis, Friends of Thornby spent weeks polishing our petition for legal "standing" at the VGMC. At last, 18 months later, the commission was about to vote on our request. Standing is a big deal, but only if you lose. With standing, you have the right to appeal a commission vote. Without standing, you have the right to hang your head and walk away.

Under oath and under the flag, I was cordially invited to face the commission, its lawyer, its planner, the crowd, and Mark Watts. The question of whether Friends of Thornby had standing hinged on whether the damages our members would incur from hundreds of condos on the property were different from those suffered by the public as a whole, and whether a "substantial number" of Friends of Thornby lived close to the property. The commission's lawyer explained this. The commission would have the final say. Like much in the legal world, its decision would be based as much on art as science. The VGMC chairman gave Scott the floor, to establish our case for standing.

"How many Friends of Thornby are there?" Scott asked me. Things were off to a rocky start. Friends of Thornby wasn't like the Mickey Mouse Club where you joined and got a set of ears. We had no dues, no money, and no meetings since those long-ago days at the kitchen table. By 2005, someone who sent supportive email, signed a petition or came to a hearing was considered a "Friend of Thornby." Like those in the audience. But I couldn't volunteer that information. I was feeling sweaty. About 200, I guessed. "Do any live in Deltona?" Well, *that* one was easy. "Do a substantial number live near the property?" "Yes, they do." (What was "near" anyway?) Commissioners began to quiz me politely from the dais: "What percentage of your members lives 'in close proximity' to the property?" I wished the crowd would find somewhere to look besides at me. Do alligators count? I was winging my way, trying for folksy and sympathetic. "I'm not very good with mileage," I apologized. Wary of coming on too strong, I sounded tentative: "I would have done research," I offered. "That's OK," said the VGMC secretary, a county appointee. She asked audience members to stand if they lived within half a mile of Thornby; then repeated her request for those within one mile. Most of the 100 people present stood.

Scott's job was to convince the VGMC that Friends of Thornby deserved standing. Mark's job was to convince them we didn't. Lawyers learn early that pressing a witness too hard can backfire on their case. Watts asked how the Thornby land use change would affect Friends of Thornby more than the general public. Increased traffic on Lakeshore Drive, I said. I got in a word about our "five years of working on this," too. Watts was gentle with me; he didn't pursue the issue of who lives where. Then the commission's attorney,

Paul Chipok, told them that the petition we had so carefully crafted in 2004 was faulty because we hadn't alleged that "a substantial number" of Friends of Thornby lived in or owned property in Deltona. I died inside. Jay Erndl asked if there would be any downside if Friends of Thornby were given standing. Commissioners asked their attorney to repeat the required elements. Scott told them we only had to meet any one of the elements. When they asked what would happen "if" we got standing, it seemed we might have aced the first round. Mark Watts must have sensed it, too. He backed off; I sat down. The vice-chair's motion to give legal standing to Friends of Thornby passed almost unanimously. The only vote opposed was the one from Deltona.

Disclosure

Land use activists tend to focus attention on facts and documents, but lawyers know how to grab human nature by the collar. Scott, veteran of many voting skirmishes, knew the path to take. "We needed to get through to the commissioners who were unfamiliar with Thornby," he recalls. "I needed to understand their position first, show them I do, work through it." His plan was easier said than done. Because VGMC members are "discouraged" from talking to the public about pending cases, most make themselves unavailable. Scott recalls that he asked his assistant to schedule a phone conference for him with each member but when she called, they expressed concern about doing so.

But DeBary appointee Jay Erndl didn't shy away. Days before the hearing, over coffee at IHOP with Scott and me, Jay was willing to listen. He was polite but wary and at first did not "get" why we asked him to meet. The VGMC staff report gave him enough information about the Thornby plan amendment, he told us. As Scott and I spread our star items, like DCA's critical ORC report, over the table, Jay turned quizzical. "I haven't seen this stuff," he told us.

At the hearing, members were routinely asked if they had discussed the amendment with anyone. Jay Erndl's unapologetic disclosure that he had met with Scott Selis and Sandra Walters drew a collective intake of breath. Instantly, Scott was on his feet. "I recognize that it's unusual to meet with members of this board before a hearing," he said firmly to the wide-eyed commissioners, "but I spoke to Mr. Chipok about this. It's not illegal, but it's discouraged — by Mr. Chipok. It's perfectly legal for Mr. Erndl to have met with us." Someone asked if he had met with other commissioners. "No," replied Scott, "I tried, but got much resistance," and left it at that.

Teri Bowley

"A lot of the information submitted by the public wasn't germane."
— **Teri Bowley**[2]

"It's not VGMC's job to determine whether this is a good or bad, popular or unpopular, plan amendment," the pretty, dark-haired planner declared pertly. She was bright and breezy and she worked for the large Orlando planning firm that had consulted for the VGMC, without competitive bidding, since Day One of the commission's existence. Her words piggybacked lawyer Paul Chipok's earlier directive: *"The question is not whether this is a good or bad plan. The question is how can it be made to be consistent?"*

It's been Florida's legacy since at least the mid-20th century to plow down that which is natural or historic and put up bland, harsh or ugly office buildings, retail centers or condominiums. Books have been written to try to stop these practices. Speeches have been given against them and political candidates elected who promised to outlaw them. Almost all to no avail. In the Florida of easy approvals, planners tread a comfortably worn path. Veteran planner Ron Paradise espouses a different approach. "For planning to be effective, it needs to be grassroots," he said in 2010. However, grassroots didn't rate with VGMC planners, who met with government representatives, but not with the public.

When we got the staff report a week or so before the hearing, we combed through it like condemned prisoners probing the governor's final message — page by page, paragraph by paragraph, line by line, word by word. The mistakes and omissions we found filled seven pages. In addition, the report asserted that Thornby is "not subject to Enterprise Local Plan policies" but Thornby condos would be considered for Deltona's "Urban Design Policy" standards. In the singsong tones of a kindergarten teacher explaining the mysteries of crayons, Bowley took commissioners through the staff report for nearly 50 minutes. Our role, she said in distinctly pass-the-buck mode, is "to review the application *'as submitted by the city'*." As for the many documents submitted by Friends of Thornby: they are "available for review at the VGMC office," she said.

---

2   Teri Bowley declined a request to be interviewed for this book.

Selective Information

"I shot an arrow in the air/It fell to earth I know not where."
-**Henry Wadsworth Longfellow**

If the poet's arrow had been dipped in misinformation, though, he would have known where to find it. Several of Deltona's factually-challenged arrows, first shot skyward in 2002, fell into the VGMC staff report in 2005. The "affordable housing on Thornby" threat was still alive. The state's last-year objection to the old Thornby plan was attached to the staff report, while its last-month objection to the new Thornby plan was not. But the most maddening scrap of tara-diddle was the statement that at a county council hearing, "a suggestion was made that the property would be best suited in Deltona." (No one interviewed for this book who was present at the 2000 county Thornby hearing remembered such a suggestion.) I wrote the VGMC planner. She did not respond.

Consistency

To the VGMC, consistency is king. The Volusia County Charter states that if a comp plan amendment is "consistent" with other governments' plans — i.e., it has "no significant adverse effects" on them — it will be certified by the VGMC. Six specific criteria for making the judgment call "what is consistent?" are in the county code. (*Volusia County, Florida, Code Sec. 90-37, (2007)*). From his window as a former consultant, Doug Kelly opines that those criteria were designed broadly so that "consultants would be needed to interpret." Consistency was a "brand new buzzword" when the VGMC was created, said a member of the 1986 Charter Review Commission (CRC), who asked not to be identified. The consistency concept was simple:

Adverse effects = not consistent = amendment not certified

After the VGMC was around for a few years, however, the simple concept got complicated:

Adverse effects = not consistent + conditions = amendment certified

Using staff-created conditions to "make a plan consistent" soon pretty much overshadowed the VGMC's charter-endowed decision-making function. At least since the early 1990s, says planner Ron Paradise, "All sides were involved in conditioning and in some cases the conditioning activity was used to justify or even augment planning products that were not well thought out." The CRC member quoted anonymously above agrees, saying she can't pinpoint when "conditions and other weasel words crept in to thwart whatever good intentions there may have been originally."

In Thornby, the VGMC planner seemed to address the required consistency criteria by shaking them into submission:

- **Water permits and capacities:** She advised the commission that "during the meeting tonight" she had been informed by the St. Johns River Water Management District that some city-supplied information was inaccurate. "Be that as it may", she concluded," there are still adequate utilities to serve this property."

- **Traffic:** The state expected the VGMC to have "plenty to say about impacts to the local roads" - but what the VGMC staff said was probably not what the state had in mind. The VGMC staff's position went like this: When the bypass road is finished (its original 2003 completion date had been pushed back three years), there won't be any problems. To mollify concerns about worsening gridlock by adding 436 new residents in one place, the planner said, "We are looking at this not only from today but a 20-year timeframe." Then she assured the commission that Deltona would do a traffic review when the Thornby property was rezoned.

- **Adverse effects on natural resources:** The report spent three pages concluding that landscaped buffers would protect the scenic road, that other agencies would protect the wetlands, and that an archeological survey would protect anything else. Historic and specimen trees would be protected, too — on the one-sixth of the property left for them. Bowley took a cavalier approach to Thornby's bald eagle nest: "An eagle has been "spotted over the years, sometimes there, sometimes not." At any rate, she assured commissioners, eagle protection would come from federal and state permits and government agencies are doing a "great job."

- **School numbers:** With schools already over capacity, the staff report had to concede that 244 new townhouses "could have adverse impacts on county schools."

- **Agreements between governments:** This issue is irrelevant, she said, because the city and county never made an agreement about Enterprise.

Wrapping up, the planner/consultant recommended "conditional" approval of the Thornby Special Area Plan. Condition: The School Board and Deltona should coordinate how to "minimize the impacts" from over-capacity schools. Condition: "Limit" total units to 151 instead of 244.

> **Activist Lesson:** When is a compromise not a compromise? When you ask initially for more than you expect to get, and then "compromise" by accepting what you wanted in the first place. Both numbers are above what is legally allowed, but sham compromises make it easier for officials to approve land use changes. Focus on bottom line numbers instead of the "compromise" dangled before officials' eyes.

The planner/consultant concluded by asking if her employers — the commissioners — had any questions. Deltona's appointee asked a canned question about affordable housing on the property. *"In certain circumstances,"* Bowley responded, the county council *could* approve "up to five per acre" for affordable housing. She interjected that the county *could* allow non-residential uses, too. She thanked Deltona's appointee for reminding her. Another commissioner asked about overcrowded middle and high schools, a subject not mentioned in the report. The planner asked the school board's Saralee Morrissey to speak "if she doesn't' mind." The always-plainspoken school official drew a chuckle from the crowd. "Why would I mind?" she wondered. "You're showing an interest in schools — I'm thrilled!" Other thoughtful questions from the dais proved that commissioners were not only still awake, but paying attention. "You're recommending 151 units. How many units are allowed there now?" The planner's answer: "41." Commissioners grilled her about traffic concerns. "Are you taking Deltona's other pending amendments into account in analyzing traffic?" Answer: "No. It's like dominoes and you can't take them out of order." "Doesn't traffic to be generated from other plans concern you?" Her answer: "There are various different ways to look at traffic impacts. Planning is a difficult job." She deflected concerns about traffic on scenic corridor Lakeshore Drive: "We can only assess information that's provided to us," she bristled. (Presumably, that did not include information provided by Friends of Thornby.) A commissioner asked lawyer Chipok what burden of proof would apply when they voted on Thornby. "Preponderance of the evidence," he instructed.

Bob Nix

"The concept here is to pay the developer to do the right thing."
— Bob Nix

Bob Nix knew his stuff. When Deltona was an infant city, he was a one-man planning staff. By 2005, he was a department head and his assistant represented Deltona on the VGMC. He regularly addressed the Deltona City Commission, advised its planning board, and steered the lesser-known Development Review Committee. For nine bustling years, he had taken the city where its leaders told him to go. But that night, he was 15 miles from Deltona City Hall.

Nix was tall, sturdy and smart, but no one would ever accuse him of being a "people person." It was said he once aspired to a legal career, but he kept his private life private. (Years later, after leaving Florida, he returned regularly to assist a family member who had significant health problems.) For six years, Thornby opponents had been putting wrinkles in his nicely ironed workdays.

That night, Nix clearly enjoyed the opportunity to convince the commission that he possessed a superior knowledge of Thornby. In the sonorous tones and rapid-fire delivery of a former broadcaster, Nix assured commissioners that the "Thornby Special Area Plan" solved the public's problems. "Density credits for saving resources," he called it.

Commissioners had already heard from their planner how the Thornby plan would satisfy their consistency criteria with only minor tweaking. They expected to hear the same from Bob Nix representing the applicant, Deltona. But Nix didn't go there, at least not in listener-friendly fashion. He talked about the economics of market-driven development and lectured about institutional constraints. (Because Deltona's VGMC appointee was a planner, Nix may have wrongly presumed that all commission members were planners.) He wandered down the lane of Professional Planner, speaking Planner-ese about complex matters like state concurrency, PUDs and school bond issues — important topics, surely, but not on point when it came to the VGMC's decision. He brought himself back to the subject of traffic. There would "probably" be impacts to Lakeshore Drive from Thornby condos, he allowed, but the city's analysis "didn't really indicate" that impacts would be "massive." Without hesitation, he declared that, "One day the region is going to develop so much that there will be traffic problems there [even] if we do nothing to Thornby." Then he was off again, tangentially speaking, musing on the philosophical question of policy-constrained roads and impact fee credits.

> **Activist Lesson:** "It's coming whether we like it or not." Why, then, do we have controls like comprehensive plans, future land use maps, zoning and proscribed land use designations?

Rather than allaying commissioners' concerns, Nix's words may have had the opposite effect. He acknowledged a "drainage problem in front of this property," that the county could fix "if they choose to do so." He agreed that school overcrowding is a "massive problem." The scenic road buffer would be taken care of later, he soothed. The VGMC staff's conditions meant the city would "take away" 47 percent of the property, he said, but "Frank is OK with that."

Surely, Bob Nix knew that in 20 years, the VGMC had certified 99 percent of the amendment proposals that came its way. He almost seemed to wink at commissioners — "Hey, we're all in this together," he seemed to be saying. He got through everything in barely 10 minutes. "Questions for Mr. Nix?" inquired the VGMC chairman. There were none.

Mark Watts

"The plan protects certain elements of the property."

— Mark Watts

Shortly before the hearing, Watts was publicly annoyed. "They had us looking for cowboys and then they had us looking for Indians," he complained in the *Daytona Beach News-Journal*. In the same story, Bob Nix groused that people were "stuck on one item — density." Kevin Finn and I fought back in the same article: What about the traffic fallout from so many townhouses, and the protective Natural Resources Management Area overlay to be lifted from the property, we countered.

> **Activist Lesson:** It's been said, "All publicity is good publicity." Keeping your cause in the public eye is essential: after all, decision-makers read newspapers too.

Watts was a clean-cut, youthful-looking 31-year old. Invoking the spirit of his father's legal vanguard, he opened with a line from Robert Frost. He introduced Bruce Andersen. He told commissioners that the Thornby property had been in his clients' family since 1911 and that things around Thornby had changed. There's the Publix, the 7-Eleven, even new cottages at the Children's Home, he said. He told the VGMC that in 2000, the county "council suggested that perhaps the future of this property and its growth would best be addressed by the city of Deltona." (Again, no one interviewed for this book who attended the council hearing recalls the council making such a suggestion.)

Watts delivered a calm, clean account of the Thornby struggles, sprinkled with plenty of "publics," "protections" and "preservations." "We need to assign [Thornby] an appropriate land use," he declared, without saying what was wrong with the one-per-acre land use it already had. We've "re-tooled," and "my clients have been reasonable working with the city," he averred. It was not clear whether VGMC members followed his technical blow-by-blow of density credits and bonuses, and it probably didn't matter anyway. The commissioners were told, "We are giving up approximately 50 percent of this property to conservation." They were not told that, according to the state, Deltona's "conservation" on Thornby would allow "intensive non-residential uses."

> **Activist Lesson:** "Truth" and "accuracy" are not the same concept. A statement can be factually true but not contain enough information to be accurate. Listeners/activists must ask questions, seek clarification, and search for the accuracy behind the truth.

The owners "have no problems going through the permitting process" for the Thornby eagle nest, Watts said. "Our analysis doesn't indicate any significant impacts to Lakeshore Drive," he averred. As to school capacity: The owners agree to work out a strategy with the school board, but "this isn't the time for it," he said. In addirion, it's premature to consider traffic impacts from other developments, he said. "First you get the entitlements." (Translation: Your planner has devised a way around all the problems. Vote yes now and rely on us to take care of everything later.) Bruce Andersen had remained silent, as did commissioners when Watts asked for questions.

The VGMC chairman then asked if anyone else wished to speak in favor of the Thornby application. The room was as silent as an old, vacant house.

Ron Paradise

"If the density doesn't FIT, find the amendment inconsisTENT."
— Ron Paradise

It was nearly 10 p.m. and the hearing was only halfway through. Ron Paradise's customary affable demeanor belied the fact that he carried the full weight of Volusia County's Thornby opposition on his shoulders. "I will be brief; it is late," he began, knowing that what he had to tell the commission could not be rushed. Time travel is never speedy.

Ron related how in 2000 the county council rejected a land use change to multi-family on Thornby; in 2001, the property was annexed into Deltona. "Those two events had a coalescent effect on the Enterprise community," he stressed. "This was the kickoff of the Enterprise Local Plan." He spoke slowly, emphasizing every word: *"It was intended to protect the character of the community of Enterprise."*

"I want to talk about the Enterprise Plan," Ron continued. The county sent out more than 800 surveys to landowners. The response rate was "really good." Overwhelmingly, Enterprise wanted to maintain and protect low density, the environment and its historical character, he said, and cited the specific county policy that discourages "increases in land use intensities and densities" in Enterprise. Before the plan became official, he said, Deltona was asked to participate. The county sent the survey and responses to Deltona. The county sent policy drafts. Members of county staff had a couple of meetings with city staff. The Enterprise Preservation Society met with Deltona. County and city officials exchanged numerous emails. Deltona didn't object when the VGMC approved the Enterprise Plan in 2003, he said.

Ron's jabs gathered force. Yes, he said, in 2000 the county staff *did* recommend changing Thornby's land use, as Mark Watts told you. But why? "By just looking at what's immediately next door without looking at the context of this property with the greater Enterprise community, we fell into the same trap that VGMC staff has," Ron said.

Ron's degree in history and 15-year planning career had taken him through county ranks from journeyman to senior planner. Along the way, he gathered stellar evaluations, customer service awards, and the respect and thanks of local activists. If you had a question about a development or a plan amendment anywhere in Volusia, Ron was your go-to guy. He looked like Charlie Sheen's Eagle Scout brother, but at the VGMC meeting, he was the county's smokejumper, packing a PowerPoint instead of a parachute.

"I want to discuss the Natural Resources Management Area on Thornby," Ron said solemnly. The NRMA overlay is intended to safeguard Thornby's wetlands, trees, listed species and flood plains, and low density is the "one prime method" to protect these resources. If the land use changes, the overlay disappears, he said.

By "chapter and verse" of county code, he splattered the years-old myths touted to justify city development plans for Thornby. Those "commercial and industrial uses" on Thornby that we're told would be welcome under the county? No. Commercial development "needs to be" on thoroughfares and Lakeshore Drive is not a thoroughfare, Ron said. "Anybody who's driven it can understand why the scenic views should be protected." Then he threw a straight right. "The possibility of there being commercial or industrial, non-residential uses on this area is nil." He debunked the scare tactic of "affordable housing on Thornby" — in 15 years, nobody in Volusia, including Deltona, has implemented the process — the same words heard from Friends of Thornby at those long-ago city hearings.

Ron had eradicated the myths and doused the VGMC staff's glowing bonfire of reasons to approve the plan. What remained was most important: the consistency criteria. One by one, he addressed them.

- **Water permits and capacities:** Deltona wants a "leap of faith" from you, Ron warned. With future city sewer capacity unknown, it is conceivable Deltona might decide to build a sewage treatment plant on Thornby.

- **Traffic:** Again, "the city is asking the VGMC to take a leap of faith," he cautioned, "that these traffic issues will be addressed sometime in the future when studies are complete."

- **Adverse effects on natural resources:** Thornby's eagle nest is part of the countywide natural resource infrastructure base, he apprised them. Under this plan, "We don't have a handle on how the area will be protected."

- **Agreements between governments:** "We want to have an agreement with Deltona over the Enterprise area; we just have never been able to come to a conclusion on that," he reported.

The room was still while Ron gave his presentation. For the Friends of Thornby, every word elicited joy combined with relief. No longer were we the rag-tag kids on the block, picking fight after exhausting fight with the heavyweight neighbors. Finally, we had reinforcements. We had backup. We had a whole county on our side.

Ron continued, "I want to close by saying this: The density proposed by your staff is still insufficient to protect the resources of this property. It's almost four times above what the county would allow. The density doesn't fit and if the density doesn't *fit*, find the amendment inconsis*tent*." When laid-back planner Ron Paradise channeled O.J. Simpson's flamboyant lawyer Johnnie Cochran, the room erupted with delighted applause. When things settled down, all ears were tuned to Ron. His voice carried empathy, a sharp sense of right and wrong, and professional competence. "Notwithstanding the jurisdictional nuances of the city of Deltona and the unincorporated county," he said, hesitating a little, and then raising his voice so the back row could hear: "The Thornby property is historically, culturally, socially and environmentally part of Enterprise. Our position is that development on the Thornby property needs to be consistent with the Enterprise Plan." The room rang with applause.

Bob Nix vs. Ron Paradise

"I have a couple of questions about the testimony that was just given." Bob Nix left his seat and inserted himself up front, where Ron Paradise was still standing. Drowsy commissioners were suddenly alert, as if each had swigged a double espresso: *this* was highly irregular! The mild-mannered VGMC chairman, who represented New Smyrna Beach, told Nix to go ahead. The room fell silent as Bob Nix loomed unfashionably close to Ron Paradise. It was a different Nix from the jaunty city planner who had confidently skimmed over Thornby issues an hour earlier.

"Looking back on it, we probably should have" objected to the Enterprise Plan, Nix told the Commission and himself. Commissioners squirmed in their seats as he cross-examined his "witness," Ron Paradise. Nix insisted that Deltona was shut out of the process while the Enterprise Plan evolved. Then: "How does one unit per acre protect resources?" he demanded, jabbing a finger in Ron's direction. The commission heard him cut off Ron's attempts to answer that question and questions about commercial uses. "Thank you for speaking for me, but that's not true," he threw at Ron, pacing back and forth in front of the dais. His face reddening, Nix went on about densities, utilities, and new cottages at the Children's Home. The demon of public opinion that trailed him like a stray dog for years was unleashed that night, and he knew it. Commissioners watched him circle a calm, stationary Ron Paradise, who stayed polite and respectful, as though Nix had every right to call the shots.

They heard Nix's voice rise while he turned Thornby's traffic problems into a wordplay seesaw over the terms "need" and "shall" in county codes. The disconcerting bout lasted no more than 10 minutes, but to those who sat through it, it seemed to drag on much longer. "Nix was in Ron's face and yelling," recalls Roy Walters. "The chairman let him hang himself." Finally, the VGMC chair, maybe sorry that he allowed the runaway train to go forward, put on the brakes. "What's the biggest issue here?" he asked. Nix seemed to deflate. Ron answered the question. The biggest issue is the 244 units proposed by the city and the 151 units proposed by VGMC staff, he said.

Friends of Thornby

The room was still reeling from the off-putting spectacle of one professional railing at another in public. To relieve the tension, our lawyer Scott Selis took a different tack: "It's hard to pay attention for more than three hours," he told commission members, confessing that, "We actually toyed with the idea as we sat over there about what should we do right now." The case to certify Thornby's land use change was spread on the commission table, served up by Teri Bowley, Mark Watts and Bob Nix. Tempting conditions placed within easy reach promised they could vote "yes" and still leave satisfied. Scott had to convince commissioners to reject that fare. And do it before more commissioners joined the long-time member from an east Volusia city who, as was his habit at hearings, dozed quietly in his seat.

Scott plunged in against the current. He had learned that, for the VGMC, approving "with conditions" was an ingrained habit, much like those quick naps. "You're being asked to determine whether the plan as proposed is consistent *now*, he insisted, not "later once those edges are removed."

Above the trees, away from political boundaries, vision clears. Look at the neighborhood from the air, he invited them, pointing to the aerial map. "These high densities you keep hearing about from your staff and others are in *Deltona*. The question before you is not whether condos on Thornby are consistent with the way *Deltona* uses its land. The question is whether the proposal before you is consistent with the surrounding county uses. What's the surrounding use? *The Enterprise Plan*."

"I have so much to say," he went on, almost apologetically. "We tried to get our side of the story out before tonight; the only side that came out was Deltona's. The staff report supports Deltona completely. Sandy went to the trouble of getting documents to the VGMC. She left them at the office for anyone who would take time out of their busy schedules and go to Daytona to see them. Paul Chipok discouraged you from meeting with us. We didn't want to present these documents tonight: We wanted you to have them in advance, but [only] Jay Erndl has them."

"If you go to a movie and all the seats are sold, they won't sell you a ticket. What's wrong with Florida? Why is it that we put the cart in front of the horse so much? Tonight is your opportunity. It's what the VGMC is here for. Enterprise Elementary is 138 percent over capacity right now and using portable classrooms. We shouldn't be building new developments or allowing land uses that will allow them until the theater is not full. The developer should be told: Come back when the theater is not full. Come back for a later show."

Scott thanked the audience for sticking it out. He said he knew how emotional this was for all of us. He asked anyone who wished to speak after Friends of Thornby's presentation to keep on point and limit their comments to three minutes. (Although the VGMC did not limit speakers' times, it was obvious their attention was flagging.) It was around 11 p.m. when Friends of Thornby were allowed to speak.

First, Stephen Wiechert told commissioners that for 30 years he had lived 10 feet from Thornby. His solid background — 25 years at Lockheed-Martin, work on Apache helicopters, father of two — gave weight to his words: One-lane Broadway and two-lane Lakeshore Drive can't handle hundreds more cars a day.

Carol Aymar reminded the commission about the last — and only — time she came before them: "It was on July 23, 2003, when you unanimously voted to certify the plan amendment to establish the Enterprise Local Plan." She originally planned to invoke history, to make them see that Friends of Thornby were "all good people," not obstructionists, not radicals. We've "never objected to development of that property at current zoning," she made it clear. She traced six years of support: from the public, from the county, from DeBary and from Lake Helen. She handed out copies of the *Orlando Sentinel's* recent editorial: "Reject Big Growth in Enterprise" and related EPS' efforts to buy the property. Now, the night's events had city-county infighting on everyone's minds. One of the VGMC's criteria was "furtherance of intergovernmental cooperation." "From what you've seen tonight," she said pointedly, "I can't imagine another amendment that could more adversely affect intergovernmental cooperation between Deltona and the county." At the end, the chairman asked her if we had a "problem with 40 units on the property." Carol repeated: "We have *never* objected to that."

If Friends of Thornby had been limited to just one witness at the VGMC, it would have to be MIT-educated Jeffrey Buckholz, Ph.D./Professional Engineer from Jacksonville. If anything could carry the day at the VGMC, we believed, it would be traffic problems — more than ruined natural resources, more than cramped schools, more than burdened utilities. Dr. Buckholz was a little younger than Bob Nix and a little older than Ron Paradise with a clean-shaven head, a dry wit, and perhaps the most high-powered resume the VGMC had ever seen. "There were lots of things wrong with the concurrency system in Volusia County and Deltona," Buckholz explained when interviewed for this story. What's "concurrency?" Simply put, it's making sure you have transportation infrastructure in place to support new developments. Sounds great, but, as he points out, concurrency drives a truckload of problems, not the least of which is, "If you want to be shifty, there are lots of ways to beat the system."

At the hearing, Buckholz used a 16-frame PowerPoint to identify at least nine major deficiencies in the Thornby traffic study, including unanalyzed intersections, miscounted traffic numbers, incorrect standards, and a too-small study area. The traffic from four nearby planned developments hadn't been taken into account, either. He noted that Thornby development would add "a substantial number of trips" to two-lane Lakeshore Drive, a scenic road without shoulders. And the "Bypass Road," long heralded by Deltona as the answer to Thornby gridlock? "The construction date continues to slip," Buckholz noted, labeling the city's Thornby traffic report as "yesterday's news." Bottom line: "Piecemeal, inconsistent and ineffective" traffic planning, said the expert.

It was "disturbing," Buckholz said, to hear Bob Nix say, "The region is going to develop so much that there will be traffic problems there, and there's nothing you can do." He ended by setting the record straight: "Yes, there *is* something you can do: Use land controls."

Introducing the next presenter, Scott told the commission: You have been hearing about densities all night, but "I promise you that the following is new information." The PowerPoint created by Roy Walters, Ph.D., a Professional Engineer, targeted "Three Real Problems" with the Thornby amendment. The first was Deltona's colored "Lot Density Map" of property densities within three miles of Thornby. By showing numbers in "square miles" rather than "acres," neighboring densities seemed supersized (calling to mind attorney Arline's observation that city documents made Thornby seem surrounded by Miami). The same map pinned questionable labels like "exurban" and "highest urban densities" on some close-by properties, and used blood red to signify the densest areas. When "per mile" was converted back to "per acre," however, the smoke around Thornby's surroundings cleared. As demonstrated, the "Thornby Special Area Plan" would load densities that were *15 times higher*, on average, than neighboring properties. "INCOMPATIBLE" read Roy's slide, in bold red letters.

The second problem noted by my husband was the proposed "landscaped buffer" between planned Thornby condos and Lakeshore Drive. It would be an open invitation to replace Lakeshore Drive's famous overhanging oak canopy with low shrubs, thus giving higher-priced condos a lake view.

Part of Dr. Buckholz's presentation

CONCLUSIONS - 2

- There is almost no meaningful coordination between the City and the County with respect to traffic concurrency.
- The Thornby Traffic Study has many problems and can not be relied upon when evaluating the traffic concurrency situation in the area.
- All future traffic studies should explicitly account for the effect of other planned developments.
- The Debary Avenue/Doyle Road corridor and the Lakeshore Drive corridor are critical traffic locations. Their operational characteristics need to be protected, either through needed improvements or through the scaling-back of future developments, or both.

Commuter traffic through Enterprise, 2005

Slide from Dr. Walters' presentation

Where will the density load go?

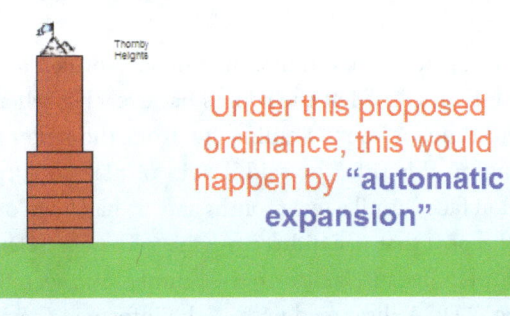

Under this proposed ordinance, this would happen by "automatic expansion"

The most startling graph turned sometimes-confusing density numbers into a real-life lesson on what the Thornby Plan meant in real-life terms. Excluding wetlands, buffers, setbacks, roads, etc., from Thornby's 41 acres left only 18 acres for the proposed 244 units — 13 condos per acre. At 2.8 people per unit (Deltona's demographics), 38 people would populate each acre. Picture three football teams, five cheerleaders and 27 cars all living on an area smaller than a football field. And they'd likely gain more neighbors, thanks to the Plan's "automatic expansion of density" that was "not subject to review." Where, oh where, to put them all? The VGMC members seemed to get a kick out of Roy's solution: "Thornby Heights," a high-rise condominium complex with commanding views of Lake Monroe.

When the St. Johns Riverkeeper and the Audubon eagle watch coordinator stepped up to help the Friends of Thornby at earlier hearings, neither Neil Armingeon from Jacksonville nor Lynda White from Orlando could foresee that one night they would spend hours in DeLand waiting to tell the Volusia Growth Management Commission the facts of life about wetlands and bald eagles. Neil, a down-to-earth, likeable man with the faint drawl of a New Orleans native, had a stinging retort to the commission staff report's *laissez faire* approach: "Let me assure you that the agencies that people talk about overseeing these projects and protecting our wetlands are *not* doing that," he said. "The Army Corps of Engineers in the last three years reviewed 12,000 wetland permits and denied two. Florida's DEP [Department of Environmental Protection] has failed in its mandate to protect state waters. I'm still waiting to see the Water Management District deny one permit." He zeroed in on what mattered: Because this project adversely affects the county's natural resources, he told the VGMC, it "violates your criteria."

Lynda, a short-haired, pleasant woman with decades of experience with raptors, briefed commissioners on Eagle Nest VO12C. "The Thornby nest is right smack-dab in the middle of the property," she advised them. Many times, state/federal agencies "will issue a 'take' [permit] and that means the developer is allowed to do whatever he plans to do," she said. "This is the only resident nesting pair of eagles in Deltona. It would be a terrible shame to lose them after 30 years."

After Lynda spoke, Scott startled the commission. "Our last speaker tonight will be Chris Elmer." With that, Chris left the room's back reaches where he had been silently biding his time for hours. Smiling, he strode the center aisle. "It's a little bit weird being on this side," he said. Looks of pleased surprise came over tired commission faces; until a few months ago, he had been one of them. "I read the first staff report that you didn't read," he told them, referring to 2004's "Thornby Oaks" plan because as [former Commission] Secretary I [got] a copy of everything." "DCA disagreed with it," he informed them, his voice rising. "They had to go back and, as Mr. Watts says, 'retool.' They retool a lot on this thing because they've been trying to get this thing through and it won't get through because it keeps failing on all the key aspects — the aspects that fall *exactly* under the jurisdiction of this commission."

"I've counted 83 questionable items in the staff report," he told his former colleagues. "One that bothered me the most was the section on the history where it says that 'Following substantial public opposition the county council denied the plan amendment at a later hearing' … (this is when they turned it down)… and 'a suggestion was made that the property would be best suited in Deltona and could be reviewed by the City of Deltona.'" In a voice knotted with controlled indignation, he re-lived that day in 2000:

> I was standing at the podium and I was looking at [County Councilwoman] Ann McFall, and her comment was that she *feared* when they turned it down, that it would be annexed into the city of Deltona and Deltona would give them what they wanted. That's what it was. She *feared* it.

Chris continued, "The bottom line is that this thing fails on every aspect and it's based on … 'theoretically' it'll work out. We're 'hopeful' that they'll do this. The school will 'hopefully' be built. The drainage will 'hopefully' be there. I … did my own traffic analysis because I drive past this thing every day. It's gridlocked now — *Now* … It's basically going to violate everything that you guys are looking at. So I'm going to ask you to basically turn this thing down cold. Thank you," said Chris, turning to join the Friends of Thornby in the front row, to hearty applause.

Scott Selis reappeared in front of the commission: "Why is Deltona trying to fit this square peg into a round hole? And why is Thornby on the city commission's agenda for their last meeting before city elections?" He kidded about the late hour, and then turned deadly serious: "This isn't a religion based on faith. This is a governmental body that makes its decisions based on facts and evidence. I respectfully request that you deny this application," he said.

The case was wrapped up, but I was not. "I want to say something," I said to our attorney. Matter-of-factly, Scott leaned over and whispered, "Save your speech, we've got them." "Scott," I retorted, "I know they're drooping and so are we. But there are a couple of things I need to say." I walked to the podium, weary commission eyes watching. "The blue folders we gave you earlier are full of documents you hadn't seen," I said. I sent them to your planning firm, as I was instructed. Your staff report talks about public input, but I've handed you Friends of Thornby's documents they say are "not germane": Dr. Buckholz's traffic report, the Department of Community Affairs' latest objections, and two letters from the Florida Department of Environmental Protection.

They were tired, but I kept going. It took five years to get here. There's an archeological report, I informed the commission, "but no one knows what it says." The state documented an Indian mound on this property, I told them, but the owners' lawyers called it "another tactic." They joked in the newspaper about "cowboys and Indians" on Thornby, and about finding beer bottles instead of a fort that was not there … sardonic words that cut like a sword buried for 100 years but nonetheless malevolent. The remarks were "very unfair," my lips said to the commission, but my heart said that, no matter what happened that night, the hateful words had, at least, been reported for the record.

Last up was Mark Watts with rebuttal. "Good morning," he greeted the commission, because it was then Thursday. "Your decision is not based on popularity but on consistency," he said in a near-scolding tone. His 12-minute wrap-up marshaled his most persuasive points: How the next-door condos were county-approved when built decades before; how Deltona had no voice in the final Enterprise Plan; how the Thornby plan protects half the property; how traffic studies prove all would be well. He referred to population hordes that were "coming no matter what," and pointedly disagreed with presentations by Roy Walters, Jeff Buckholz, Lynda White and me. Still, his most potent weapon was not Bob Nix, or even his own lawyerness. It was the commission's own planner's report, which favored approving the amendment with conditions. Six times, he reminded commissioners of that fact. "I ask for your support," he said in closing. No one had a question.

The Time Has Come

Five incredible years of hearings, meetings, phone calls, e-mails, speeches, travel, bills, experts, bureaucrats, politicians, letters, lies, arm twisting, civic campaigns, tears, elation, and disappointment came down to this moment. Final words, an anxious "Hail Mary" on my Nana's rosary, a lawyer's last entreaty to the Volusia Growth Management Commission, and its plain response — "approve" or "deny." That night, our fight to preserve the 40-acre historic Thornby property would be won or lost for good.

My thoughts floated… flammable gas, fateful hurricanes, fatuous T-shirts, a story too incredible to invent. Save Thornby? Of course. Save Enterprise, too. Back then, I thought the story of Thornby began with its Friends. Later, I came to understand that the story of Thornby has always lived in the history of Enterprise.

Time Stands Still

Eleven seconds after the hearing was closed, a motion and second were on the floor. The motion was to deny the Thornby application.

A handful of members advertised their thoughts. The amendment doesn't meet our criteria addressing natural resources, traffic or school capacity, they said. The vice-chair, who represented Ormond Beach, said the scenic road buffer and the Enterprise Local Plan were issues that "stick in my mind." It took a few seconds for the words to sink in. Scott was right: they *were* on our side! I closed my eyes, thanking every saint I could muster, and then realized that most of the members hadn't said a word.

In the front row, we were holding hands and squeezing arms. My dead grandmother's rosary beads hung around my neck. I looked at the floor because I couldn't look at their faces. The chair wanted a roll call. Sixteen voting members were present. Voice after voice said "yes" — to *deny* the amendment, but three went the other way. One, naturally, was from Deltona. At 16.54 percent, her vote carried the most weight. The others who voted for the plan were Orange City and Ponce Inlet. "Motion carries," announced Merry Chris Smith, the VGMC administrator, then hesitated: "Let me just verify that." The room turned to stone. Two minutes later, Paul Chipok retracted: "The motion did *not* carry. It was 48.63 percent in favor, which is less than 50 percent, so the motion [to deny] fails." Since Daytona Beach didn't have a representative, and one county appointee was absent — as were members from Pierson, South Daytona, and Port Orange — under the "wacky voting rules" that considered an empty seat's vote as "no," there weren't enough "yes's" to deny the amendment! A black tunnel opened at my feet and it led straight to Hell. "So what do we have to do?" the chair coolly asked the commission's lawyer.

"You need to make a final decision this evening," Chipok replied, dangling the easy solution. "You have a staff report before you," he offered more than once, but no one seemed inclined to go there. The minutes ticked by. Some commissioners questioned their understandably nonplussed lawyer ("how would you re-word the motion?") He offered another option: Reverse the motion so you are voting to *approve* the amendment. With the "empty seat votes," there might be enough "no's" to defeat it. However, he warned, even if that happened, "that still leaves open 'what is the action being taken.'" Friends of Thornby had been wrapped in stunned silence since the first motion faltered. Several commissioners talked at once; side conversations gave the aura of a neighborhood carnival. Time seemed to shut down, the way it had years before while the flustered city planning board sorted out Q. L. Snook's vote. The witnesses just stared. Mark Watts didn't utter a word. Scott offered a suggestion, but it went nowhere. Commissioners batted comments around like a plastic ball at a Beach Boys concert. A motion was made and seconded to *approve* the Thornby comp plan amendment. The normally unflappable Merry Chris carefully asked for clarification. She wasn't alone in her confusion. The commission secretary, when assured by Chipok that the motion to approve included the staff's conditions, drew an anemic chuckle when she responded, "That doesn't mean I have to vote for it, right?"

They voted again. The chairman wanted another roll call. Chipok slowly explained that this time, a "yes" vote would approve the amendment. Deltona and Orange City voted "yes;" everyone else voted "no." "Motion carried. Motion didn't carry," said Ms. Smith. "My head's all screwed up, excuse me," she apologized for misfiguring the voting percentages. After her 15-hour workday, it was forgivable.

"OK, so that motion also failed," Chipok said. "Do you want to leave it at that? Or do you want to bring it to some type of —" A chorus of commissioners interrupted. "I'm a little —" His words were drowned in a sea of agitated outbursts. From the audience where he had been sitting for five hours, Jack Hoyt piped up: "Is this a democracy or what?" The secretary's plea: "Why can't we just say we're not accepting this?" was met with applause from her fellow commissioners (and quoted in news stories). "I understand that the intent of the board is that you want to deny the application, but you voted to *deny* the application and it did not pass with a majority vote," Chipok spoke more deliberately. "Then, the motion to *approve* the amendment did not pass. So you could extrapolate that it's an open question because you have two failed motions. You don't have an approved motion yet. You've opened the door very wide for Mr. Watts to have a great big entry into circuit court," he cautioned. Shrill voices emerged. "Mr. Chairman —" one member began. Another said, "Let somebody else talk here."

Scott Selis directed his words not to the lawyer, but to the VGMC chairman:

> The only question on appeal, Mr. Chairman, will be whether there is competent, substantial evidence to support this group's denial of this application. There is no question. I stand on my reputation and every dollar that this lady has paid to me that there is competent and substantial evidence. That's the standard of review. There's not going to be any question by the appellate court. It's obvious that the motion to deny failed because of the absent folks... Don't be intimidated by threats.

Scott's words, and the hand clapping that met them, roused Mark Watts from his funk: "I disagree with the standard that's just been quoted, but I'll leave it with Mr. Chipok to advise you how best to proceed." "Good night," called a couple of rascally voices from the crowd.

"My understanding is that as a board, we're done with that issue," said the chairman. At 12:40 a.m., the "long, strange and surprising" Volusia Growth Management Commission hearing was put to sleep. Emotionally and physically depleted, we went home to wait: either for the lawsuit that would arise from tonight's chaos, and/or for a year to pass, when Thornby could come back to the VGMC and we would have to go through it all over again.

PART THREE

Enterprise Returns What It Received

Opposing Thornby Amendment	Supporting Thornby Amendment
City of Lake Helen	Deltona City Commission
Daytona Beach News-Journal	
Deltona Planning & Zoning Board	
Enterprise Preservation Society	
Environmental Council of Volusia-Flagler	
Florida Bicycle Association	
Florida Dept. of Community Affairs	
Florida Dept. of Environmental Protection	
Friends of Thornby	
Mayor of DeBary	
Orlando Sentinel	
St. Johns Riverkeeper	
School Board of Volusia County	
Sierra Club	
Seminole Audubon Society	
University of Central Florida	
Volusia County	
Volusia-Flagler Environmental Action	
Volusia Growth Management Commission	
Volusia Historic Preservation Board	
Volusia Soil & Water Conservation District	
West Volusia Audubon Society	
West Volusia Historical Society	

For in the end, our society will be defined not only by what we create, but by what we refuse to destroy.
John Sawhill, President & CEO
The Nature Conservancy

CHAPTER SIXTEEN

Out of the Frying Pan and into the Mire

On the groggy morning after the rambunctious Wednesday night meeting that melted into Thursday, the Volusia Growth Management commissioners faced their own version of a disputed presidential election. Instead of "hanging chads," though, the culprit was "weighted votes." While newspapers speculated about a possible appeal, attorney Mark Watts was coy. "We have 30 days to file an appeal in circuit court. We haven't made a decision yet," he parried.

In the Aftermath of the VGMC Hearing

On the night before Election Day 2005 (see Chapter 14), I addressed the Deltona commission. The next day, the city would have a new mayor and maybe new commissioners, but my words were intended for the "old" officials on the dais. The Volusia Growth Management Commission failed to certify the Thornby project, I said. Undoubtedly, they already knew it, but it still felt damn good to say the words, out loud on the record. There were no "Sandy Walters T-shirts" in the room.

At the meeting, Commissioner David Santiago decried Deltona's "lack of recreational facilities" and Mayor John Masiarczyk suggested building another ball field. Thornby had been taken off the commission's agenda. "We don't want to antagonize the [Volusia Growth Management] Commission," Bob Nix explained to the *Daytona Beach News-Journal*.

VGMC's Faults

With the Thornby hearing fresh in her mind, Suzanne Steiner presented the Volusia County Charter Review Commission with a VGMC member's perspective. She saw an inherent conflict of interest in government employees representing their employer on the VGMC, she told them. In addition, the VGMC rule that absent members' votes count as "no" should be changed, she said.

Thornby on Hold

To our great relief, the 30-day deadline for the Thornby owners to appeal the VGMC's midnight vote came and went without a lawsuit, meaning that the "no certification" would stand — at least until the owners could reapply in November 2006.

In Deltona, new city officials' seats were barely warm when Cindy Sullivan, Enterprise Preservation Society director, waved a white flag at a commission meeting. Let's start out on the right foot, she implored officials: "Enterprise wants to begin 'a new tradition of brotherhood' with our neighbor, Deltona." Larry French's guest column in the *Orlando Sentinel* echoed her sentiments: "Yes, Thornby, there is a Santa Claus!" He hoped the "direction would change with the election of a new mayor and city commissioners."

As the outnumbered Thornby tug-of-war team grappled for a foothold in deep political mud, newly elected Commissioner Janet Deyette grabbed the rope. Deyette, a tax accountant, had been investigating what Thornby could do for her city since her planning board days. She contacted Thornby owner Frank Knight, who told her he was open to a city purchase. After that, she asked for a workshop to "re-visit" Thornby, reminding fellow officials that grant funds might be available. "I would like it to be a park, to have walkways with museum-like labels pointing out unusual plants; something that would not disturb the eagles' nest," she envisioned. New mayor Dennis Mulder concurred. Commissioners directed city staff to research grant funding. The *News-Journal* gave a shout-out: "Saving the property, touted for its environmental and historic values, is a worthwhile goal."

Thornby Back from the Brink

Despite those encouraging words, on January 3, 2006, Thornby was back on the city commission agenda for two votes — one to amend the comprehensive plan, the other to change the zoning to multi-family. Because the VGMC denied the plan amendment with less than a 50 percent weighted vote, and even though the owners had not appealed the denial, some Deltona commissioners were considering having the city adopt the amendment anyway, without the required certification. If the city did that, then Volusia County, the VGMC, the Friends of Thornby and Steve Wiechert would face a costly legal battle to defend the VGMC's decision.

Before the meeting, Scott Selis spoke with city officials (except Lucille Wheatley) in an effort to convince them that pursuing the Thornby amendment without the VGMC's certification would be ill-advised and expensive. He remembers Bill Harvey as "noncommittal and somewhat challenging: I felt I wasn't getting his complete view." The commission followed Scott's advice, however, (with Harvey dissenting) and voted to table the Thornby amendment again. Commissioner Michele McFall said the delay would give the city "more time to look into the possibility of purchasing the property."

Is the Tide Turning?

After nine years' employment with the city, Bob Nix resigned as Deltona's director of development services. Nix and planning board member-now-commissioner Janet Deyette had many conversations over the years. They talked about Thornby and about "several really good ideas he hoped to accomplish in the city," she says. "He and I had always respected each other. He did not always agree with the commission, but he worked for them." On his last day, they met in the city hall elevator. "I told him he should stay, but he said he'd made up his mind to leave. He said he was fed up with Thornby." Janet was "stunned" by what he said next. Before the doors opened and Bob Nix left Deltona for good, "He told me that right after the election, he'd directed his staff to quietly, privately start working on a grant to buy Thornby." Today, Nix explains:

> After changes on the city commission ... we came full circle right back to my [1999] proposal ... to acquire the site and develop it as an historical waterfront public access area... in a more favorable political environment I started looking to find a program to assist us in moving in that direction.

Several months later, the *News-Journal* reported, "After a proposal that would allow the development of 227 townhomes on the property failed to get a majority vote at the VGMC, the developer informed city officials he would be willing to sell the property for $6.8 million."

Janet Deyette

Janet Deyette and her husband "Mac" moved to "nice and quiet" unincorporated Deltona from Seminole County's "congested mess" in 1986. Raised on a farm in upstate New York, she had always been intrigued by the past. "I knew of the history on the shores of Lake Monroe. I started to work on it as soon as I got elected," she recalls. "I couldn't wait to present it." "It" was a professionally-styled, 44-page, spiral-bound booklet that she'd created, titled "The Question to Purchase Thornby," and it was the centerpiece of an April 24, 2006 commission workshop held at her request. For months, she had researched and gathered statistics on the hard economic facts of historic preservation in Florida. Although her work featured Enterprise and West Volusia history, its main purpose was to hammer home the numbers on direct (purchases) and multiplier (jobs, income) dollar benefits of ecotourism and destination tourism. The history came from the Enterprise Preservation Society; the statistics came from the University of Florida and The Center for Urban Policy Research.

"Bill Harvey was especially impressed with the professional-looking brochure," Deyette remembers. "He said the [city] commission should give it serious attention because it was a 'scholarly' report. That was his highest compliment." [1]

Meanwhile, Mayor Mulder didn't equivocate about his support for Thornby preservation. "I want to keep some sort of gem in Deltona. Sky-rises can be nice, but there's nothing quite like Thornby," he said, adding that he would like to acquire it "without having to pay the price." At the workshop, the commission discussed applying for a $5 million grant from Florida Communities Trust (FCT), the same agency that EPS had previously sought for grant funding when the asking price was $2.5 million. In three years, thanks to Florida's building bubble, Thornby's price had almost tripled. Kathy Culligan, the city's grant writer, advised the commission that Deltona would need $1.8 million in matching funds.

Thornby is "important to the county as well," the mayor said, revealing that he had discussed a possible partnership with county officials whereby Deltona wouldn't have to contribute. Commissioner Harvey responded by patronizingly reminding the young mayor that he "was not allowed to make commitments without discussing the matter with the full commission."

---

[1] In 2007, Deltona established the "William S. Harvey Scholarship Fund" to acknowledge the late commissioner's dedication to education.

Title page of Commissioner Deyette's presentation

THE QUESTION TO PURCHASE THORNBY

Providing Economic Benefit

To

The City of Deltona

&

Critical Missing Link

for

Volusia County Trails System

A Collection and Compilation
Of Economic Data

and

Historic Information

Prepared by

Commissioner Janet Deyette

for

The Thornby Workshop

April 24, 2006

The commission majority, however, was intractable on the subject of Thornby. Commissioner Santiago "did not feel it appropriate to expend taxpayers' funds" to buy riverfront property for a city park. Commissioner Denizac "would not support using city funds." Similarly, Commissioner McFall said her main concern was that "the property would come off the city tax rolls." (City taxes on the Thornby property amounted to about $300 per month.) Commissioner Carmolingo called it "a very good project for the city" that he wouldn't support with city money. It was a hard-line stance because FCT grants, like virtually every grant, require "matching funds" as a prerequisite to receiving money. The commission's consensus was that the city would seek a grant, but only if the needed match came from somewhere else (the county, for instance).

Dissension

Janet Deyette visualized trails on Thornby, and maybe a dock for ferry service across the lake to Sanford as had once existed. She said residents would enjoy a park "not focused on [organized] recreational activities. Some of us want a quiet park where we can walk and see historical exhibits. With the trailhead, those things can tie together nicely," she said. Mayor Mulder said, "There needs to be compromise." Others, however, didn't share that view. McFall pitched "more important projects to focus on, such as the Partnership Center."[2] Santiago beat the "taking the property off our tax rolls" drum. Larry French observed, "A lot of these [financial barriers] are smokescreens."

"[Mulder's] first six months in office have produced some of the stormiest moments in the city's brief history," opined Mike Lafferty in the *Sentinel*.

What the Well-Dressed Blogger Wears

At the May 1, 2006 city commission meeting, the "new tradition of brotherhood" was AWOL and Santa Claus was MIA. Looking in the rear-view mirror, Commissioner Santiago, president of a construction company, wanted to take the city "back to its original plan." He extolled the "luxury town homes" and "open space" of "Thornby Oaks" — the Andersen plan rejected by the state in 2004. He said that Deltona needed to "diversify the type of homes provided" without acknowledging that the city had recently annexed several hundred vacant acres. Preserving Thornby wasn't "a priority for him *or the city*," he announced, bemoaning the "organized effort from people outside of Deltona to design this park."

> **Activist Lesson:** A government's priorities are supposed to be the goals and policies set out in its comprehensive plan.

---

2 The Partnership Center project, beset by political and financial problems, was abandoned in 2007.

Likewise, Commissioner Denizac was "having second thoughts;" she represented a different district than the one in which the Thornby property was located. Commissioner McFall (the daughter of former County Councilwoman Ann McFall, who had championed Thornby and Enterprise years before) *did* represent Thornby's district. She said she "wouldn't be supporting the grant application," but she would do so at "a better price" because she thought the "developer" was taking advantage of the city. Unwillingness to contribute city dollars; unspecified needs at other parks; better places to use general funds; and the property's cost were cited as obstacles to Thornby's purchase.

The mayor was blindsided by the mass defection. "We were all at the same workshop last week," he said. "I thought we directed staff to prepare a grant application for the Thornby property with no funds coming directly from the city." Calling it a "fear and smear campaign," he saw their agreement to seek grant funds unwinding before his eyes.

Commissioner Deyette pointed out that submitting an application to Florida Communities Trust for a possible $5 million in free money carried no risk and no commitment. The city's grant writer was researching other funding sources, such as the county's ECHO (Environmental, Cultural, Historic, Outdoor) program, she told them. Deltona doesn't have a passive park, she reminded them. This could be a chance to link the multi-use "rail trail" through Deltona from Gemini Springs Park. And "there is real history there." She jogged their memories: "The desire for a park on this property goes back to 1999 when Bob Nix was first instructed to pursue a grant proposal." Deyette recognized a practical reason for buying Thornby, as well. The only city access to Lake Monroe was a small boat ramp. Adding 1,000 feet of shoreline "would give our citizens more access to the lake," she said.

The public had its say. The *News-Journal* noted that the meeting "included booing and yelling from the audience." Kevin Finn eloquently asked his city to "demonstrate how a community can grow not only in size, but in quality of life," and railed against the "outrageous slam against a citizen from outside of Deltona." The citizen was me, and the "slam" he referred to was the "She Doesn't Live Here Gang" attired in their "Sandy Walters T-shirts," who filled two front rows at City Hall. Their aim, they said, was to send "a clear message to Janet Deyette" that "outsiders" shouldn't be heard.

Richard Ellison of Deltona encouraged the city to apply for the grant. Deltonan Michael Williams expressed concern that many people have been "misinformed about the project." One of two residents who spoke against a Thornby park said the property was "prime real estate" and a perfect place for town homes or condominiums, that "the native plants can be saved or moved," and questioned how the city would "replace the tax money from the development of this property." (The resident did not question how much tax money it would take to provide city services to hundreds of new Thornby residents.)

Larry French wondered why the city's parks advisory board, of which he was a member, had not been invited to give input on Thornby. The trees, flora and fauna on the property are priceless, said the naturalist, encouraging Deltona to proceed with the grant process. Carol Aymar clarified that EPS' prior efforts to buy Thornby dissolved when the owners decided not to sell for the appraised value. EPS is ready to help Deltona in "any way we can," she emphasized. "We have 20 experts willing to volunteer their time and talents on this project." Carol reminded Commissioner McFall that she once supported efforts to protect the area. Once again, Thornby stalwart Jack Hoyt spelled it out for his city: "Let this thing go forward. It'll be an asset."

Deyette's motion to seek grant funding to purchase Thornby squeaked by, miraculously, on one vote. The unexpected tiebreaker was Bill Harvey, who'd never been pro-anything on Thornby but paving. "The presentation was a big deal in getting him to OK applying for a grant to buy Thornby," Deyette confirms. Her statistics on the financial benefits of preservation and nature-based tourism convinced him that a park would be "great"— as long as it was free to the city.

Carol, who helped Deltona's grant writer prepare the application, says she "didn't see how the application could be successful if the city did not put up matching funds." Yet the 4-3 vote to seek grant money brought cheers from the crowd — I suppose because, for the first time in five years, the Deltona City Commission threw us a crumb.

The next day, Scott Maxwell of the *Sentinel's* "Political Pulse" column called to tell me about the "Walters-dissing" T-shirts on display at the commission meeting — hoping, I assumed, for a colorful quote from me. But the surprise was on him when I said that I already knew about the shirts. In fact, I told him, I have one of my own! "The shirts are hilarious. I've been waiting for a good time to wear mine," were my words quoted in the paper.

> **Activist Lesson:** Humor is one way to disarm a bully — or even two rows of them.

More Dissension

Thornby was back on the front (news) burner. The *News-Journal* praised the city's attempt to purchase "a natural enclave within an area facing heavy development pressure."

The *Sentinel's* Mike Lafferty chided, "Don't blame the mayor for all of Deltona's woes," a shot that might have been fired straight at anti-Mulder bloggers. Referring to "a Deltona city commissioner's recent attempt to derail a park purchase," he wrote, "The debate over whether to apply for a grant to buy the Thornby property on Lake Monroe produced Mulder's 'fear and smear' remark, which was directed at Commissioner David Santiago. The rivalry between Mulder and Santiago is obvious to anyone who has seen or heard recent meetings."

Deltona's Grant Application

At a Thornby workshop days after the May 1 fracas, city commissioners circled the campfire of cooperation. Said Commissioner Santiago, "It's no secret that I fought hard not to make this project go to the next step; however, the commission decided to go forward and now I will make sure the city does it right." Furthermore, he said, he supported the Enterprise Preservation Society's offers of help. Carol Aymar, who was invited to the workshop, remembers being "somewhat surprised" at his more conciliatory stance.

City planner Lisa Wargo briefed commissioners on the details of Florida Communities Trust funding. "The grant is based on points," she explained. Carol told the commission that in 2003, EPS' Thornby grant application scored 165 of a possible 200 points, but the owners would not meet the appraisal price, so it was never submitted. According to Wargo, the city's application, as it now stood would rate 180 points. She praised the property as a "biologist's dream with seven different vegetative groups," and mentioned that county ECHO grant funds would be appropriate for this project. She reminded them that the purchase price was negotiable.

The commissioners shared visions of a boat dock, picnic tables, playground, trails, and walkways as potential features of Thornby Park, without disturbing the wetlands or the eagles' nest. When Aymar asked if the Indian midden had been mentioned in the grant application, the answer was "no."

The commission decided that an application for a $5 million grant would be submitted without dedicated matching funds. Commissioner Santiago said he was looking for a "dollar commitment" from the county. Commissioner Carmolingo said, "The commission decided not to expend any taxpayer dollars for this project." Commissioner McFall repeated, "The commission had said no to putting up monies for such a match." Carol relates that McFall seemed to be the most cautious — even reluctant — participant at the meeting.

"She was adamant about 'no matching funds.' I was a little disappointed with her demeanor, after having been encouraged in the past, in a face-to-face meeting and an email, by her supportive tone about Thornby's historical value." Today, Janet Deyette says that, "The majority didn't care enough, or realize the value, to purchase Thornby so it was a convenient excuse to say, 'We're not going to spend city money,' while acting as if they wouldn't waste taxpayer money on something frivolous. It didn't matter that support for Thornby was growing."

The *Sentinel* Speaks

Mike Lafferty had more to say to Deltona. A few days after the workshop, he briefed *Sentinel* readers on "Government Spending 101," with Thornby as a regrettable case history. The Thornby property on Lake Monroe is an "exquisite Southern setting, all filled with fat live oaks and towering magnolias," he described. "This waterfront property is worth buying and preserving, just as it was when the opportunity first presented itself in 1999, with a price tag significantly less than it is today." He related how "city officials did everything in their power to help drive up the purchase price" — first by annexing it, then approving hundreds of townhouses on it. No doubt about it, he said, "Deltona still needs the Thornby property." However, even "free" grant money comes from taxes, he stressed. "If the city commissioners had shown the capacity for vision a few years ago," he remonstrated, "they might have saved taxpayers a bundle."

A Man with a Plan

Mike Fleming was a Deltona resident and computer whiz. Like most people, he was too busy working and raising a family to give much time or thought to politics. That is, until 2004 when Hurricane Charley hit.

As Fleming tells it, his family, like thousands in the city, was without power or essential services and he was desperate for information. With the city in chaos, and unable to get needed help, he headed for City Hall. Inside the front door, there was a visitors' desk and a woman behind it. To her right were two sheriff's deputies. Upon asking to see the mayor, he was told that he could either go to a city meeting or call to make an appointment. He explained how he felt that the city had failed to provide support or information to its residents. The clerk said she understood his frustration, but again referred him to the meeting or telephone. "I went home and told my wife that not being able to see the mayor is wrong," Fleming says. "Mark my words, I'll get involved in city politics and make sure the mayor knows my name."

"I will never forget that day since it was the one single event that drove me past just talking about Deltona politics," he says. He soon got his chance to do more than talk.

Elections were approaching, and West Volusia's county council seat was up for grabs. John Masiarczyk, so far unopposed, wanted the spot. That the former mayor who "did not like dissension," as Jack Hoyt put it, might represent Thornby's district at the county level gave chills to many people, Mike Fleming included. Although there was talk of Deltona's Pat Northey (a two-term council veteran with a good environmental record) as a candidate, she was hesitating, and time was passing.

True to his word, Fleming jumped into the race against his former mayor who he couldn't see that day at city hall. Like Mulder the year before, he had to bone up on local issues, fast. Also like Mulder, he didn't know much about Thornby, but he says that, "After researching Thornby and seeing the property, I felt a strong pull to be a part of protecting the land."

Ultimately, Pat Northey entered the race and Mike Fleming withdrew to clear her way. Though no longer a candidate, he gave Friends of Thornby a huge boost by launching the "Save Thornby" website with everything Thornby: photos, facts, history, updates on the latest political developments — and music. Linked to the site was local songwriter Rog Lee's "St. Johns Lullaby," its lyrics a sweet promise:

> "Some day I'll meet you down at Thornby Park/
> We'll watch the sunset slowly turn to dark."

The website was long overdue and badly needed to raise Deltonans' awareness of why such remarkable land shouldn't be turned into a staging area for condos, a clubhouse and swimming pool. On Wednesday nights, you could hear Mike Fleming in a live Internet broadcast dishing on local topics, with Thornby getting a hefty share of time. He hosted guests who knew all about Thornby, like Pat Northey. I can still picture the magical images in his words:

> Hello. This is Mike Fleming with Deltona online.com.
> When most people think of Deltona they do not think about it as being rich in history. But what if I could tell you there was a place you could walk where ancient Americans lived? What if there was a place where you could see what pioneer Floridians once saw? What if there was a place where you could stand where there'd been a Seminole Indian war fort? What if there was a place where you could walk along where an 1800s-era railway ran? What if there was a place where you could look out onto Lake Monroe and imagine the steamboats that once plied the waters there? What if there was a place where you could see how a Florida pioneer family once lived?
> There is such a place, and it's RIGHT HERE IN DELTONA.
> All of these things could have been seen had you been a visitor back in time to what is today called the Thornby Estate. Would you like to imagine and see some of those things today? There's a chance you can, but you need to let your city commission know you want them to save Thornby. Contact them today.[3]

---

3 Words written by Larry French

Fleming's broadcast attracted lots of attention, including some unwanted attention from those who wished to strangle the Thornby park plan. "There were personal comments about me posted online," he recounts. At least once, he reported to the sheriff an unsuccessful attempt to hack into his server. (Author's note: I, too, experienced a similar, unsuccessful hacking attempt around that time.)

He eventually left Florida to be closer to his wife's family, settling in a small New York town coincidentally near Dr. Glass' lifelong home in Utica. Hurricane Charley turned Mike Fleming into an activist, much like the park/CVS issue did for Larry French and the American bald eagles Nest VO12 did for Sandy Gallagher. Mike's bad day at City Hall turned into an online boost for Thornby.

Money Talks

In Deltona, money — what to do with it — was still the main topic of conversation. "There was almost $17 million in city undesignated reserve funds [at the time]. That was the most in city history," recounts then-mayor Dennis Mulder. Although the price of the Thornby property was the only thing on the menu, opponents mixed unfounded fears with unsubstantiated future estimates for uncertain items, dishing up an anti-preservation stew hyped to cost $9.8 million when the bill came. Bill Harvey reflexively worried that the whole thing was now "out of the city's reach." Even so, on June 19, 2006, Deltona's city commission voted unanimously to seek funds from Volusia Forever (a taxpayer-approved county program providing funds to buy environmentally sensitive lands) to buy Thornby. If they got the funding, Volusia County and Deltona would co-own the property. Commissioner Denizac expressed "concerns" and Commissioner Carmolingo was "not happy" with that arrangement. Commissioner Deyette reminded everyone that the commission had wanted the county to "step up its involvement" in the first place.

In six tumultuous years, citizen activists had persuaded officials, commissions and agencies not to flatten a beloved corner of creation called Thornby. When the VGMC turned down the high-density land-use amendment for Thornby, we were touching heaven. Now, we found ourselves relegated to the sidelines while a tenuous purchase deal bucked like a wild mustang intent on unseating its rider. In the *Sentinel*, Larry French wondered, "How much of a good bargain will a purchase of Thornby become before some commissioners stop insisting on rejecting it?" In the same paper, I challenged city pursestring squeezers: "Grant money will provide practically all needed funds and Friends of Thornby will contribute. How about it, Deltona?"

Playing Second String at Volusia Forever

Soon after the city applied, the Volusia Forever Advisory Committee declared Thornby eligible for up to $1.8 million in funds. Deltona's grant writer rhapsodized over the property: "It's gorgeous. It's some of the prettiest property I've seen. It's totally unique. It's a gem." (Ironic words, in light of Mark Watts' assessment years before that a shopping development on Thornby would be the "gem of Enterprise.") Pat Northey was a member of the committee, which would make final recommendations to the county council on what properties to buy.

"GRADE A" hailed the *News-Journal*, lauding the decision. Thornby "may yet become what it deserves to be — a permanent nature preserve that new generations can enjoy. If it all works as it should, the Thornby land will have trails, a pavilion and other nature-park amenities." Friends of Thornby were over the moon, even though matching funds would still be needed to make it work "as it should." We were so thrilled with the advisory committee's decision that we didn't think much about the Volusia Forever staff report. We didn't realize that the committee's eligibility awards had an air of "sure, why not?" because eligibility was only half the battle. Like Hollywood, Volusia Forever has an "A List" and a "B List." Though in movie land, even "B Listers" get attention and dazzling jewels for Oscar night, it's different with Volusia Forever. Properties that don't make their "A List" get little attention, and the only shiny thing coming their way will be the sun's reflection off the bulldozers clearing the property when the owner gets tired of waiting for the county to buy it. In other words, "B-Listing" is a doorway to nowhere. Which is where Thornby was headed, because staff recommended that it be assigned to "B List" Siberia.

Telling it Like it Is

At the time, Enterprise wasn't the only West Volusia community under the gun. Deltona also had annexation sights on tiny Osteen. In a letter to the *Sentinel*, Carol Aymar deplored Deltona's incursions into rural Osteen, leading to Commissioner Michelle McFall's printed retort that "Ms. Aymar has never given Deltona a chance to prove ourselves." Lashing out at "Ms. Aymar and others who oppose anything Deltona does," her words rubbed hot salt into Friends of Thornby's wounds. Lani Friend shot back, citing the "struggle by Deltona and Enterprise residents to prevent the upzoning of the Thornby property... on a unique environment tract in the heart of historic Enterprise." Bob Sayre's assessment was blunter: "Each time the folks in Enterprise have given Deltona a chance to act hand-in-hand with us to preserve the special beauty of our area, we have been given the cold shoulder — or worse."

Parks & Rec Meeting

In August 2006, the Chairman of Deltona's Parks & Recreation Advisory Board invited Kevin Finn to make a presentation on Thornby. Kevin accepted, even though the newly appointed chairman was a rabid anti-Thornby blogger. With the mayor, several commissioners, and about 25 Deltona and Enterprise residents in attendance it seemed, [the chairman] "tried to embarrass me," Kevin recalls.

Mike MacHardy served on the parks advisory board for nine years, but that meeting stands out from all others. "I was vice-chair," he recalls. "I tried to temper everything the chairman did." As for Thornby, "I was sold on it," he says staunchly, because "Deltona has no real history." MacHardy allows that Kevin's presentation made a strong impression on him. He describes condos on Thornby as "a terrible idea" and says he wanted his city to buy it for a park from the beginning.

Beatrice Ludvick of the city's parks senior subcommittee said Deltona parks offered "very little for adults to do" and that senior citizens could use Thornby's walking trails. Some Deltona folks said they came "to become more informed about Thornby." Normally, committee meetings are tame, but this was an exception. Reporting on the meeting, the *News-Journal* berated the chairman for failing to follow parliamentary procedure, chiding him for "inappropriate" remarks. "He had his mind made up," said Cindy Sullivan of the chairman (who announced, and later withdrew, as a city commission candidate). In a follow-up interview, Stetson University political science professor Dr. T. Wayne Bailey admonished that a committee chair should "certainly not get into a debate or banter with citizens." Reporter Sara Kiesler wrote that the chairman "debated each speaker who had an opinion of Thornby different than his." Kevin shakes his head over the whole experience. "It was nasty," he confirms. He was surprised when Commissioner Santiago cornered him in the hallway after the meeting. "Maybe we're not that far apart," he told Kevin in the course of their private conversation, indicating that he might support a Thornby purchase after all.

Online, the blogs kept the kettle on high simmer. Ed Sullivan of Enterprise observes, "There was a lot of vitriol on the local Web site forums, most of which was initiated by three or four people who seemed to have a very specific agenda — to tear down the new mayor, Sandy Walters, or Thornby. Online supporters were immediately set upon by this gang and harassed incessantly." Ed's wife Cindy affirms, "There were numerous mentions about the fact that Ed and I shouldn't say anything about Thornby because we lived in Enterprise. I explained that we lived around the corner; it was almost literally in our backyard, and as a result, we had every right to have an opinion. But they disagreed." Copy-catting the inflammatory rhetoric of some commissioners, any semblance of reasonable online debate about Thornby vanished. Postings turned childish (making fun of a commissioner's physical appearance) or potentially libelous (accusing an official of adultery). From Mike MacHardy: "The blogs were very anti-Dennis." Commissioner Deyette was mocked by derogatory cartoons. Mud was tossed at two commissioners accused of having an extra-marital affair. Deceitful comments were posted briefly, and then pulled. One item, though, never made it online: the city planner's statement that Deltona "does not have enough parks or urban open spaces."

Saved Again

In September, the appointed Volusia Forever Advisory Committee would rank the latest properties eligible for county purchase. Pat Northey warned us of the death-knell consequences of "B Listing." "It has to go on the 'A List,'" she warned. "Otherwise, it will never be funded." There isn't enough money to buy all the "A" properties, let alone the "B" ones, she explained. Even "A" listing doesn't guarantee funding, but it opens the door for negotiations, surveys and appraisals, all prerequisites to a purchase deal. If Thornby were "A-Listed," even without city matching funds, it would be ready and waiting if and when the city found a grant source, Northey said, but if the committee accepted its staff's "B" listing, Thornby would be without a funding source. Then the owners would likely repeat the cycle, wearing us down with a new development plan while waiting for city and county decision-makers, staff and policies to change. I honestly did not know if we could go through it all again.

From her home in Georgia, Carolyn Watson Langley wrote to the committee, explaining that she grew up on Thornby and that its massive oaks, acres of woodlands and natural habitats had prompted her to establish an environmental education area at the elementary school where she used to teach. "I implore you to seriously consider saving this pristine piece of Volusia County," she wrote.

The committee met in late afternoon on a weekday, when most working people could not attend. Roy and I were there. Once again, we faced the challenge of persuading a group of decision-makers not to follow their staff's report. If we failed to get Thornby on the "A List," there was no foreseeable tomorrow. Thornby was one of eight properties to be rated; there were too many parcels waiting for too little money. Three of the seven committee members were familiar: Pat Northey was one; the late Ken Russell, an activist from Ponce Inlet with whom I had previously discussed Thornby, was another. The third was Dennis Bayer, the attorney who, years before, advised Valerie Grill about annexation and talked to Allen Watts about public purchase of Thornby (See Chapter 8).

The staff report acknowledged Thornby's active bald eagle nest, location on the St. Johns River, natural communities, gopher tortoise burrows, and archeological sensitivity, but decried the property's "exotic vegetation" and "disturbed areas" — so-called "issues" that had never surfaced in seven years and 10 public hearings. The report dismissed the archeological investigation because "the results are not available for review." Some of its conclusions, for instance that the property lacked "significant areas of high water recharge rates," were technically questionable, at best. In short, like every Thornby staff report over the years, it seemed tailored to frustrate public preservation. Why did the Volusia Forever staff report appear to discourage committing county funds for a Thornby purchase? Possibly, after years of county-city wrangling over Thornby and other issues, some county staffers were reluctant to co-manage the land with Deltona. With Thornby shunted to the "B List," they would not have to.

The committee chairman called attention to the "significant amount of disturbance to the property." Other members questioned Deltona's low-scoring Florida Communities Trust grant application. Janet Deyette, the only Deltona representative present, was honest: Not every city commissioner favors this application, she told them. The city has not made matching funds available, but "an effort is being made by the community to preserve this property and to create a passive park with a historical element," she said. She echoed the assessment by Deltona planner Lisa Wargo that Thornby was a "biologist's dream." She mentioned the fact that Thornby's owners had not disclosed what their archeologists found.

Committee member Northey tapped into the diplomatic skills that put her in office and kept her on the county council for eight years. Low-key at first, she said, "Development pressures are significant" in the Enterprise area. She talked about Lakeshore Drive's scenic road status and confirmed, "The community has been working for years to put this property into public ownership." Finally, she laid it on the line: "Politically, this property will be dead if it is placed on the B List."

I still have the speech I gave that day— messy lines of handwriting squeezed on both sides of a page, jammed with cross-outs, arrows, highlights and margin notes. I was desperately re-writing as the committee deliberated. These folks must care about history or they wouldn't be here, I decided. Therefore, in addition to talking about Friends of Thornby and EPS' dead-end attempt to buy the property, I tried to put a face on Thornby history. I presented articles about Dr. Glass and told of his philanthropy and his professional achievements, including the still-active fellowship he established at Hamilton College. I distributed copies of 19th century maps showing Fort Kingsbury on Lake Monroe's north shore. I requested that they place this property on the "A List" so the acquisition process could move forward.

Roy Walters, was (and, at this writing, is) an appointed member of Volusia County's Bicycle-Pedestrian Advisory Board. With that in mind, he discussed the county's trails plan, a portion of which was proposed to adjoin the Thornby property. He also touted Thornby history by providing facts and photos of the railroad trestle and canal on the property. He requested that the property be listed as "A," adding, with monumental understatement, "There is a tremendous amount of community support for the preservation of this property."

One committee member commended our presentations, but others strongly opposed putting Thornby on their "A List" without a commitment of matching funds from Deltona. In addition, two members expressed concerns regarding Thornby's "ecological value." (Since Volusia County, the Volusia Growth Management Commission, the Florida Department of Environmental Protection and the Florida Department of Community Affairs all recognized Thornby as being environmentally sensitive and worthy of protection, their opinions were — and still are — inexplicable.) The same members also balked at providing funds to buy environmental land like Thornby where something, even a passive park, might one day be built. The chairman renewed his pitch for "B-Listing" — evidently, nothing we said had touched him.

Eventually, committee member Dennis Bayer, who had been waiting for five years to rescue Thornby, moved to assign it to the "A List" of eligible properties. The motion, seconded by Ken Russell, passed 5-2.

You Have One More Chance

One month after the Volusia Forever Advisory Committee put Thornby on its high-priority list, Deltona elected officials brainstormed their "hopes and aspirations" for the city at a two-day retreat. Commissioner Deyette's proposed city motto, "On the Shores of History" (referring to Deltona's southern border on Lake Monroe) met with indifference. "I don't think some commissioners wanted to attribute any good coming to Deltona from either Enterprise or Thornby," she suggests. The mayor, possibly hoping to change some minds about city matching funds, unveiled a conceptual plan for Thornby featuring a banquet hall, an outdoor stage, and a rebuilt Thornby house that resembled Monticello — a new home for Deltona's Arts and Historical Center. Other commissioners shared more general visions for the city — Carmolingo: retention of some natural areas; McFall: additional recreational facilities/parks. Denizac, the mother of a disabled daughter, wanted accessible parks for all residents.

At the same time Volusia Forever pushed Thornby onto its "A List," Florida Communities Trust pulled the rug out. Deltona's application for a grant to help buy Thornby ranked in the crowded middle of about 100 candidates — far too low to qualify. FCT staff offered to help the city resubmit the application next year. Larry French blamed his city's "lack of unified support."

The grant writer was more precise, admitting to the *News-Journal*, "The city would have stood a better chance if city commissioners had committed city funds."

At that point, I thought the Thornby owners should be pretty well soured on Deltona. I emailed Allen Watts, jokingly (?) suggesting that, since Volusia County was easier to deal with than Deltona, maybe they should de-annex back into the county. His response was a polite lecture about the value of his clients' property (with a harrowing reference to "private offers we have received") followed by this conjecture: "My sense is that we have one more window that will allow public or nonprofit ownership, and the right forces and checkbooks would have to align soon after the [next county] elections."

The stars aligned. The right force was on the scene. Her name was Pat Northey.

> *Destiny is not a matter of chance; it is a matter of choice. It is not something to be waited for; it is something to be achieved.*
>
> **William Jennings Bryan**

CHAPTER SEVENTEEN

Indecision: The Thief of Opportunity

"Most Deltona residents don't even know what Thornby is."

Deltona resident quoted in the *Orlando Sentinel*'s October 2006 article: "Thornby Vision — Can it Work?"

In November 2006, Volusia County Council District 5 would elect a new representative for Deltona, Enterprise, Osteen and DeBary. I hit the ground running (not literally; I'd recently injured my left foot in a fall) on behalf of Deltona resident Pat Northey's candidacy. I was determined that Deltona's former mayor, John Masiarczyk, would never represent me, or anyone in Enterprise, at the county level. If slogging alone with a broken foot to every front door in an unshaded DeBary subdivision on a 96-degree Florida afternoon would keep that from happening, that's what I would do.

Masiarczyk campaign sign on SR415 as altered by a concerned Osteen resident

Northey's name was as familiar to Volusia County residents as the Daytona 500. As a popular eight-year council member before term limits forced her out of office in 2004, she was known for her quick responses to residents' concerns. She was a proponent of trails and environmental protection, and "Thornby" was a name she knew well. Her campaign had the human touch. Wearing green "Northey for Council" T-shirts, a large group of her supporters — a broad spectrum of colors, ages and backgrounds — smiled for a campaign photo under the live oaks outside the Osteen Diner. Captioned "Hi, We're Your Neighbors and We Support Pat Northey," it made an impressive mailer. Her opponent ran on his record as mayor and made few campaign appearances.

On November 7, 2006, Patricia Northey was elected to represent Volusia County Council District 5.

Failed Experiment?

In the same election, voters had the chance to follow the Charter Review Commission's recommendation by disbanding the Volusia Growth Management Commission and replacing it with an "advisory only" board. The *Sentinel* editorialized its opinion of the VGMC:

> The commission hasn't stopped much of anything. Oh, in 2005 it did. It stood up to Deltona and rejected plans to develop the historic Thornby property ... Well, we can't have that now, can we?

It was a Gordian knot for voters: Should they keep a potentially effective but failed system, or replace it with a toothless tiger? They kept it intact. Later, the *Sentinel* observed:

> Armed with renewed backing from the voters, the panel would now take tough stands, right? Wrong.

Looking Back/Looking Ahead

Writing about election issues, *Sentinel* columnist Mike Lafferty called Deltona's former mayor John Masiarczyk "enormously popular." I disagreed in print, saying that Masiarczyk's legacy of failing roads and constant annexations still rippled through Deltona. What about the illegal Leffler annexation of 5,000 acres? I asked. What about all the tax money spent fighting to "upzone" Thornby? I concluded: when Doug Horn lost the race for Deltona mayor, and John Masiarczyk lost the race for county council, it showed voters are fed up with "the kind of policies that gave the city of Deltona the black eye its residents are trying hard to overcome."

I guess the *Sentinel* didn't take my barbs personally. In December, I was included in the paper's year-end "Leaders Look to 2007" and described as "not shy about speaking against uncontrolled growth at government meetings." Asked about my goals for 2007, I responded that I planned "to continue pushing for preservation of the historic Thornby property" and that Deltona "should take a more active role."

Deltona Takes a More Active Role

At a November 14, 2006 workshop, Deltona City Manager Steve Thompson presented the city commission with a list of proposed capital projects. "Thornby property acquisition" topped the list.

Opinions and ideas floated among officials and residents. Mayor Mulder's plan to preserve Thornby history with "functional buildings" clashed with Volusia Forever's vision of more passive uses for the property — and Volusia Forever held the "strings," as the mayor put it, because it would provide funding. Commissioner Harvey objected that "bottom line costs" weren't identified. Commissioner Denizac said she would like to poll residents to see their interest level for acquiring the property. Deltona resident Joanne Gehring asked that city funds be diverted from the stalled Partnership Center project "for the Thornby property."

With Thornby heading the city's wish list, Mulder approached state officials in Tallahassee about funding. But legislators told him they were not accepting budget requests for local projects.

A House Divided

Thornby started 2007 like a mail-order bride waiting for someone to claim her. Things were so peaceful — in print anyway — that the *Daytona Beach News-Journal* stepped back to take an upbeat look at how Enterprise was faring. The Enterprise Heritage Center (old schoolhouse) project, the Lakeshore Scenic Corridor, and a planned Enterprise Historic District, it was reported, were all progressing nicely. "The major change last year was the regime change in Deltona," reported Mark Matzinger, Enterprise Preservation Society chairman. "Thornby was the biggest issue," he said, echoing Valerie Grill's words seven years before, "and we made some headway there. It's a testimony to the tenacity of a group of people coming together," he said.

Unfortunately, things did not stay tranquil. Lest anyone doubt they were deadly serious about selling, Thornby's owners hired a Realtor, Bernie Senez, and gave Deltona right of first refusal. With the stakes higher than ever, the city commission scheduled a Thornby workshop on the fly, prompting the *News-Journal* to note that, "Advocates say they're a little shocked at the short notice." The paper said the property was "worth preserving."

The asking price for Thornby was $6.8 million. At the city workshop on February 12, 2007, comments were all over the place, but the main question was whether Deltona should pay to have the property appraised. The city grant writer gave a presentation on Thornby. Commissioner Denizac asked if they could skip the history part, since "the commission has seen the pictures before." A conceptual plan prepared by city staffer Lisa Wargo was "based on the uniqueness of the property and the idea that the city could get more grant funds by pursuing this sort of a park," she said. The city manager said he had been directed "not to spend any more money" on Thornby. The mayor said U.S. Rep. John Mica would be asked for "help with federal funding." Two commissioners wondered if Thornby could become a state park. Commissioner Santiago commented that residents were "desperate for ball fields for their kids" and he was "not convinced that the [Thornby park] project is a benefit to the community." "I haven't had people knocking down my door saying, 'I need trails,'" he remarked. Santiago said he was not against preserving Thornby or a trailhead on the property or re-building the house, and that if Deltona could get "stronger financial partners" he was "not opposed to the city spending some funds on this project." Mulder reaffirmed his commitment to find funds and his desire for "a facility the city can rent out." "Now is decision time," said Commissioner Deyette, pointing out Thornby's 1,000 feet of river frontage would make it unlike other city parks. She suggested rebuilding its old dock in conjunction with water taxi service across Lake Monroe to Sanford, an idea she had long pursued. Commissioners Harvey and McFall brought up project costs. Commissioner Carmolingo said that Deltona would need ballparks "continuously" and reiterated that he wouldn't use taxpayer dollars for Thornby.

During public comment, Deltonan Ed Gable said a park on Thornby would be "the most beautiful and memorable place in the city," while Kevin Finn called it "the crown jewel of the city if done right." Another resident brought up "lost tax revenue from city ownership."

The suggestions for rented banquet halls, arts centers and other traffic-and-pavement-intense uses plopped on Lakeshore Drive's delicate landscape made Friends of Thornby feel we were being stretched on the rack. Officials were still arguing about whether to pay for an appraisal; however, we decided not to make waves and hoped things would work out for the best.

After the workshop, the *Sentinel* chided Deltona "for not having the foresight years ago to preserve the land when it was much cheaper." At a city budget forum where residents were asked to prioritize desired spending, they were divided as ever. One group wanted "passive parks" and one wanted "more sports parks."

Councilwoman Northey weighed in on Thornby, cautioning that the county couldn't help unless Deltona came up with matching funds. "We're not really the leaders. It's a Deltona project," she said.

Small Step

In hindsight, playing officials' recorded voices on a boombox and calling them "liars" at a public meeting might not have been a first-rate plan. With Thornby on the city commission's February 19, 2007 agenda, one Deltona resident did just that to protest the thought of spending tax dollars on Thornby. The minutes reflect the reactions of the mayor (being called a liar may not be "such a bad thing, considering other names I've been called") as well as Commissioners Harvey ("a rough thing") and Carmolingo ("character assassination"). Discussion on whether Deltona should pay for a Thornby property appraisal turned into a "chicken-or-egg" debate. Commissioner Santiago argued that the city should get the grant and then the appraisal, while others felt the city needed the appraisal to get the grant.

"Residents may not know where Thornby is, but they know where the St. Johns River is," said Deltona resident Catherine Madden, disputing claims that Deltonans didn't know or care about the waterfront Thornby property. Other residents weighed in: one wanted money spent on existing parks and said residents should be polled on whether to buy the property. Kevin Finn said the city could spend *his* tax money on the project. Joanne Gehring urged the commission to "not lose this valuable property." Mike Fleming talked about city spending priorities when he addressed his city commission for the first time:

Educating residents about proposed charter amendments — $80,000

Fighting an illegal annexation of county land — thousands of $s

Saving Thornby — PRICELESS

Mulder, Harvey and Carmolingo were part of the 6-1 vote to pay for an appraisal of the Thornby property.

Big Gap

"This latest headache." That's how the *Sentinel* described the city's Thornby appraisal. It came in at $2.3 million — $4.5 million below the owners' asking price — making heads ache all over the county. Deltona commissioners' heads hurt because the asking price was too high to start with. Pat Northey's skull was throbbing from the "big gap" between the sales price and the appraised value. The Realtor's noggin ached, too. The appraisal was "unrealistic," he said, because it didn't take into account that Lake Monroe "leads into the St. Johns River."[1] The owners will get their own appraisal, the Realtor promised, adding that they "want it sold soon" and that he had a sales contract from "a development group" at a "much higher price." Commissioner Deyette retorted, "Just because a developer is willing to pay doesn't mean they'll get what they want." Thornby's greenery was conspicuously studded with big "FOR SALE — WATERFRONT" signs. We looked away when passing the property, as if loath to see an old friend who had long fought a serious illness, now potentially terminal.

Fear and Loathing in Deltona

In June 2007, I was appointed as a county representative to the Volusia Growth Management Commission. Pat Northey nominated me, and the county council approved my nomination. The VGMC had been given a new lease on life in the last election. I had learned all about the VGMC process from the "outside" as an ordinary citizen working to stop the Thornby comprehensive plan amendment. Now I wanted to help make changes from the "inside" as a commission member. My biggest concerns were the planning staff's influence on commission decisions and the practice of city employees representing their employer on the VGMC.

I had only been a VGMC member for two months when the boombox-playing blogger sent a "public record request" to me by email, seeking "any and all emails dated 2005 to present that were either sent from or sent to you regarding the Thornby property." I referred the email to the VGMC attorney, who confirmed what I already knew. Although VGMC members are subject to state laws requiring disclosure of correspondence relating to "official business," my Thornby emails were sent to the VGMC years before I became a

---

1 Lake Monroe is actually *part of* the St. Johns River.

commissioner. Thus, they were private, just like anyone's emails. (Of course, all VGMC files are public record and available for inspection through the VGMC. The email requester chose not to review the VGMC's files.)

Pro-Thornby commissioners were being rapped by "anti" forces, both online and in public. Between January and November 2007, close to 400 Thornby comments were posted on one Deltona blog. Commissioners who supported a Thornby purchase were labeled "stooges;" ordinary people were called "Thornby money people." A broad brush slapped negative paint around indiscriminately with comments like:

- Do you ever stop thinking about how you Enterprise residents can spend Deltona's money?
- Perhaps a modern-day landfill would be appropriate for Thornby.
- "They" got the people in power they bought off.

On July 31, the *Sentinel* reported that Thornby's owners had a "nearly $6 million" purchase offer from Orlando-area developer Allan Keen. Keen, former director of the powerful Orlando-Orange County Expressway Authority, was then making news for his involvement in developing The Carlisle, a highly-contentious "four-story structure out of proportion from the rest of the surrounding area."

That story broke the day after yet another city workshop on Thornby. Commissioners debated Thornby's potential, ranging from "a passive park like we do not have" to "private use," but were acres apart on whether Deltona should buy it. Commissioner Santiago seemed especially agitated, complaining, "The commission gives a lot of attention to trails and preservation, but [has] failed to protect the community's youth." And, he said, "We have a lot more priorities than pushing for a project like that on the outskirts." (Thornby was in the southern part of the city; Santiago's commission district was in the north.) My comments that day were probably the most dispassionate I had ever made. I simply reminded the commission that after six years of trying, they were no closer to changing Thornby's land use than when they started. At this point, they had two options, I told them: approve a development density no higher than one residence per acre, or buy it for public use.

"Can it get any uglier at City Hall ... ?" wondered the *News-Journal* in early August 2007. Even without Thornby in the mix, commissioners' disagreements over such issues as city credit card charges and youth curfews were so unruly that Commissioner McFall opined that a "long-awaited decision on whether the city will buy ... Thornby ... will help" cool things down. Along those lines, the notion of a Thornby public forum had been tossed around for months — online, in print and in public. Maybe commissioners hoped that the public's voice would shine a spotlight on the murky waters of political indecision.

The Public Has its Say

The two-hour forum at City Hall was like other Thornby events for the crowd size (more than 50), the number of speakers (32), and the speaker consensus (4:1 in favor of purchase). Of those who didn't support an outright city purchase, one agreed it should be a park — just not a city park. One resident presented a proposal for a performing arts center, and another wanted to see a "yacht club and marina" on Thornby. Another became so incensed while watching the televised meeting at home that he drove to City Hall to denounce purchase of the property as "fiscally irresponsible."

NOTICE
OF
PUBLIC FORUM
ON THE

HISTORIC THORNBY PROPERTY

City commission wants to hear from you

SHOULD THE CITY USE GRANT FUNDS TO BUY THE PROPERTY?

When: Tues. Aug. 14
           7:00 pm
Where: City Hall
           2345 Providence

Friends of Thornby flyer

On the other side, Councilwoman Patricia Northey reaffirmed the county's support and referred to Volusia Forever's "stringent standards" for the "only land left on the river for this type of acquisition." Evelyn Sheldon said she spoke for "312 [nearby] condominium owners who were anxious to have the Thornby property made into a historical park." Other speakers in favor were: Kevin Finn, Jane Trimmer, Dan Trimmer, Robin French, Larry French, Carol Aymar, Eric West, Olga Flores, Joanne Gehring, Lani Friend, Allison Thomas, Bill Nanstiel, Jim Glanz (Deltona's Bicycle-Pedestrian Board representative), Ed Gable, Veronica Kenny, and (future city commissioner) Heidi Herzberg. Johnathan Kenny, a high school student, offered a unique perspective. "What would New York City be like without Central Park?" he asked, pleading that his city pursue Thornby's purchase. Mark Watts and the Thornby Realtor, Bernie Senez, joined the chorus of support. No earthquakes hit Central Florida on August 14, 2007, and the moon didn't switch places with the sun. But that night, as in a romance novel where sworn enemies become ardent lovers, Friends of Thornby aligned with John Clapp, Frank Knight and Mark Watts in the quest to put Thornby into public ownership. Senez told the commission that Thornby's owners "really wanted the city to have the property." It would "mean a lot to them," he said.

Afterwards, Commissioner Harvey deplored that more Deltona residents didn't turn out for the meeting. Larry French was disappointed that the forum seemed to be a one-way street; residents could comment on the city's PowerPoint presentation, but not "ask questions and get answers" about the property. Indeed, one Deltonan said she "would not be leaving the meeting any better educated" than when she came in. Still, French allowed, "It was a first," though his question remained: "Did commissioners hear what the public was saying, and will they act upon what they heard?"

"And Just Like That, Years of Work Appear to be Lost"

In September 2003, the Thornby house died. Almost exactly four years later, the Thornby purchase died. The home, at least, had a lifespan; the deal died *in utero*, when a motion by Commissioner Deyette to negotiate for purchase, assuring that the city would pay no more than 12.5 percent of the price, failed. Voting against the purchase, Commissioner Denizac questioned, "If there was an active eagles nest there or not." Commissioner Harvey felt like he was being "pushed." Commissioner McFall-Conte said she "absolutely wants this property" but the money would be better applied elsewhere. Commissioner Santiago didn't think they should be "jeopardizing the city's financial position." At the same meeting, the commission approved Deltona's budget for Fiscal Year 07/08, which included $17.4 million for capital projects like parks.

Jack Hoyt told his commission that he didn't understand how "two teachers could be set against the purchase of this property." Before the vote, three residents came forward to oppose buying the property, one of whom talked about "Sandy Walters not living in the city but donating to election campaigns." The vote was 5-2 against negotiating with the owners. "It's dead," pronounced the assistant city manager. In two months, John Clapp could return to the VGMC for another shot at getting his project approved.

In the *Sentinel*, former commissioner Joe Perez likened Thornby to a taxicab waiting at the curb with its meter running through "many periods of debate and indecision," then puzzlingly he seemed to conclude that the city wouldn't have resources for "economic development" if it helped buy the waterfront property. Thornby was "hacked to death," Larry French wrote, at the same time noting that Deltona had 17 established parks with more than 20 sports fields, but "no walking or biking paths or trails." Wrote the *News-Journal*: "Commissioners argued that there were too many unknowns — even though the purchase had been studied for at least seven years." Volusia activist Eric West said:

> Commissioners voted down a chance to purchase the historic Thornby property, the last large piece of land along the Lake Monroe waterfront, because they couldn't figure out what it was going to cost! Yep, that's right. Five years of talking and nobody ever thought to make the sellers an offer and see what they said ... they didn't even table it for a week or so until they would know for sure about one of the grants they had applied for ... Did it occur to them to just make a lower, safer offer and see if it would fly?

The *Sentinel* printed the highly charged sentiments of one of Deltona's most vehement anti-Thornby bloggers, who accused Mulder and Deyette of being "willing to spend whatever it took to acquire this property without any regard for other priorities." The total cost to taxpayers, the blogger wrote, would have been "about $10 million. All of this for mulch (sic) trails." All the while, it looked as if public purchase was improbable because Deltona wasn't interested; Pat Northey still kept busy on the phones, seeking support.

Hanging in the Balance

"Mayor Dennis Mulder ... has been on the losing end of key votes recently," the *Sentinel* reminded readers. Life and politics were looping back around. Two city commission seats — Harvey (term-limited) and Santiago (not seeking re-election) — would open in November. The coming elections offered faint hope that Thornby, cold and dead in Deltona's political graveyard, could be resurrected — *if* the owners didn't sell to a developer first, and *if* we got more Thornby support on the commission.

In District 4, retired Marine Paul Treusch was running against two opponents — one of whom, he says he was told, didn't know where Thornby was.

Treusch had noted student Johnathan Kenny's remark at the public forum that Thornby would be Deltona's Central Park and says, "It made perfect sense to me." In District 2, Ed Gable, a retired police officer, was running against an opponent who thought, "The money would be better spent elsewhere."

> **Activist Lesson:** This simplistic verbiage disregards the realities of line items, grants and allocations. Often, government funds are earmarked for a single purpose, or a fund source may be a "use it or lose it "proposition. Activists should challenge this kind of rhetoric by demonstrating how a specific project fits in the budget and how it will economically benefit residents.

Gable wanted to buy Thornby and turn it into a park. The elections were "largely penned as a determination of Mayor Dennis Mulder's vision for the city," said the *News-Journal*. We needed more Thornby votes on the city commission. I joined door-knocking teams on long, humid twilight evenings trudging through Deltona suburbs and sign waving on traffic-heavy streets at morning and afternoon commute times. The *Sentinel* reported on donations to Treusch's and Gable's campaigns from Mayor Mulder and "from Enterprise resident Sandy Walters, who has passionately supported the city's purchase of Thornby."

Along with political campaigns, "Destination Deltona" was in full swing. Destination Deltona was a series of visioning sessions where residents shared their concerns and priorities for the community. In the *News-Journal*, Larry French praised the concept, but opined, "Deltona has seldom if ever followed any of the vision plans or citizen mandates." He decried the city's sale of half of DuPont Lakes Park for commercial development; displacement of an Osteen historic marker for Deltona development; and the Thornby public forum where "the city commission ignored everything that was told them."

> **Activist Lesson:** Deltona isn't alone in that mindset. In fact, you would be hard pressed to find a city or county that, after using tax dollars for "visioning sessions" and facilitators, actually put their residents' compiled suggestions to use as something other than pricey bookends.

Ed Gable lost his election. Paul Treusch won his. Thornby was still out on a ledge, but maybe not too far to be hauled back in. The Thornby owners requested that Volusia Forever keep the property on its "A List." With another potential vote in place, Mayor Mulder said, "The timing is perfect" to bring the issue up again. Commissioner Deyette was "thrilled to hear the plan may be revived." Newly elected Commissioner Treusch said, "A partnership with the county is probably a good idea." Commissioner Carmolingo seemed to have had reconsidered. "We really need to protect some of the environmental property ... it's absolutely beautiful," he enthused. Commissioner Denizac said, "I've never been against Thornby being preserved."

Yet, on the same day the *Sentinel* printed those words, *News-Journal* reporter Sara Kiesler wrote about her visit to Thornby with John Clapp (in town "to complete negotiations") and Frank Knight. Two offers from developers were on the table, both in the $5 million range, and the Thornby owners were "ready to cut a deal." As they toured the property, Clapp and Knight reminisced about their Thornby childhood, their "beloved caretaker" Miss Doris, and the Clapp family — "the original tree huggers," Knight called them. "The owners still hold out hope it will be purchased by the public," the story said. As he staked a "No Trespassing" sign in the ground, Knight imagined a restaurant on the property along with picnic areas, bathrooms, parking and trails so that people could "admire its giant 350-year-old magnolia tree."

"No one dreams but us," Knight complained.

Re-elected Commissioner McFall-Conte's opposition to buying Thornby hadn't softened. She told the *News-Journal* that she didn't want to spend city tax dollars amid uncertainty over future property tax revenues. In December, Deltona's city manager, Steve Thompson, (who would soon leave his job) said 2007 had been a "rocky year." His words came at a commission meeting at which "Thornby discussion" was an agenda "add-on" by Commissioner Deyette, drawing the accusation of a few that she was "sneaky."

Deyette explains:

> Pat Northey was working to keep the county interested. Volusia Forever had just voted to keep Thornby on its A List for a while to see what Deltona might be willing to do. I was positive that time was running out for that opportunity. I also knew the real estate market had drastically reduced land values, and I felt we could negotiate a better price than ever. An exasperated and weary Frank Knight had asked me if I thought I could get the city interested again. I felt a strong sense of urgency to bring this before the commission as quickly as possible.

Residents Joanne Gehring, Veronica Kenny, Johnathan Kenny and Phil Giorno spoke in favor of a Thornby purchase. Pat Northey formally asked Deltona to look at a partnership with the county. Thornby's newest "Friend" spoke, too: Realtor Bernie Senez urged commissioners to walk the property. Seven Deltona residents spoke against purchase, for reasons ranging from "we need ball fields" to "the city should not partner with anyone." Mark Watts' account sounded incredible, but it was all too true:

> The one thing that has never happened is the opportunity to sit down with the city and entertain pricing and funding options ... *the actual price has never been discussed between the two parties.*

(At that juncture, Thornby's numbers were all over the board. The asking price was $6.8 million, the owners' appraisal $5.2 million, and the city's appraisal $2.3 million.)

Deyette revived her motion that had failed three months earlier, before Treusch was on the commission. She moved to authorize city staff to negotiate price and terms with the owners, find out how much the county would contribute, and bring a proposal back to the commission in 90 days. Denizac was among those opposed, expressing her "concern about any additional partnerships with Volusia County," but this time, the motion passed. And, like so many Thornby turning points over the years, it passed by one vote. Mulder says jump-starting Thornby negotiations was "one of the reasons the election of Treusch was so important."

Later, when we took Thornby "on the road" in an effort to reach Deltonans' hearts and minds, the *News-Journal*'s opinion was posted front and center on the presentation board:

> The heavy and still-growing density of human population in southwest Volusia will, if not now certainly a generation from now, compel appreciation for the foresight in preserving that historical and ecological treasure.

> *How wonderful it is that nobody need wait a single moment before starting to improve the world.*
>
> **Anne Frank**

CHAPTER EIGHTEEN

Politics: The Art of the Possible

"Fund and Implement Boundless Playground" was a priority at a January 2008 planning retreat for Deltona's elected officials and department heads. A "boundless" or "all-inclusive" playground has features like rubberized surfaces, wide slides and ramps that make it accessible to all children, with or without disabilities. Bringing such a play facility to Deltona had been a goal of Commissioner Zenaida Denizac for at least two years.

Form invitation mailed to nearby residents

Dear Edgewater/Lakeside Resident:

For some time, the 40-acre Thornby property, on Lakeshore Drive between Providence and Broadway, has been advertised for sale by a realtor. You may wonder what the plans are for this historic property. You may recall that three years ago, the owners tried to increase the allowable density on this property and build approximately 250 houses, a clubhouse and swimming pool, with entrance and exit onto Providence Blvd. The plan was approved by the city of Deltona but rejected by the Florida Department of Community Affairs in 2005.

Since then, Deltona mayor, Dennis Mulder, as well as several city commissioners, have been working toward city purchase of the property, using state and county grant funding combined with city funds, in order to develop it as a passive park. Passive parks typically feature picnic tables, nature trails and other amenities for quiet enjoyment of nature, rather than ball fields or more active recreational uses.

It's estimated that as much as **88%** of the cost of this 40-acre, waterfront property would be paid for by state and county funds; however, Deltona will have 100% ownership of the property and the park. If you agree that the city should proceed with negotiating a price and obtaining grant funding to purchase Thornby, please contact your elected officials at:

(emails and phone numbers)

FRIENDS OF THORNBY is a group of residents from Deltona, Enterprise, and other Volusia communities, who have been working for years to "Save Thornby" from inappropriate, high-density development on Lake Monroe.

YOU'RE INVITED

WHAT: THORNBY "OPEN HOUSE"
WHEN: Sat. Feb. 2 - 10:30 am to 3:30 pm
WHERE: Deltona Community Center, Lakeshore Dr.

Enjoy FREE food & entertainment and learn more about this unique and historic property. Who originally owned it? How much is wetlands? How old are the trees? Where is the eagle's nest? What about the Indian midden? Is there really an old single-gauge railroad on the property? Plenty of maps and info.

CAN I SEE IT FOR MYSELF?

YES , you can. With permission of the Thornby owners, we'll also be giving GUIDED TOURS, weather permitting. Walking will be on trails; comfortable shoes are all you need!

Involve Me and I'll Understand

As soon as Pat Northey was elected to the county council, she started brainstorming with Friends of Thornby about how to make Thornby Park happen. Pat combined a deep understanding of human nature with an objective viewpoint. She knew that Friends of Thornby had been immersed in preserving the property for years, trudging from one step to the next, always playing defense. She lived in Deltona and saw that most residents did not know much about the property. Without knowing what Thornby is, residents will never support a Deltona purchase, she told us, and offered a suggestion: Why not have a public event and let people see for themselves why Thornby is so important? Once they see that their city includes such a handsome, serene spot, they will picture themselves enjoying it and be supporters all the way — especially when they realize the price works out to about $18 per Deltona resident.

We wondered why the heck we hadn't thought of it ourselves.

> **Activist Lesson:** Involving/informing people about your cause is vital. Hold an information session if feasible, or consider taking your message "on the road" to homeowners' associations, civic groups, etc.

Pat's eye-opening idea inspired Kevin Davidson and me to plan a Thornby Open House at the Deltona Community Center. The center, a somewhat worn-looking building with an unpaved parking area, was small, but its well-lighted main room and kitchen were rentable. By far, its biggest asset was its location: very close to Thornby and just across tree-lined Lakeshore Drive from gleaming Lake Monroe, where nature provides its own special panache.

Weeks before the event, Roy and I spent days designing, printing, copying and mailing hundreds of flyers. We mailed one to every property owner at the nearby condos.

> **Activist Lesson:** Names and addresses of property owners can be obtained from the local property appraiser's office, usually online.

We sent flyers to every Deltona resident we knew personally. I scoured Deltona public meeting minutes to find names of interested persons to invite. Friends of Thornby posted flyers at the Community Center, as well as the Deltona Library and the Enterprise Post Office. We sent announcements to the local papers and Pat Northey put the word in her monthly council newsletter. We planned for informative, eye-catching exhibits, lively music and free food, but the piece de resistance would be guided tours of Thornby. Three years before, John Clapp had said he didn't want "those people" on his property. Now, he not only gave permission for tours, but also arranged for paths to be bush-hogged through the underbrush, clearing the way for "those people" and lots of others to access the property. Mark Watts prepared a liability release to be signed by everyone entering the property (in case of falls or snakebite?) Roy spent hours on the property, clearing away the foot-tripping vines that stretched across the trails. Kevin Davidson, often with his young daughter Leeanne in tow, scouted the property for the "best of the best" photo ops, ending up with literally hundreds of striking photos. He says Leanne didn't like sticks brushing against her legs, but he made her laugh with "sticks and stones may break my bones, but developers won't get it." One morning, he says, they were awestruck to see "a magnificent spider web stretched between two small trees. Facing east, every inch of the web threads had dewdrops attached and the drops acted like many small prisms for the sun's rays, with hints of different colors outlining the web in the most detailed way."

Saturday, February 2 dawned blue-sky perfect. At 10:30 a.m., we opened the doors. Tables were spaced around the large, bright room, each one displaying 5'x3' poster boards that Kevin and I had made, each one displaying a different aspect of Thornby. There were close-ups of colorful wildflowers and greenery taken by Kevin and Deltona nature photographer Susan Young; exhibits illustrating Dr. Glass' life and career; shots of the Thornby eagles' nest; information on the property's history from Indians to the 20th century; a display of the Volusia County recreational trail slated to adjoin Thornby; material on the St. Johns as an American Heritage River, the Indian midden, and the old railroad spur. We pinned up photos, newspaper clippings, letters, documents, and other interesting items, all designed to demonstrate Thornby's past, present and future, all arranged for visual appeal. On a side table sat Roland Peloquin's scaled-down model of a mule-pulled orange cart as must have been used on the Thornby railroad spur in the 1800s, along with his intriguing re-creation of how Fort Kingsbury may have looked.

As a few people stepped inside, we were as anxious as schoolgirls at a dance. Did we have too much "stuff" displayed, or not enough? Would anyone even care? Would they eat and run? Thanks to Larry, the Florida Department of Community Affairs sent "a boxload of brochures and printed material," including a DVD, "Our Legacy," on saving community resources through grant/preservation purchases. Thanks to Veronica Kenny's laptop and projector, we looped the state's DVD continuously all day. A long table held sandwiches, chips, brownies and sodas; in the kitchen, Kevin's stepson Billy Davidson was busy dishing up hot dogs (donated by Ed Gable) with all the trimmings. Award-winning singer/songwriter Rog Lee generously donated his time and love for Thornby to entertain guests with songs like Thornby's "official" theme song, "St. Johns Lullaby." (Rog wrote "St. Johns Lullaby" in response to Mike Fleming's request for a Thornby song he could use on his online radio show.)

Colorful spider web on Thornby property

Roland Peloquin's models of Fort Kingsbury and mule-drawn cart

As it turned out, we had underestimated the outpouring of community curiosity and interest in Thornby. When people began flocking into the center, we couldn't get them back out fast enough. Folks lined up so they wouldn't miss "their" next tour. The guides (Roy, Kevin, and Larry French) worked non-stop for hours, loading up the vans, shuttling people one-half block to Thornby, and leading them for half an hour by way of narrow, rough paths to sites they couldn't have found on their own. From bounding little kids to shaky oldsters, they pushed through the underbrush to see the enormous old trees that Rich Vail calls "truly God's wonders and miracles." They saw the Indian midden and the loveliest wildflowers, while Roy, Kevin or Larry narrated the sights, the property's history, and community efforts to save it from inappropriate development. Since it was the winter dry season, those who were able clambered down into the empty drainage canal to look up at the old trestle. They visited the old keyhole pool and the remains of the old dock. People were in awe, the guides reported, taking photos, exclaiming they had no idea the property was so beautiful and the trees so magnificent. The guides heard, "I never knew this was here!" so many times that it got to be "old hat."

Colleen "Coe" Chamberlain of DeBary came as a guest with husband Rog Lee but was soon recruited as greeter and people mover. The always-sociable Coe made sure releases were signed, kibitzed with folks as they waited, managed the lines, and talked to almost everyone who took a tour. "Most of the people I talked to were very impressed with the information and history of Thornby. Many had never heard of it; some came out to downplay the importance of saving it, and came away saying it had to be saved," she remembers.

Pat Northey was there, of course. In the *West Volusia Beacon,* she had called Thornby "a little piece of heaven that needs to be preserved." Commissioners Paul Treusch and Mike Carmolingo toured the property. Commissioner Deyette came, as did Mayor Mulder. With the blogs producing folderol like "Thornby Park Cost to Deltonans Could be $10-$20 Million," I'd felt some trepidation that disruptive anti-Thornby bloggers might show up. At least two very vocal ones did, but there were no problems — in fact, after touring the property, one Deltona anti-Thornby blogger, a vintage railroad fan, ventured that he might change his mind, after all.

As Frank Knight and his wife peered intently at the board illustrating Dr. Glass' life, career and philanthropy, I asked Frank if he could identify any of the people posing in front of the Thornby house in an old photo. He said he didn't know who they were. It occurred to me then that out of my passion to save Thornby, I may have come to know more of its history than even Frank, who had played there as a child, known Anna Glass and Doris Faber, and lived next to the property for years.

Nancy Siebert of Deltona signing the Big Board

The Big Board was another of Pat Northey's powerful ideas. She knew that people love to express themselves and that anything "supersized" makes a great photo op. Sure enough, this shot made the *Beacon's* front page.

Some Big Board comments:

- Please preserve this for our children's children
- Do the right thing… no developing
- Don't sell our history to the developers…save Thornby
- Save natural Florida before it all disappears….save Thornby
- Can't wait for this to develop into a park
- Heavenly … wonderful … a treasure for future generations
- Save this historic property. It's community! It's historic! It's beauty!
- Really enjoyed tour
- Preserve our biodiversity please
- Fantastic property

Tour guide Roy says, "I could hardly walk when it was over, I was so exhausted." He remembers an elderly woman with severe leg problems. "She was going to go!" he says, and she did, even though she could barely keep up. The hot dogs vanished, but people didn't eat and leave, as we had feared. They scanned the exhibits, enjoyed the music, and watched "Our Legacy."

Larry French admires a 500-year-old historic live oak tree on the property during the Thornby open house tour.

To help Deltona residents lobby their elected officials, we asked them to fill in their name and address on pre-printed postcards expressing support for a city purchase. We collected hundreds of cards. Afterward, I organized the cards by city commission district and sent each commissioner the cards signed by their own constituents — a message hard to ignore.

At 4 p.m., the remarkable event was winding down. I had been on my feet for eight tiring hours, answering questions and guiding people through the exhibits; to me, the opportunity to talk about Thornby was sheer delight. I knew how those virgin Thornby visitors felt, because I felt the same way when I first saw it. We estimated that more than 250 people came through the doors that day; at least 150 toured the property. I was elated that the open house had turned out so well; it gave me solid hope that, since a few hundred more Deltona people were now tuned in to Thornby, maybe we really *could* make it happen. Still, says Coe, "A few grumbled and griped about cost, 'already had too many parks,' tired of Enterprise people telling them what to do with Deltona's money."

Nancy Siebert (shown in photo above) and Esther (former Mole) Dobens did not think their city had too many parks. Both had supported Mulder for mayor for his "new, fresh ideas and energy." Neither had been to Thornby before. "I was blown out of my mind when I walked the property for the first time at the Open House," Esther says. She and Nancy came to the Community Center in high heels, straight from a church meeting. Nancy says she just wanted to see the displays, "but then I thought, 'what the heck?' and took the tour." Like Esther, Nancy had her doubts when she first heard the controversy over buying Thornby. She had campaigned for Janet Deyette when Deyette ran in her commission district, and says, "I'd listened to Esther and Janet talk about Thornby, and I wondered, why a park? — a park brings no income and no jobs."

"Truly, it was the tour," she continues. "That was what turned me. The tour made it come to life. We could see all these things as he [Larry French] talked. He was so knowledgeable; he explained the history and how it all fit together. It was a natural part of Florida, with the river. We saw what was there, and what could be, like the ferry across Lake Monroe. I went home and told my family, 'I've got to take you down there'. I supported it because it would be a passive park. No ball games." And, adds Esther, "it's right in our backyard."

That day, Esther and Nancy ran into Deltona friends who had brought their kids to the open house because of the eagles: "They came to see things they were learning about in school." Both women deem the event "excellent" and say they were "totally impressed." So much so, that they had a brainstorm. "The poster boards impressed me," says Esther. "That's where we got the idea to have a program on Thornby at the church [First United Methodist of Deltona]. I said, 'we need this.'"

Thornby is "the elephant in the room," said Larry French in the *Beacon*. "The Commission tried to argue it away. They can't." Commissioner Paul Treusch recalls:

> During my campaign [for city commission] Thornby was a high-profile issue. Most of the citizens I talked to did not care much one way or the other, but after a few minutes, most understood and agreed with me that saving Thornby was something that we should do. There were some that, no matter what I said or did, would not change their minds. However, when Friends of Thornby hosted a tour to educate the uninformed, they changed their positions.

Thornby on the Road

Activist, lobbyist, campaign worker, sleuth, historian, rabble-rouser — now I donned my newest Thornby hat: guest lecturer. "We wanted you to come and speak because church members are to be involved in social and environmental causes," Esther explains. Like most other Deltonans, the Methodist churchwomen had "heard arguing about" Thornby, but weren't familiar with the issues. So, on a sunny afternoon a few weeks after Friends of Thornby's invigorating Open House, Pat Northey and I gave a joint Thornby presentation to about 50 women from the United Methodist Women's group. I had 20 minutes, poster boards and an easel to introduce the property to a non-political audience. I used a hand-drawn map to point out Thornby's location. I mentioned Bob Nix's 1999 statement that Thornby "has some history of local significance," and brought them through state, city and other agency actions over the years, careful not to criticize officials or get boringly political. I kept to the straight facts — this happened and then that happened. I emphasized that condos on Thornby were not "property rights" — the owners were trying to get their existing property rights changed. I talked about the eagles, the Indian midden, the wetlands, the possible fort and the old railroad spur, and passed around photos they could see while they listened. I told them about the grant funding process. The women seemed receptive to my main message: they needed to contact their mayor and city commission if they wanted the property saved. I had handouts with City Hall contact information.

Pat Northey put the Thornby property in a regional context for them, expounding on the county's trails network and how the property tied in with the 50-mile paved recreational trail planned to stretch from Enterprise to Titusville. Esther says that for "most of the people, it was probably the first time Thornby meant anything to them." Nancy adds that our Thornby talk was "the only time they heard about current events [at a meeting]." Both women say that the members said "good things" afterward and that "they were all interested and nobody fell asleep."

Every day, it seemed, brought more public support, but we still didn't have enough commission votes to buy Thornby.

Working Every Angle

After the Open House, Kevin Davidson posted scores of impressive Thornby photos on an "anti-Thornby" website. Amid shots of Phoenix palms, giant oaks, mammoth ferns, wild ginger, old railroad and dock remnants, he invited anyone interested to meet him on the property for a tour. As usual, comments were divided. One blogger posted: "A lot of people seem to have the mentality of Mayor John. If there is a vacant piece of property, pave it over. Look what that mentality did to Deltona." Another wrote, "Treusch thinks a Boy Scout camp might be a good thing for Thornby. One stray campfire and there goes the tree huggers (sic) Paradise. Not to mention many $$$$$$$$$."

Local newspaper readers may well have wondered, as Larry French did in the April 9, 2008 *Daytona Beach News-Journal* "What's up with Thornby?" After more than five years, he said, "Thornby is still waiting for Deltona to decide what it will do." At the same time, a Deltona resident (and long-time anti-Thornby speaker) wrote in the *Beacon* that she wished more residents would visit the Deltona Arts and Historical Center "to see the history of their hometown." (Presumably, she was referring to the Center's displays highlighting the founding of Deltona in the 1960s.) She seemed not to realize that when Deltona annexed the Thornby property, it brought history with it. I pounced on her words in my own letter to the editor, pointing out that *"The oldest history of Deltona is that of the historic Thornby property,"* and if this riverfront jewel is preserved for public use, then the letter writer and others will never find themselves staring at high-rise development on Lakeshore Drive wondering, "How did this happen? This was our history."

Meanwhile, Pat Northey was working hard to win commitments from the county manager and other key managers to keep Thornby alive. On May 5, she updated the Deltona City Commission on the county's network of multi-use recreational trails[1], explained how trails draw people to local shops and businesses, and said that a trail will run "right by the Thornby property." [2]

People Who Need People

Pat had another astute idea on how to gain support for Deltona's purchase of Thornby. If Commissioner Zenaida Denizac saw Thornby for herself, she reasoned, she would surely recognize it as the ideal site for her long-desired boundless playground. (Pat was thinking like her former council colleague, Jim Ward, who says, "I can't learn enough from looking at a map.") Pat arranged a tour and so, on a sunny summer afternoon, Roy Walters escorted the sneaker-clad city commissioner/English teacher and the jeans-wearing county council representative around Thornby. The paths cleared for the Open House were still walkable, and so they followed the same trails past the keyhole pool, midden, old railroad, duck pond. "Zenaida was very impressed with the plant life," Roy says, and identified native plants she had tasted as a child in Puerto Rico. "She was deep in the woods loving it, and at the same time sad that her [physically challenged] daughter could not keep up with us," Pat says. After the tour, Zenaida re-joined her waiting husband and daughter Yaitza — the young adult who had inspired her quest to establish a Deltona playground that would be accessible to everyone.

---

1 Paved, multi-use trails, sometimes called "linear parks," are used by cyclists, walkers, runners, baby strollers and wheelchairs, among others.
2 This refers to the East Coast Regional Rail Trail, a 50-mile trail linking Enterprise with Titusville.

The Thornby aura

In June, Sandy Gallagher was appointed to represent Deltona on the Volusia Growth Management Commission. "Eagle Sandy," once quiet and self-conscious, now had the most heavily weighted vote on the county's most omnipotent board.

As a member of Deltona's parks advisory board, Larry French had been bringing up the need for a parks master plan as called for in the city's comprehensive plan. The city hired a well-regarded planning firm, Glatting-Jackson, to update its parks plan. During the six-month process, consultants evaluated city facilities, met with residents, conducted a telephone survey, and met with commissioners. As part of their report, the consultants highly recommended that Deltona buy the Thornby property, noting that existing Deltona parks "do not embrace the natural landscape and provide little water access." Planner Allison Crnic said, "I don't know a city that has ever regretted having bought their lakefront property."

At a parks visioning session, Commissioner Denizac said, "I am all for the boundless playground; there is nothing else like it in Volusia County." She added that she wished that such a facility had existed when her disabled daughter was a child. Thus, an all-inclusive playground became part of Deltona's Master Parks Plan.

Be careful what you wish for — you might get it? Commissioner Deyette and everyone else who yearned for a lower Thornby offer got one, but barely. The new, reduced price was $5.5 million. "Fantasy," scoffed the mayor, and several commissioners agreed. "Reasonable," said Mark Watts.

"Deltona went from being led by a hurly-burly mayor who rarely tolerated dissent to a neophyte who rarely earns agreement," said a *News-Journal* editorial. True enough, but even as the words appeared, a grant-funded "boundless playground" was something all commissioners agreed on. The seed, planted by Commissioner Denizac, had been nurtured through countless budgets, workshops and visioning sessions. By mid-2008, it was no longer a question of *"should* we build it?" but *"where* should we build it?" With county and state grant deadlines looming, on August 25, 2008 the commission held an arduous "Boundless Playground Site Selection" workshop. Of the 10 city-owned sites discussed, a 17-acre plot on Beechdale Drive got the most support. No one breathed the word "Thornby" until Denizac broke the ice. She told her colleagues that, after visiting a heavily treed playground in Lake County, she "thought about the Thornby property and contacted County Councilwoman Northey." Northey says she believes that the Thornby tour is "when the spark lit" for Denizac's support of a Thornby purchase. (Nevertheless, she apparently was under enormous pressure from some of her supporters to vote against it.) Today, Denizac says she remembers, "How beautiful this land was. It reminded me of back home, since I grew up in a place very similar to the Thornby property. I always knew that the property was worth preserving, but the actual tour confirmed it."

Mayor Mulder, anticipating a reduced Thornby sale price, said, "If the opportunity presents itself for Thornby, the city may be able to do something." At the same time, he wanted city matching funds committed for a playground on Beechdale. "I really liked the [Beechdale] location [for the playground] and thought Thornby should be purchased anyway," he says. The consensus at the time was to "move forward with the Beechdale Drive site for the boundless playground" — a move that sent both Pat Northey and me to the brink of a nervous breakdown. She wasn't at all confident that Deltona could work up grants for *two* properties at once. With weeks of keyed-up calls and animated conversations, she kept Thornby, seemingly so close, from slipping away, with Friends of Thornby watching from the political sidelines. The whole process "taught me patience and the art of negotiation," she says.

The city commission postponed its vote on buying Thornby. The community's wrangling continued. On a blog: "It's going to be developed and I am going to laugh my butt off," a poster predicted, while railing at the "$16 million cost." At a commission meeting, teenager Johnathan Kenny urged the city commission to buy the property. And at Deltona City Hall, a new assistant director of planning and development services started work. He was up to speed on city land use issues in no time. The job fit him like a glove because his name was Ron Paradise — the same Ron Paradise (now a *former* county staffer) who initially recommended a Thornby land use change in 1999, revised his thinking, helped write the Enterprise Local Plan, and led the county's fight against the Thornby amendment at the VGMC in 2005. He was now the second-in-command planner for the city of Deltona.

Friends of Thornby flyer

DELTONA RESIDENTS:

There are "For Sale" signs on the historic Thornby property in the city of Deltona – 40 waterfront acres of heavily wooded land with an American bald eagles' nest and 7-1/2 acres of wetlands, directly on Lake Monroe (St. Johns River) adjacent to Providence Blvd. The plans for development hav include strip shopping on the river and a multi-family project of approx. **250 units.**

Your City Commission will decide whether the *city* should apply for state grant funds to buy the historic Thornby property and preserve it as a PARK ! ! !

* * * * * * * * * *

DO YOU WANT A PARK ON THE HISTORIC THORNBY PROPERTY?
!! TELL YOUR ELECTED OFFICIALS !!

Contact:

Deltona City Commissioners

City Hall: (386) 561-2100
City Hall FAX: (386) 789-7230

OR: Send to the Commissioner for your District. Don't know who that is? Check city website at www.ci.deltona.fl.us

MORE INFO?
FRIENDS OF THORNBY (407) 328-8556

This is the way the Struggle Ends/ Not with a Condo but a Playground

On October 20, 2008, the Deltona City Commission's regular meeting was held not at City Hall, but at the Community Center on Lakeshore Drive, where eight months before Friends of Thornby held our Thornby Open House. It was an extraordinary night. Kevin Finn told the commission:

> Tonight, it might be a little different. Tonight you likely won't be bombarded by the people of Enterprise. Please understand they have stated their case, put their cards on the table. Time after time, they have argued the traffic, they have argued the eagles, they have argued the soil, the trees and plants, the impact on the quality of life, the water quality, the historical significance, the schools, so on and so on.

That night, the Deltona City Commission would hear just from Deltona residents. As always, Thornby supporters filled nearly every seat.

Pat Northey made a presentation on the Thornby purchase. The $3 million price would be split 50-50 between the city and county. By city ordinance, a commission "supermajority" — five votes instead of the usual four — was required to approve the purchase, since the *total* cost was higher than the city's $2.3 million appraisal. At public comment, the words of the lone dissenter — the same person who had said she wanted more Deltonans to appreciate their history — were overshadowed by supportive ones from Finn, Robin French, Larry French and Sandy Gallagher.

"The possibilities for the park are endless," Mayor Mulder said, "and it makes perfect sense to put the boundless playground on this [Thornby] property." Commissioner Denizac said, "The timing is right." Northey said later, "The idea for the boundless playground on Thornby was Zenaida's. She really wanted that playground and she wanted it on Thornby, but she was getting a lot of [outside] pressure not to support it. I promised I would move stones to put the playground there, but we had to get the property first." Commissioner Treusch said he didn't think there was a better project for the city to get involved in. Today, he adds, "I hoped that my fellow commissioners would listen to reason. I was concerned that some were influenced by developers." Commissioner McFall said the boundless playground should go on Thornby. (She later observed that she changed her mind about buying Thornby "because of the public input that came out.") Commissioner Carmolingo called the property "beautiful" and the price "unbelievable." Commissioner Zischkau, who cast the sole dissenting vote, said that under the contract "the special playground couldn't be placed on the property." Pat Northey disagreed with his interpretation. Later, she says, he told her that he "probably should have voted for it."

On October 20, 2008, the commission voted 6-1 to use city funds to pay half the cost of the historic Thornby property. With that vote, it was assured there would be no condos, no strip shopping, no swimming pools or clubhouses on Thornby. it only took eight years of backbreaking grassroots work to get there.

I remember sitting in the back of the room. I remember crying when they took the vote. The staggering drama unfolding on the dais must have mesmerized me, because I remember nothing else about that night and have relied almost exclusively on minutes, newspaper articles, and interviews to write about it. Kevin Finn says: "I was in front and Sandy Gallagher was beside me. I was ecstatic when the vote came. They had to gavel the meeting — it was pandemonium. Frank Knight and his wife congratulated me. Allen Watts congratulated me. On the way home, I called my mom in Ohio. I had tears in my eyes: 'WE WON, MOM! We did the impossible!' I think that was when I finally believed we'd saved Thornby." Jack Hoyt agrees. "For me, that was the deciding moment," he says, "because the city's vote took it off the market."

"The stars aligned," Pat Northey said in the *News-Journal*. This time, they weren't dark stars. "It would have been a travesty to bulldoze this property for more condominiums and strip malls. Instead, it will be preserved as a passive park that will provide a glimpse of old Florida for generations to come," she said, crediting "the economy and the negotiating skills of county land-preservation staff for striking an affordable deal" to buy the historic Thornby property. Modestly, she left herself out of the equation, but "that should never be." From the time of her election to the county council in 2006, she worked tirelessly to keep alive the goal of saving the Thornby property for public use. The county council's 2008 vote to approve using Volusia Forever funds to pay for half of Thornby rated little public fanfare. Few people knew what it took to get there, or that Pat was behind the wheel. "Getting it [Thornby] past the staff and to the attention of the county manager was a major big deal," she recounts, "and getting Jim [Dinneen, county manager] to understand the importance of the project took some doing." After that came discussions with county staff over the Thornby playground. "We [customarily] don't put playgrounds on Volusia Forever lands," she says. "We manage those footprints very naturally. The purchase, the playground, the carve-out… it wasn't an easy deal on the county end, either." She continues, "Sandy (Walters) was the cheerleader, and I worked behind the scenes. Everything has been difficult."

> *From time to time little men will come along to find fault with what you have done.... They will go down the stream like bubbles; they will vanish. But the work you have done will remain for the ages.*
>
> **Theodore Roosevelt**

CHAPTER NINETEEN

Some Day I'll Meet You Down at Thornby Park

After eight years under threat of Florida-intense development, Thornby's old trees were still trees, not cypress mulch or oak firewood, and its wetlands were still wet, not dried-out runoff basins — no small miracle, for sure. In 2008, when good things started to happen, they happened fast.

In September, Ron Paradise went to work for Deltona. In October, Deltona agreed to buy Thornby. In November, Volusia County agreed to pay half its purchase price. In December, Chris Bowley, the planner who, years before, shared his time and knowledge with the neophyte activists known as the Friends of Thornby, became Deltona's Director of Planning and Development Services, assuming the job Bob Nix held for nine years. "Will the Circle be Unbroken?" asks one of my favorite traditional songs. After all this time, Thornby's circle of Friends was strong and unbroken.

Obstacle Course

At this point, we should have been able to enjoy the view from the top. After all, it took eight years to reach it. As close as we were, though, the summit remained frustratingly out of reach, wrapped in a chilling fog of complication.

"Grant Mistake Complicates Proposed Thornby Playground" declared the *Daytona Beach News-Journal* headline. "Plans for a playground . . . have already hit a snag in Deltona," announced the *Orlando Sentinel*. Just one month after the city commission voted to buy Thornby, Commissioner Denizac put the property back on the agenda. She had "heard comments the [playground] project would take more than a couple of years" and wanted "a timeline in black and white showing the time table from today to the ribbon cutting." Commissioner McFall-Conte said the playground was the only reason she voted to buy Thornby, and that, if the project could not be completed by the end of 2009, she would "ask that her vote be reconsidered."

"There is only one location for the boundless playground: Thornby," opined Commissioner Deyette. The commission decided to forget about Beechdale and concentrate on just one playground site — Thornby — even though they had already sent grant requests to the county and state for equipment at Beechdale. Because of the mid-stream change, the state application had to be withdrawn, leaving only one grant source for playground equipment: the county. For Deltona to build an all-inclusive playground on Thornby as fast as some commissioners directed, the city needed a county ECHO (Educational, Cultural, Historic, Outdoor) grant, and they needed it right away. But the Thornby closing was delayed because the property's total acreage had been miscalculated. Therefore, in essence, Deltona was applying for a grant to buy playground equipment for property it did not own.

That was just one in a slew of problems cited by the ECHO advisory board in February 2009 when Patrice Murphy, Deltona's grants coordinator, defended the city's application. She was the only city representative at the meeting. Reviewing Deltona's application, one member said, "I'm unimpressed with [the city's stated] goals." Another referred to items "mistakenly inserted." Still another commented that the grant application "did not address historical resources on the property," calling it a "major defect" for the city to rely on the Thornby owners' archaeological survey. "You're under the gun," the board told Murphy, and quizzed her for 40 minutes about "missing pieces" in the city's paperwork. They considered the all-inclusive playground an "admirable" project, they said, and agreed that Deltona had a shortfall in parks, but "Given the omissions in this government presentation, do you honestly feel the city is ready?" the board chair asked her. She did her best to reassure sceptical board members that Deltona staff and officials were prepared to do whatever it took to accept ECHO funds and finish the playground within 12-18 months, including obtaining required permits and a new "more meaningful [archaeological] examination of the site." Because of board members' concerns, the city's grant application scored only 73 points out of a possible 100, but fortunately, grant money was still abundant in 2009. Deltona received an ECHO award of $393,750 to build an all-inclusive playground on Thornby. The city matched the sum with an equal amount of cash. By the terms of the ECHO grant, Deltona agreed to maintain playground facilities at Thornby until November 2048.[1]

Kevin Finn says, "After the city agreed to buy Thornby, I knew in the back of my mind there would be some speed bumps, but the major roadblocks were clear as long as the closing happened as scheduled." However, the closing did not happen as scheduled. It was postponed when the latest survey showed that the property was 1.2 acres larger than everyone had thought. The owners wanted more money, saying that the price had been calculated "per acre." After a lot of back-and-forth, the county agreed to pony up extra funds, but the city said "no deal." The skittish sale was headed out to pasture. Once again, Pat Northey stepped in, spending weeks with a phone at her ear, holding hands and slogging gamely through political quicksand. She was finally able to lead county officials, city officials, Frank Knight, John Clapp, Bernie Senez, Mark Watts and Deltona City Attorney George Trovato to a creative compromise. The owners would "donate" the extra acreage's value ($121,827) to the city as a charitable contribution in exchange for a tax deduction. Says Trovato:

> Initially, I did not think the city would ever buy Thornby because the majority of the commission wanted the revenue from the development. But things changed dramatically when the economy suddenly came to a halt and the county stepped up to cover half the cost. The persistence of local citizens is what truly kept it alive. Without public opposition to the development, the historic environment would have been destroyed forever to make way for condos on the river.

---

1 The Thornby property itself must be "permanently devoted to conservation" under the terms of Volusia Forever's purchase grant.

Thornby Purchase "Giant Check"
Left to Right: Deltona City Commissioner Paul Treusch; Volusia County Councilwoman Pat Northey; Deltona Mayor Dennis Mulder; Deltona City Commissioner Janet Deyette; Volusia County Land Acquisitions Director Doug Weaver; Thornby Property Owner J. Frank Knight

Mother Always Wanted a Park

On Monday, March 9, 2009, pens were clicked, papers signed, hands shaken and photos snapped. After that, Thornby was not owned by Widow Summers or Dr. James H. Glass or Catherine Clapp or Frank Knight. "Signed, Sealed, Delivered, It's Yours" said Pat Northey, calling Thornby "the people's gift to themselves." Frank Knight told the *West Volusia Beacon,* "The family wanted the property preserved and turned into a park."

"I only felt good about our success in saving Thornby after the closing, because then we knew that somebody else owned it," says Roy Walters. "The push [to buy Thornby] lasted through several City Commission elections and changes in Deltona administration," reported the *Beacon,* as Commissioner Janet Deyette agreed: "It's been a long, long battle." The Deltona-Volusia Forever agreement designated Thornby as a passive park (A "passive" park accommodates activities like walking, picnicking and bird watching in a natural setting, as opposed to a more active park with sports fields and organized activities) connected to county recreational trails, with a small part set aside as an all-inclusive playground. Deltona had one year to create a Thornby Park management plan. Ed Sullivan voiced Friends of Thornby's roller-coaster emotions: "It's been so long that we are still a little cautious. It's really good, but we now want to see it developed into a park. Then we [will] know that it definitely will not be sold." After so long, could anyone fault us for being watchful?

Reactions and Relics

In the *News-Journal*, a couple who had lived in Deltona for less than a year professed themselves "shocked" that the city bought Thornby. On the blogs, the split continued. "Money for a stupid piece of land that NOBODY wanted... I bet 95 percent were not deltonans!" (sic) read one post. Another opinion: "What do we get? Boundless playgrounds. Idiots." Buying Thornby was "a terrible waste of taxpayer money," said a Deltona resident's letter to the *Beacon*. Yet, one resident rejoiced: "I am so glad they finally decided to buy the Thornby estate. This is a great piece of property for the city."

A *Beacon* editorial endorsed Thornby's purchase, referring to Thornby supporters who "claimed it would be an irreplaceable park site." The article, I thought, missed the point. We did not fight for years to build a park on Thornby, but rather, we fought to halt a land use change that would have sanctified a colossal density increase on the land. The park, though wonderful, was icing on the cake. I sent a letter to the editor. "Deltona's Planning and Zoning Board (twice), the Volusia Growth Management Commission, and the Florida Department of Community Affairs all rejected a six-fold density increase on the Thornby property," I wrote. My message: The owners chose to sell their land for a park rather than develop it at the allowed density because, by holding official feet to official fires for eight years, Friends of Thornby kept the allowed density unchanged.

In April, members of Deltona's Citizen Accessibility Advisory Sub-Committee raised $105 from the sale of teddy bears donated by member Tom Dockery "in the hopes these monies will be used for the Thornby All Inclusive Playground project." It was a thoughtful act that helped dilute the on-line bitterness of a blogger who did not understand that Thornby was privately owned property in the city. "Paying millions to the county for a county project THEY SHOULD HAVE PAID FOR," he/she raved.

As required by ECHO, a new Thornby archaeological survey was performed by Environmental Services, Inc., a consulting firm with offices in five states. Carolyn Watson Langley provided ESI with background information on the Thornby house and the features she remembered from her 18 years there, like the arbor, woodshed, driveways, duck pond and chicken coop. On-site tests confirmed the existence of the "Thornby Park Midden," as well as historic and prehistoric artifacts. Historic objects include pre-1900 cut nails, bottle glass and items "possibly associated with Ft. Kingsbury." Prehistoric objects include ceramic and grog (clay) fragments from the St. Johns Period (1500 BC-1565 AD).

Don't Bother to Ask

In the midst of my three-year term on the Volusia Growth Management Commission, some local officials made a push for significant commission rule changes. The resulting process included repeated reviews, drafting and re-drafting of proposed rules and meetings, and stretched for 18 months at a cost to county taxpayers of more than $50,000 in lawyer's fees. One especially repugnant proposal would have erased the public's right to simply *ask for* standing at the VGMC, as Friends of Thornby and Steve Wiechert had done four years earlier. Local officials who pushed for this change wanted only local governments to be parties to VGMC proceedings, not residents. At the public hearing, more than 30 people spoke in opposition to the rule changes, including former VGMC members Chris Elmer and Suzanne Steiner. Deltona Commissioner Janet Deyette testified that " if the Thornby property in Deltona, now destined to be an undeveloped public park, had been [considered] under these rule changes, the land would be sporting condominiums now instead of live oaks and wildlife." After much public pressure, the commission ultimately decided — although not unanimously — to retain the public's right to request legal standing at the Volusia Growth Management Commission. At this writing, the right remains intact.

A Low-Impact, Passive Recreational Facility

At a joint meeting of the Deltona Commission and the city's Economic Development Board, Chris Bowley's statistics showed that the planned recreational trail adjacent to Thornby would draw more than 60,000 users per month. Meanwhile, Larry French, now chair of the city's Parks and Recreation Advisory Board, arranged for board members to tour Thornby.

Commissioner Denizac asked about connecting with interested organizations and businesses for help in funding the playground to "move the timeline along," but the Thornby Park Management Plan was finished on schedule. Deltona's new parks director, the hard-working and enthusiastic Steve Moore, says Thornby was on his plate his first day on the job. "The city manager, Faith Miller, stressed to me that this project was a big thing," he says. He wrote the 68-page document over several months, submitting drafts to county staff and re-working it to ensure their approval. The plan detailed the property's history, ecology, wildlife, and natural communities, the playground footprint, and future park possibilities like walking trails. The onsite playground wouldn't be "an impediment to the heritage and environmental requirements of Thornby, as it is not vertical construction," the plan read. Some of the Plan's components were very familiar; for instance, the Thornby soils report and the onsite wetlands map. This data, entered into the record by the Friends of Thornby at every hearing since 2001, was now a permanent part of the property's official DNA.

Under the management plan, Deltona would be responsible for all operational aspects of maintaining and managing the park. "It is hoped that the property will remain an ecological and environmental gem of Volusia County and become a cornerstone in the region," the plan states. It also called for public participation in the project. Development Services Director Chris Bowley recommended a "task force of representatives from the community" as well as groups like the Deltona Accessibility Board and potential trail users. Commissioner McFall-Conte "suggested they be citizens of Deltona" and Commissioner Denizac suggested nominating "residents of Deltona." Those sentiments clouded the horizon a bit. Still, on October 20, 2009, the Deltona City Commission approved the Thornby Park Management plan by a vote of 6-1. Also sanctioned by the county, the plan guarantees that nothing but a park can happen on the Thornby property. For me, when the management plan was adopted, the fog finally lifted. Then I knew for sure: WE WON!

For years, Deltona claimed that the new "Bypass Road" would be the panacea for traffic jams created from adding 500 new residents on Thornby. In 2005, architect Bruce Andersen had "no doubt" that the road would be "in place and well used" before Thornby condos were built. The same year, traffic expert Dr. Jeff Buckholz pointed out that the road had already slipped off the timetable. When construction of the Bypass Road finally began in 2009, it was four years behind schedule.

> **Activist Lesson:** Every phase of a road project requires separate financing: planning, land purchase, design and construction. Construction/improvement schedules are often subject to political winds and priorities.

In May 2010, Chris Bowley advised the Deltona City Commission that the Thornby playground was on target for an October construction start. He envisioned two community meetings before construction began. Bowley reminded commissioners that the all-inclusive playground would serve a wider geographical area than Deltona.[2] Not even the chance for disabled kids to have fun tempered the furor of the blogger who blasted "the two teachers who sold out their vote because they were enamoured by some vision of a boundless playground." That post may have been the impetus for a Deltona resident's public complaint about online "defaming remarks made about residents and members of the commission."

Focusing on the Good

At Commissioner Deyette's "town hall" meeting on June 14, Chris Bowley honed in on the economic benefits of paved, multi-use trails, citing Winter Garden and Dunedin as examples of Florida towns that got a second wind

---

2 According to the *News-Journal*, in 2008 there were only 10 all-inclusive playgrounds in Florida, and none in Volusia County.

when a recreational trail came through. In addition to tying into Volusia County's recreational network, he said, Thornby's future may include nature trails and a small gazebo. He showed how the playground was sited on the property with regard for wetlands and archeologically sensitive areas. Then, out of the blue, he announced, "The city is looking for a permanent name for the park." Although the remark caused some consternation among Friends of Thornby, it was short-lived. The idea of Thornby being named anything but Thornby was as preposterous as re-thinking the name of the Washington Monument. And so we forgot about it.

In July, the city commission voted 6-1 to approve the Thornby playground construction contract. Pat Northey's monthly newsletter spread the marvellous news: "The park, overlooking the St. Johns River, will be a passive oasis for families and will feature a children's playground that will be completely handicap accessible," she wrote. "Partial funding came from Volusia ECHO. Your tax dollars coming back to Southwest Volusia."

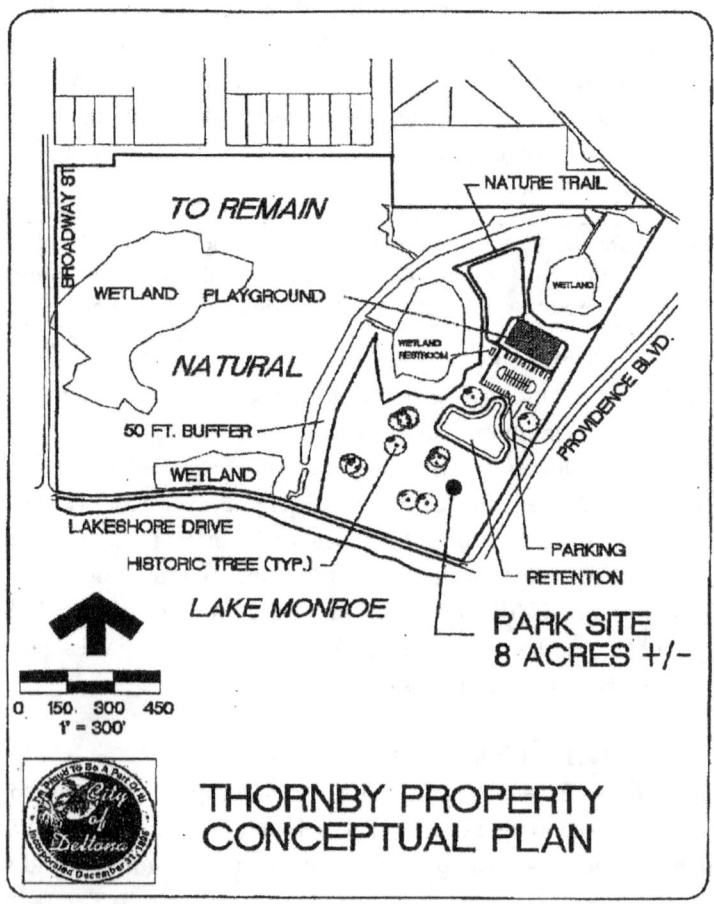

Thornby Park conceptual plan

In September, Commissioner Zischkau talked about "capital projects that do not make any sense as in the $1.5 million for the Thornby property," and an extremist Thornby opponent said the whole thing was a waste of money. Still, naysayers were miniscule dark clouds in a vast blue sky. The park was secure, the playground was getting off the ground, and Thornby, we felt sure, was finally sheltered from fickle political winds.

That fall, inspired by the 10th anniversary of the Enterprise Preservation Society, the *News-Journal*'s Mark Harper wrote a long and lovely story entitled, "Enterprise Charms Like 1970 All Over Again." "It might be impossible to find a more historic place in Volusia County" than Enterprise, he wrote, delving into the days of Cornelius Taylor, Jacob Brock and the county-seat-that-was.

> The incorporation of Deltona in 1995 and subsequent development and annexation plans were the cold water that awoke its residents. Battles were fought and won by both sides ... But the formation of the Enterprise Preservation Society in 2000 led to a unified opposition when landowner Frank Knight started making noises about developing the Thornby property. The preservation society waged a six-year war against plans to develop Thornby commercially.Deltona's City Commission ultimately relented and agreed to purchase the land and develop it as a park.

"You need places like this to clear your brain," said a visitor to Enterprise's Green Spring Park, interviewed for the story. The accompanying photo showed why, as did the shot of Thornby's "two-lane canopied" Lakeshore Drive. Harper continued,

Enterprise is making progress on the restoration of a 1934 schoolhouse partly funded by Volusia ECHO money ... and [thanks to the Bypass Road], where more than 40,000 cars crawled [through Enterprise] every day, wild turkeys are said to now scurry across newly christened Jacob Brock Avenue ... and community development standards have been put into the county's master plan.

The struggle to save Thornby contributed to a "fervor for Enterprise that's similar to the love some college football fans have for their programs," said Kevin Finn, EPS chairman. For me, the article was very special because it sang the praises of EPS and everything we had worked toward for 10 years.

Four Minutes to Say Thank You

"The story of Thornby has a beginning and a middle, but no end." It was October 18, 2010. Again, I was in front of the Deltona City Commission, but this time I was there for Mayor Dennis Mulder and Commissioner Janet Deyette. It was the next-to-last meeting before city elections. Mulder was not seeking re-election. He and I had clashed over Thornby at times, mostly when I didn't think he was moving fast enough. Deyette was fighting for her commission seat in a race that could go either way.

It was time for me to give the CliffsNotes version of Thornby's story to the commission. In four minutes flat, I took them through the early days, of Dr. Glass and "local legend" Doris Faber and how the Thornby owners tried to change its land use under the county. Then begins the middle of the story, I said — the best-known part. I talked about the "massive grassroots effort" from 2001 to 2009: 200 people at a P&Z hearing; enormous amounts of correspondence to the city; Channel 9-TV and WDBO Radio reports; two hours of speakers at three minutes each with not one in favor of development; the room packed for a VGMC hearing; hundreds showing up for an open house to see and learn about the property. "In the face of overwhelming governmental and public opposition, however, thousands of city staff hours were expended in a push for commercial development on a two-lane rural road lined with massive oaks on Lake Monroe, and then a push for a 250-condo complex on wet land with hydric soils that flooded the road in hard rains."

As a planning board member, I said, Commissioner Janet Deyette "repeated that Deltona had the legal right to annex the property, but with rights come responsibilities. She never stopped pointing out that an eight-fold density increase on Thornby directly violated city comprehensive plan policies, goals and objectives dealing with protection of environmentally sensitive lands and intergovernmental cooperation."

I quoted Dennis Mulder's words when he ran for mayor: "Residents and those who live in rural communities near the city are frustrated because commissioners are dismissing their concerns about annexations." His words were not just political rhetoric, I pointed out. The annexation binge years are over — the city is directing its energies toward improving existing infrastructure and development that suits its location. "Mayor Mulder, without your leadership, today the historic Thornby property would be a sea of concrete with retention ponds, speed bumps, dumpsters, suburban roads and too many empty windows. Instead, it will be a shady spot where disabled kids and their families can play and relax under the massive oaks. One day we will see walkable trails, picnic tables spread out on the quiet acres with a view of Lake Monroe and maybe even a water taxi across the lake — Commissioner Deyette's idea."

I looked at Mulder and Deyette. "The end of the story has yet to be written," I said, "but whatever the future holds for Thornby and for you, you can be proud of what you've accomplished. Some people in public office say they made a difference, but not everyone can point to what their efforts have done. Thornby is Deltona's brightest and greenest place, to the credit of the mayor and the five commissioners who cast that historic 'yes' vote to put it forever in public ownership. I thank you." In the commission chambers you could hear a pin drop. Mayor Mulder thanked me and perhaps I just imagined the slight catch in his voice. For him, it had been four bumpy years.

Before he left office, Mulder sat down with the *News-Journal*'s Mark Harper to review "The Mulder Years." In the interview, the mayor said that "Purchasing the Thornby property ended up working out better than we could have imagined … it changed the perception of Deltona … to more of a "conservation kind of city-can-meet-nature too." He cited Thornby as one of the benefits of what had become a "far more workable" relationship between Deltona and Volusia County. While acknowledging that it would have been "more productive" had he handled some things "more politically," he considered increased citizen involvement in city government to be one of his key achievements.

Officially, the 2010 Deltona mayor's race featured former mayor John Masiarczyk vs. former commissioner David Santiago. Given the "pave Thornby" records of both men, however, it felt more like Frankenstein vs. Godzilla. We told ourselves that no matter who won, at least we had already saved Thornby. I would not get involved in this campaign, I told myself. Then I read the "Why did we spend money on this Thornby thing?" posts of a third candidate, Robert Desmond. Factual mistakes in his message prompted me to respond — not very politely, I confess. In our resulting email exchanges, Desmond, who said he loved history, admitted he didn't know much about the property; like others, he had looked at Thornby and seen only dollar signs. When he learned about Thornby's history — especially the possible Seminole Wars fort on site — and that it would become a passive park, he came to appreciate its value, as well as the public's high-profile fight to save it.

To Carol Aymar goes the credit for approaching Enterprise's old nemesis, John Masiarczyk. When they met pre-election, she was pleased at his new, peaceful tone. "I know I've made mistakes in the past," he told her, referring to his unrestrained drive to get condos on Thornby. If elected mayor, he said, he wanted to put the disputes to rest and see Deltona and Enterprise work together. Likewise, the *News-Journal* reported that Masiarczyk "thinks he was wrong during his earlier stint as mayor when he proposed controversial annexations as a way for Deltona to get more land suitable for commercial development." "That was not well accepted by our neighbors, and I learned my lesson," he said. Santiago's stance, however, had not changed. In a campaign video, he stood on city-owned empty land and challenged the camera: "They keep buying more and more park sites and I say, 'Why?' "

In November 2010, John Masiarczyk became mayor of Deltona for the second time. In the city commission race, Janet Deyette's opponent, the pastor of a large church on the north side of Deltona, called for "eliminating unnecessary spending such as purchasing Thornby." To our knowledge, he had never toured the property and was not (nor did he try to become) familiar with its history, its environmental significance or its place in the community. With "dollars" the watchword in many races that year, Deyette lost her re-election bid and Thornby lost its longtime champion at City Hall. Although her years of elected service ended, at this writing she serves on several city and county advisory boards.

Don't Confuse Me with Facts

Early in December 2010, a friend called with exciting news. An Orlando TV station would be taping a short segment about the Thornby park and playground. The purpose, he said, was to air favorable news about Deltona in contrast to all the media-spotlighted city controversies in the last few years. "Wow, I'd really like to talk to the reporter first, to give him some background and explain why Thornby means so much to so many people," I said. A few hours later, the TV reporter called. I did my best to squeeze Dr. Glass / Miss Doris / Enterprise Plan / annexation / condos / land use change / Friends of Thornby / VGMC / State of Florida / arson / elections / wetlands / fort / midden / eagles nest / county / park / playground into a 10-minute conversation, but the resulting piece aired that night bore no resemblance to the story I had related. Instead of being a happy-ending story, it was a waste-money story. The lead-in:

> A piece of prime waterfront land in Volusia County could have made taxpayers money, but instead leaders spent $3 million to buy the land on Lake Monroe from a developer for a playground and park!

Viewers who stayed tuned for more details got an earful of sloppy journalism. First was the false statement that Thornby was purchased "from a developer." Then, "the city and county decided the lakefront land was too pristine to allow development on" and "the city wanted it protected, too" — where in God's name did that come from? The land had "Indian mounds" — plural — the reporter said. "Why did you spend so much on land nobody else could build anything on anyway?" demanded the microphone-holding reporter, displaying astonishing ignorance. Lee Lopez, Deltona's public information officer, responded that Thornby was "an investment in the city of Deltona." He did not correct the factually challenged reporter's premise by explaining that, in fact, one residence per acre could legally have been built on Thornby. Two "taxpayers" interviewed for the story were solidly in support of the purchase. Maybe that's why, at a city workshop the following day, Mayor Masiarczyk noted the "great story last night on the Thornby property."

> **Activist Lesson:** "When you are dealing with newspeople there are no guarantees that any coverage will be exactly what you wanted. Be prepared for the fact that any news story done on your issue may not be 100% of what you wanted." [Quoted with permission from *www.Boatus.com*]

True Believers

Until the fall of 2010, when work on the playground actually started, Bob Sayre did not believe that Thornby was saved, he says. Like every construction job, the project had its share of delays. Sometimes, progress seemed as slow as the Enterprise snail.[3] When the day finally came that a big, green, proudly- beautiful sign announcing "Thornby Park" to the world appeared on the property, it was like Shangri-La rising from the mist. "I wasn't sure we would see the day. What a beautiful sight!" wrote Sandy Gallagher. It would be smooth sailing from now on. We thought.

And We Sang: "Here We Go Again"

Just two months before, I told the Deltona commission, "The end of the story has yet to be written." However, I was expecting it to be written by Hans Christian Andersen, not Stephen King.

On January 3, 2011, the *News-Journal* reported: "After months of referring to the park as 'Thornby Park' in city documents, Deltona's contractors constructed a sign using that name. But Commissioner Zenaida Denizac wrote a letter last week to commissioners suggesting the park be named 'Inspiration Playground' and told the *News-Journal* that [City Manager Faith Miller] erred

---

3 The Enterprise siltsnail, also known as the Enterprise spring snail, scientific name *Floridobia monroensis*, is a *species* of very small *freshwater snail* identified by naturalist William H. Dall, curator at the National Museum of Natural History, in 1885.

in assuming the 'Thornby Park' name had been finalized." Further, the commissioner said, "The manager should be fired, with the park's naming being the final straw." A city spokesman told the newspaper that some officials were "uncertain if Denizac's intent was to rename the park or simply the playground." If the commission wants to re-name the park, he offered helpfully, we could change the sign.

Deltona resident Michael Kiepert ended the guessing game. He mailed Denizac, asking her point-blank if what she wanted was to "simply name the playground within Thornby Park." Her response was biting. "Mr. Kiepert, we have no 'Thornby Park,'" she wrote. "The Deltona City Commission has not named the 'Thornby' property ...*This land needs to be named by the Commission.*" Suddenly it was 2004 all over again.

The one good thing about 2004, 2002, 2005 and all the other years, was the Friends of Thornby in action. As if stepping back into our activist roles without missing a beat, the emails started flying. "Now we know what we gotta do," got things started. "I'm now researching the city minutes since 1995 for all references to 'Thornby' estate or property," reported Carol Aymar. Kevin Finn phoned Commissioner Carmolingo. I went through Anna Glass' will to find early mention of the 'Thornby' property name. Carolyn Langley sent the city commission a "historically-based letter regarding the naming of Thornby by Dr. Glass." And it was all done in one day.

"I was upset and puzzled by the controversy over the name change," Pat Northey says. "The name Thornby had graced the property for as far back as we could find records ... Everything that had been submitted by the city ... referred to this property as Thornby." She sent a letter to the city commission and made a few calls, and soon came to realize that it wasn't about the name at all, but was "an internal issue." The name Thornby had become "the football between opposing teams," she says.

The "new business" agenda item for the commission's January 3, 2011 meeting read like gibberish: "Commissioner Denizac ... is suggesting that the *park* be called "Inspiration *Playground*." During discussion, Denizac said she was "shocked to see a sign in place knowing that the commission had not officially discussed naming the *property*." She called the name "Thornby" a "point of reference only" and asserted that the city manager had "taken it upon herself to name the park." In response, Mayor Masiarczyk said that the property "has always been Thornby." Commissioner Carmolingo said that if changes are made to the park's name, "then history will be changed." Commissioner Herzberg noted that Thornby was her inspiration to get into politics and she "has never known this park or property as other than Thornby." Commissioner Treusch pointed out that on the plans, the park was identified as "Thornby Park."

On a motion by Herzberg, the commission voted unanimously to "name" the park on Thornby as "Thornby Park." After the vote, the mayor thoughtfully allowed those of us who still wished to speak about the name to do so, even though the issue was now moot. Kevin Finn, Jack Hoyt, Johnathan Kenny, Veronica Kenny, Janet Deyette and I talked about why the name "Thornby" is inseparable from those 40 acres on the St. Johns River. Thornby is here today thanks to "years of struggle, heart and soul, money, time and effort by the people of Enterprise and Deltona," I said. "We've become better neighbors; let's not mess things up now." When I finished, Masiarczyk said he hoped we knew that Deltona was now trying to be a good neighbor.

The upshot of the whole brouhaha? As Mark Lane reported in the *News-Journal*:

> City Manager Faith Miller had approved a sign identifying Thornby Park as, well, Thornby Park and not Inspiration Playground, as Commissioner Denizac preferred. This gave Denizac the inspiration to call for Miller's firing. In a compromise, the playground will be identified as Inspiration Playground and the Thornby sign stands for overall park.

Sandy Gallagher says she didn't feel that we had saved Thornby "until after the commission meeting when they finally agreed upon the name of the park." As for the city manager, she kept her job by one vote — 4-3.

Dennis Mulder on Thornby

> There were times ... that I doubted we would ever get it done... but ultimately the result was a great deal for the public... It will be nice to be able to show my own children what can be accomplished with enough determination. Thornby faced every possible obstacle and prevailed because of the work of many people determined to keep this gem intact for future generations.

World Without End, Amen

"Nothing has been easy." Pat Northey's words filled my thoughts on the achingly lovely Saturday morning when Deltona held the Thornby Park ribbon-cutting. The ceremony started half an hour late due to a minor accident featuring a falling flagpole and a bruised head. Never funny, but certainly ironic.

I remember a red-shouldered hawk soaring overhead in one of the bluest skies I've ever seen, his wings swooping like the playground swings far below where brightly dressed little kids squealed with glee, happily oblivious to the official ceremony a few yards away.

"Some day I'll meet you down at Thornby Park." I'd heard those lyrics countless times — at parties, in bars, on outdoor stages. I always cheered when Rog Lee sang the line; it was a little joke between us. But the words had never sounded so clear, or meant so much, as they did that morning, when a smiling Rog sang them in the bright, warm sunlight, a breeze ruffling his long brown hair as shining Lake Monroe peeked through the tall trees under a crisp blue sky. He sang it to dignitaries and regular folks alike that day — down at Thornby Park.

Until the last moment, I was not sure if I would be allowed to speak. Certainly, I was not part of the official program for the "Thornby Park Grand Opening/Ribbon Cutting Ceremony." Janet Deyette wanted to say something, too. So many times, Jan and I had spoken out for Thornby. Today, with our Thornby friends gathered for this, the culmination of everything we had worked for, we ached to open our hearts one last time. Steve Moore, Deltona's parks director, had graciously agreed to try to slip us into the program.

Thornby Park
Grand Opening/Ribbon Cutting Ceremony
February 12, 2011
10:00 a.m.

AGENDA

Welcome and Introduction of City of Deltona City Commission	Mayor John Masiarczyk City of Deltona
St. Johns Lullaby, Someday I'll Meet You Down at Thornby Park	Rog Lee
Introduction of the Volusia County Council and Acknowledgements from District #5	Patricia Northey, Vice Chair County Council
Introduction of Volusia ECHO Advisory Committee Members	Margaret Hodge ECHO Program Coordinator
ECHO "Preserving our Quality of Life"	Eugene Gizzi ECHO Board Member
Dedication of Inspiration Playground	Zenaida Denizac, District 1 Deltona Commission
Development of Thornby Park Improvements, and Recognition of Support by:	Steve Moore Director, Parks & Recreation

Parks & Recreation Advisory Committee
Citizens Accessibility Advisory Sub Committee
Senior Advisory Sub Committee
Youth Advisory Sub Committee
Southern Building Services, Contractor
Play Space Inc., All Inclusive Playground Contractor
Parks & Recreation Department
City of Deltona Staff

The dedication ceremony was brief. Vice Mayor Paul Treusch filled in for Mayor John Masiarczyk, who sent word that he was ill. Among Deltona officials in attendance were Commissioners Herb Zischkau, who had voted against the property purchase, against the park management plan and against the playground construction contract, and Fred Lowry, who had labeled the Thornby purchase "unnecessary spending." Pat Northey spoke, as did representatives from ECHO, the project's "bankers." Commissioner Denizac dedicated the playground area. Steve Moore recognized the support received by city committees and staff members.

Then, true to his word, Moore detoured from the pre-ordained schedule so Jan and I could speak. Jan's words acknowledged the perseverance of "so many of us who refused to give up" — including Larry French, "the Eagle lady," Pat Northey and me. She rightly included herself as one who never quit the fight. She says, "I wanted to make sure that all would know how far back it all began."

I was the last person to speak that day. Was it symbolic that, for the first time in 10 years of Thornby speech-giving, the crowd was in front of me, the officials behind? For two days, a Psalm had been ringing in my non-religious ears. Maybe Dr. Glass or Doris Faber put it there, I decided, and began:

"This is the day that the Lord has made. Let us rejoice and be glad in it."

Then, "It all started in 2001 with a big bowl of popcorn and some friendly cats. Ordinary people sitting around an ordinary kitchen table started something extraordinary. Today, we see the results… "

I read the names of the original Friends of Thornby: Carol Aymar, Kevin Finn, Lani Friend, Sandy Gallagher, Jack Hoyt, Mark Matzinger, Gisela Oeffen, Debra Richardson, Bob Sayre, Grace Stamile, Patrick Stamile, Rich Vail. Most were in the crowd. Gisela Oeffen and Jack Hoyt sat front and center, as they had at every hearing. This time, though, they were grinning.

I thanked others by name: Chris Bowley, Janet Deyette, Larry French, Doug Kelly, Dennis Mulder, Ron Paradise, Roy Walters, and the commissioners who voted to buy Thornby: Carmolingo, Denizac, McFall-Conte and Treusch. Then, to my eternal embarrassment, I forgot to include Pat Northey's name in the Thornby Honor Roll. My nervous screw-up aside, the fact remains that Volusia County Council member Patricia Northey was Valedictorian of the Graduating Class of Thornby.

Carol Aymar had found a Theodore Roosevelt quote and sent it to me while I was working on the speech I hoped to give. His words open this, the last chapter of Thornby's story. The crowd heard these final words before the red ribbon was cut to officially open Thornby Park:

> From time to time little men will come along to find fault with what you have done…. They will go down the stream like bubbles; they will vanish. But the work you have done will remain for the ages.

And the Beat Goes On

Every day, drivers head slowly east along rural Lakeshore Drive under a spreading umbrella of tight-knit live oak trees. On the right, the sensuous beauty of nature's watery art gallery, Lake Monroe. On the left, beautiful Thornby: Nature's green haven, comforting and mysterious at the same time, unspoiled and unruined. Simply existing, whether or not we use it.

***

On the white-columned front porch of a Southern-style home in a small town west of Atlanta, a healthy green fern in a tall gray pot greets visitors at the door. The house belongs to Carolyn Watson Langley and her husband, Jay. The thriving plant, like Carolyn herself, was transplanted from her childhood home. "It is a living part of Thornby, like a little piece of yesterday that continues to live with me today," she says. "I am a child of the Thornby legacy and the experience is forever with me."

***

Doris Faber is part of Thornby's legacy, too. "She couldn't have children of her own, but she had more children than anyone could ever dream of," Carolyn says. As long as Thornby Park exists where James Glass, Anna Glass and Doris Faber lived, worked, played and prayed, children and grown-ups alike will share the legacy of community spirit, hope, and kindness they imprinted on ever-welcoming, wonderful Thornby. And that should *always* be.

Epilogue

In May 2011, the Florida Legislature dealt a fatal blow to the sole state agency charged with preventing irresponsible development. Governor Rick Scott, elected the prior November, had labeled the DCA as a "job killer." Behind the scenes, reported the *Orlando Sentinel,*

> ... lobbyists for some of the state's biggest developers already had outlined a game plan to make it easier for large-scale projects to spread across the rural and exurban landscape...

Many of the DCA's community planning staff, like those who diligently analyzed and applied the state's rules in reviewing the Thornby comprehensive plan amendment, were sacked.

In the last four years of its existence, the "job-killing" DCA approved more than 90 percent of plan amendments it reviewed. Occasionally, as with the Thornby plan, the DCA issued a finding of "not in compliance" with state law. Still, that wasn't good enough for big-money interests like the Florida Chamber of Commerce, which paraded feel-good language like "too much red tape" to justify dissolving one of the strongest growth management laws in the nation.

The hard reality that Florida's economy tanked from over-development was shoved under the table. Billy Buzzett, Scott's appointee as Secretary of the Department of Community Affairs, was formerly an executive of one of Florida's largest land development companies. He touted control by local officials as the magic elixir for economic woes. After all, he said, "they know their communities best." Indeed. The department was reinvented as the "Department of Economic Opportunity."

Florida's former Department of Community Affairs was indispensable in the public's fight against an inappropriate land use change on Thornby. At this writing, it remains to be seen whether future grassroots groups in Florida can successfully thwart ill-conceived land use changes without the state's intervention and assistance.

Selected Pages from the Thornby Guest Book

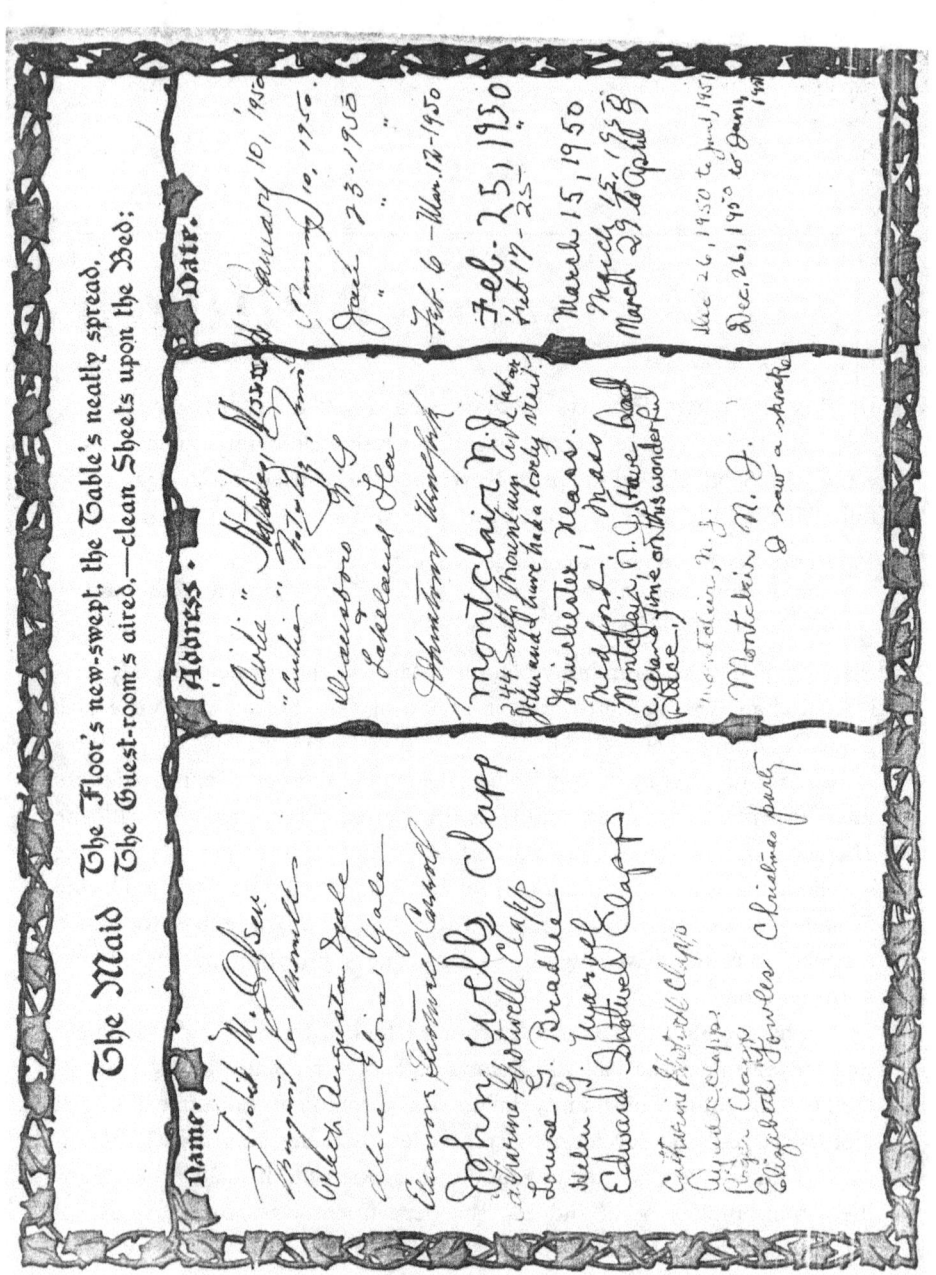

The Pipe-Rack 1977

Choose:—Creamy Meerschaum, Corncob sweet as Hay,
The long Church-warden framed of short-lived Clay.

Name:	Address:	Date:
Dorothy and Caroline Potter	420-70 Ave. 6S - S.A. Calif. Had a nice visit with our friend Doria, whom we hadn't seen in thirty years.	Jan. 1, 1977
	Liverpool, New York First time we have seen her	
John, Shirley, Lisa, Jack, David Allen Lillraine	enjoyed visiting Jack	Feb 24, 1977
Gene Schad	308 Jerry Ave, Spring Lake Heights, New Jersey	Feb 28 - 4 days
John Clapp	Ocean Ave. Sea Girt, N.J.	April 7-12, 1977
Mrs Sharon Allen — Tamara — Andrew and Allyson — friends of John Clapp	A very special place to live among a faithful group of Annie Brown.	April 7-10, 1977
	Sea Girt N.J.	
Jasper C Yates		June 20 - 1977
James P Eddy Morris	Wilmington N.C.	Wed. 30 - 1977

The Stairs

Asceno,—s. ce [or Ascent] the summer muse
Our roomy Treads and sweeping Balustrade.

Name.	Address.	Date.
Jr. W. Clapp / Catherine Shotwell Clapp	Syracuse N.Y. / Montclair N.J. — "Bill said one morning gets frogs, the Play's will lay lots of eggs. Doing Nothing at all — Collecting today at Cow"	1-21-72 1st Clapp? / Merry Guest Rest / I like to see Ayre and Bill ride Horse-back.
Bill N. Clapp / Anne D. Clapp	Marythol N.J. / New Vernon / Marythol N.J.	"72 Hell of a surge / -23 / Feb. 16-23
Catherine S. Clapp → Mrs Geo. 23 Wallace / Jr. W. Clapp / Jay Mellor – Samuel, aged 3 / Aguer, C.S.C. – Jane straight on over —	I had fun with all. / A short treat is much felt. / Sea Gut. Glad to see Guy / to miss Doris — / Thankyou, Boris will. / So long if last time. / stayed 3 days with Bill in Tampa / Sea Gut – Found	of animals. / than man. / Have again. Thanks / wonderful place / 26 Feb. 1973 / 26 " – 28 th Feb
Jr. W. Clapp		out but property / gold mine, but no / estate get to will will / allowed.
George Fink / Pat Fink	west Hollywood the pier / " " / " "	June 30- / July 1-1973 / Sunny half to Sunny seventh.

Away, thou Gnat! Each humming, stinging Pest
Begone! My Bars repel thee from our Guest. The Screen

Name:	Address:	Date:
Fauzyn Baley Sturges	Fairfield, Conn.	So lovely a visit—
Catherine R. Evans		I'll be back?!
John W. Clapp	Johnstown N.J. april	Maud our friend
Catharine—	Burlington Vt 4-1970	Doris — You are a
Jane, Joan, Andrew, Charlotte Loving	From trout bass Wed Apr 22	real Hostess —
John and David "Patterby" Friends	For one week—	stopped in last year
Morris and Elaine Wing	Tue: Sunday Apr 26 - Charlotte's	at this time — will
Farmington, Maine	seventh birthday	be the most beautiful
Emily O. Wing		time!
Farmington, Maine	July 16, 1971	
Susan Bugg Tucson, Arizona		Here for
	July 27, '70	Emily & Ernie's
		wedding
Julia Nelson	Tampa, Florida	All remember your
Jennifer Nelson	Tampa, Florida	beautiful place & you for
Marjorie Nelson (Mrs. Henry)	Tampa, Florida	being the Guest
		That I am.
		July 27, 1970
		July 27, 1970
		July 27, 1970

List of Sources

ORGANIZATIONS
Bentley Historical Library, University of Michigan, Ann Arbor
Deltona Arts & Historical Center
Enterprise Preservation Society
Florida Humanities Council
Hamilton College, Hamilton, New York
Herkimer County New York Historical Society
Museum of Seminole County History
Oneida County New York Historical Society
Peabody Museum of Archeology and Ethnology, Harvard University
Tampa Historical Society
West Volusia Historical Society
Wisconsin Historical Society

NEWSPAPERS
Daytona Beach News-Journal
DeLand Sun
Enterprise Herald
Florida Times-Union
New Smyrna News
Orlando Sentinel
Richfield Springs Mercury
Sanford Herald
Utica Daily Press
Utica Herald-Dispatch
Utica Observer
Volusian

PUBLICATIONS
American Medical Directory, American Medical Association Press, 1916
A Bibliography of the History and Life of Utica, 1986
Centennial History of Volusia County, Florida, Ianthe Bond Heber, College Publishing Co., 1955
Encyclopedia of Historic Forts, McMillan, 1988
Florida Forts, James M. Gray, 1972
Florida Place Names, Allen Morris, Pineapple Press, 1995
Florida's Seminole Wars 1817-1858, Dr. Joe Knetsch, Arcadia Publishing, 2003
Gazetteer and Business Directory of Herkimer County, New York for 1869-70

History of Oneida County, New York, S. J. Clarke Publishing Co., 1912
History of Volusia County, Florida, Pleasant Daniel Gold, Higginson, 1927
Hopes, Dreams and Promises: The Story of Volusia County, Florida, Michael Schene, News-Journal Corp., 1976
New York and Its Institutions 1609-1871, John Francis Richmond, E. B. Treat, 2009
Notable Men of Central New York, D. J. Stoddard Publishers, 1903
Polk's Medical and Surgical Register, R. L. Polk & Co., 1900
Reflections of West Volusia County, M.E. Ross, 1976
Under the Sheltering Tree, Stephen T. Hartsfield, 2008
Volusia County, Past and Present, T. E. Fitzgerald, E. O. Painter, 1937
Volusia: The West Side, Arthur E. Francke, Jr., Alyce Hockaday Gillingham, Maxine Carey Turner, West Volusia Historical Society, 1986.
Whitney's Florida Pathfinder, 1875-6
Who's Who in America, A. N. Marquis & Company, 1922-3; 1926-7; 1930-1

OTHER

City of DeBary Archeological Survey, Stewart, Jones and Jones, 1999
City of Deltona City Commission Minutes
City of Deltona Parks and Recreation Department
City of Deltona Planning and Zoning Board Minutes
Cultural Resources Assessment Survey of the DeBary Avenue Pond C Parcel, Environmental Management Systems, Inc., 2006
Cultural Resource Assessment Survey of the Thornby Park Tract, Environmental Services, Inc., 2009
Cultural Resource Survey, Thornby, Southeastern Archeological Research, Inc., 2005
"The Doris Story," Doris Faber, date unknown
"Enterprise, Florida" CD, West Volusia Historical Society, 2006
"Enterprise Historical Trail," Steve Rajtar, 2006
Essex County, New Jersey Probate Records
"The Florida Anthropologist," December 1994
Florida Death Records
Florida Department of Community Affairs
Florida Department of Environmental Protection
Florida Department of Historic Preservation
Florida United Methodist Childrens Home Archives, including:
    The Orphans Friend, February 1927
    The Florida Methodist, November 1941
    History of Barnett Memorial United Methodist Church, 2008
Florida State Census Records

Letter from Doris Faber to West Volusia Historical Society, 20 July 1973
Mohawk Village Business Directory Map, 1868
New York State Census Records
Texas State Death Records
Thornby Guest Register
United States Census Bureau Records
United States Social Security Death Records
Volusia County Clerk of Court:
    Probate Records
    Property Records
Volusia County Council Meeting Minutes
Volusia County Historical Structures Survey, 1989
Volusia County Planning Commission Meeting Minutes
Volusia Growth Management Commission Meeting Minutes

WEBSITES

http://chestofbooks.com/gardening-horticulture/American-Horticultural-Manual-Vol2/The-Orange-Family.html (Enterprise seedless orange)
http://www.citruscountyfl.org/devservices/landdev/community/springs of_florida.pdf (Florida springs)
www.cypressloghomes.com (cypress related to sequoia)
http://www.delandchamber.org/newsite/cities.htm (city history)
http://www.deltonafl.gov (city history)
http://www.fumch.org/fumch/WhoWeAre/History.aspx (Florida United Methodist Children's Home)
http://www.jstor.org/pss/3492441 (malaria)
http://melvinsembler.blogspot.com/2006/10/semblers-shameful-dalliance-with.html (Allan Keen)
http://www.mystjohnsriver.com (St. Johns Riverkeeper)
http://www.oldenterprise.org (Enterprise Preservation Society)
http://www.outintheboonies.com/Tosohatchee/time_line.html (Armed Occupation Act)
http://www.poynter.org (historic newspapers)
http://www.roglee.com (singer/songwriter Rog Lee)
http://www.volusia.org/history (Enterprise history)
http://volusia.org/parks/green.htm (Green Spring Park)
http://en.wikipedia.org/wiki/Edward_VII_of_the_United_Kingdom (Prince of Wales)
http://en.wikipedia.org/wiki/Editorial_board (editorial boards)
http://140.247.102.177/col/shortDisplay.cfm?StartRow=1 (Enterprise Midden artifacts)

Acknowledgments

Just as saving Thornby required the hard work, dedication and commitment of many people, this book was shaped by the answers, assistance and courtesy of many who went out of their way to help me tell our grassroots story. I especially thank the following:

- *Carol Aymar,* for her insight and advice and for being in the trenches all those years while we fought to make the dream come true.
- *Janet Deyette,* for being a true friend to Thornby and to me, whatever the political climate.
- *Larry French,* for his love of history, the natural world and writing.
- *Carolyn Watson Langley,* for sharing her story, her family and her knowledge of Thornby, no matter how many questions I asked.
- *Pat Northey,* for moving heaven and earth and for making the stars align.
- *Ron Paradise,* for being a true gentleman, endlessly helpful and a modest hero.
- *Grace and Patrick Stamile,* for the gift of Faber family items that reveal the human side of Thornby's story.

To those who invited me into their homes, patiently answered my questions, shared their memories, offered their expertise and/or generally helped put the pieces together, I offer my heartfelt thanks:

Dennis Bayer; Montye Beamer; Catherine Bruce; Wilbur Bruce; Paul Camp; Coe Chamberlain; Pam Cook; Kevin Davidson; Esther Dobens; Ben Dyer; Chris Edmonston; Mike Fleming; Valerie Grill; Roxann Hardin; Wise Hardin; Wesley Kihlmire; Paula Lewis; Mike MacHardy; Saralee Morrissey; Dennis Mulder; Todd Peetz; Roland Peloquin; Joe Perez; Steve Rajtar; Mark Rakowski; Brian Schieck; Scott Selis; Kimberly Selis; Nancy Siebert; Suzanne Steiner; George Trovato; Jim Ward; Dwayne Watson; Emily Watson; Ernie Watson

To those who went above and beyond, took a personal interest in the project and made sure I got the facts straight:

- *DeLand House Museum:* Billy Desilva and Rhonda Janitch
- *Deltona Arts & Historical Museum:* Lloyd Marcus
- *City of Deltona:* Marlene Brown; Sherri Campbell; Joyce Kent; Lee Lopez; Faith Miller; Steve Moore; Chief Robert Staples
- *State of Florida:* Erin Bailey, James Stansbury and Ryan Wheeler
- *Florida United Methodist Children's Home:* Reverend Stephen T. Hartsfield and Ann King
- *Herkimer County, New York, Historical Society:* Susan Perkins and Steve Knight
- *Oneida County, New York, Historical Society:* Richard Williams
- *Tampa Historical Society:* Maureen J. Patrick
- *The Trust for Public Land:* Grant Gelhardt, Doug Hattaway, Alanna Layton and Kevin Mooney
- *Volusia County:* Bill Gardner; Morgan Gilreath; Sedrick Harris; Alan Horne; Ed Isenhour; Julie Scofield; Carol MacFarlane; Marsha Naber; Merry Chris Smith; Rob Walsh; Marcy Zimmerman
- *Westminster Presbyterian Church, Utica, New York:* Linda Jennings

Special Thanks to:

- Chris Bowley, Tom Brooks and Doug Kelly, for their time, knowledge and experience, always needed and always generously shared.
- John White and Lynda White for caring about our national symbol, the American bald eagle.
- Neil Armingeon for caring about the St. Johns River
- Pat Hatfield of the *West Volusia Beacon*, Mark Harper and Mark Lane of the *Daytona Beach News-Journal* and Mike Lafferty of the *Orlando Sentinel:* fine journalists and, more importantly, good people, all.
- Michael Kiepert, for keeping Thornby in the online news
- Rog Lee, for sharing his heart and voice with Thornby.

And of course, thanks to my world-class editor, David Wiggins. As editorial director for the *News-Journal*, he and his team wrote many pro-Thornby editorials. Neither of us could have imagined that years later he would end up editing my book about Thornby. David believed that the story was worth telling and never stopped reminding me that, first and foremost, I was recording local history. His wisdom, common sense and guidance in shaping this ragged writer's efforts into a finished dream prove that Friends of Thornby still appear when you need them. Thank you, David!

Thanks to all over the years who put their hearts, souls and hands into this beautiful place, and thanks to Dr. James Henderson Glass, whose spirit inspired me every step of the way.

Photo Credits
All photographs and graphics are from the author's collection unless otherwise noted. Thanks to all those who provided photographs.

Aymar, Carol – Chapter 8, p. 138
Brock, Dorothy – Chapter 1, p. 26
Bruce, Wilbur – Chapter 2, p. 45; Chapter 4, p. 64
Davidson, Kevin – Chapter 18, p. 309
City of Deltona – Chapter 11, pp. 189, 190; Chapter 19, pp. 324, 328, 336
Deltona Fire Department – Chapter 10, p. 180
Deyette, Janet – Chapter 16, p. 277
Enterprise Preservation Society – Title page; Chapter 7, p. 120; Chapter 8, p. 131; Chapter 11, p. 197
Finn, Kevin – Chapter 8, p. 140
Florida Humanities Council, Chapter 1, p. 14
French, Larry – Chapter 12, p. 224
Florida United Methodist Children's Home – Chapter 2, pp. 32, 33
Gallagher, Sandy – Chapter 8, p. 142
Langley, Carolyn Watson – Front cover; Chapter 3, p. 53; Chapter 5, p. 81
Richardson, Debra – Chapter 8, p. 148
Sanford Herald – Chapter 5, p. 83
Siebert, Rena – Chapter 10, p. 178
Stamile, Grace – Chapter 2, p. 41; Chapter 3, p. 57; Chapter 4, pp. 62, 64; Chapter 5, pp. 74, 76, 86; Chapter 8, p. 151
Stamile, Patrick – Chapter 8, p. 151
Sullivan, Cindy – Chapter 1, p. 24
Vail, Rich – Chapter 8, p. 150
Volusia County – Chapter 1, p. 17; Chapter 11, p. 189
West Volusia Beacon – Chapter 18, pp. 311, 312
West Volusia Historical Society – Chapter 1, pp. 20, 27

WALTERS' TOP 11 LIST
of statements made at hearings.

11. We've been good stewards of the land.
10. You just don't want anything built here.
9. This is smart growth like we want.
8. Other boards/commissions approved it.
7. It's compatible with the surroundings.
6. If we don't build this, something worse will be built.
5. This is our property right.
4. The area is already overcrowded/polluted/ruined.
3. We've scaled it back from what it was.
2. It's coming whether we like it or not.
1. Everything will be taken care of later.

APPENDIX

The ABC's Of Land Use Activism

The following is an ever-expanding and inconclusive, but hopefully useful list, of sources and techniques that a citizen activist should know and use when engaged in serious opposition to an inappropriate land use change/development or rezoning.

A

Activist Network: Anyone you know is a possible supporter. Let your friends, locally and in other communities, know what you are doing and why. Most people don't keep up with current local land use issues that don't personally affect them, but often they will agree to send an email or attend a hearing when they understand the issues.

Annexation: Attorney Tanner Andrews explains, "The common reason for annexing is that the present land use is something fairly harmless where the developer wants something like a strip center or high-density housing."

Attorneys: From the American Bar Association's Model Rule 4.1, Truthfulness in Statements to Others:

In the course of representing a client a lawyer shall not knowingly:
(a) make a false statement of material fact or law to a third person

B

"Biostitute": A job title coined by an activist to describe expert biologists whose reports often "miss' things. The words "cherry picking" might apply. In one case, underwater vegetation sampling was done strategically in areas lacking vegetation. In another case, experts reported a lack of a protected species, but looked out of season.

Blogs: With a controversial project, inaccurate information can be posted by proponents of the project, without fear of accountability. It's easy to get "in the weeds" with personal attacks. Usually better to focus your efforts elsewhere.

Buzz Words: BEWARE feel-good words like "vision," "conservation," "open space," "sustainable," "public use" and "smart growth." BEWARE generic words like "official," "suggested," "policies," "possible" and "potential."

C

Contact Person: Usually there's one person in a government office with overall responsibility for a particular matter. Get to know that "go-to" person, who can be a source of vital information, especially when last-minute complications arise.

Courthouse Records: Research public records and court records of corporations or individuals involved in your land use issue. Corporate information is available from each state, as are lawsuit records. They are often online.

Cut & Paste Emails to Officials: What you lose in quality by not sending individual emails, you make up for in quantity. Most people won't compose their own email, but will forward one. Form emails should be brief (two paragraphs) and attention-getting, but not tacky. Provide contact information and space for senders to add their own comments, if they would like.

D

Deadlines: Most government items have a deadline for submitting comments, becoming an interested party or filing an objection. Be cognizant of the time constraints at every step.

E

Email Contact List: Scrounge every local email address you can find, from whatever source. Use this list to update the public about an issue. While some people will ask to be removed from your list, more will thank you for keeping them informed. Include a link to your Facebook page or website where you provide more details.

Experts (hired): Planners and traffic engineers are the most common types of experts you may need. You might find one who will help a grassroots group at a reduced rate. You might have to search out of town to find them.

Experts (other): Identify any private groups or associations whose interests and passions might provide people willing to help. Local history buffs, for example, might get involved with a land use issue of historical significance, or Civil war re-enactors, metal detecting clubs, or fisherman might identify with your issue.

F

Facts: Just because a statement is made on the public record does not make it true. In one case, an out-of-town developer claimed that a new marina would provide needed boat slips. Calls to local marinas showed that, in fact, space was plentiful. It's not "official" evidence, but you can still present it at a public hearing. At the least, it gives decision-makers something to think about.

Flyers: A low-tech wonder. Make them short and snappy with plenty of "white space." Add visual interest by using bright-colored paper and colored ink and a photo of the property. Give phone, email and fax contacts for decision-makers. You can even include the property owner/developer. Put flyers on windshields in parking lots near the planned development and tape them to mailboxes in the area. (Some people, even though it's illegal, put flyers inside mailboxes or tape them to prominent traffic signs.) Post them at libraries, on church bulletin boards and at community centers. Mail them to the property's neighbors. (See Neighbors, below)

G

Governments: Know if other local governments have a stake in the issue, for example, from traffic problems. Educate other officials about the issues.

H

Half-Truths and Omissions are often presented as the whole picture. Eric West, an experienced citizen-activist, calls it "the sin of omission" and warns that, even if what you hear is true, frequently "what you hear is only half the story."

Homeowners Associations: Some counties have a master file of all homeowners associations in their jurisdiction. Consider addressing a homeowners association meeting to make residents aware of your issue.

I

Investigate: Knowledge is power. Google the names of the main players who are backing development. In one instance, online searching led to Securities & Exchange Commission filings that provided valuable information about a would-be developer's corporate structure and pending merger.

Investors: We were surprised to learn that, in one project, a large Ivy League school's pension fund was an investor in a Florida development corporation. In a case like this, contacting the fund's trustees with information about the detrimental project might be helpful if you can get one trustee to stir the pot.

J

"Just Because We Can" often seems the only rationale behind a decision that, while technically legal, is missing stringent analysis of its costs and benefits.

K

Knocking on Doors: Talking to neighbors can bring big rewards. Do not assume that people who live nearby are aware of the project. In one case, I met a sweet 80-something widow facing a land use change/high density development in the neighborhood where she had lived for decades. I was as flabbergasted as everyone else when she appeared at the public hearing and spoke out against it. (The land use change was denied.)

Knowledge: If you have learned an issue "inside and out," there's a good chance you know more about it than the officials you will be addressing. They do not have the time to understand the complexities of every issue before them. Use your knowledge as a positive force, either to support the staff's recommendation or demonstrate its flaws.

L

Lawyer: Seriously consider hiring a good land use attorney — if not at the beginning, even in the middle or near the end of the process. Your cause will be taken more seriously and the "intimidation factor" alone could be worth the expense.

Legislators: State legislators rarely involve themselves in local land use issues.

Letters: You can get nearby property owner information from the property appraiser's website to use for a form letter advising them of an upcoming hearing.

Letters to the Editor: It goes without saying that you will be writing these. Have different people write letters at intervals, to keep the issue in the public eye. Guest editorials are a very potent vehicle, as well.

Lobbying: Find out the names and contact information of every person who will vote on the development. Ask if they are allowed to talk to you; rules differ. If they are allowed to talk but "discouraged" from doing so, call anyway. Some will ignore you, some will say "no," but occasionally, a conscientious soul will talk about the project and how he/she feels about it. Then, you know what areas to work on. Certainly, you can be assured that the opposition is doing its own lobbying.

Local Groups: Tell your story to local groups who would be affected by the project; for instance, environmental groups, bicycle clubs and homeowners associations. Ask if you can make a short presentation. Bring flyers. Collect names and contact information from those at the meeting and add them to your contact list.

M

Media — Reporters: Get to know the local reporters, but remember, their job is to emphasize conflict, so they often seek inflammatory comments. Don't talk "off the cuff" unless you are experienced. Only say what you want the world to know. You don't have to answer every question. If caught off-guard by a phone call, say you'll call them back right away and then write down exactly what you want to say before you call. Then do it, because reporters have tight deadlines.

Minutes from Other Meetings: Research past minutes in the same jurisdiction to find names of people who objected to past developments. Call them. If they cared enough to attend a hearing and speak about a land use issue, they might do the same for your cause.

Minutes from Past Proceedings: If a land use matter was heard at a lower level, for example, before a planning board, read those minutes. Look for quotes that contradict, or support, your position. Talk to someone who voted at the meeting, if you can, for added insight on the issues.

Money: A few dollars from many people adds up. You may need some funds to hire a lawyer or other experts.

N

National Agencies: Explore the possibilities. For instance, the Army Corps of Engineers may have jurisdiction over wetlands in some cases. Do not assume every agency cognizant of your issue.

Negative Information: "Negative information in almost every context that we know about stays with people longer. People may not remember the source or specifics of a negative message, but they will remember there was something negative weeks, months or even years later," says Ruthann Weaver Lariscy, Ph.D., Professor of Public Relations, University of Georgia.

Negotiations: "Attorneys who negotiate typically puff, bluff, embellish, and intentionally over- or understate the value of particular items for strategic purposes. Under Model Rule 4.1, a lawyer may not knowingly misrepresent material law or fact, but the Rule's Comment 2 acknowledges that in the negotiation context, individuals have different expectations." From the American Legal Institute/American Bar Association description of a course in "Negotiation Ethics."

Neighbors: Since nearby residents can be your biggest asset, it's crucial to reach out to as many as you can. The goal is to inform everyone about what's going on.

Newspaper Archives: Worthwhile for searching for anything written about the issue or key players. For a developer, you might research newspapers in cities where the company has done other projects, or where the business is headquartered. You might be surprised what you find. Many newspapers have online chats. Post the name, ask for information, and see what you come up with. In one case, online sleuthing led me to a phone conversation with the former neighbor of a high-profile, sleazy Miami developer, which gave some insight to the developer's modus operandi.

O

Officials: Background research can reveal telling details: for instance, that an elected official owns an electrical contracting company, or another's spouse is a licensed Realtor.

Officials, Part 2: An elected official has the right to speak on an issue as an individual, even when their viewpoint goes against the majority of their own board. In one instance, a commissioner spoke her personal viewpoint at a hearing in a different forum than her own city. It brought her a lot of grief from her fellow commissioners, but it was a remarkably gutsy act that helped to defeat the proposal.

P

Petitions: Not worth the time, but people like to sign; they feel they are doing something worthwhile with little effort. This is true for written, as well as online, petitions.

Phone Calls: If you have volunteers, phone calls to inform people about hearings are excellent. Use member lists for groups like Sierra, or voter lists of the street you want to target. If you have access to automated voice messaging, use it.

Photos: Visit the property. Walk it, if possible. Take photos of its features: tree cover; shoreline; adjacent properties; standing water, etc. If you cannot access the property, take the best photos possible from the outside.

Press Release: Simply, it's a statement of what you want the world to know. Make it short (a few paragraphs) and succinct. There must be a news angle; for instance: "Indian Mound Just Discovered on Property." Email press releases to the contact people at each newspaper, TV or radio station, online newspaper and blogs. That contact list should be checked frequently to keep the names current, as reporters are re-assigned often.

Public Records Request: Your best friend, and the only way to be sure you have every relevant document. You may well end up sitting at a desk for hours, poring over thick files, rather than pay for hundreds of copies. Remember to re-submit requests from time to time to keep up with the latest developments. In some jurisdictions, a friendly staffer might respond to a verbal request, but resist the temptation to short-cut. Put your request in writing. You can find sample request forms online.

Q

Question Everything: Who supports this change/development? Why is it being presented now? Most importantly, follow the money!

R

Radio: A local talk show or Internet broadcast might be willing to put you on the air.

Reporters: Reporters tend to use the same "sources" frequently. If a reporter knows he or she can count on you for the facts, you will be surprised how often you hear from them. That said, never assume that a friendly relationship with a sympathetic reporter will color their story. Their job is to report all sides of an issue.

Ride: Offer to drive elderly residents to a hearing. Many times, they want to get involved but don't like to drive alone at night.

S

Social Network Sites: e.g. Facebook. Social sites are useful for explaining issues in-depth at no cost as a paid web host is not needed. Also, they are far easier and faster to make and update than web pages.

Staff Reports: A staff report is presented as advisory to decision-makers and is often the basis for their decision. In preparing their report, staff should do extensive analysis of any plan, especially a large or complicated one, before making a recommendation, rather than simply accepting data from the developer's hired guns. Often, such data is unsupported or sketchy. You must obtain the latest version of the staff report, as they are often updated days, or even hours, before the public hearing, and you won't know it unless you ask. Be sure to obtain copies of any reports referenced in it, such as traffic reports.

State Statutes, City Ordinances, Comprehensive Plan Sections: The goal is to quote the law or policy that is being ignored or misconstrued. Research laws, codes or regulations that have bearing on the subject.

Strategic Misrepresentation: An element of "Competitive Decision Making," a class once taught at Harvard Business School by Professor Emeritus Howard Raiffa, who referred to the "analytical need to misrepresent." Lawyers often seem to excel at this.

T

Topics: Officials at public hearings expect to hear repetitive testimony that they can tune out. Surprise them. Each member of your group who speaks at a hearing should focus on a separate issue. The usual examples are traffic, schools and flooding. Some lesser-known examples are noise pollution, security issues and developer insolvency/reputation

Traffic: If traffic is an issue, consider doing an informal "traffic count" of vehicles passing by the property in a ten-minute period, preferably at peak traffic times. Of course, you will be told that such figures are unscientific and worthless — but in the meantime, decision-makers will hear the results. Traffic reports are highly technical, but you can at least question if the opposition's traffic report took peak service hours into account. At one hearing, a traffic expert admitted that his project would make an already-bad situation worse, but justified it on grounds that "it's already messed up." (Approval was not granted).

U

"Undecideds": Don't waste time on official decision-makers known for their "pro-development" stance or connections. Target the fence-sitters, those without an agenda.

V

Volunteers are best recruited by asking for specific help. "Can you address 100 envelopes?" "Will you share your email list?"

W

War: An experienced activist once summed it up this way: "Activism is war, and you must be prepared to fight on three fronts: at the government, in the media and in the courts."

Websites for The Cause: Start one. For a complicated project with high public visibility, a website is a godsend. You control the content, so every word is factual. Project history and photos are helpful. Include a "contact" link to increase your contact base, but not a space for comments — it should be a "one-way website."

Websites of Others: Some big projects rate their own developer's website (or Facebook page). Expect them to be slick and manipulative. From them, you can learn what the key arguments will be.

XYZ

Any Idea, no matter how far-fetched, is worth a try, e.g., are there possible onsite burials?

Does the developer own the property in question, or is the deal contingent on a land use change?

About the Author

I was born in Pittsburgh, PA and moved to Florida in 1971, where I worked as a paralegal in Miami, Pensacola, St. Petersburg and Orlando. My husband, Roy A. Walters, and I moved to Stone Island in Enterprise in 2001. I once was a normal person; that is, not really involved in government or politics. But when we moved to Enterprise, the Thornby fight was just heating up and I found myself in the thick of the struggle to keep this beautiful, historic place from "death by high-density development." The "Friends of Thornby" grassroots group was formed, and I was soon leading the fight, hiring lawyers and planners, researching, speaking at hearings, rounding up experts. Along the way I was appointed to the Volusia Growth Management Commission, where I served as a county representative for three years.

Fighting an enormous land use change on Thornby taught me more than I ever thought possible for an ordinary citizen to know about the workings of government, and how politics informs everything from road-widening to rezoning and personal relationships.

www.ingramcontent.com/pod-product-compliance
Lightning Source LLC
Chambersburg PA
CBHW070823250426

43671CB00036B/1843